U.S. ECONOMIC HISTORY

U.S. ECONOMIC HISTORY

A Survey Of The Major Issues

★★★★★

Albert W. Niemi, Jr.
University of Georgia

RAND McNALLY COLLEGE PUBLISHING COMPANY/Chicago

Rand McNally Economics Series
Ralph E. Beals, *Advisory Editor*

Printed in U.S.A.
Library of Congress Catalog Card Number 74-19518

*For Maria, Bert,
and Eddie*

Contents

List of Figures

List of Tables

Preface

This text presents a concise review of the major forces in American economic development. Economic forces receive primary emphasis; non-economic considerations such as political, social, and cultural changes command attention only when they are relevant to the discussion of the economic growth and development process. The book's limited objective stands in sharp contrast to the encyclopedic coverage of many standard textbooks of American economic history and, in my opinion, this is its strength. The comprehensive approach in many standard works fails to provide adequate isolation of economic forces, and consequently, the process of economic growth and development is enmeshed in a mass of detail.

The book's short length results from its limited objective and concise expression. Tables and charts are used liberally to elaborate, clarify, and defend the verbal argument in the text. The prose is simple and avoids unnecessary use of jargon. No prior knowledge of economics is required. Economic terms are carefully defined as they are introduced, and a complete glossary of all economic terms used in the book is provided in an appendix. Suggestions for further reading are included at the end of each chapter.

Although the book is written from the perspective of an economist, it has no strong methodological bias. I have attempted to integrate the quantitative-theoretical contributions of the "new" economic historians with the rich stock of research generated by the "traditional" economic historians. In most chapters, the treatment involves a synthesis of the most relevant research by the new and traditional schools; in the several areas where the new economic history has brought about a sharp revision of opinion, the traditional view has been altered according to the evidence supplied by the new economic historians.

Here American economic development is described from a topical approach, the treatment involving a detailed examination of key periods, sectors, and issues. Economic development is a complicated process, achieved through simultaneous solution of many problems; the American experience is the classic success story. Nineteenth century economic conditions in America were quite different from conditions in present-day underdeveloped countries, and the United States was endowed with many advantages, including a favorable mix of public and private enterprise, favorable land/labor ratio, productive land, access to foreign capital, selective population developed through immigration, early transportation development, heavy borrowing of British technology, and a free and open society conducive to individual initiative. There is no single theory that can explain the unique success of the United States, and the following chapters will reveal that the American achievement involved a combination of special circumstances.

The book is intended as the major text for the basic survey course in American economic history. At the same time, the broad coverage of the book and its synthesis of the most recent literature should also make it extremely useful to advanced students and researchers in American economic history. American historians interested in the current state of knowledge in American economic history will find the book a valuable reference piece and a useful supplement in advanced courses in American history.

I am heavily indebted to the many economic historians who have contributed to the rich stock of knowledge that has been used in writing this text. I am grateful to John W. Kendrick, Irving Gershenberg, and John Thorkelson, my former teachers who first aroused my interest in economic history. I have benefited from the advice of my colleagues and students at the University of Georgia. I am also grateful to Stanley Engerman, Robert Gallman, William Parker, and Paul Uselding, who read various portions of the manuscript and offered valuable criticism.

Finally, I owe a special debt to my wife, Maria, who read the entire manuscript and offered many valuable suggestions concerning content and style.

I am grateful to all of my critics, but I have not followed all of their suggestions. Any errors of omission, interpretation, or fact are mine.

Albert W. Niemi, Jr.

1 Introduction

This chapter surveys the various approaches to economic history, the nature of economic development, and the operation of a market economy. The relationship between new economic history and traditional or "old" economic history and their contributions are examined. Past accomplishments of the American economy are placed in perspective by reviewing the current state of world economic development. The major sources of economic development are specified, and a distinction is made between economic development and economic growth. Finally, the basic flows that occur in the everyday operation of a market economy such as the United States are reviewed. The concepts introduced in this chapter provide a handy frame of reference for the analysis that follows in later chapters.

Approaches to Economic History

The scientific revolution that has swept over the social sciences during the past several decades has had a great impact on the writing of economic history and the training of economic historians. Traditionally, economic historians were trained as interdisciplinary specialists, and they combined the talents of the historian and the economist. Refinements in economic theory and statistical methods have spawned a new approach to economic history which emphasizes training in the use of quantitative-theoretical analysis of the past.[1] Much research in the new economic history has in-

[1] The most precise statements concerning the objectives and techniques of the new economic history are contained in the following: John R. Meyer and Alfred H. Conrad, "Economic Theory, Statistical Inference, and Economic History," *Journal of Economic History,* Decem-

volved the formulation of hypotheses concerning the past and the utilization of statistical techniques to test their validity. In addition to using economic theory and statistics to refine our understanding of the development of the American economy, the new economic historians have made liberal use of counterfactual propositions of which the following are examples: what if the South had won the Civil War? what if slavery had not been introduced into the United States? and what if the British colonial system had endured into the twentieth century?

The rise of new economic history began in the late 1950s and, initially, traditional economic historians strongly resisted it. Some of them charged that the liberal use of econometric models, computer techniques, and counterfactual propositions did not result in history but rather in "quasi-history," and some described the new economic history as an exercise in hypothesis testing.[2] The new school's attack on several central tenets of American economic history heightened the conflict. For example, most standard traditional treatments of American economic history reached the following conclusions:

- British imperial policy had a significant negative impact on American economic development during the colonial period.
- On the eve of the Civil War, slavery was an unprofitable and non-viable institution.
- The railroad was indispensable to American economic development.
- The American Civil War was a major watershed in the economic development of the nation and insured the triumph of industrialization.

The early research of the new economic history minimized the importance of British colonial restrictions, viewed slavery as a viable and profit-making institution, reduced the significance of the railroad in American economic development, and viewed the Civil War as a major disruption in the progress of the American economy.[3] With the exception of the railroad's indispensability, a subject still under some debate, the available evidence supported the revisions of the new school, and this sharp break with traditional views created dissension in the field during the decade of the 1960s.

---

ber 1957; Douglass C. North, "Quantitative Research in Economic History," *American Economic Review*, March 1963; Douglass C. North, "The State of Economic History," *American Economic Review*, May 1965; and Robert W. Fogel, "The Reunification of Economic History with Economic Theory," *American Economic Review*, May 1965.

[2] For a good example of issues raised against the new economic history, see Fritz Redlich, "New and Traditional Approaches to Economic History and Their Interdependence," *Journal of Economic History*, December 1965. For a full treatment of the use of counterfactual propositions, see Meyer and Conrad, "Economic Theory, Statistical Inference."

[3] British colonial policy is treated in Chapter 3; slavery is discussed in Chapter 9; the question of the indispensability of the railroad is examined in Chapter 6; and the Civil War is treated in Chapter 10.

The methodological debate between traditional and new economic history appears to have run its course, and both schools are now directing their attention to achieving a better understanding of American economic development. Each recognizes the other's merit, and the distinction between old and new economic history appears to be diminishing. The sophisticated econometric models of the new economic history are difficult to apply without a solid foundation in traditional economic history; similarly, traditional economic history cannot ignore the theoretical models and empirical evidence generated by the new economic history. Traditional economic history has provided us with a vast store of important and useful information and, in spite of several major revisions in thinking, in most instances the new economic history has corroborated traditional opinion and supplemented it with empirical evidence.

In the discussion that follows, an attempt has been made to integrate the contributions of both the new and traditional schools. With respect to most issues, the treatment is straightforward, summarizing the current state of knowledge without specifying the contributions of old or new economic historians. Concerning the several issues on which there has been a major revision of opinion, a summary of the traditional view has been provided, and this has been modified in light of the evidence supplied by the new economic history.

The Problem of Economic Development

Economic development, encompasses many facets of an economy and must be distinguished from economic growth. Measures of economic growth reflect changes in aggregate output. In the United States, the accepted accounting concept for aggregate production is gross national product (G.N.P.), defined as the sum of the value of all goods and services produced for final sale. The growth rate of the American economy usually refers to the average annual percentage rate of increase in real G.N.P. Using this definition of economic growth, it is possible to argue that most countries in the world today are growing, many at relatively rapid rates.[4] On the other hand, development economists argue that many of the world's nations are not experiencing economic development and that the large majority of nations are currently classified as underdeveloped. The apparent paradox here stems from the rigid requirements that most economists believe must be fulfilled before a nation can be considered fully developed.

In measuring economic development we are concerned with the welfare aspects of growth, as reflected in per capita income levels, as well as with improvements in technology, investment in human capital, efficiency in economic organization, institutional stability, and other related factors. Per

---

[4] See Edward Marcus and Mildred Rendl Marcus, *Economic Progress and the Developing World* (Glenview, Ill.: Scott, Foresman, 1971), p. 13.

capita income is the most commonly used measure of a country's standard of living, and it is often used to categorize countries as developed or underdeveloped. The figures in Table 1–1 point out the tremendous disparity in standards of living that exists between the rich and poor countries of the world at the present time.[5] Economists who have examined per capita income movements over time have suggested that the standard of living gap between the rich and poor countries has widened in recent years and that, despite absolute gains by poor countries, their relative per capita income position has deteriorated.[6]

In order to raise the standard of living there must be an increase in the efficiency with which resources are combined in the production of goods and services. Productivity change, defined as an increase in the ratio of output to input, generally results from improvements in technology, investment in human capital, and greater efficiency in economic organization. Increases in productivity are often accompanied by a shift in emphasis away from primary economic activity (agriculture, forestry, fishing, mining) and toward manufacturing and the service industries.[7]

Technological improvement has occurred at a rapid rate since the Industrial Revolution and has been a major contributor to the high standard of living currently enjoyed in the developing countries. On the surface, it might appear that modern communication and transportation facilities have created a situation that would foster an easy transfer of technology from the developed to the less developed nations. However, utilization of the latest techniques of production requires more than just a transfer of knowledge. The rate of adoption and implementation of modern technology is largely determined by the quality of labor, the quantity of capital, the efficiency of economic organization, and social and political conditions. The labor force must be educated and trained so that it can use the latest techniques; capital must be available in adequate supply to introduce the new technology; the system of economic organization must be capable of adopting the new techniques; and the social and political institutions must be receptive to these changes.

When a nation has progressed to the point where its standard of living is above a certain level, where it has adopted the latest advances in technology, where education is widespread, where the form of economic organization provides a system of rewards that perpetuates the growth process, and where social, cultural, and political institutions are stable

---

[5] Per capita income and per capita output are very similar in concept and, for purposes here, they can be used interchangeably.

[6] See Robert E. Baldwin, *Economic Development and Growth,* 2nd ed. (New York: Wiley, 1972), pp. 3–9.

[7] Some countries have achieved economic development by concentrating their efforts on the export of agricultural staples (Denmark, New Zealand), but generally development is accompanied by industrialization.

Table 1-1 Per Capita National Income, Selected Countries, 1970
(U.S. dollars)

Area	Per Capita Income
All Market Economies	$ 920
Developed Market Economies	2,660
Underdeveloped Market Economies	210
United States	4,274
Sweden	3,695
Canada	3,214
Denmark	2,875
Germany	2,698
Australia	2,629
France	2,606
Norway	2,550
New Zealand	2,004
United Kingdom	1,993
Finland	1,952
Japan	1,658
Israel	1,636
Italy	1,587
Ireland	1,246
Greece	998
Argentina	978
Spain	889
Venezuela	836
South Africa	728
Mexico	632
Chile	613
Portugal	610
Colombia	366
Peru	363
Turkey	348
Brazil	341
Philippines	327
Korea	241
Ghana	238[a]
Bolivia	190
Thailand	169[a]
Vietnam	163[b]
Kenya	131
Uganda	105
Indonesia	89
India	86[a]
Nigeria	83[a]

Source: *Yearbook of National Accounts Statistics, 1971*, Vol. III, United Nations, 1973.
[a] 1969
[b] 1968

and consistent with economic growth, that nation is considered to be developed.

Economic Organization in the American Economy

The American economy is organized according to the market system as opposed to the planning system. In the planning system, decisions concerning prices, wages, profits, production, and related factors are made by some central planning agency. In the market system, these decisions are made in the competitive market place. The market brings together the individual decisions of everyone in the economy and develops a rationing system (competitive market prices) which apportions factors of production and goods and services throughout the economy.

It is essential for the student of American economic development to understand the operation of a market economy. Figure 1–1 shows the major flows involved in the everyday functioning of the market system. Three major sectors are involved in the diagram: business, households, and government. Financial institutions have been separated from the business sector to depict more clearly the savings-investment linkage. The top portion of the diagram exhibits the operation of the factor market and shows the flow of factors of production (labor, capital, land and resources, and risk) from

Figure 1-1 The Circular Flow of a Market Economy

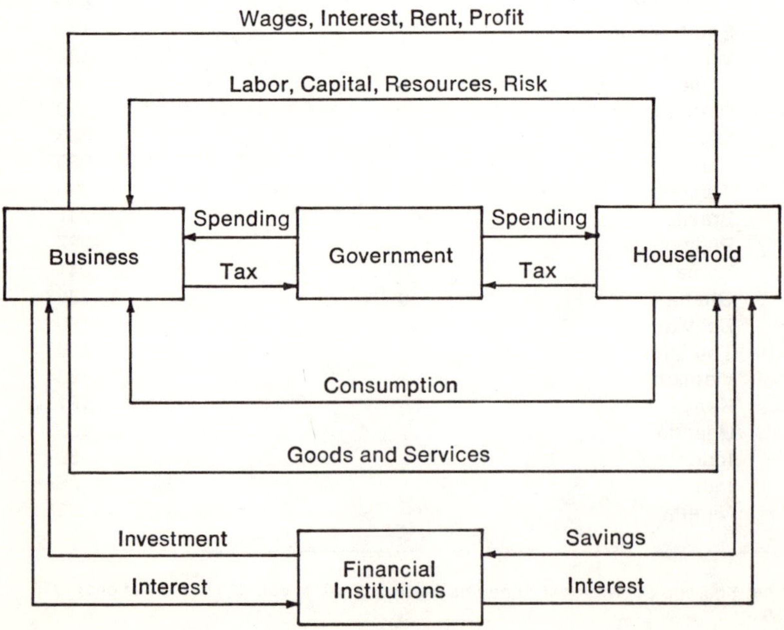

the household to the business sector. The business sector competes for factors of production, and a set of factor payments is determined. Wages are returned to labor, interest is returned to capital, rent is returned to land and resources, and profits are returned to the entrepreneur or risk bearer. The reward system established in the competitive factor market conveys to the household the current value placed on the various factors of production. The bottom portion of the diagram, excluding for the moment financial institutions, shows the operation of the goods market. Consumers enter the goods market with a stock of dollar votes to purchase goods and services. The competition of dollar votes establishes a price system which reflects current consumer preference.

Financial institutions are included in the diagram to demonstrate the link between household savings and business investment. It is assumed that households save a portion of their income and deposit these savings in financial institutions in order to earn interest. The individual savings of many households are pooled to make investment loans to the business sector.

The major fiscal operations of government are also included in the diagram. Government taxing and spending policies directly affect the aggregate level of economic activity and the pace of economic growth. In a pure market economy, there is very little direct government interference. However, the mixed economy of the United States has a long tradition of government involvement, and it is appropriate to include government in the diagram.[8]

Summary

This chapter has discussed the methodological debate that occurred in the middle 1960s between traditional and new economic historians. In recent years, the dispute over approaches to economic history has subsided, and both traditional and new economic historians have recognized the shortsightedness of a single approach to economic history. In addition to highlighting the current state of economic history, this chapter also has developed some basic notions of economic growth and development, and it has outlined the broad flows that characterize the everyday operation of a market economy.

Suggested Reading

Davis, Lance E., " 'And It Will Never Be Literature': The New Economic History, A Critique," *Explorations in Entrepreneurial History,* Fall 1968.

[8] The role of government in American economic development is treated in Chapter 8.

Fishlow, Albert, and Robert W. Fogel, "Quantitative Economic History: An Interim Evaluation, Past Trends and Present Tendencies," *Journal of Economic History,* March 1971.

Fogel, Robert W. "The Reunification of Economic History with Economic Theory," *American Economic Review,* May 1965.

Meyer, John R., and Alfred H. Conrad, "Economic Theory, Statistical Inference, and Economic History," *Journal of Economic History,* December 1957.

North, Douglass C., "Quantitative Research in Economic History," *American Economic Review,* March 1963.

———, "The State of Economic History," *American Economic Review,* May 1965.

Redlich, Fritz, "New and Traditional Approaches to Economic History and Their Interdependence," *Journal of Economic History,* December 1965.

———, "Potentialities and Pitfalls in Economic History," *Explorations in Entrepreneurial History,* Fall 1968.

2

The Long-Run Pattern of American Economic Development

This chapter begins with an assessment of the long-run growth trend in America's per capita income, and it analyzes the issue of smooth versus discontinuous growth. The second portion of the chapter provides a summary of statistical trends in a number of variables which reflect the pace and pattern of the nation's development. Attention is given to trends in population, immigration, production, employment, technology, and foreign trade. The overview provided by this chapter is a convenient reference point from which to begin the study of specific features of American economic development.

The Issue of Discontinuity in Economic Development

W. W. Rostow is most closely associated with the thesis that economic development takes place in discontinuous fashion. Rostow attempted to formalize the long-run process of economic development by identifying five separate stages that a country passes through in becoming a fully developed nation.[1] These five stages are: traditional society, preconditions for take-off, take-off, drive to maturity, and age of high mass consumption. For our purposes, the most interesting stage is the take-off, since it is during this period that a country is transformed from an underdeveloped to a developed nation.

---

[1] W. W. Rostow, *The Stages of Economic Growth: A Non-Communist Manifesto* (Cambridge: At the University Press, 1960).

Rostow described the take-off as a period of several decades of intensive development. The conditions which set the take-off in motion are the following:

1) An increase in the rate of investment (share of output committed to capital formation) from 5 percent or less to 10 percent or more.
2) The development of one or more substantial manufacturing sectors with a high rate of growth (manufacturing is defined to include processing of agricultural products by modern methods).
3) The existence or emergence of a political, social, and institutional framework conducive to economic development.

Rostow dates the take-off for the major developed countries of the world as follows: Great Britain, 1783–1802; France, 1830–60; Belgium, 1833–60; United States, 1843–60; Germany, 1850–73; Sweden, 1868–90; Japan, 1878–1900; Russia, 1890–1914; and Canada, 1896–1914.[2] In examining Rostow's take-off thesis, we wish to determine whether the American economy experienced a discontinuous shift, dating from the 1840s, in its long-run per capita output trend.[3] If Rostow is correct, one would expect to see a significant upward surge in the long-run growth trend in per capita output during the 1843–60 period.

Raymond Goldsmith's work on long-run growth trends in the American economy is the most thorough empirical investigation of nineteenth- and twentieth-century growth available to the economic historian.[4] However, since Goldsmith's work concentrated on the period 1839–1959, it does not yield data with which to test the Rostovian hypothesis of discontinuity. Goldsmith demonstrated that during the period 1839–1959 real per capita output in the American economy grew at an average annual percentage rate of 1.64 percent; this suggests that the standard of living was doubling approximately every forty years. Goldsmith also demonstrated that growth had been quite smooth during the 120-year time span. The following 60- and 40-year subperiod rates of growth in real per capita output were calculated: 1839–99, 1.67 percent; 1899–1959, 1.62 percent; 1839–79, 1.55 percent; 1879–1919, 1.76 percent; and 1919–59, 1.64 percent.

---

[2] According to Rostow, the American take-off was primarily the result of railroad expansion. Chapters 5 and 6 take a close look at the impact of transportation developments on the American economy, and Chapter 6 pays specific attention to the issue of the railroad's indispensability.

[3] For a more detailed treatment of the take-off stage, see Rostow, *The Stages of Economic Growth,* Chapter 4.

[4] See Raymond Goldsmith, "Historical and Comparative Rates of Production, Productivity, and Prices," United States Congress, Joint Economic Committee, *Hearings,* Part 2, 86th Congress, 1st Session, 1959.

Using Goldsmith's work as a starting point, George R. Taylor examined pre-1840 American economic growth.[5] Taylor's analysis was highly qualitative and contained a rather meager amount of empirical support. He indicated that some growth had occurred during the latter part of the colonial period, 1710–75, but that the pre-1840 period as a whole was one of slow growth. Taylor argued that there was virtually no change in the standard of living during the first three decades of the nineteenth century. Douglass North reached the same conclusion and suggested that there had been appreciable change in the standard of living during the first half of the nineteenth century.[6] On the surface, the work of North and Taylor, in conjunction with that of Goldsmith, appeared to corroborate the Rostovian argument of discontinuity in per capita output growth.

Recent study has rejected the notion of take-off for the American economy, and, at present, the thesis of a discontinuous jump into economic development is generally disregarded. In an excellent paper, Paul David developed a model to analyze American economic growth during the period 1800–1860.[7] The theoretical framework and empirical support David developed allow for much more rigorous analysis of early growth than the methods of North and Taylor. David's analysis suggests that American economic growth during the first half of the nineteenth century was characterized by cycles of expansion and retardation rather than a discontinuous change in the 1840s. David cited three separate periods of expansion during the pre–Civil War era: early 1790s–1807, early 1820s–1834, and middle 1840s–late 1850s. The following average annual percentage rates of growth in real per capita output were estimated for 20 year intervals: 1800–1820, 0.24 percent; 1810–30, 1.54 percent; 1820–40, 1.96 percent; 1830–50, 1.37 percent; 1840–60, 1.59 percent. David demonstrated that growth during the decades of the 1840s and 1850s was not significantly different from that of the early nineteenth century; therefore he concluded that the thesis of a discontinuous change in the long-run trend of growth in the form of a Rostovian take-off is not relevant to the American experience.

A Statistical Reconstruction of the Past

Now we turn to a survey of the broad trends in population, immigration, production, employment, technology, and foreign relations that have characterized our past. American population has grown rapidly throughout our

---

[5] George R. Taylor, "American Economic Growth Before 1840: An Exploratory Essay," *Journal of Economic History*, December 1964.

[6] Douglass C. North, "Early National Income Estimates of the United States," *Economic Development and Cultural Change*, April 1961.

[7] Paul A. David, "The Growth of Real Product in the United States Before 1840: New Evidence, Controlled Conjectures," *Journal of Economic History*, June 1967.

history, and this was especially true during the heavy immigration period from colonial times until World War I. (See Table 2–1.) Population growth during the colonial period consisted largely of British migration to America. The majority of migrants came to America voluntarily, but many came under one of several forms of temporary servitude. In addition, slaves were brought from Africa to the American colonies to augment the labor supply

Table 2-1 United States Population, 1630-1970

Year	Number of Inhabitants
1630	4,646
1640	26,634
1650	50,368
1660	75,058
1670	111,935
1680	151,507
1690	210,372
1700	250,888
1710	331,711
1720	466,185
1730	629,445
1740	905,563
1750	1,170,760
1760	1,593,625
1770	2,148,076
1780	2,780,369
1790	3,929,214
1800	5,308,483
1810	7,239,881
1820	9,638,453
1830	12,866,020
1840	17,069,453
1850	23,191,876
1860	31,443,321
1870	39,818,449
1880	50,155,783
1890	62,947,714
1900	75,994,575
1910	91,972,266
1920	105,710,620
1930	122,775,046
1940	131,669,275
1950	150,697,361
1960	179,975,000
1970	203,805,000

Source: *Historical Statistics*, U.S. Bureau of the Census, Series Z 1-19 and A 17-21; *Statistical Abstract*, U.S. Department of Commerce, 1972, p. 14.

in the South in order to maximize the flow of resources to England. Immigration contributed large shares to American population throughout the nineteenth and early twentieth centuries, with heavy inflows from Great Britain, Ireland, Germany, and Scandinavia during the nineteenth century and eastern and southern Europe, especially Italy, in the early twentieth century. In absolute numbers, immigration reached a peak shortly before World War I with the annual flow to the United States exceeding one million people in 1905, 1906, 1907, 1910, 1913, and 1914. Migration was significantly curtailed after 1914 and again after 1930, and it has not been a major factor in American population growth since the early twentieth century. (See Table 2–2.)

Table 2-2 Annual Flow of Immigrants to America, 1820-1970

Year	Immigrants
1820	8,385
1830	23,322
1840	84,066
1850	369,980
1860	153,640
1870	387,203
1880	457,257
1890	455,302
1900	448,572
1910	1,041,570
1920	430,001
1930	241,700
1940	70,756
1950	249,187
1960	265,398
1970	373,326

Source: *Historical Statistics,* Series C 88-114; *Statistical Abstract,* 1972, p. 93.

In addition to migration, one must take note of changes in the natural factors affecting population growth: the birth rate and the death rate. (See Table 2–3.) The birth rate, defined here as the number of total live births per one thousand population, declined sharply during the nineteenth and early twentieth centuries, reaching a trough in the depression of the 1930s. More recent times have witnessed a rise after World War II and a decline during the 1960s. The death rate remained stable during the nineteenth century, and results from improvements in health care did not show up until early in the twentieth century. Advances in medicine and health care are also reflected by the significant increase in life expectancy at birth shown in Table 2–3.

Table 2-3 Birth and Death Rates and Life Expectancy, 1820-1970

Year	Birth Rate[a]	Death Rate[b]	Life Expectancy at Birth
1820	55.2	—	—
1840	51.8	—	—
1860	44.3	—	—
1880	39.8	—	—
1900	32.3	17.2	47.3
1910	30.1	14.7	50.0
1920	27.7	13.0	54.1
1930	21.3	11.3	59.7
1940	19.4	10.8	62.9
1950	24.1	9.6	68.2
1960	23.7	9.5	69.7
1970	18.2	9.4	70.8

Source: *Historical Statistics,* Series B 19-30, B 92-100, B 129-142; *Statistical Abstract,* 1972, pp. 50, 55, and 57.

[a] Live births per 1000 population.

[b] Number of deaths, excluding fetal deaths, per 1000 population.

The nineteenth and twentieth centuries have witnessed a tremendous change in the industrial structure of the American economy. At the beginning of the nineteenth century, the majority of Americans were employed in such primary economic activity as agriculture, forestry, and fishing. Since that time there has been a steady decline in primary activity's share of national production and employment. Robert Gallman has provided us with a valuable reconstruction of sectoral developments in commodity output during the period 1839–99.[8] Gallman's data clearly point to the dramatic nineteenth-century rise of manufacturing and the steady relative decline of agriculture. (See Table 2–4.) Recent data show a continuation of these trends and also document the significant relative advance of service industries. (See Table 2–5.)

Industry employment trends corroborate the results suggested by output and national income data. Occupational data indicate that a significant shift toward white collar occupations accompanied the rise of manufacturing and service industries. At the beginning of the twentieth century, the large majority of Americans were either categorized as blue collar or farm laborers; by 1970, 48.3 percent of all Americans were employed as white collar workers. (See Table 2–6.)

[8] Robert E. Gallman, "Commodity Output, 1839–1899," in *Trends in the American Economy in the Nineteenth Century,* Conference on Research in Income and Wealth, Studies in Income and Wealth, National Bureau of Economic Research, Vol. 24 (Princeton: Princeton University Press, 1960).

Table 2-4 Sectoral Shares in Commodity Output, 1839-99 (percentages)

Year	Agriculture	Mining	Manufacturing	Construction
1839	72%	1%	17%	10%
1849	60	1	30	10
1859	56	1	32	11
1869	53	2	33	12
1879	49	3	37	11
1889	37	4	48	11
1899	33	5	53	9

Source: Robert E. Gallman, "Commodity Output, 1839-1899," in *Trends in the American Economy In the Nineteenth Century*. Conference on Research in Income and Wealth, Studies in Income and Wealth, National Bureau of Economic Research (Princeton: Princeton University Press, 1960), p. 26. Reprinted by permission of the National Bureau of Economic Research.

Table 2-5 Percentage Distribution of National Income by Industry, 1930-70

Industry	1930	1940	1950	1960	1970
Agriculture	8.3%	7.6%	7.4%	4.1%	3.1%
Mining	2.1	2.3	2.1	1.4	0.9
Construction	4.3	3.2	4.9	5.0	5.3
Manufacturing	24.3	27.4	30.9	30.5	27.6
Trade	16.3	17.6	17.8	15.6	15.4
Finance, Insurance and Real Estate	14.1	10.1	9.0	11.2	11.0
Transportation, Communication, and Public Utilities	11.2	9.9	8.5	8.5	7.6
Services	12.3	11.0	9.6	10.8	13.1
Government	7.1	10.9	9.8	12.9	16.0

Source: *Historical Statistics*, Series F 22-33; *Statistical Abstract*, 1972, p. 318.

The structural changes characterizing the American economy during the nineteenth and twentieth centuries have been associated with a marked increase in efficiency. The most easily calculated productivity measure is real output per manhour; the trend in this measure for the total economy during 1890–1955 is shown in Table 2–7. In a pioneering study of productivity change in the American economy, John W. Kendrick pointed out that productivity increases have been widespread in all industries, and that the rate of advance in productivity, which has been substantial, increased after World War I.[9]

American economic development has always been strongly tied to foreign trade and foreign capital flows. Significant changes in America's bal-

[9] John W. Kendrick, *Productivity Trends in the United States* (Princeton: Princeton University Press, 1961).

Table 2-6 Percentage Distribution of the Employed Labor Force, by Major Occupation, 1900-1970

Occupation	1900	1910	1920	1930	1940	1950	1960	1970
White Collar	17.6%	21.3%	25.0%	29.4%	31.1%	36.6%	43.1%	48.3%
Professional and Technical	4.3	4.7	5.4	6.8	7.5	8.6	11.2	14.2
Managerial	5.9	6.6	6.6	7.4	7.3	8.7	10.6	10.5
Clerical	3.0	5.3	8.0	8.9	9.6	12.3	14.7	17.4
Sales	4.5	4.7	4.9	6.3	6.7	7.0	6.6	6.2
Blue Collar	35.8	38.2	40.1	39.6	39.8	41.1	39.7	35.3
Craftsmen	10.6	11.6	13.0	12.8	12.0	14.2	13.8	12.9
Operatives	12.8	14.6	15.6	15.8	18.4	20.4	20.1	17.7
Laborers, excluding Farm	12.5	12.0	11.6	11.0	9.4	6.6	5.8	4.7
Service	9.1	9.6	7.9	9.8	11.7	10.5	10.9	12.4
Farm	37.5	30.9	27.0	21.2	17.4	11.8	6.4	4.0

Source: *Historical Statistics,* Series D 72-122; *Statistical Abstract,* 1972, p. 230.

Table 2-7 Index of Real Output per Manhour, 1890-1955 (1929 = 100)

Year	Productivity Index
1890	45.7
1895	50.7
1900	55.6
1905	59.9
1910	64.4
1915	67.2
1920	78.3
1925	91.6
1930	97.5
1935	108.0
1940	124.0
1945	159.0
1950	175.4
1955	204.8

Source: *Historical Statistics*, Series W 1-11.

ance of trade and in the composition of items involved in foreign trade occurred during the nineteenth and twentieth centuries. Table 2–8 exhibits the nation's merchandise exports and imports and the resulting surplus or deficit in foreign trade from 1790 to 1970.[10] Since the late nineteenth century, the American economy has always been successful in maintaining a large surplus in merchandise trade.[11] Figures in Table 2–9 indicate that a significant change in the composition of America's exports and imports has taken place during the past decades. In the early years, America was primarily an exporter of raw materials and an importer of finished manufactured goods. Recent trends have altered this situation, and currently the nation's exports and imports consist primarily of manufactured items.

The international investment position of the United States has changed from one in which the nation was traditionally an importer of capital to one in which it has become an exporter of capital. The net assets or liabilities of the United States, defined as American investment abroad minus foreign investment in the United States, are shown in Table 2–10; the figures clearly demonstrate the improved American investment position. The nation incurred net liabilities in international investment until the end of World War I; the only net liabilities since that time occurred during World War II.

---

[10] Merchandise trade excludes movements of gold and silver.

[11] Figures for 1971 indicate a deficit in merchandise trade of −$1465 million, the first deficit since 1889.

Table 2-8 Merchandise Exports and Imports, 1790-1970 (millions of dollars)

Year	Exports	Imports	Surplus (+) or Deficit (−)
1790	20	23	−3
1800	71	91	−20
1810	67	85	−19
1820	70	74	−4
1830	72	63	+9
1840	124	98	+26
1850	144	174	−30
1860	334	354	−20
1870	393	436	−43
1880	836	668	+168
1890	858	789	+69
1900	1394	850	+544
1910	1745	1557	+188
1920	8228	5278	+2950
1930	3843	3061	+782
1940	4021	2625	+1396
1950[a]	14354	10501	+3853
1960	20575	14654	+5922
1970	43224	39952	+3272

Source: *Historical Statistics,* U 1-14; *Statistical Abstract,* 1972, p. 776.
[a]The figures for 1950 represent the average for 1950-55; 1950 was an atypical year for the early fifties with a surplus of only +1423.

Summary

The above overview of long-run trends in population, output, employment, productivity, and foreign trade provides a convenient starting point for the study of American economic history. The United States has achieved a standard of living unparalleled in the world, and this has not been due to any single factor or isolated event, but, instead, it has resulted from an almost ideal combination of circumstances. In the early stages of development, the American economy was endowed with a rich natural resource base, a high land/labor ratio, a favorable mix of public and private enterprise, access to British capital and technology, selective inflow of European migration, and early transportation development; the joint operation of these and other favorable circumstances created a solid base for United States economic development. To be sure, there have been periodic fluctuations in the rate of progess, but these have been temporary setbacks, and the overriding trend has been one of unparalleled growth and development.

Table 2-9 Value of Merchandise Exports and Imports, by Economic Class, 1830-1970 (millions of dollars)

Year	Crude Materials	Crude Foodstuffs	Manufactured Foodstuffs	Semi-Manufactures	Finished Manufactures
Exports					
1830	37	3	10	4	5
1840	76	5	16	5	11
1850	84	8	20	6	17
1860	217	12	39	13	36
1870	214	42	51	14	56
1880	243	266	193	29	93
1890	309	132	225	46	133
1900	340	226	320	153	332
1910	574	110	259	268	499
1920	1883	918	1117	958	3205
1930	829	179	363	513	1898
1940	464	74	167	900	2330
1950	1886	760	634	1121	5741
1960	1475	2569	416	2531	13155
1970	3427	4181	691	2628	30026
Imports					
1830	5	7	10	5	36
1840	12	15	15	11	44
1850	13	18	21	26	95
1860	40	46	60	35	172
1870	57	54	96	56	174
1880	142	100	118	111	197
1890	180	128	133	117	231
1900	282	98	133	134	203
1910	578	145	182	285	368
1920	1784	578	1238	802	877
1930	1002	400	293	608	757
1940	1011	285	277	559	409
1950	2465	1750	898	2126	1504
1960	1486	2403	967	2970	6845
1970	1966	4409	1870	4527	25907

Source: *Historical Statistics,* Series U 61-72; *Statistical Abstract,* 1972, p. 777.

Suggested Reading

Budd, Edward C., "Factor Shares, 1850–1910," in *Trends in the American Economy in the Nineteenth Century,* Conference on Research in Income and Wealth, Studies in Income and Wealth, National Bureau of Economic Research, Vol. 24. Princeton: Princeton University Press, 1960.

David, Paul A., "The Growth of Real Product in the United States Before

Table 2-10 International Investment Position of the United States, Selected Years, 1790-1970
(millions of dollars 1790-1900; billions of dollars 1908-70)

Year	Assets (+) or Liabilities (−)
1790	−61
1800	−83
1810	−85
1820	−88
1830	−75
1840	−261
1850	−217
1860	−377
1870	−1252
1880	−1584
1890	−2894
1900	−2501
1908	−3.9
1914	−3.7
1919	+3.7
1927	+7.2
1935	+7.1
1940	−1.2
1945	−0.8
1950	+13.3
1955	+37.2
1960	+44.7
1965	+61.6
1970	+69.1

Source: *Historical Statistics,* Series U 193-206 and U 207; *Statistical Abstract,* 1972, p. 765.

1840: New Evidence, Controlled Conjectures," *Journal of Economic History,* June 1967.

Easterlin, Richard A., "Interregional Differences in Per Capita Income, Population, and Total Income, 1840–1950," in *Trends in the American Economy.*

———, *Population, Labor Force, and Long Swings in Economic Growth: The American Experience* (New York: Columbia University Press, 1968).

———, "Regional Income Trends, 1840–1950," in Seymour Harris, ed., *American Economic History.* New York: McGraw-Hill, 1961.

Gallman, Robert E., "Commodity Output, 1839–1899," in *Trends in the American Economy.*

———, "Gross National Product in the United States, 1834–1909," in *Output, Employment, and Productivity in the United States after 1800,* Conference on Research in Income and Wealth, Studies in Income and

Wealth, National Bureau of Economic Research, Vol. 30. New York: Columbia University Press, 1966.

Goldsmith, Raymond, "Historical and Comparative Rates of Production, Productivity, and Prices," United States Congress, Joint Economic Committee, *Hearings,* Part 2, 86th Congress, 1st Session, 1959.

Kendrick, John W., *Productivity Trends in the United States.* Princeton: Princeton University Press, 1961.

Meeker, Edward, "The Improving Health of the United States, 1850–1915," *Explorations in Economic History,* Summer 1972.

———, "The Social Rate of Return on Investment in Public Health, 1880–1910," *Journal of Economic History,* June 1974.

North, Douglass C., "The United States Balance of Payments, 1790–1860," in *Trends in the American Economy.*

Simon, Matthew, "The United States Balance of Payments, 1861–1900," in *Trends in the American Economy.*

Soltow, Lee C., "Evidence on Income Inequality in the United States, 1866–1965," *Journal of Economic History,* June 1969.

Taylor, George R., "American Economic Growth Before 1840: An Exploratory Essay," *Journal of Economic History,* December 1964.

3
The Colonial Period

The disintegration of feudalism in Europe resulted in the concentration of political power in nation states, and the rise of European nationalism was, in part, a reaction against the decentralized system of political organization that had characterized feudalism. The nature of the feudal system, with its emphasis on privileges and obligations at the local level, had stymied the development of strong centralized nation states. Machiavelli, Bodin, and other leading writers in the formative period of the nationalist movement stated the case for concentration of political power, and associated with the rise of nationalism was a collection of pragmatic economic policies intended to aid in the creation of a strong national state. These economic policies, generally referred to as mercantilism, flourished throughout Europe from the late 1500s to the late 1700s, between the end of the feudal period and the rise of laissez faire. Mercantilist doctrines are of interest to us because they set in motion world exploration and the settlement of colonies, including America.

Mercantilist Economic Policies

There was never a formal school of economic thought calling itself mercantilism, but most mercantilist writers were concerned with several pragmatic policies aimed at increasing the political strength of the nation state. Mercantilists were very much aware of competition with other nation states and consequently developed economic policies aimed at enhancing their nation's political strength relative to that of other nations. Mercantilists measured political power in terms of the amount of wealth a nation had accumulated. The most desirable form of wealth was gold, and the major means of acquiring gold were mining and trading. In the absence of indigenous or colonial mineral wealth, a country was forced to turn its attention to trading, and mercantilists argued that a nation should always seek to maintain a favorable balance of trade, that is, an excess of exports over imports. The difference between exports and imports is the gold flow to settle accounts. By running a favorable balance of trade, a mercantilist country could increase its stock of gold and, thereby, insure its political strength.

Mercantilist thinking emphasized government controls and direct government economic activity. In order to guarantee a favorable balance of trade, mercantilists argued that the government should encourage exports, through bounty payments and subsidies, and discourage imports, through tariffs and direct prohibition. The government should also establish a hierarchy of occupations consistent with a favorable trade balance: trade would rank first, manufacturing second, and agriculture last. The mercantilists viewed agriculture as a sector unable to generate surpluses beyond domestic consumption needs and, therefore, not conducive to maintaining a favorable balance of trade.

The mercantilists viewed the world's stock of wealth as fixed. In order to become wealthy a nation had to increase its influence relative to that of other nations. The mercantilists viewed the world as one of extreme national competition and failed to recognize that all nations could benefit from trade. They wanted to be self-sufficient and independent of their neighbors. This view of the competitive nature of the world, along with the desire to be self-sufficient, led to the search for colonies that could supply products the mercantilist country needed. Colonies also were viewed as a source of demand for manufactured goods produced by the mercantilist country. This outside demand could increase exports and thereby contribute to a favorable balance of trade and stimulate industrial growth in the mercantilist country.[1]

Establishment of the American Colonies

Chartered companies representing economic interests stimulated the earliest permanent settlements in America. The settlements by the English (Virginia and Massachusetts), the Dutch (New York), and the Swedes (Delaware) were all supported by merchant and trading companies. It is true that religious idealism motivated some settlement such as that in Massachusetts, but all the early settlements depended on economic interests for their livelihood. The proprietorship formed the other major type of colonial organization. Proprietary colonies were established by individuals who had obtained large grants of American land from the English government. During the latter half

[1] For an excellent summary of mercantilist doctrine, see Alexander Gray, *The Development of Economic Doctrine* (New York: Wiley, 1961).

of the seventeenth century, proprietary colonies were established in Maine, New Hampshire, New Jersey, Pennsylvania, Maryland, and Carolina.

Outmigration from the original colony in Massachusetts extended British settlement throughout New England. British influence was further extended during the 1660s when the English took New York and Delaware by force from the Dutch and the Swedes. The debtor settlement in Georgia in 1732 became the last British colony established in America. Earlier, the Spanish had established colonies in Florida, Mexico, the West Indies, and in the southwestern part of North America, and the French had established colonies or trading posts along the St. Lawrence River, the Great Lakes, and the Mississippi and Ohio rivers.

Land Tenure and Settlement

Despite several early attempts in Virginia and Massachusetts to develop a communal type of economy where all production was pooled and distributed by a central authority, individual land tenure developed very early in Colonial America. The size of individual land holdings varied greatly among the colonies. In New England, the average holding was generally less than 20 acres; in the middle colonies, the majority of plots was between 100 and 300 acres; and in the southern colonies, tracts in excess of 1000 acres were common. Southern settlers on the whole attempted to institute a feudal system of organization, and this was reflected in the region's large land holdings. The economical production of southern crops afforded by large-scale units gave further inducement to large holdings.

Throughout the colonial period, scarcity of labor relative to land characterized the American economy. As a result of this factor imbalance, several methods of inducing migration to the colonies became popular during the 1600s. Land in New England was largely settled as an outgrowth of earlier settlements, and new towns were continually being established. Each new town petitioned for a certain acreage of land which was distributed to town members according to needs and planned use.

In the proprietary colonies, land settlement was left to the discretion of the individual proprietor. Proprietors established a headright system whereby a certain number of acres (generally fifty) was provided for every freeman brought to the colonies. Small farmers used the headright system to obtain family-sized units, and shippers, merchants, and financiers used it to earn rights to land by transporting individuals to the colonies. During the 1600s, the headright system was used extensively to settle areas of New York, New Jersey, Pennsylvania, Maryland, Virginia, the Carolinas, and Georgia. However, by 1700, the system had fallen out of use, and most land in the middle and southern colonies was sold.

The indentured servant system became another means of inducing migration to America. An indentured servant would obligate himself to work for the person who paid his passage; the work obligations generally ran for two to seven years. This system opened avenues for employment in America to those who could not afford to bear the costs of migration. Indentured servants often could obtain land at the end of their servitude. Furthermore, those who paid the passage of indentured servants could qualify for land under the headright system, and this encouraged an active search for volunteers to migrate to America. The system flourished during the 1600s, and it is estimated that at least one-half of all those who migrated to America during the seventeenth century came as indentures.

Slavery replaced the indentured servant system on the large southern estates. Blacks were first brought to America in 1619, but the figures in Table 3–1 show that slavery expanded very slowly until the 1690s. However, between 1700 and 1780 there was a tremendous increase in the American slave population, particularly in Virginia, Maryland, and the Carolinas, and slaves replaced indentured servants in southern agriculture.

Regional Differences Among the American Colonies

Methods employed to encourage migration to America were highly successful, and the colonies were settled at a rapid pace. Most of the early migration was concentrated in Virginia and Massachusetts, and, until 1700, these colonies accounted for 50 percent or more of the total colonial population. (See Table 3–2.) Virginia's population expansion was especially impressive, and, at the end of the colonial period, she still accounted for approximately 20 percent of total population. Connecticut, New York, Pennsylvania, Maryland, and North Carolina underwent significant population growth during the 1700s, and, by 1780, each of these colonies had a population in excess of 200,000 .

Three distinct groups of American colonies can be distinguished: New England, middle, and southern. The New England colonies did not readily fit into the ideal mercantilist mold. The agricultural resource base in New England was rather poor, and there was little surplus output that could be sent to England. During the early colonial period the region was mainly known for such maritime activities as fishing, shipping, and shipbuilding; later in the period, household manufacturing also became important. In both shipping and manufacturing, the New England colonies periodically came into competition with the British, and the region was often at odds with the mother country. Similarly, the middle colonies were not ideally suited to the mercantilist ambitions of the British. The area was capable of generating an agricultural surplus, but goods available for export—basic grains and livestock—were not in short supply in England. Nevertheless, the New England and middle colonies were not engaged in much significant

Table 3-1 Estimated Negro Population of the American Colonies, 1630-1780

Year	New England	Middle Atlantic (excluding Maryland)	Maryland	Virginia	North Carolina	South Carolina	Georgia
1630	—	10	—	50	—	—	—
1640	180	232	20	150	—	—	—
1650	380	515	300	405	—	—	—
1660	562	630	758	950	20	—	—
1670	375	790	1190	2000	150	30	—
1680	470	1480	1611	3000	210	200	—
1690	950	2472	2162	9345	300	1500	—
1700	1680	3661	3227	16390	415	2444	—
1710	2585	6218	7945	23118	900	4100	—
1720	3956	10825	12499	26559	3000	12000	—
1730	6118	11683	17220	30000	6000	20000	—
1740	8541	16452	24031	60000	11000	30000	—
1750	10982	20736	43450	101452	19800	39000	1000
1760	12717	29049	49004	140570	33554	57334	3578
1770	15367	34929	63818	187605	69600	75178	10625
1780	14427	42365	80515	220582	91000	97000	20831

Source: *Historical Statistics*, Series Z 1-19.

Table 3-2 Estimated Population of the American Colonies, 1630-1780

Colony	1630	1640	1650	1660	1670	1680	1690	1700
Maine[a]	400	900	1000	—	—	—	—	—
New Hampshire	500	1055	1305	1555	1805	2047	4164	4958
Vermont	—	—	—	—	—	—	—	—
Plymouth[b]	390	1020	1566	1980	5333	6400	7424	—
Massachusetts	506	8932	14037	20082	30000	39752	49504	55941
Rhode Island	—	300	785	1539	2155	3017	4224	5894
Connecticut	—	1472	4139	7980	12603	17246	21645	25970
New York	350	1930	4116	4936	5754	9830	13909	19107
New Jersey	—	—	—	—	1000	3400	8000	14010
Pennsylvania	—	—	—	—	—	680	11450	17950
Delaware	—	—	185	540	700	1005	1482	2470
Maryland	—	583	4504	8426	13226	17904	24024	29604
Virginia	2500	10442	18731	27020	35309	43596	53046	58560
North Carolina	—	—	—	1000	3850	5430	7600	10720
South Carolina	—	—	—	—	200	1200	3900	5704
Georgia	—	—	—	—	—	—	—	—
Kentucky	—	—	—	—	—	—	—	—
Tennessee	—	—	—	—	—	—	—	—
Total	4646	26634	50368	75058	111935	151507	210372	250888

[a]Maine is included in Massachusetts for 1660-1760.
[b]Plymouth is included with Massachusetts after 1690.

Table 3-2 *Cont.*

Colony	1710	1720	1730	1740	1750	1760	1770	1780
Maine[a]	—	—	—	—	—	—	31257	49133
New Hampshire	5681	9375	10755	23256	27505	39093	62396	87802
Vermont	—	—	—	—	—	—	10000	47620
Plymouth[b]	—	—	—	—	—	—	—	—
Massachusetts	62390	91008	114116	151613	188000	222600	235308	268627
Rhode Island	7573	11680	16950	25255	33226	45471	58196	52946
Connecticut	39450	58830	75530	89580	111280	142470	183881	206701
New York	21625	36919	48594	63665	76696	117138	162920	210541
New Jersey	19872	29818	37510	51373	71393	93813	117431	139627
Pennsylvania	24450	30962	51707	85637	119666	183703	240057	327305
Delaware	3645	5385	9170	19870	28704	33250	35496	45385
Maryland	42741	66133	91113	116093	141073	162267	202599	245474
Virginia	78281	87757	114000	180440	231033	339726	447016	538004
North Carolina	15120	21270	30000	51760	72984	110442	197200	270133
South Carolina	10883	17048	30000	45000	64000	94074	124244	180000
Georgia	—	—	—	2021	5200	9578	23375	56071
Kentucky	—	—	—	—	—	—	15700	45000
Tennessee	—	—	—	—	—	—	1000	10000
Total	331711	466185	629445	905563	1170760	1593625	2148076	2780369

Source: *Historical Statistics*, Series Z 1-19.
[a]Maine is included in Massachusetts for 1660-1760.
[b]Plymouth is included with Massachusetts after 1690.

large-scale manufacturing, and both regions depended on external supplies of manufactured goods.[2]

The southern colonies were much better suited than the northern colonies to the British mercantilist goals in America. The South produced surpluses of such products as rice, tobacco, indigo, and naval stores; all these were not produced in England or Europe and were in great demand. A direct shuttle trade between England and the South developed, involving the exchange of southern resources for British manufactured goods. Mercantilists viewed this as the ideal type of commercial relation between the mother country and her colonies. (See Table 3–3 for figures on trade between England and the American colonies.)

Table 3-3 Value of Exports to and Imports from England by the American Colonies, 1700-1774 (pounds sterling)

Year	Exports	Imports
1700	395,021	344,341
1705	150,961	291,722
1710	249,814	293,659
1715	297,246	452,366
1720	468,188	319,702
1725	415,650	549,693
1730	572,585	536,860
1735	652,326	668,664
1740	718,416	813,382
1745	554,431	535,253
1750	814,768	1,313,083
1755	939,553	1,112,997
1760	761,099	2,611,764
1765	1,151,698	1,944,114
1770	1,015,535	1,925,571
1774	1,373,846	2,590,437

Source: *Historical Statistics,* Series Z 21-34.

Colonial Trade Routes

Regional differences in resources, climate, and economic activity exercised an important influence on commercial relations between England and the American colonies. The South traded heavily with England, and, until re-

[2] Later in the colonial period American manufacturing did compete with England, and restrictions were placed on wool and woolen textiles (1699), hats (1732), and iron (1750). The nature of these restrictions on manufacturing are explained later in this chapter.

cently, historians viewed the direct shuttle trade with England as the region's only important commercial route. On the other hand, the northern colonies were not suited to direct shuttle trade with England. Consequently, historians regarded them as being involved in several important triangular patterns of trade that enabled them to buy British manufactured goods. The triangular trade thesis suggested that the northern colonies sought out third markets in which they could trade their surplus products for goods that were in demand in England; they could then ship these goods to England in exchange for manufactured goods. The West Indies and the southern European countries were viewed as the two most significant third markets involved in the triangular trade. Another important commercial route in the colonial period was that which involved the African slave trade, molasses, and rum. New Englanders bought molasses from the middle colonies, converted this to rum, and sent the rum to Africa to purchase slaves to be sold in the West Indies and in the South. The British encouraged the institution of slavery as an expedient means of increasing the labor supply which would enhance the flow of southern resources to England.[3]

Recently, there have been some important revisions regarding colonial commerce. Gary Walton, in a detailed study of American trade during the colonial period, has raised serious doubts concerning the validity of the triangular trade notion.[4] Walton examined the routes followed by American ships that embarked for the West Indies. He found that almost all of the trade between America and the West Indies was a direct shuttle-type operation; in other words, American ships returned to the American colonies after trading in the West Indies. Walton found no evidence to support the notion that American ships went to the West Indies, stocked up with goods that were in demand in England, and then set sail for England. Of course, the Americans may have returned home with West Indian products and then re-exported these to England; however, this is not triangular trade. Due to insufficient data, Walton could not test for the existence of triangular trade with southern Europe.

Walton also examined the trade flows between the three groups of American colonies and major foreign markets and other American colonies, and he raised some serious questions about the degree of British monopoly of southern trade. (See Table 3–4.) The figures in Table 3-4 show that the South was actively engaged in trade with the West Indies, southern Europe, and the other American colonies. In fact, the South exported more com-

---

[3] This is the standard view found in most textbook treatments of colonial commerce; for example, see Dudley Dillard, *Economic Development of the North Atlantic Community* (Englewood Cliffs, N. J.: Prentice-Hall, 1967), pp. 197–98, and Ross M. Robertson, *History of the American Economy,* 3rd ed. (New York: Harcourt Brace Jovanovich, 1973), pp. 83–84.

[4] Gary Walton, "New Evidence on Colonial Commerce," *Journal of Economic History,* September 1968.

Table 3-4 Average Annual Tonnage Entered and Cleared, by Region, 1768-72

Group of Colonies	Other American Colonies	West Indies	Africa	Southern Europe	Great Britain (including Ireland)
New England					
Entered from	22112	45566	14	6883	14001
Cleared to	26809	50496	1023	5424	15164
Middle					
Entered from	16156	21817	78	11894	16493
Cleared to	17081	21642	171	11968	13987
South					
Entered from	25426	34568	1882	9574	60568
Cleared to	18954	34001	92	13970	70248

Source: Gary Walton, "New Evidence on Colonial Commerce," *Journal of Economic History*, September, 1968, p. 366.

modities to southern Europe than any other group of colonies and exported more commodities to the West Indies than the middle colonies did; between 1768 and 1772, one-half of the region's total exports were shipped to non-British ports. Walton's results suggest that British controls in colonial commercial activity allowed a considerable degree of freedom and did not discourage initiative. Later in this chapter, the assessment of the economic burden of British imperialism on the American colonies will reflect the flexible nature of British restrictions.

British Colonial Policy

The implementation of mercantilist policies in colonial America began with the Navigation Acts. The several versions of the Navigation Acts (1651, 1660, 1663) contained policies aimed at promoting British self-sufficiency and a favorable balance of trade. Their major provisions were:

1) All trade between England and her colonies had to be carried in English or colonial ships, and three-fourths of the crew had to be English or colonial.
2) Most European imports into the colonies had to pass through England.
3) A list of enumerated goods was drawn up; goods on the list could be shipped only to England.
4) Colonies were prohibited from selling manufactures abroad.

5) Bounties were to be paid for the production of certain enumerated goods.

The first provision was intended to discourage America's use of foreign shipping, especially Dutch. Use of a foreign country's shipping services enters the balance of payments as an import,[5] and by allowing the Americans to use Dutch shipping, the British had been failing to capitalize on an important source of exports to her colonies. The first provision was designed to force Americans to purchase British shipping services in order to aid the British balance of payments.

The second provision of the Navigation Acts was intended to eliminate direct trade between the colonies and the European continent. The colonies imported many manufactured goods directly from Europe; many of these could have been purchased from England. In order to force her colonies to buy British manufactured goods, most European goods going to the colonies were routed through England, where a duty was levied. The purpose of the duty was to raise prices of European manufactured goods so that Britain would be an attractive market for the colonists. British exports would be increased and a favorable balance of trade encouraged.

The enumerated goods list included those goods that England could not produce but considered essential for her self-sufficiency. Enumeration gave England exclusive control of the surplus production. The fourth provision of the Navigation Acts was also tied to British self-sufficiency. By eliminating foreign markets for colonial manufactures, England hoped to discourage manufacturing and encourage production in those areas consistent with British self-sufficiency. The bounty payment system that was established was a further attempt to promote colonial activity in areas conducive to British self-sufficiency.

In addition to the Navigation Acts, the British developed numerous other policies. However, many of these were revenue-raising measures rather than policies aimed at altering the economic activity of the colonies, and legislation such as the Stamp Act, Townsend Acts, Molasses Act, and Sugar Act need not concern us. Several American manufacturing industries came under British control after the restrictions imposed by the Navigation Acts, and these do deserve mention. The American wool and woolen textile industry (1699) and the hat industry (1732) came into competition with British manufacturing in foreign markets and were prohibited from exporting their products abroad. The colonial manufacture of finished iron products was prohibited by the Iron Act of 1750, but American pig and bar iron were to be

[5] The balance of payments is a financial statement showing a country's international receipts and expenditures, including trade in goods and services, gold transactions, and capital movements.

admitted into England duty free. This policy resulted in a large flow of pig and bar iron to England, as evidenced by the figures in Table 3–5.

Economic Impact of British Colonial Policy

The basic burdens on the American colonies in the British mercantilist system were the enumeration of certain commodities, especially tobacco and rice, and the routing of European imports through Britain. Exploitation resulting from the enumeration of colonial goods came about because Britain paid the colonists at levels below the world market price for goods on the enumerated list. Many enumerated goods, particularly tobacco, were re-exported by Britain and sold at world market prices in Europe. (See Table 3–6.) A measure of the exploitation resulting from enumeration would have to approximate this loss in income to American producers. The routing of American imports from Europe through England raised the prices paid by Americans for imports, either by forcing them to pay duties on European goods or by altering their preferences and forcing them to buy relatively expensive British goods. Restrictions placed on American manufacturing have not been viewed as bearing any great negative impact, and although the revenue-raising measures passed in the last years of British colonialism created political unrest, they did not represent major economic burdens.[6]

The major direct benefits to the Americans in the mercantilist system were the bounty payments, British use of American shipping services, and British military and naval protection. Bounties were paid to individuals engaged in certain designated occupations, and they provided the Americans

Table 3-5 Pig and Bar Iron Exports to England, 1730-70 (tons of 2240 pounds)

Year	Pig Iron	Bar Iron
1730	1717	9
1735	2561	55
1740	2275	5
1745	2274	4
1750	2924	6
1755	3441	390
1760	3265	127
1765	3264	1079
1770	4233	1716

Source: *Historical Statistics,* Series Z 131-135 and Z 159-164.

[6] Douglass C. North, *Growth and Welfare in the American Past* (Englewood Cliffs, N. J.: Prentice-Hall, 1966), p. 46.

Table 3-6 American Tobacco Imported and Re-Exported by Great Britain, 1710-73 (millions of pounds)

Year	Imports	Re-Exports
1710	25	16
1721[a]	41	30
1730	41	33
1740	41	42
1752[a]	78	69
1760	85	64
1770	78	73
1773	100	97

Source: *Historical Statistics,* Series Z 230-237.
[a]Figures were not available for 1720 and 1750; the closest year available was chosen to represent these periods.

with a free source of income.[7] American shippers earned extra income by providing shipping services to the British, particularly in the trade between America and the British West Indies. Throughout the colonial period, the British met the costs of American military and naval protection. In addition to these direct benefits, membership in the British Empire provided America with such indirect advantages as easy access to British markets and British capital.

Lawrence Harper has done the path-breaking work in measuring the net economic impact of the Navigation Acts on the American economy.[8] Harper provided estimates, in the form of a balance sheet, depicting the burdens and benefits stemming from the Navigation Acts; his results appear in Table 3–7. The figures suggest that British colonial policy imposed a rather heavy net burden on the colonies, and this conclusion found its way into many of the standard textbooks. The net burden suggested by Harper varied between $2.5 million and $7.0 million—his estimate of the annual net loss in colonial income that resulted from British exploitation. However, in order to interpret the significance of Harper's results, the exact nature of his counterfactual proposition must be fully understood. Harper was concerned with burdens and benefits to the Americans if they had continued their membership in the British Empire but had not been controlled by the Navigation Acts. Therefore, he purposely excluded national defense from the benefits side of the

[7] Some bounties were spent on industries which had little future in America such as the silk industry, and their value can be questioned.

[8] Lawrence Harper, "The Effects of the Navigation Acts on the Thirteen Colonies," in Richard B. Morris, ed., *The Era of the American Revolution* (New York: Columbia University Press, 1939).

Table 3-7 Harper's Estimates of the Burdens and Benefits of the Navigation Acts, 1773

Burdens and Benefits	Lowest	Intermediate	Highest
Burdens			
Enumerated Goods			
Tobacco	$2,177,000	$2,428,000	$3,401,000
Rice	186,000	231,000	517,000
European Imports	521,000	997,000	3,444,000
	2,884,000	3,656,000	7,362,000
Benefits			
Bounties (indigo, naval stores, and lumber)	324,000	324,000	324,000
Net Burden	$2,560,000	$3,332,000	$7,038,000

Source: Lawrence Harper, "The Effect of the Navigation Acts on the Thirteen Colonies," in Richard B. Morris, ed., *The Era of the American Revolution* (New York: Columbia University Press, 1939), p. 37.

ledger because under his counterfactual proposition the Americans would still have received this benefit.[9]

Douglas North, Robert Thomas, Gary Walton, Peter McClelland, and others have re-examined the issue of British exploitation of the American colonists.[10] The counterfactual proposition examined in most of these recent studies was different from Harper's, and, therefore, the results are not comparable. North, Thomas, and Walton attempted to measure the burdens and benefits of British colonial policy when viewing America as a free and independent nation operating in a mercantilist world; therefore, all benefits such as defense that would have been forfeited upon independence are included in the estimation. North suggested that an appropriate measure of the benefits of British military and naval protection would be the actual expenditure incurred by the Americans after the Revolutionary War; these expenditures exceeded $2 million per year. The accuracy of the data used by

[9] Harper also excluded the extra shipping income that Americans might have earned as a result of membership in the British Empire. However, Robert P. Thomas, "A Quantitative Approach to the Study of the Effects of British Imperial Policy Upon Colonial Welfare: Some Preliminary Findings," *Journal of Economic History,* December 1965, argued that on balance the colonial shipping industry neither gained nor lost due to the Navigation Acts. He suggested that increased American shipping directly to Europe would have compensated for the loss in shipping income that would have occurred had America been free.

[10] See North, *Growth and Welfare,* pp. 43–49; Thomas, "A Quantitative Approach"; Gary Walton, "The New Economic History and the Navigation Acts," *Economic History Review,* October 1971; and Peter D. McClelland, "The Cost to America of British Imperial Policy," *American Economic Review,* May 1969.

Harper to measure the price burden to Americans on tobacco, rice, and European imports has been questioned, and recent data suggest that narrow differentials existed between prices received by Americans for enumerated goods or prices paid for European imports and the world prices for these items. For example, when calculating the tobacco burden, Harper assumed a difference between the price received by America and the world market price of 2½–3¼ cents per pound; latest evidence suggests that the price difference was between ½ and 1½ cents per pound.[11]

Robert Thomas has recalculated the burdens and benefits of British mercantilism, taking into account all benefits of membership in the British Empire, and he expressed the results in terms of a net per capita burden. For the period 1763–72, he calculated the net per capita burden at 26 cents; for 1770, the net burden was calculated at 42 cents. Given that per capita incomes during this period were approximately one hundred dollars, Thomas argued that it is very difficult to make a case that any significant economic exploitation of the Americans resulted from British colonial policy. Thomas's attempt to measure the net burden of British colonialism has stirred a great debate in the literature, and there has been a vigorous discussion of his methods and data.[12] However, there has been no serious challenge to Thomas's conclusion that the net burden of British colonialism was rather small.

Summary

The desire for national self-sufficiency and political strength prompted the British to colonize America. The British attempted to control colonial economic activity through legislation, primarily through the Navigation Acts. A number of burdens were imposed on the colonies, but there were a number of offsetting benefits too, and the net degree of economic exploitation was rather small. Given the size of the burden, it does not appear that the pace of economic development would have been significantly more rapid during the colonial period had America been a free and independent nation.

---

[11] There has been a great deal of debate about the price burden on tobacco. See Walton, "The New Economic History and the Navigation Acts"; McClelland, "The Cost to America of British Imperial Policy"; and Frank J. A. Broeze, "The New Economic History, the Navigation Acts, and the Continental Tobacco Market, 1770–90," *Economic History Review*, November 1973.

[12] See Walton, "The New Economic History and the Navigation Acts"; McClelland, "The Cost to America of British Imperial Policy"; Broeze, "The New Economic History, the Navigation Acts"; Roger L. Rabsom, "British Policy and Colonial Growth: Some Implications of the Burden from the Navigation Acts," *Journal of Economic History*, September 1968; Peter D. McClelland, "The New Economic History and the Burdens of the Navigation Acts: A Comment," *Economic History Review*, November 1973; and Gary Walton, "The Burdens of the Navigation Acts: A Reply," *Economic History Review*, November 1973.

Suggested Reading

Broeze, Frank J. A., "The New Economic History, the Navigation Acts, and the Continental Tobacco Market, 1770–90," *Economic History Review,* November 1973.

Harper, Lawrence, "The Effects of the Navigation Acts on the Thirteen Colonies," in Richard B. Morris, ed., *The Era of the American Revolution.* New York: Columbia University Press, 1939.

Loschky, David J., "Studies of the Navigation Acts: New Economic Non-History," *Economic History Review,* November 1973.

McClelland, Peter D., "On Navigating the Navigation Acts with Peter D. McClelland: A Reply," *American Economic Review,* December 1970.

———, "The Cost to America of British Imperial Policy," *American Economic Review,* May 1969.

———, "The New Economic History and the Burdens of the Navigation Acts: A Comment," *Economic History Review,* November 1973.

Ransom, Roger L., "British Policy and Colonial Growth: Some Implications of the Burden from the Navigation Acts," *Journal of Economic History,* September 1968.

Reid, Joseph D., "On Navigating the Navigation Acts with Peter D. McClelland: Comment," *American Economic Review,* December 1970.

Shepherd, James, "Commodity Exports from the British North American Colonies to Overseas Areas, 1768–1772: Magnitudes and Patterns of Trade," *Explorations in Economic History,* Fall 1970.

———, and Gary Walton, "Trade, Distribution, and Economic Growth in Colonial America," *Journal of Economic History,* March 1972.

Thomas, Robert Paul, "A Quantitative Approach to the Study of the Effects of British Imperial Policy Upon Colonial Welfare: Some Preliminary Findings," *Journal of Economic History,* December 1965.

———, "British Imperial Policy and the Economic Interpretation of the American Revolution," *Journal of Economic History,* September 1968.

Walton, Gary, "New Evidence on Colonial Commerce," *Journal of Economic History,* September 1968.

———, "The Burdens of the Navigation Acts: A Reply," *Economic History Review,* November 1973.

———, "The New Economic History and the Navigation Acts," *Economic History Review,* October 1971.

4
The Early National Period and the Napoleonic Wars

With the end of the Revolutionary War in 1783, the new nation turned to the task of establishing a workable form of political-economic organization. The most immediate problem concerned the basic orientation of the economy. Would the economy be modeled after the mercantilist system, with an extreme degree of government control, or would individual initiative and private enterprise prevail?

The American economy had been spawned in a mercantilist world. At the time of the American Revolution, however, there was a growing body of thought favoring a greater degree of individual freedom and a relaxation of government controls. This spirit of laissez faire, meaning that government should intervene in the economy as little as necessary, can be traced to the writings of David Hume, but it is generally associated with Adam Smith's classic statement of the workings of the competitive system in *The Wealth of Nations.*[1]

Smith attacked mercantilism as an inefficient system of economic organization. He claimed that it was not in the best interest of any nation concerned with efficiency to attempt to achieve self-sufficiency. Smith criticized mercantilist efforts to control the balance of trade, and he proposed instead that all nations would be better served by free trade. The main stimulus to growth, in Smith's mind, could be found in the division of labor and in specialization. If all nations specialized on products in which their relative efficiency was greatest, they could all benefit by trade. Mercantilists,

[1] Adam Smith, *The Wealth of Nations* (New York: Random House, 1937). Book I outlines the principles of laissez faire and Book IV, Chs. I–VIII, presents an attack on the principles of mercantilism.

with their narrow view of the world, never appreciated the notion of mutual gains through trade.

Smith glorified individual economic freedom. He believed that each person should be allowed to maximize his personal profit; this would result in the maximization of the economy's total wealth. Fear of retaliation would restrain individuals from exploiting their fellow man.

America's decision with respect to a system of political economy took place in the formative years of laissez faire economics, and, essentially, the decision was favorable to the establishment of a market economy or a private enterprise system. Government was awarded limited goals and granted limited powers to achieve them. However, unfettered private enterprise has never existed in any modern economy, and, in some areas, the American economy had strong mercantilist overtones. The *Report on Manufactures,* in which Alexander Hamilton advocated a strong role for the federal government in promoting American industrialization, including a system of bounties and subsidies, certainly indicated this.

Economic Conditions, 1783–93

There has been some debate concerning economic growth during the post-Revolutionary War period. Curtis Nettels has claimed that the period was one of depression; Merrill Jensen, on the other hand, has suggested that the period was one of significant growth.[2] Recently, Gordon Bjork has presented a middle view which sees the period as neither one of new growth nor one of depression.[3] Owing to lack of adequate income data, Bjork utilized data concerning America's foreign relations. He defended the use of trade data on the grounds that America's economic health during this period was strongly tied to foreign demand for American products.

Bjork focused his analysis on the two major markets for American products, Britain and the West Indies, and the international price position of American goods as reflected in the terms of trade. Table 4–1 exhibits Bjork's estimates of the market value of British imports from the United States. The figures suggest that exports to Britain were only marginally lower after the Revolutionary War than they had been during the period of mercantilist control, and it appears that America's commercial ties with the British were relatively unaffected by the political separation.

British legislation prohibited American trade with the British West Indies during the period 1783–92, but Bjork found that a substantial market for American goods still existed. He calculated the average annual value of

---

[2] Curtis P. Nettels, *The Emergence of a National Economy, 1775–1815* (New York: Holt, Rinehart & Winston, 1962); Merrill Jensen, *The New Nation* (New York: Knopf, 1950).

[3] Gordon Bjork, "Weaning of the American Economy: Independence, Market Changes, and Economic Development," *Journal of Economic History,* December 1964.

Table 4-1 British Imports from the United States, 1770-92 (thousands of dollars)

Year	Imports
1770	$3248
1771	5978
1772	5078
1773	4960
1774	4842
1775	6555
1784	4429
1785	4901
1786	4134
1787	4488
1788	4901
1789	4901
1790	4905
1791	4724
1792	4311

Source: Gordon Bjork, "Weaning of the American Economy: Independence, Market Changes, and Economic Development," *Journal of Economic History,* December 1964, p. 550.

American exports to the British West Indies as follows: 1771–73, $2.2 million; 1785–87, $1.4 million; 1793, $1.2 million. Bjork pointed out that American exports to the British West Indies were greater during the period of restriction than they were during 1793, after the trade restrictions had been raised. Nevertheless, there was a post-war decline in American exports to the British West Indies, although this was partially offset by substantial gains in trade with the non-British West Indies.

Bjork also found that America's net barter terms of trade improved substantially in the postwar period.[4] His calculated values for the net barter terms of trade are shown in Table 4–2, and it is clear that America's international price position was substantially improved with the demise of mercantilism. With the end of British control in America, exporters were able to sell their merchandise at world prices rather than being forced to sell to Britain at below market prices; similarly, importers were now able to

[4] The net barter terms of trade are calculated as follows:

$$\frac{P_{x_t} / P_{x_o}}{P_{m_t} / P_{m_o}}$$

where P=a weighted price index, x=exports, m=imports, and o and t refer to the base period and terminal year. They show the change over time in the average price received for exports relative to the change in the average price paid for imports.

Table 4-2 America's Net Barter Terms of Trade, 1770-92 (1790 = 100)

Year	Terms of Trade
1770	63
1771	72
1772	81
1773	72
1774	68
1775	64
1784	112
1785	105
1786	96
1787	91
1788	88
1789	88
1790	100
1791	89
1792	78

Source: Gordon Bjork, "Weaning of the American Economy," p. 554.

buy directly from Europe at world prices rather than being forced to pay the world price plus some arbitrary duty imposed by the British.

Bjork concluded that the period 1783–93 was one of mixed economic activity somewhere between the optimism of Jensen and the pessimism of Nettels. He indicated that aggregate exports increased during the period, but export growth did not keep pace with population growth, and the per capita level of exports declined. Of course, the mercantilist effort in America was aimed at maximizing the outward flow of goods from the colonies. The new political situation in America most likely would bring about some change in the orientation of the economy. In this regard, less emphasis on the export trade and more concern with domestic needs would be expected, and Bjork cites the restructuring of the economy, especially in the South.

The Economics of the Constitution

The Articles of Confederation formed the framework within which the American economy functioned during the period 1781–89. There were numerous defects in the Articles, most serious of which was the failure to create a strong central government, and they were shortly replaced by the Constitution. The Constitution vested much more power in the federal government and represented a major movement away from the earlier emphasis on state government controls.

Charles Beard has argued that the overwhelming majority of those in attendance at the Constitutional Convention were personally interested in the outcome.[5] He also insisted that the vote on ratification of the document took place on class or sectional lines. Beard demonstrated that those who attended the Convention represented various forms of personal or real wealth; no one from the small farming or mechanic classes was present. He argued that the Constitution was built on the economic interests of those who participated in drafting the document and that the powers given to the federal government prevented any attack on the position of the wealthy. Beard's views have been widely criticized, and critics have emphasized that many noneconomic factors were involved in the drafting of the Constitution and many groups without personal interest or wealth voted for ratification of the document.[6]

Regardless of the motivations behind the writing of the Constitution, it is clear that the document changed the political features of American life. The following economic powers were granted to the federal government: collection of revenue, payment of debts, provision of national defense, promotion of general welfare, borrowing money, regulation of all foreign and domestic commerce, coining of money and the regulation of its value, determination of a set of weights and measures, granting of copyrights, and establishment of a postal system.

Curtis Nettles has argued that the new constitutional powers played a significant role in American economic growth during the early national period.[7] He claimed that the idea of a national economy was in danger of being discarded in favor of states' rights; ratification of the Constitution destroyed this possibility and entrenched the idea of a strong central government. Nettels suggested that federal regulation of commerce, uniformity in the set of weights and measures, creation of a national postal system, and federal government access to state militias created a more favorable business climate and a more stable atmosphere in which growth could take place. Nettles also cited several new federal powers in the realm of money and credit, and he argued that uniformity here helped create an integrated trading area with few barriers to interstate trade. The specific and implied powers over money and credit cited by Nettels include the following: coin and regulate the value of money, enact bankruptcy laws, establish courts authorized to set aside state laws impairing the obligation of contracts, issue bills of credit, charter banks, and determine legal tender.

It must be admitted that the Constitution did create a strong central gov-

---

[5] Charles A. Beard, *An Economic Interpretation of the Constitution of the United States* (New York: MacMillan, 1913).

[6] See Robert E. Brown, *Charles Beard and the Constitution* (Princeton: Princeton University Press, 1956).

[7] See Nettles, *Emergence of a National Economy*, Ch. V.

ernment, and the concentration of power in the federal government acted to promote a more stable environment for the development of the American economy. However, in the areas of control over the money supply and federal taxation, the improvements introduced by the Constitution were marginal. Under the Constitution, the states retained the right to charter banks, and these banks floated their own notes. As a result, the federal government did not obtain control over the money supply but instead shared this with state governments, and the lack of homogeneity in the money supply retarded interstate and interregional trade. (See Chapter 12.) In the area of taxes, the Constitution allowed only for taxation on an equal basis, and, in effect, regressive taxation became the accepted means for the federal government to raise revenue. It was not until the Sixteenth Amendment to the Constitution (1913) that a progressive tax structure was introduced in America.[8]

The Federalist Economic Program

The first national administration was that of the Federalists in which George Washington served as president. Washington, along with Alexander Hamilton, developed several significant programs, and in this section we will consider the Federalist endeavors in three areas: tariff protection for American industry, inflation and the Revolutionary War debt, and the issue of a national bank.

In 1789, Congress passed a tariff designed to protect and encourage American industry. The tariff was an outgrowth of Hamilton's *Report on Manufactures,* and it demonstrated the presence of mercantilist sympathies in America.

The Revolutionary War debt was still outstanding when the Federalists took power, and there was talk of forfeiting on the debt. Despite an inadequate supply of gold to retire the Revolutionary War bonds, Hamilton developed a debt payment plan. Hamilton was concerned with increasing the money supply, and he thought that a government-controlled inflationary bias would help stimulate the economy. He believed that public securities could circulate as money and create inflationary pressure. His proposal called for the payment of all federal and state war debt. He hoped that this would promote faith in the new government and demonstrate its ability to honor its debts, thereby creating public confidence in government bonds and underscoring their value as money. The debt payment plan consisted of an exchange of Revolutionary War bonds for a new series of high-interest

---

[8] Among other things, Beard cited the federal tax structure as an example of unwillingness on the part of the writers of the Constitution to attack the position of the wealthy.

government bonds. This would spread the new money—government bonds —throughout the economy and bring about the desired inflation.[9]

In 1791 the Federalists created a type of national bank, the Bank of the United States, and gave it a twenty-year charter. The Bank was a private institution that was given control of a portion of the federal government's revenues and asked to perform some of the functions of a central bank. Hamilton was opposed to direct government control of the money supply, and he thought that a private bank would be more likely to adhere to sound management practices.[10]

By using the new constitutional powers, the Federalist economic program entrenched and broadened the influence of the federal government. However, the Federalists were not particularly successful in stimulating manufacturing development or in promoting an inflationary bias. Aggregate manufacturing output increased steadily, but per capita manufacturing output levels remained unchanged after the passage of the tariff. Furthermore, the basic structure of American industry, with heavy emphasis on extractive activities, went unchanged, and the techniques of production were those of the pre-Revolutionary War years.[11] There was an inflationary spiral during the early national period, but this largely reflected the issue of notes by state chartered banks and not the positive actions of the Federalists. Inadequate controls on state bank operations resulted in excessive note circulation, and, by 1791, the main monetary concern of the Federalists was to curtail state bank note issue and curb inflation.

The Napoleonic Wars

It became quite clear during the Napoleonic War period (1793–1815) that despite the Revolutionary War and the constitutional changes, the American economy was still tied to Europe. The war years can be broken into two separate periods, 1793–1807 and 1808–15. During the first period, the conflict had a positive impact on the American economy. Both England and France were concerned with keeping trade open with their colonies, and they turned to neutral nations to provide the bulk of their shipping services. According to an agreement between England and France, neutral shipping was not to be subjected to attack by the warring parties. The type of trading

---

[9] For a much fuller discussion of this issue and for an assessment of an alternate debt payment plan offered by James Madison, see Nettels, *Emergence of a National Economy,* Ch. VI.

[10] An examination of the Bank's policies and success in carrying them out can be found in Ch. 12.

[11] See Ross Robertson, *History of the American Economy,* p. 184. It is difficult to assess the merits of the tariff since the Napoleonic Wars, 1793–1815, followed closely behind its passage.

pattern that developed became known as the re-export trade. Goods from the British and French colonies, destined for the mother country, first had to be imported to a neutral port and then re-exported to their final destination. Similarly, manufactured goods shipped from England and France to their colonies were first sold to an importer in a neutral nation and then re-exported to the colonies. During the period 1793–1807, the neutral Americans fulfilled the majority of Europe's shipping needs. America dominated the re-export trade because of her reputation for low-cost, efficient shipping, her geographic closeness to the West Indies, and her ability to produce resources and foodstuffs needed in England and France.

American shipping, shipbuilding, and agriculture experienced tremendous growth during the early part of the Napoleonic Wars. The degree of this growth is shown by the data in Table 4–3 concerning the value of

Table 4-3 Exports and Re-Exports from America During the Napoleonic War Period (millions of dollars)

Year	Exports of U.S. Merchandise	Re-Exports
1791	19	1
1792	19	2
1793	24	2
1794	27	7
1795	40	8
1796	32	26
1797	24	27
1798	28	33
1799	33	46
1800	32	39
1801	46	47
1802	36	36
1803	42	14
1804	41	36
1805	42	53
1806	41	60
1807	49	60
1808	9	13
1809	31	21
1810	42	24
1811	45	16
1812	30	8
1813	25	3
1814	7	0[a]
1815	46	7

Source: *Historical Statistics*, Series U 1-14.
[a]Less than $500,000.

America's exports and re-exports during 1790–1815. During 1791–1807, exports of American merchandise increased from $19 million to $49 million, and re-exports increased from $1 million to $60 million. The economic boom ended in 1808 as a result of British and French interference with American shipping. President Thomas Jefferson did not have the naval strength to protect American shipping, and he was fearful that the nation might be drawn into the war. To insure peace, he declared an embargo—designed to keep American ships at home—which prohibited all American exports. American shipping and agricultural interests felt that this complete restriction on foreign trade was too severe. The Embargo Act was rewritten as the Non-Intercourse Act (1809) and prohibited only trade with England and France. Interference with American shipping continued and became one cause of the War of 1812.

The imposition of commercial restrictions put a serious crimp in America's world trade. Because of the tremendous decline in the re-export trade, American shipping interests were especially hard hit. Foreign demand for American agricultural goods continued to be high, but there was a relative decline from pre-embargo export levels. In addition to limiting foreign markets for American goods, the trade restrictions brought about a decline in the flow of foreign goods to America. The depressed economic conditions created by the trade embargo soon gave way to an American attempt to produce manufactured goods. Much of the business capital that had been funneled into the shipping, shipbuilding, and agricultural export industries was now turned to the development of import substitution manufacturing.

The composition of America's imports from Britain in the period just before the embargo provides an indication of those domestic industries that trade barriers stimulated. Victor Clark's study of American manufactures suggests that most of our imports from Britain in the period 1806–8 consisted of cotton or woolen textiles; in fact, textiles accounted for 86.3 percent of our total import of British manufactured goods during this period.[12]

The American attempt to substitute domestic production for goods which previously had been imported was concentrated on textiles, especially cotton, and most of this activity was localized in southern New England. There had been some expansion in the cotton textile industry during 1793–1807, but it was not until the trade embargo that manufacturing began in earnest. The number of spindles involved in cotton textile production increased from 20,000 in 1809 to 135,000 in 1815, and the domestic consumption of cotton by the American textile industry increased from 500 bales in 1805 to 90,000 bales in 1815.[13] In 1816, with the return to relatively

[12] See Victor S. Clark, *History of Manufactures in the United States,* Vol. I (New York: McGraw-Hill for the Carnegie Institution of Washington, 1929), p. 247.

[13] Clark, *History of Manufactures,* p. 538.

free trade, British competition forced most of the American textile manufacturers to close their doors, and the nation returned to shipping, agriculture, and other resource intensive forms of economic activity.

There were many factors favoring the short-run spurt in cotton textile production in the American economy. Trade restrictions associated with the Napoleonic Wars had cut off foreign products and left a large unsatiated demand for textiles. On the supply side, American cotton exports declined from 66 million pounds in 1807 to 12 million pounds in 1808, and raw cotton was readily available. Labor was also in abundant supply since the great decline in commercial activity had resulted in a large amount of unemployment, particularly in southern New England. The technology of the industry was simple, and the southern New England area had a great abundance of available water-power facilities.

The woolen industry received less stimulus from the war than the cotton textile industry, but still there was a significant increase in activity. Clark estimates that by 1816 there was $12 million invested in the woolen textile industry, and the annual output had reached approximately $19 million.[14] The fate of this industry was similar to that of cotton textiles, with the major portion of the industry succumbing to foreign competition after the War of 1812.

One other notable industrial development during the second half of the Napoleonic wars was the increased processing of raw materials; this is most evident in the wheat industry. In 1790, wheat exports equaled one million bushels; during 1810–17, the average annual export was 100,000 bushels. However, during this latter period, flour shipments increased from 620,000 barrels to 1,500,000 barrels.[15]

Summary

British colonial rule in America ended in 1775 with the outbreak of the Revolutionary War. During the decade following the war, economic conditions in America were relatively stable and commercial ties with England and the West Indies remained strong. Shortly after the war's end in 1783, national leaders turned their attention to the creation of a stronger national government, and, in 1789, the Constitution was ratified and became the law of the land. The Constitution introduced a number of new economic powers at the federal level, and, despite the failure to achieve progressive taxation and a homogeneous money supply, the Constitution did entrench the notion of a strong central government and created a stable environment for future development.

[14] Clark, *History of Manufactures,* p. 562.

[15] Clark, *History of Manufactures,* p. 237.

The Napoleonic War period followed closely behind the constitutional changes, and this era was separated into two subperiods: 1793–1807 and 1808–15. The first period was much more prosperous for the nation than the second. Given the comparative advantage of the United States in the early nineteenth century, the nation's growth and welfare could be maximized by specializing in an exchange of resources for foreign manufactured goods. With the artificial trade situation that developed because of foreign interference with American shipping, the economy was forced to diversify its activities and to attempt some import-substitution-type manufacturing. Once trade returned to normal after the war, the American economy returned to the export of natural and processed resources. The mass failure of American manufacturing in 1816 bears testimony to the artificial nature of this short-run spurt of industrialization. It also demonstrates that the United States was still not a mature market economy but rather was extremely sensitive to European economic conditions. The main directions of American economic growth were still very clearly tied to the foreign sector.

Suggested Reading

Beard, Charles A., *An Economic Interpretation of the Constitution of the United States.* New York: Macmillan, 1913.

Bjork, Gordon, "Weaning of the American Economy: Independence, Market Changes, and Economic Development," *Journal of Economic History,* December 1964.

Brown, Robert E., *Charles Beard and the Constitution.* Princeton: Princeton University Press, 1956.

Fishlow, Albert, "Discussion of Bjork Paper," *Journal of Economic History,* December 1964.

Nettels, Curtis P., *The Emergence of a National Economy, 1775–1815.* New York: Holt, Rinehart and Winston, 1962.

North, Douglass C., *The Economic Growth of the United States, 1790–1860.* New York: W. W. Norton, 1966, Chs. II-VI.

Post, John D., "A Study in Meteorological and Trade Cycle History: The Economic Crisis Following the Napoleonic Wars," *Journal of Economic History,* June 1974.

5

Transportation Improvements During the Nineteenth Century

The American economy underwent a fundamental change in economic structure during the latter half of the Napoleonic Wars. For the first time the nation experienced a significant industrial boom, and agriculture and staple exports ceased to be the chief sources of economic growth. Immediately after the cessation of the conflict, the American economy returned to its prewar structure. However, the short run spurt of industrialization during 1807–15 signaled the future direction for the nation's growth, and, as soon as an efficient and inexpensive interregional transportation system was developed, a vigorous industrial expansion ensued.

The Appalachian Mountains, separating the eastern seaboard region from the West, impeded the interregional distribution of commodities. The Northeast's relative scarcity of productive agricultural land and relative abundance of labor and capital dictated that the region's comparative advantage *vis-à-vis* the rest of the nation was in manufacturing. However, in order to specialize in manufacturing, the Northeast needed western food supplies which were being produced in surplus. To reach eastern markets, western food producers had to bear the heavy expenses of overland wagon transportation or endure the very slow route by river to New Orleans and ocean shipping to Atlantic seaboard ports. The market potential for eastern products in the West was also limited by the inadequate transportation system, and only high-value, low-weight products could be exchanged profitably in interregional trade.

Until the early nineteenth century, this spatial separation of markets hampered American economic development. During the 1820s canals broke the natural geographic barrier between East and West and provided the first inexpensive means of East-West trade. At the same time, steamboats were developed and were used extensively to facilitate the distribution of goods within the West. All this created a national market which encouraged distinct patterns of regional economic specialization, namely production of staple agricultural commodities in the West and manufactured goods in the East. East and West produced for the market according to their comparative advantages, and improved efficiency in resource allocation raised consumer welfare in both regions. The basic direction of America's internal trade changed from a North-South orientation to a strong East-West flow. Railroad expansion during the middle nineteenth century acted to reinforce these earlier developments, and, during the late nineteenth century, the railroad extended interregional commerce to the Far West.

This chapter surveys the major developments during the nineteenth and early twentieth centuries in each of the following forms of transportation: road, canal, river, lake, and ocean. The discussion devotes specific attention to consideration of the impact of canals on regional economic specialization and the rationality of public investment in canal construction. Railroad developments are treated in Chapter 6, and special attention is given to an analysis of the competitive advantages of railroads over alternative forms of land and water transportation.

Road Transportation

Roads were not a major factor in the interregional distribution of goods until well into the twentieth century. However, there were numerous attempts to develop profitable toll roads during the early nineteenth century, and, by 1815, toll roads linked most important northeastern population centers. In fact, New England had completed many of its important toll roads by the first decade of the nineteenth century, and the Middle Atlantic states undertook their most rapid period of construction during the 1820s. Toll road construction lagged outside the Northeast, but, by 1816, a major North-South route was in operation between Maine and Georgia. By the 1820s, all sections of the country had developed some low-quality country roads, which provided access to local markets or to other forms of transportation.

In the populous sections of the nation, private road companies which were organized as corporations financed most road construction. Corporate privileges required approval of state legislatures, but owing to the desire to improve transportation facilities, charters were generally easy to obtain. Toll road companies mobilized private capital by issuing securities, and, although the total amount of investment in roads was considerable, most road companies were capitalized for less than $100,000.[1]

Outside the Northeast, state governments financed most road con-

[1] See George R. Taylor, *The Transportation Revolution* (New York: Holt, Rinehart and Winston, 1951), p. 25.

struction. The greater role for the public sector in the South and West resulted from the inadequate local demand for transportation services and the absence of adequate supplies of private capital. Although there was some direct ownership of roads by state governments, the typical pattern of aid was state government investment in the securities of private road companies. Aggregate aid from local governments was relatively minor, but significant financial support was given to several turnpike developments. The federal government gave limited support to road construction, and there was never a commitment of federal funds to develop a national highway system. In fact, throughout the early nineteenth century, there was constant debate concerning the constitutionality of federal activity in road construction. The most ambitious federal project was the National Road, which was built from Cumberland, Maryland, through Wheeling, West Virginia (1818), and Columbus, Ohio (1833), to Vandalia, Illinois (early 1850s).

Individual travelers used toll roads but the high rate charges discouraged freight traffic. Public resentment made tolls difficult to collect, and maintenance expenses were higher than anticipated. Toll receipts on most roads were insufficient to cover the initial construction costs; revenue on many roads was not even sufficient to cover the annual maintenance expenditures. Toll roads were clearly financial failures, and even among the roads that attracted a large volume of traffic, many found it difficult to make a profit.

The advent of plank roads stimulated road construction during the 1840s and 1850s. These were roads built by placing large wooden planks on cross-ties to form a path approximately eight feet wide. Plank roads were generally intended for short-haul traffic, and they often were built as feeder lines into railroads and canals. Their main advantages were low initial cost and ability to support heavy loads. However, plank roads suffered from very heavy maintenance expenditures, and, like other roads, they proved to be unprofitable and declined rapidly in the late 1850s.

Nineteenth-century roads were characterized by very high user costs relative to alternative forms of transportation, and the relative cost disadvantage of long-haul road transportation lasted until the 1920s. During the early twentieth century, the trucking industry acted as a complement to the railroads, and the railroads supported highway development programs. However, by the 1920s, it was becoming apparent that trucking would offer effective direct competition to the railroads, and, since that time, an increasing share of America's goods have moved by truck.

Canal Development

From the time of the Revolutionary War, canal development had been recognized as a feasible means of integrating the American economy and creating a national market. However, canal construction lagged due to the heavy initial capital requirements and engineering difficulties. Finally, in 1817, the state of New York undertook the construction of the nation's first major interregional canal. The Erie Canal was planned to run from Albany on the Hudson River to Buffalo on Lake Erie, a distance of almost four hundred miles. The proposed route had the natural advantages of relatively level terrain and abundant water. A portion (75 miles) of the canal was opened to central New York in 1819, and the project was completed in 1825. The original canal was forty feet wide and four feet deep, but, in 1835, plans were adopted to enlarge its dimensions to seventy feet by seven feet. Many smaller canals and feeder lines which tied into the Erie were also built during the 1820s and 1830s, and the state of New York also financed most of this construction.

New York's canal construction created national interest in this form of transportation, and many states quickly responded with construction projects of their own. A number of eastern seaboard states built canals designed to connect the interior with tidewater, and New York City faced direct competition from Baltimore and Philadelphia, both of which tried to develop a through route to the West.[2] Western states were also caught up in the canal fever and developed a system of canals which linked the Great Lakes to the western rivers. (See Table 5–1.)

Among the numerous canal projects undertaken during the 1820s and 1830s, the most important to the integration of the American market were the five major East-West canals built by New York (Erie), Pennsylvania (Pennsylvania Mainline), Ohio (Ohio and Erie, Miami and Erie), and Indiana (Wabash and Erie.)[3] The Pennsylvania Mainline paralleled the Erie's route, running East and West from Philadelphia to Pittsburgh and eventually tying into the Ohio canal system. The Mainline was built through much more uneven terrain than the Erie, and a cable-car-type of railroad was constructed to carry canal boats over the most rugged mountainous areas. The two major Ohio canals were designed to link the Ohio River to Lake Erie. The Ohio and Erie ran through the eastern portion of the state and was completed between Cleveland and Portsmouth in 1833; the Miami and Erie ran through the western portion of the state and was completed from Cincinnati to Dayton in 1832 and through to Toledo in 1845. The Wabash and Erie canal tied into the northern section of the Miami and Erie canal and connected Lake Erie with the Ohio River in southwestern Indiana. (See Figure 5–1.)

Most new canal construction occurred during the 1820s and 1830s. By 1840, most of the natural water routes had been utilized, and the majority of expenditures went into maintenance and improvement of existing

[2] Baltimore tried to build a canal route to the West (Chesapeake and Ohio), but this did not prove successful, and eventually a railroad (Baltimore and Ohio) was built.

[3] See Taylor, *Transportation Revolution,* Ch. III, for an excellent detailed survey of canal construction.

Table 5-1 State Canal Mileage by Decade, 1830-50

State	1830	1840	1850
Maine	21	21	29
New Hampshire	—	11	—
Vermont	—	1	1
Massachusetts	74	89	89
Rhode Island	11	11	11
Connecticut	34	36	36
New York	546	640	803
New Jersey	20	142	142
Pennsylvania	230	954	954
Delaware	14	14	14
Maryland	10	136	136
Ohio	245	744	792
Indiana	—	150	214
Illinois	—	—	100
Virginia	—	216	216
North Carolina	—	13	13
South Carolina	52	52	52
Georgia	16	28	28
Kentucky	2	2	2
Alabama	—	52	52
Louisiana	—	14	14

Source: George R. Taylor, *The Transportation Revolution* (New York: Holt, Rinehart and Winston, 1951) p. 79

canals. Prior to 1840, 3326 miles of canal had been built at a cost of $125 million. After 1840, only 400 miles of new construction were added, and, by 1850, annual new construction was exceeded by canal closings.[4] George R. Taylor suggests that most of the $75 million spent on canals during the 1840s and 1850s went into maintenance and improvement of old facilities.[5] Harvey Segal has examined the various cycles of canal construction, and his figures also suggest that there was a concentration of effort prior to the early 1840s.[6] He estimated the total canal investment prior to the Civil War at $188.2 million and claimed that $130 million was spent before 1844.[7] (See Table 5–2.)

Advantages of Canal Transportation

The canals brought about a tremendous revolution in interregional trade and production because they created the first feasible means of direct

[4] Taylor, *Transportation Revolution,* p. 52.

[5] Taylor, *Transportation Revolution,* p. 53.

[6] See Harvey Segal, "Cycles of Canal Construction," in Carter Goodrich, ed., *Canals and American Economic Development* (New York: Columbia University Press, 1961).

[7] Segal, "Cycles of Canal Construction," p. 172.

Figure 5-1 Major Canals Built by 1860

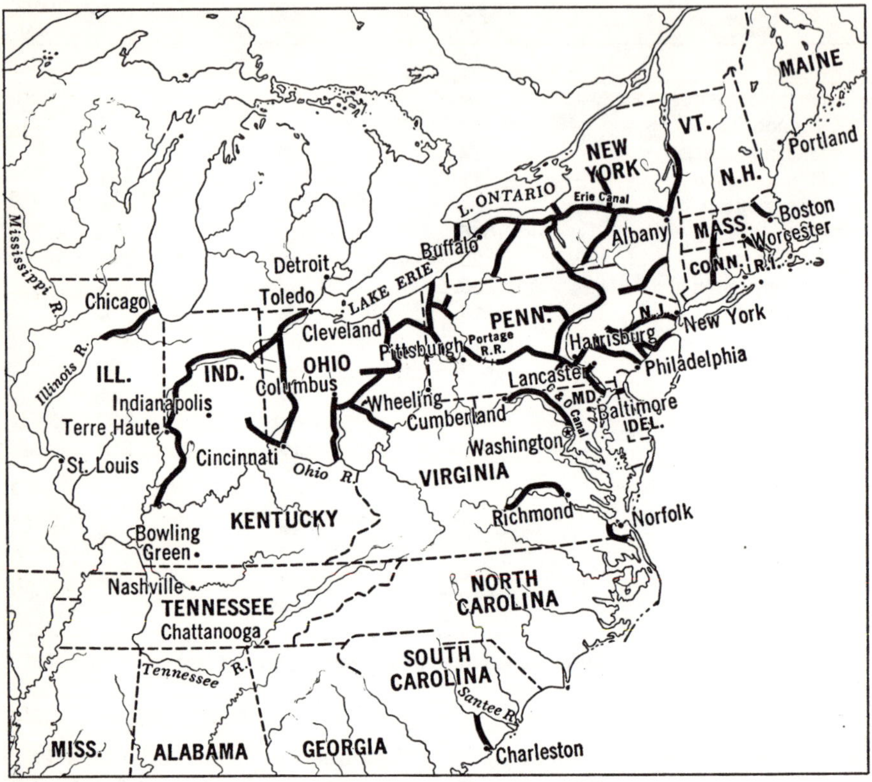

Source: Adapted from Henry F. Graff and John A. Krout, *The Adventure of the American People*, 2nd ed. (Chicago: Rand McNally, 1970), p. 210.

Table 5-2 Canal Investment in the United States, 1816-60 (millions of dollars)

Period	Expenditures
1816-20	$ 2.68
1821-25	12.24
1826-30	31.53
1831-35	16.47
1836-40	51.64
1841-45	18.66
1846-50	19.36
1851-55	22.04
1856-60	13.55

Source: Computed from Harvey Segal, "Cycles of Canal Construction," in Carter Goodrich, ed., *Canals and American Economic Development* (New York: Columbia University Press, 1961), pp. 208-9.

East-West transportation. During the period 1830–50, eastward rate charges on the Erie averaged 1.7 cents per ton-mile, and westward rates averaged 3.4 cents per ton-mile.[8] Average rate charges for wagon transportation varied greatly, depending on local road conditions, but, in 1830, the average charge for freight wagons was approximately 20 cents per ton-mile. Canal rates were steadily lowered, and, in 1853, the following average ton-mile rates prevailed: Erie, 1.1 cents; Ohio and Erie, 1.0; Wabash and Erie, 1.9; and Pennsylvania Mainline, 2.4 cents.[9] At that time, wagon rates were approximately 15 cents per ton-mile. Further rate reductions were made on the Erie, and, by the late 1850s, the average ton-mile rate was 0.8 cents.[10] Attractive canal rates encouraged regional economic specialization, and a great interregional trade involving exchange of western agricultural products and eastern and foreign manufactured goods developed during the 1830s and 1840s.

Canal transportation was very slow, and even the better canals averaged less than two miles per hour on through traffic. Consequently, canals were used almost exclusively for freight shipment. The cost and speed characteristics of canals made them ideally suited to the carriage of high-weight, low-value bulky items such as grain, lumber, ore, and coal. Before the advent of the railroad, the majority of East-West trade moved by canal, and the bulk of it moved on the Erie. (See Table 5–3.) Initially, the railroads competed away the canals' trade in low-weight, high-value items; however, well after the railroads had become entrenched, bulky items continued to be shipped by canal.[11] Freight traffic reached a peak on most canals during the 1850s, but the New York canal system continued to expand its volume of East-West trade until 1880. Available data indicate that the freight moving over the Erie averaged 2 million tons during the 1850s, almost 3 million tons during the 1860s, peaked at 4.6 million tons in 1880, and remained in excess of 2 million tons until 1910.[12]

Canals and Regional Economic Specialization

It is generally asserted that canals and other internal improvements during the antebellum decades brought about rather sharp patterns of regional

---

[8] Taylor, *Transportation Revolution,* p. 137.

[9] Taylor, *Transportation Revolution,* p. 442.

[10] Taylor, *Transportation Revolution,* p. 137.

[11] See Douglass C. North, *Economic Growth of the United States, 1790–1860* (New York: W. W. Norton, 1966), pp. 251–54, for figures that show a decline in canal trade in eastern exports to the West and a steady increase in canal trade in western grains; also see Taylor, *Transportation Revolution,* Ch. VIII.

[12] See *Historical Statistics,* Series Q 243–44.

Table 5-3 Percentage Distribution of the Northwest Commodity Trade, by Shipping Routes, 1835-53

Year	Northeastern Route[a]	Eastern Route[b]	Southern Route[c]
1835	23.7%	14.1%	62.2%
1839	38.2	16.4	45.4
1844	44.1	12.0	43.9
1849	52.7	8.9	38.4
1853	62.2	8.9	28.9

Source: Harvey Segal, "Canals and Economic Development," in Goodrich, ed., *Canals and American Economic Development,* p. 231.
[a] Lake Erie and Erie Canal.
[b] Pennsylvania Mainline, Pittsburgh Turnpike, or National Road.
[c] Mississippi River System.

economic specialization.[13] The Northeast supposedly undertook a rapid industrial expansion to capitalize on the new markets in the West, and the West, similarly market oriented, concentrated on the production of staple commodities for sale in the East or overseas. Recently, I subjected this assertion to statistical testing in order to determine the nature and degree of structural change that occurred during the canal-building era, 1820–40. The states chosen for analysis were those served by the Erie, Pennsylvania Mainline, Ohio and Erie, and Miami and Erie canals. I found that all areas in New York, Pennsylvania, and Ohio were heavily concentrated on agriculture in 1820, but some significant shift away from agriculture and toward manufacturing and commerce had occurred in the eastern seaboard regions of New York and Pennsylvania by 1840. (See Table 5–4.) The data also revealed that the West had experienced some slight decline in the importance of agriculture relative to manufacturing during the 1820s and 1830s. However, further analysis showed that this expanded manufacturing activity in the West was concentrated in several population clusters on the major canals.

Roger Ransom recently has argued that 1840 manufacturing in western canal regions largely represented a simple extension of agriculture into processing industries.[14] It is true that much western manufacturing was concentrated on the processing of such resources as timber, grain, and leather, which were exported to the East in finished form. However, the

[13] See the following: North, *Economic Growth in the United States,* Appendix 2; Albert Fishlow, "Antebellum Interregional Trade Reconsidered," *American Economic Review,* May 1964; Roger Ransom, "Interregional Canals and Economic Specialization in the Antebellum United States," *Exploration in Entrepreneurial History,* Fall 1967; and Harvey Segal, "Canals and Economic Development," in Goodrich, ed., *Canals and American Economic Development.*

[14] Roger Ransom, "A Closer Look at Canals and Western Manufacturing in the Canal Era," *Explorations in Economic History,* Summer 1971.

Table 5-4 Percentage Distribution of Total Employment by Major Sector, 1820 and 1840

Area	Agriculture	Manufacturing	Commerce
1820			
New York	78.2%	19.0%	2.8%
Eastern New York[a]	64.2	29.3	6.5
Western New York	84.4	14.3	1.3
Pennsylvania	67.7	28.9	3.4
Eastern Pennsylvania[b]	61.9	33.6	4.5
Western Pennsylvania	78.8	19.9	1.3
Ohio	84.5	14.4	1.1
1840			
New York	67.7	25.7	6.6
Eastern New York	49.3	38.1	12.6
Western New York	76.8	19.6	3.6
Pennsylvania	62.0	31.7	6.3
Eastern Pennsylvania	48.9	41.8	9.3
Western Pennsylvania	74.6	22.0	3.4
Ohio	77.5	18.8	3.7

Source: Albert W. Niemi, Jr., "A Further Look at Interregional Canals and Economic Specialization: 1820-1840," *Explorations in Economic History,* Summer 1970, p. 502.

[a] Eastern New York included the area between New York and Albany; Western New York included the area west and north of Albany.

[b] Eastern Pennsylvania included Harrisburg and all counties to the east; Western Pennsylvania included all counties to the west of Harrisburg.

bulk of canal region manufacturing activity took place in more sophisticated manufactures such as textiles, apparel, and machinery, and the relevant data suggest that a rather diversified manufacturing structure developed along the canal routes.[15] In fact, the differences in manufacturing structure between western canal counties and the eastern seaboard counties of New York, Pennsylvania, and New Jersey were minor. For these regions, I estimated that 30.2 percent of western manufacturing employment and 28.4 percent of eastern manufacturing employment was engaged in the processing of food, tobacco, lumber, and leather in 1840; the residual of approximately 70.0 percent in each region was engaged in nonprocessing types of manufacturing. (See Table 5–5.)

The above results are not in conflict with the traditionally accepted notion of eastern specialization on manufacturing and western specializa-

[15] See Albert W. Niemi, Jr., "A Closer Look at Canals and Western Manufacturing in the Canal Era: A Reply," and Roger Ransom, "A Rebuttal," in *Explorations in Economic History,* Summer 1972. Harry Scheiber, *Ohio Canal Era* (Athens: Ohio University Press, 1969), has suggested that the rise in demand for manufactured goods along canal routes was generally met by indigenous production; see pp. 190–99.

Table 5-5 Percentage Distribution of 1840 Manufacturing Employment

	Western[a] Canal Counties	Western Noncanal Counties	Eastern[a] New York, Eastern Pennsylvania, and New Jersey
20 Food	3.8%	2.0%	3.6%
21 Tobacco	1.3	0.4	1.7
22 Textiles	20.9	11.8	28.5
23 Apparel	6.3	2.6	5.2
24 Lumber	2.7	13.2	1.7
25 Furniture	7.6	4.1	5.2
26 Paper	1.3	1.3	1.7
27 Printing and Publishing	4.2	2.2	5.2
28 Chemicals	0.7	0.2	1.5
29 Petroleum	—	—	—
30 Rubber	—	—	—
31 Leather	7.6	10.5	6.6
32 Stone, Clay and Glass	9.6	7.2	11.1
33 Primary Metal	3.2	0.7	2.0
34 Fabricated Metal	2.5	1.4	1.5
35 Nonelectrical Machinery	4.8	1.5	6.7
36 Electrical Machinery	—	—	—
37 Transportation Equipment	7.4	7.4	6.9
38 Instruments	—	—	—
39 Miscellaneous	0.6	0.2	1.7
20 + 24[b]	14.8	33.1	8.2
28 + 39[c]	0.7	0.1	0.9
Subtotals			
20 + 24	21.3	48.3	13.5
22 + 23	27.2	14.4	33.7
33 – 35	10.5	3.6	10.2

Source: Albert W. Niemi, Jr., "Interregional Canals and Manufacturing Development in the West Before 1840," *Revue Internationale D'Histoire De La Banque,* 1974, Table 1.

[a] The West included Western New York, Western Pennsylvania, and Ohio; Canal counties include those contiguous to the Erie, Pennsylvania Mainline, Ohio and Erie, and Miami and Erie canals. Eastern New York and Eastern Pennsylvania were as defined in the notes to Table 5-4.

[b] Category 20 + 24 was specified simply as "mills" in the 1840 Census. Since no breakdown was provided, it is included exclusive of categories 20 and 24.

[c] Category 28 + 39 was specified as "soap and candles" in the 1840 Census. Since no breakdown was provided, it is included exclusive of categories 28 and 39.

tion on agriculture. It should be obvious from the earlier treatment in this chapter that regional specialization developed and created a large East-West trade flow. My results simply indicate that the canal-building era brought increased manufacturing to western canal regions. However, these pockets of industrialization represented a rather small percentage share of the West's total economic activity.

Financing Canal Construction

State governments raised most of the investment funds for canal development, and they usually financed canal construction by the sale of bonds issued on the credit of a state. Further, state governments retained canal ownership and operation. Local governments also built and furnished financial aid for the construction of canals, although not on the same scale as state governments. The federal government played a minor role in canal construction; the direct subscription of federal funds to canal stock amounted to only about $3 million. In addition, the federal government also made some small land grants (four million acres) for canal projects in Ohio, Michigan, Indiana, Illinois, and Wisconsin. The private sector participated in the canal boom by providing an active source of demand for government canal bond issues.[16] However, very little private capital was involved in direct construction operations because of the heavy capital requirements, speculative nature of the investment, and absence of short-run profits. An active market for state canal bonds existed overseas, and Segal has estimated that foreign capital underwrote one-third of the total construction cost in the antebellum period. Foreign investment was clustered during the peak building boom, and Segal suggests that 60 percent of the capital raised between 1834 and 1844 came from foreign sources.[17]

It is generally recognized that the canal boom resulted in an overcommitment of public funds to canal investment.[18] As a result of this overspending, many states were on the verge of bankruptcy in the early 1840s and could not meet their debts. Pennsylvania, Ohio, and Indiana were the most overextended, and Segal has estimated that approximately $60 million of worthless canal bonds were outstanding in 1844.[19] As a result of state forefeiture on canal-related debt obligations, foreign capital avoided American canal bonds during the late 1840s, and it was not until the railroad expansion of the 1850s that foreign capital showed a strong interest in American transportation development.

Profitability of Canal Investment

Most canals were financial disasters. The Erie, which earned an annual rate of return of 10 percent during 1825–82, was the only major canal to

---

[16] See Scheiber, *Ohio Canal Era,* Chs. 2 and 6.

[17] Segal, "Cycles of Canal Construction," p. 179.

[18] See Taylor, *Transportation Revolution,* Ch. III; Segal, "Cycles of Canal Construction"; and Roger Ransom, "Canals and Development: A Discussion of the Issues," *American Economic Review,* May 1964.

[19] Segal, "Cycles of Canal Construction," p. 202.

yield a respectable profit rate throughout its life as a state enterprise. The Pennsylvania Mainline, on the other hand, never generated enough revenue to cover the initial construction costs. The Mainline ($16 million) was much more expensive to build than the Erie ($7 million), and the relatively high initial cost was reflected in relatively high rate charges. In addition, the uneven terrain through which the Mainline was built resulted in very slow-moving traffic. As a result of the high rate charges and low speed, the canal was never able to attract a large enough volume of traffic to yield a profit.[20] The Ohio canals carried a substantial volume of goods, but they were subject to periodic flooding and other maintenance problems which made profitable operation difficult. The Wabash and Erie was a financial failure and suffered from light traffic and flood damage.

In general, canals were financial failures because their promoters overestimated revenues from tolls and underestimated construction and maintenance expenditures. Initial construction costs were high, averaging $20,000–30,000 per mile, and the liberal use of natural waterways resulted in high maintenance and repair expenses due to flood damage. Canals required an extremely heavy volume of traffic in order to generate enough revenue to amortize the debt and cover operating and maintenance expenses. For many canals, superfluous construction depressed revenues to the point at which profitable operation was impossible. In addition, revenues were affected by natural phenomena such as floods, drought, and winter freezing.

Rationality of Government Investment in Canals

The rationality of government involvement in canal construction has been debated at great length in the literature. Roger Ransom has concluded that possibly as much as 85 percent of the total government canal investment may have been a social waste.[21] The only major interregional canals that Ransom viewed as probably successful were the Erie and the Ohio and Erie. Harvey Segal has also studied the merits of government canal building, and he has concluded that benefits greatly exceeded costs on approximately 80 percent of the projects, and, therefore, government action represented a socially responsible utilization of public funds.[22] Segal clearly stated, however, that the only major canal which satisfied a strict accounting concept of profit was the Erie. Albert Fishlow has criticized Segal's methods of calculating benefits relative to costs, but he concluded that the canal transportation system carried many benefits.[23]

---

[20] See Ransom, "Interregional Canals and Economic Specialization."

[21] Ransom, "Canals and Development," p. 375.

[22] Segal, "Canals and Economic Development."

[23] Lance E. Davis, Richard A. Easterlin, William N. Parker, et al., *American Economic Growth* (New York: Harper & Row, 1972), pp. 517–18; also see Ransom, "Canals and Development," pp. 371–73.

The merits of any public investment are difficult to measure because of the problems encountered in quantifying social returns. It is relatively easy to demonstrate that in almost all instances revenue generated by canals was insufficient to cover the initial construction debt, the interest charges on the debt, and operating expenses. However, the canals brought many special advantages to the areas which they served, although these advantages are difficult to evaluate. The Pennsylvania Mainline canal was the largest single financial failure of all the major state projects. Even in this case, though, there were still many benefits, and the canal stimulated a great intrastate transportation of coal and ore that encouraged concentration of the iron industry in Pennsylvania. It is very difficult to quantify the value in dollars and cents of the regional concentration of this basic industry, and, depending on one's biases and assumptions, one could conclude that the canal investment was rational or irrational. Earlier in this chapter, it was shown that the East-West system of interregional canals was a prime contributor to the creation of an industrial base in the Northeast. To determine exactly how much of our industrialization should be attributed to the canals presents a difficult measurement problem, but it is obvious that the canal effect was significant. Fishlow and others have argued that the market creation and population redistribution that resulted from canal development during the 1820s and 1830s had a large controlling influence on the pace and pattern of railroad development during the 1850s.[24]

Some economists will continue to discount the rationality of public expenditures on canals because of their unprofitability. However, in view of their strategic role in widening the market in the American economy during the first half of the nineteenth century, it seems appropriate to conclude that canals carried many benefits and stimulated the economy's development. At the same time, we should be aware that there was an element of state and urban competition present during the canal era which encouraged overbuilding and resulted in some superfluous construction.

Antebellum Developments in River and Lake Transportation

American river transportation before 1815 was archaic and, except for sail transportation on several of the broad rivers, most commerce was limited to downstream navigation by raft and flatboat. There was some upstream navigation by keelboat, but this was difficult and expensive, and there was a clear need for an innovative form of cheap river transportation. During the latter half of the Napoleonic Wars, there were numerous experimental attempts to harness steam power for transportation, and, by 1815, the era of the steamboat was beginning. Throughout the remainder

---

[24] Albert Fishlow, *American Railroads and the Transformation of the Ante-Bellum Economy* (Cambridge, Mass.: Harvard University Press, 1965), Ch. IV.

of the nineteenth-century steamboats were an important means of internal transportation in America.[25]

During the antebellum period, the steamboat had its greatest impact on western economic development. There were alternative means of freight distribution in the East, and eastern steamboats were largely used for passenger transportation. Western steamboats attracted a heavy volume of passenger traffic, and almost immediately they captured virtually all upstream freight carriage. The volume of western river downstream freight carried by rafts and flatboats expanded until the late 1840s. By the early 1850s, however, most upstream and downstream freight on western rivers moved by steamboat. While steam did revolutionize western river transportation, the total amount of freight carried by steamboats was never very large, and most western commodities were shipped to the East by canal rather than down the Mississippi to New Orleans. By the 1850s, western steamboats were most heavily involved in trade between the South and the lower West.

Advantages of Steamboat Navigation

The major advantages of steamboats over alternative forms of river transportation were speed and economy. Labor costs were high for pre-steamboat river transportation, and rafts and flatboats were often scrapped at their downstream destination, adding to the cost of shipment. Average charges per ton-mile in the 1850s for most rivers were approximately one cent.[26] Taylor claims that rate charges on shipments on western rivers during the 1850s were 25–30 percent (downstream) and 5–10 percent (upstream) of their pre-steamboat level.[27] In addition to the tremendous cost reduction, steamboats also offered relatively rapid upstream and downstream navigation. The average rate of speed of western river steamboats was approximately 10 miles per hour, and the average rate of speed on the Mississippi and Ohio Rivers approached 15 miles per hour.[28]

Sailing vessels provided a viable alternative to steam power on the Great Lakes because the steamboat's higher operating costs offset its slight speed advantage. Taylor estimates that by 1860 the Great Lakes steamship tonnage equalled 137,771 tons compared to sailing tonnage of 255,449.[29] It was not until the development of large-scale barge operation

---

[25] An excellent treatment of steamboats is provided by Louis C. Hunter, *Steamboats on the Western Rivers* (Cambridge, Mass.: Harvard University Press, 1949); also see Taylor, *Transportation Revolution*, Ch. IV.

[26] Taylor, *Transportation Revolution*, p. 442, gives the following ton-mile charges for 1853: Ohio River, 0.8¢; Hudson River, 0.7¢; and Illinois River, 1.2¢.

[27] Taylor, *Transportation Revolution*, p. 136.

[28] See Taylor, *Transportation Revolution*, pp. 138–39.

[29] Taylor, *Transportation Revolution*, p. 62.

in the late nineteenth century that steam navigation replaced sailing vessels on the Great Lakes.

Financing Steamboat Development

The amount of capital required to enter steamboat navigation was small, and the industry was almost exclusively financed by private capital. In the large-scale operations that developed on the Great Lakes and in the East, the corporate form became a popular means of capital mobilization. However, the majority of eastern and Great Lakes steamboats and most western steamboats were owned by individuals or by partners. Government investment was not needed in the steamboat industry because of the low initial capital requirements and the heavy demand for steamboat services. Government provided little or no land or direct financial support to steamboat companies; instead, public assistance was largely confined to improving the conditions of steamboat navigation. State and federal funds were spent on harbor and river deepening and dredging, and the majority of this indirect aid came from state governments.[30] In addition, the federal government regulated the steamboat industry during the 1850s. According to the Steamboat Act of 1852, the federal government was to establish standards for the construction and operation of steamboat boilers. The Act also prescribed measures to prevent fires and collisions and established federal inspection teams to enforce compliance with the Act's provisions.[31]

End of the Steamboat Era

The small amount of capital required to enter the industry was a major factor in the rapid expansion of steamboat navigation. Since steamboats used natural waterways, the only cost of entering the industry was the boat's expense. However, since steamboats depended on natural waterways, floods, drought, winter freezing, snags, and sandbars created problems and interrupted the regularity of service. The lack of dependable year-round operation was a major factor in the conversion from steamboats to railroads. Railroads also built spur lines directly to warehouses and loading docks to facilitate distribution of commodities. The conversion to railroads was also encouraged by another factor: the cooperative agreements be-

---

[30] See Taylor, *Transportation Revolution*, pp. 67–68; for federal expenditures on harbor and river improvements see *Historical Statistics*, Series Q 245.

[31] Hunter's figures show that between 1811 and 1849, 520 steamboats were destroyed on western rivers, and between 1860 and 1889, 1.4 million tons of shipping were destroyed and 6270 lives were lost in steamboat accidents; see *Steamboats*, pp. 654–56.

tween major railroad lines concerning long-distance hauling. The initial push of railroads into the West acted as a complement to the steamboat industry and stimulated its expansion. By the late 1850s, however, the cost difference between steamboat and railroad transportation had narrowed, and railroads built competing routes. The railroad's advantages of speed, dependability, year-round operation, and direct routing attracted a great deal of traffic from the steamboats and eventually led to their demise.

Western river traffic increased absolutely until the 1880s, but this was followed by a rapid decline. (See Table 5–6.) During the late nineteenth and early twentieth centuries, much river transportation converted to a barge operation, which provided low-unit cost. River freight became highly concentrated on bulky items that could not be shipped economically by rail. Lake transportation was also concentrated on bulky freight such as ore, coal, grain, and lumber, and the volume of lake traffic expanded rapidly throughout the late nineteenth and early twentieth centuries. (See Table 5–6.) By 1900, most of the nation's internal water transportation was restricted to hauling bulky commodities; the rest of the nation's freight moved by railroad.

Table 5-6 Gross Tonnage of Vessels on Northern Lakes and Western Rivers, 1816-1910
(tons)

Year	Northern Lakes	Western Rivers
1816	5217	9930
1820	7482	27269
1825	7027	19393
1830	13183	32664
1835	16851	72697
1840	48598	117952
1845	85897	187740
1850	181235	302829
1855	205894	129387
1860	463123	167739
1865	671004	245858
1870	684704	398206
1875	837892	418964
1880	605102	473792
1885	749948	346055
1890	1063063	294446
1895	1241459	281219
1900	1565587	258456
1905	2062147	174319
1910	2895102	153716

Source: *Historical Statistics*, Series Q 169-74.
Note: Figures include only vessels of five tons or more.

Population Redistribution and Western Urbanization

Nineteenth-century improvements in transportation linkage between East and West stimulated a significant westward population movement. In the early decades of the century, the bulk of Americans lived in the eastern seaboard states. The figures in Table 5–7 show that in 1820, when improvements in transportation were in their formative stages, almost 80 percent of our population lived in the eastern seaboard regions of New England and the Middle and South Atlantic states. By 1840, the eastern seaboard's share of total population had fallen to 63 percent; by 1860, it had fallen to 51 percent; and, by 1880, to 44 percent. The tremendous spurt in western population growth is clearly mirrored by the relative expansion that took place in the North Central region; the area's population share increased from 1 percent in 1800, to 8.9 percent in 1820, to 19.6 percent in 1840, to 28.9 percent in 1860, and to 34.6 percent in 1880.

The rise of many areas of urban concentration accompanied the sharp upsurge in western population. Table 5–8 shows trends in population growth between 1840 and 1890 for selected cities directly involved in the East-West trade. Among the western cities, Chicago, St. Louis, Cincinnati, Cleveland, Pittsburgh, Detroit, and Milwaukee showed the most impressive expansion. By 1890, there were sixteen cities in the United States with population exceeding 200,000; six of these were in the North Central region, and nine were western cities. Eastern urban growth was also substantial during the nineteenth century, especially in New York and Philadelphia. By 1890, however, Chicago had replaced Philadelphia as the second largest city in the United States, and St. Louis had surpassed both Boston and Baltimore.

Ocean Transportation

Whereas steam power revolutionized river and lake transportation in the early 1800s, it was not until the very late nineteenth century that steamships became the major carriers of ocean freight. Throughout the antebellum period, the bulk of ocean freight moved by sailing vessels owing to their advantages of low initial outlay and low fuel and maintenance expenses. For a long time, the cost advantages of sailing vessels were enough to offset the faster and more dependable ocean shipment offered by steamships. At the time of the Civil War, sailing vessels averaged thirty-five days to cross the Atlantic from Liverpool to New York City compared to ten to thirteen days for steamships.[32] Throughout the nineteenth century, the size and speed of steamships increased, resulting in a steady decline in

---

[32] See Taylor, *Transportation Revolution,* pp. 145–47.

Table 5-7 Regional Distribution of Population, 1800-90

Region	1800	1810	1820	1830	1840	1850	1860	1870	1880	1890
New England	23.2%	20.3%	17.2%	15.2%	13.1%	11.8%	10.0%	9.1%	8.0%	7.5%
Middle Atlantic	26.4	27.7	28.0	27.9	26.6	25.3	23.6	22.8	20.9	20.2
East North Central	1.0	3.8	8.2	11.4	17.1	19.5	22.0	23.6	22.3	21.4
West North Central	–	0.3	0.7	1.1	2.5	3.8	6.9	10.0	12.3	14.2
South Atlantic	43.1	37.0	31.8	28.4	23.0	20.2	17.1	15.2	15.2	14.1
East South Central	6.3	9.8	12.4	14.1	15.1	14.5	12.8	11.4	11.1	10.2
West South Central	–	1.1	1.7	1.9	2.6	4.1	5.6	5.3	6.7	7.5
Mountain	–	–	–	–	–	0.3	0.6	0.8	1.3	1.9
Pacific	–	–	–	–	–	0.5	1.4	1.8	2.2	3.0

Source: Computed from the figures in *Historical Statistics*, Series A 123-80.

Table 5-8 Population in Selected Cities, 1840-90

City	1840	1850	1860	1870	1880	1890
Albany	33,721	50,763	62,367	69,422	90,758	94,923
Baltimore	102,313	169,054	212,418	267,354	332,313	434,439
Boston	93,383	136,881	177,812	250,526	362,839	448,477
Buffalo	18,213	42,261	81,129	117,714	155,134	255,664
Chicago	4,470	29,963	109,260	298,977	503,185	1,099,850
Cincinnati	46,338	115,436	161,044	216,239	255,139	296,908
Cleveland	6,071	17,034	43,417	92,829	160,146	261,353
Columbus	6,048	17,882	18,554	31,274	51,647	88,150
Dayton	6,067	10,977	20,081	30,473	38,678	61,220
Detroit	9,102	21,019	45,619	79,577	116,340	205,876
Indianapolis	2,692	8,034	18,611	48,244	75,056	105,436
Louisville	21,210	43,194	68,033	100,753	123,758	161,129
Milwaukee	1,700	20,061	45,246	71,440	115,587	204,468
New Orleans	102,193	116,375	168,675	191,418	216,090	242,039
New York	312,710	515,547	805,651	942,292	1,206,299	1,515,301
Philadelphia	220,423	340,045	585,529	674,022	847,170	1,046,964
Pittsburgh	21,115	46,601	49,217	86,076	156,398	238,617
Rochester	20,191	36,403	48,204	62,386	89,366	133,896
St. Louis	16,469	77,860	160,773	310,864	350,518	451,770
Syracuse	6,500	22,271	28,119	43,051	51,792	88,143
Toledo	1,222	3,829	13,768	31,584	50,137	81,434
Troy	19,334	28,785	39,232	46,465	56,747	60,956

Source: *Seventh Census of the U.S., Population,* p. lii; *Eighth Census of the U.S., Population,* pp. xxxi-ii; *Ninth Census of the U.S., Population,* p. 380; and *Eleventh Census of the U.S., Population,* Part 1, p. lxvii.

freight charges. By the latter part of the century, the cost difference between steam and sail had narrowed to the point where the speed and dependability of steamships encouraged a rapid conversion to this form of ocean shipment.

Throughout the late nineteenth century, America's merchant marine suffered a sharp decline relative to foreign competition. During the antebellum decades, generally 80 percent or more of America's foreign trade was carried in American vessels. By 1860, the share had fallen to less than 70 percent and, by 1900, to approximately 10 percent. The tremendous decline during the late nineteenth century partially reflected America's commitment to sailing ships. As a result, technological development in steamship construction had occurred much faster in Britain, and the British maintained technical superiority over the Americans through most of the nineteenth century. It has also been argued that government subsidies to American steamship lines were rather small compared to foreign subsidies.[33] Another factor that hindered expansion of the American merchant marine was the prohibition on purchase of the cheaper and technically superior foreign ships. America's relative decline as a shipping nation was partially reversed after World War I, but the dominant position that the American merchant marine enjoyed during the era of sailing vessels was never approached again.

Summary

During the antebellum decades, canal and steamboat developments brought about a significant improvement in America's internal transportation system. Distinct patterns of regional economic specialization had been established by the late 1830s, and the United States began to approach the status of a self-sufficient national economy. Coincident with th specialized patterns of regional production, there occurred a large-scale internal migration from east to west as population was redistributed to conform to the nation's resource structure. However, the strong regional linkages created by canals and steamboats promoted a search for improved means of distribution and encouraged rapid development of the railroad. As the next chapter will show, railroads had many advantages over water-based transportation systems, and, by the 1870s, railroads had replaced canals and steamboats on virtually all important commercial routes.

---

[33] Mail subsidies were granted during the 1890s, but they came too late and were not large enough to have a significant impact.

Suggested Reading

Cranmer, H. Jerome, "Canal Investment, 1815–1860," in *Trends in the American Economy in the Nineteenth Century,* Conference on Research in Income and Wealth, Studies in Income and Wealth, National Bureau of Economic Research, Vol. 24. Princeton: Princeton University Press, 1960.

Haites, Erick F. and James Mak, "Ohio and Mississippi River Transportation, 1810–1860," *Explorations in Economic History,* Winter 1970–71.

———, "The Decline of Steamboating on the Antebellum Western Rivers: Some New Evidence and an Alternative Hypothesis," *Explorations in Economic History,* Fall 1973.

Hunter, Louis C., *Steamboats on the Western Rivers.* Cambridge, Mass.: Harvard University Press, 1949.

Mak, James and Gary Walton, "Steamboats and the Great Productivity Surge in River Transportation," *Journal of Economic History,* September 1972.

Niemi, Albert W., Jr., "A Further Look at Interregional Canals and Economic Specialization: 1820–1840," *Explorations in Economic History,* Summer 1970.

North, Douglass C., *Economic Growth of the United States, 1790–1860.* New York: W. W. Norton, 1966, Chs. VI-XV.

Ransom, Roger, "Canals and Development: A Discussion of the Issues," *American Economic Review,* May 1964.

———, "Interregional Canals and Economic Specialization in the Antebellum United States," *Explorations in Entrepreneurial History,* Fall 1967.

———, "Social Returns from Public Transport Investment: A Case Study of the Ohio Canal," *Journal of Political Economy,* September/October 1970.

Scheiber, Harry N., *Ohio Canal Era.* Athens: Ohio University Press, 1969.

Segal, Harvey, "Canals and Economic Development," in Carter Goodrich, ed., *Canals and American Economic Development.* New York: Columbia University Press, 1961.

———, "Cycles of Canal Construction," in Goodrich, ed., *Canals and American Economic Development.*

Taylor, George R., *The Transportation Revolution, 1815–1860.* New York: Holt, Rinehart and Winston, 1951, Chs. II–IV and VI–VIII.

6

Railroads and American Economic Growth

The means of internal transportation—roads, steamboats, and canals—surveyed in the previous chapter gradually gave way to railroad competition during the middle and late nineteenth century. A great deal of discussion concerning the role of transportation improvement in American economic development has focused on the impact of the railroad. The emphasis on railroads was carried to an extreme in Rostow's analysis of the American growth experience; he argued that it was mainly the railroad that set the take-off in motion (1843–60).[1] As noted in Chapter 2, Rostow's notion of take-off in the American economy has been subjected to empirical test and has been rejected. Albert Fishlow and Robert Fogel have attacked the specific issue of the crucial and indispensable role of railroads in American economic development.[2] Fishlow restricted his analysis to the antebellum period whereas Fogel was concerned with the impact of the railroad in the late nineteenth century. They argued that the railroad was an extremely important nineteenth-century transportation development, but alternative forms of transportation could have handled the distribution of commodities without substantially altering the American economy's rate of progress. The Fogel and Fishlow conclusions have not gone unchallenged, and most economic historians still regard the railroad as the most strategic investment of the late nineteenth century. It is also widely recognized, however,

[1] W. W. Rostow, *The Stages of Economic Growth* (Cambridge: At the University Press, 1960).

[2] Albert Fishlow, *American Railroads and the Transformation of the Ante-Bellum Economy* (Cambridge, Mass.: Harvard University Press, 1965). Robert W. Fogel, *Railroads and American Economic Growth: Essays in Econometric History* (Baltimore: Johns Hopkins, 1964) and "A Quantitative Approach to the Study of Railroads in American Economic Growth: A Report of Some Preliminary Findings," *Journal of Economic History*, June 1962.

that railroads lagged behind fundamental developments in the antebellum economy and mainly duplicated routes of alternative forms of transportation. During the 1850s, the railroads' competitive advantages attracted customers from alternative carriers, and railroads came to dominate late nineteenth-century interregional transportation in the United States.

This chapter will focus on the following aspects of nineteenth-century railroad development: the rate and geographic pattern of rail expansion, the competitive advantages of railroads over alternative methods of transportation, construction financing, the importance of federal land grants, the industry-linkage effects of railroads, the railroad's role as leading growth sector, and the indispensability of railroads to American economic growth.

Nineteenth-Century Railroad Development

Railroad construction began in 1830, and most of the early activity was concentrated in the eastern seaboard states. Table 6–1 shows state railroad mileage by decade for 1830–60, and Table 6–2 shows the regional distribution of railroad mileage for 1840–60. Railroads linked the major eastern seaboard cities during the 1830s, and, by 1840, there was a nearly complete route between Boston and Wilmington, North Carolina. During the 1840s, approximately 60 percent of the nation's new railroad construction took place in New England and New York. By 1850, southern New England possessed a large integrated network of railroads, and, by the early 1850s, New York had two east-west routes. The New York Central roughly paralleled the Erie Canal and the Hudson River, and the Erie traversed southern New York through to Buffalo. The 1840s also witnessed a small beginning of railroad development in the Midwest, mainly concentrated in Ohio and Michigan.

During the 1850s, the nation's railroad mileage increased from approximately 9,000 miles to almost 31,000 miles. Much of this construction was centered in the Midwest; by 1860, over one-third of the nation's railroads were in the North Central states, and Chicago had become the railroad hub of the United States. In 1860, the leading railroad states were Ohio (2,946), Illinois (2,799), New York (2,682), Pennsylvania (2,598), and Indiana (2,163). During the decade of the 1850s, there was also considerable railroad expansion in the South, particularly in Virginia, Georgia, Tennessee, Alabama, and Mississippi. Most southern railroad development was intended to connect the interior with the coast in order to facilitate the export of cotton and other staples. It was not until the eve of the Civil War that attempts were made to integrate the South's railroads with the North's. With the exception of Pennsylvania, there was very little large-scale construction in the Northeast during the final antebellum decade. During the fifties, both Pennsylvania (Pennsylvania Railroad) and Maryland (Baltimore and

Table 6-1 State Railroad Mileage by Decades, 1830-60

State	1830	1840	1850	1860
Maine	–	10	257	472
New Hampshire	–	15	471	661
Vermont	–	–	366	554
Massachusetts	3	270	1042	1264
Rhode Island	–	47	61	108
Connecticut	–	94	436	601
New York	–	453	1409	2682
New Jersey	–	192	332	560
Pennsylvania	70	576	900	2598
Delaware	–	16	16	127
Maryland	–	273	315	386
Ohio	–	39	590	2946
Indiana	–	20	226	2163
Illinois	–	26	118	2799
Michigan	–	114	349	779
Wisconsin	–	–	20	905
Iowa	–	–	–	655
Missouri	–	–	4	817
Virginia	–	341	341	1731
North Carolina	–	247	249	937
South Carolina	–	136	270	973
Georgia	–	212	666	1420
Florida	–	52	52	402
Kentucky	–	32	80	534
Tennessee	–	–	48	1253
Alabama	–	51	112	743
Mississippi	–	50	60	862
Arkansas	–	–	–	38
Louisiana	–	62	89	335
Texas	–	–	–	307
California	–	–	–	23
Total	73	3328	8879	30636

Source: George R. Taylor, *The Transportation Revolution,* (New York: Holt, Rinehart and Winston, 1951, p. 79.

Ohio) completed east-west railroad lines and joined New York (Erie and New York Central) in direct rail trade with the West. By 1860, most of the major railroad lines east of the Mississippi were completed. However, much of the antebellum development had taken place in an atmosphere of independence and competition, and eastern and western railroads were not fully integrated until the 1870s, and northern and southern railroads were not integrated until the 1880s. (See Figure 6–1.)

Lack of a uniform track gauge posed a major barrier against the integration of the various railroad lines. During the antebellum period, many

Table 6-2 Percentage Distribution of Railroad Mileage, by Region, 1840, 1850, and 1860

Region	1840	1850	1860
New England	13.1%	29.7%	12.0%
Middle Atlantic[a]	45.4	33.5	20.7
South Atlantic	29.6	17.8	17.8
North Central[b]	6.0	14.7	36.1
South Central[c]	5.9	4.3	12.3
Far West	0.0	0.0	1.1

Source: Calculated from figures in Taylor, *Transportation Revolution*, p. 79.
[a] Delaware and Maryland are included in the Middle Atlantic states.
[b] Includes East and West North Central states.
[c] Includes East and West South Central states.

Figure 6-1 Major Railroads Built by 1860

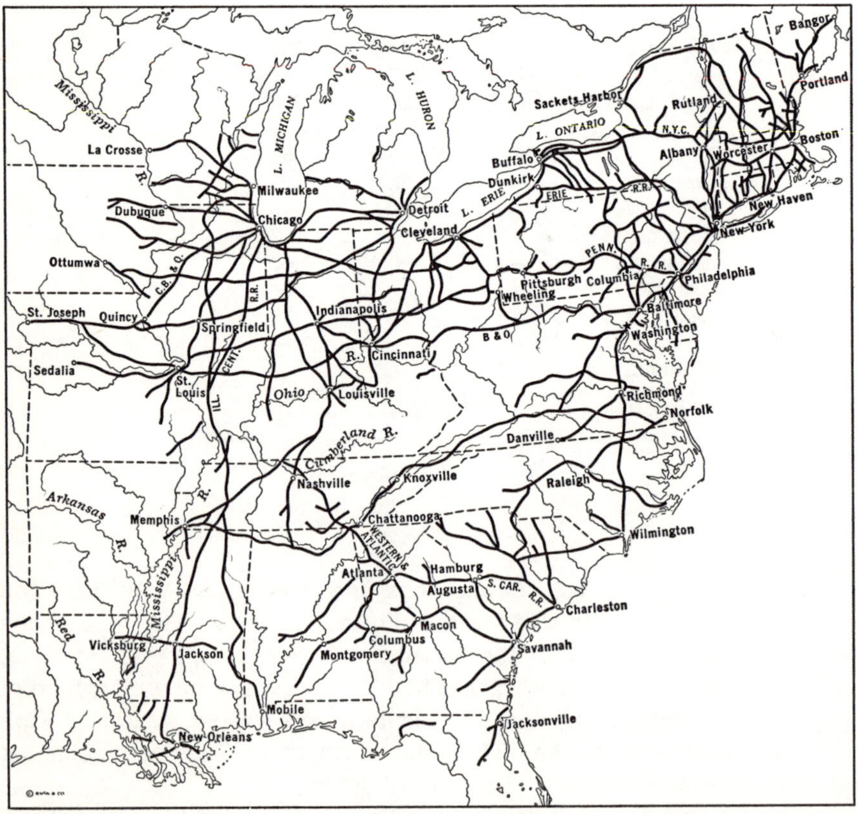

Source: Adapted from Henry F. Graff and John A. Krout, *The Adventure of the American People*, 2nd ed. (Chicago: Rand McNally, 1970), p. 212.

different gauges were built; Taylor has concluded that eleven different gauges existed in the North in 1860.[3] A portion of the variation in gauge was deliberately planned in order to allow railroads and locomotive producers to secure monopoly power over certain routes; in large part, however, the gauge variation simply represented an absence of planning. During the 1870s, all railroads except those in the South converted to a uniform gauge; in 1886, the South's railroads also adopted the standard gauge.

In the antebellum and Civil War years, several technical advances were made which increased the carrying capacity of freight trains. During the 1830s and 1840s, roadbed designs were improved to support heavier loads. Many different rail designs were tried, and the standard T rail was adopted in the late 1840s. During the Civil War and immediate postwar period, engine capacity was expanded, and steel construction in railroad cars, locomotives, boilers, and rails was developed.

There was a sharp decline in the rate of new railroad construction during the Civil War. By the middle 1860s, however, the construction boom had begun in earnest, and railroad mileage expanded at a tremendous pace throughout the late nineteenth and early twentieth centuries. (See Table 6–3.) The decade of the 1880s was the period of most vigorous construction; over 73,000 miles of new track were put into operation during this time. Much construction between the late 1860s and early 1880s represented the development of three transcontinental routes which tied the East to the Far West. The first transcontinental route ran through the central portion of the country to San Francisco; a second route went from St. Louis through Texas to southern California; and a third traversed the northern states from Chicago to Seattle.

A great deal of post–Civil War railroad construction in the central portion of the United States accompanied the establishment of the transcontinentals. A complex rail network developed between the western cities of Chicago, St. Louis, Kansas City, Omaha, Minneapolis and Denver, and these cities had strong ties with both East and West. Disruption associated with war in the South continued through the 1870s, and postwar railroad development in the region did not increase until the 1880s.[4] National railroad mileage expanded at a rapid rate until World War I; in fact, the decade 1900–1910 was the second most active period of railroad construction in the nation's history. During this time, local areas tied into the major trunk lines, and, by the beginning of the twentieth century, railroads monopolized American transportation.

Land grants played a major role in the post–Civil War expansion of railroads, and examination of the exact magnitude of these grants and consideration of the rationality of this form of government subsidy to private

---

[3] George R. Taylor, *The Transportation Revolution* (New York: Holt, Rinehart and Winslow, 1951), p. 82.

[4] See Chapter 10 for an assessment of the Civil War's impact on the South.

Table 6-3 Railroad Mileage in Operation, 1830-1950

Date	Mileage
1830	23
1835	1098
1840	2818
1845	4633
1850	9021
1855	18374
1860	30626
1865	35085
1870	52922
1875	74096
1880	93262
1885	128320
1890	166703
1895	190094
1900	206631
1905	236855
1910	266185
1915	291231
1920	296835
1925	299593
1930	303182
1935	294846
1940	287113
1945	280544
1950	277313

Source: *Historical Statistics,* Series Q 15-22 and Q 44-72.
Note: Mileage figures do not include yard tracks and sidings.

industry is deferred until later in this chapter. It is generally admitted that land grants greatly increased the rate of American railroad development, and, by the late nineteenth century, the railroad industry was characterized by excess capacity. By 1890, profits were down to the point where many railroads could not meet their debt obligations, and financial problems led to a consolidation movement in the industry.

Competitive Advantages of Railroads

The railroads' major advantages over steamboat and canal transportation were speed and flexibility of operation. The average rate of speed on the early freight trains was 10–15 miles per hour, and on certain routes, the average was as high as 20–30 miles per hour.[5] Augmenting the railroads'

[5] Chapter 5 showed that east-west canals averaged less than 2 miles per hour. Steamboats could attain speeds of 15 miles per hour, but the average speed on western rivers was less than 10 miles per hour; see Taylor, *Transportation Revolution,* pp. 138–39.

Table 6-4 Average Freight Rates per Ton-Mile, 1853

Method and Route of Transportation	Cents per Ton-Mile
River	
Ohio River	0.8¢
Hudson River	0.7
Illinois River	1.2
Canal	
Erie	1.1
Ohio and Erie	1.0
Wabash and Erie	1.9
Illinois	1.4
Pennsylvania Mainline	2.4
Railroad	
New York Central	3.4
Erie	2.4
Pennsylvania	3.5
Western: Buffalo-Chicago	2.5
Boston-Albany	2.3

Source: Taylor, *Transportation Revolution*, p. 442.

speed advantage were the shorter distances traveled by railroads compared to canals or steamboats on competing routes. Railroads used man-made roadbeds, and they generally ran in straight lines; canals and steamboats, on the other hand, followed natural waterways as much as possible. As an example of the mileage savings, Taylor points out that the distance between Cincinnati and Pittsburgh was 470 miles by river and 311 miles by railroad.[6] In addition to reducing the time required to travel between points, the railroads also offered year-round operation. Canal, river, and lake transportation was subject to periodic interruption due to droughts and floods, and winter freezing closed the northern water routes for three to four months. Railroads were also characterized by much less transshipment in long-haul trade owing to cooperative agreements between major railroad companies. Railroads offered more direct service than water alternatives, and companies often built spur lines directly to loading docks or warehouses in order to attract customers.

Despite the railroads' advantages in speed and flexibility, throughout the antebellum period, the cost advantages were with water transportation. However, during the antebellum decades, differences narrowed between railroad, canal, and steamboat cost/ton-mile rate charges, and, by the early 1850s, ton-mile rate differences were generally less than two cents. (See Table 6–4.) The cost comparisons shown in Table 6–4 do not take into ac-

[6] Taylor, *Transportation Revolution*, p. 139.

Table 6-5 Railroad Passenger and Freight Revenue, Selected Years, 1839-1920 (millions of dollars)

Year	Passenger Revenue	Freight Revenue	Percent Freight
1839	$4.5	$2.5	36
1849	13.6	14.1	51
1859	45.8	66.5	59
1871	108.9	294.4	73
1875	139.1	364.0	72
1880	147.7	467.7	76
1885	200.9	509.7	72
1890	272.3	734.8	73
1895	252.2	730.0	74
1900	323.7	1049.3	76
1905	472.7	1450.8	75
1910	629.0	1925.6	75
1915	646.5	2037.9	76
1920	1304.8	4420.8	77

Source: The 1839-59 estimates were obtained from Albert Fishlow, *American Railroads and the Transformation of the Ante-Bellum Economy* (Cambridge, Mass.: Harvard University Press, 1965), Appendix A; the 1871-1920 estimates were obtained from *Historical Statistics,* Series Q 23-32, Q 44-72, and Q 73-86.

count the long-haul rate reductions that were given by railroads on certain bulky commodities.[7] Furthermore, on competing routes, the shorter distances traveled by railroads compared to canals and steamboats tended to reduce the cost/ton-mile disadvantage of rail transportation.

By the middle 1850s, the speed and flexibility advantages of railroad transportation were enough to offset its higher cost, and, in all but bulky commodities, there was a rapid conversion to the railroad. Bulky items such as coal, grain, and lumber continued to move by water throughout the nineteenth century, but the railroads had little trouble attracting light freight and passenger traffic from the water alternatives. During the early years of railroad development, passenger fares earned most of the revenue; by 1849, however, freight earnings equaled receipts from passenger traffic, and, by the post–Civil War period, freight earnings provided 70 percent or more of railroad revenues. (See Table 6–5.) Taylor has stated that the westward shipment of manufactured goods over the Erie Canal reached a peak in 1853, and, by 1860, these shipments had declined by more than 50 percent.[8] In addition, most trade in flour, livestock, meat products, and other

[7] Taylor, *Transportation Revolution,* p. 135, claims that railroad charges on Chicago to New York wheat shipments were 1.2 cents per ton-mile in 1860.

[8] Taylor, *Transportation Revolution,* p. 165.

Table 6-6 Routes of Direct East-West Grain Shipments, 1860

Route	Wheat (000 bu.)	Flour (000 barrels)	Corn, Rye, Oats, and Barley (000 bu.)
New York Central RR	1500	2000	1000
Erie RR	501	543	653
Pennsylvania RR	500	427	364
Baltimore and Ohio RR	80	352	46
Total Railroads	2581	3322	2063
Erie Canal	19673	901	18779

Source: Fishlow, *American Railroads,* p. 264.

Table 6-7 Percentage of Chicago's Exports of Selected Agricultural Commodities Moving by Rail, 1860 and 1862

Commodity	1860	1862
Flour	65.1%	38.8%
Wheat	3.1	2.1
Corn	4.2	0.4
Cattle	98.8	99.3
Hogs: Live	99.9	99.9
Dressed	100.0	100.0
Beef (barrels)	91.2	85.1
Pork (barrels)	94.6	43.5
Lard	98.5	100.0

Source: Fishlow, *American Railroads,* p. 266.
Note: The residual percentage was moved by lake transportation.

high-value, low-weight items converted from water to rail during the 1850s. (See Tables 6–6 and 6–7.) According to Taylor, the volume of freight carried by railroads and internal waterways was about equal in 1860, and the value of trade carried by railroads greatly exceeded that of water freight.[9] Even in the grain trade, canals lost out to railroads during the late nineteenth century, and Fishlow points to the following downward trend in the percentage share of western grain carried by canals: 1868, 96 percent; 1880, 48 percent; 1890, 32 percent; and 1898, 12 percent.[10]

[9] Taylor, *Transportation Revolution,* pp. 164–65.

[10] See Fishlow's treatment of internal transportation in Lance E. Davis, Richard A. Easterlin, William N. Parker, et al., *American Economic Growth* (New York: Harper & Row, 1972), p. 484.

Financing Railroad Construction

By and large, the private sector built the railroads. The initial capital required for railroad construction could not be raised by individual capitalists and, therefore, most railroad companies were organized as corporations. State legislatures granted corporate charters, and these generally contained rather liberal provisions regarding the type of securities to be issued, tax exemptions, and privileges of eminent domain. Despite heavy capital requirements, railroads needed much less public support than canals because they were faced by a great deal of existing demand. The private sector was willing to undertake railroad construction because of the guaranteed demand and potentially high profits.[11] On the contrary, the interregional canals were built ahead of demand and were faced by an almost certain gestation period during which no profit could be earned.

During the 1830s and 1840s, most private support for railroad construction was local and represented vested interests. Competition between eastern seaboard cities promoted strong local support for railroads, and most of the private capital committed to early railroad development came from those who hoped to gain direct benefits from the railroads. To be sure, there was some private capital that was primarily concerned with the return on the investment, but it was not until the 1850s that eastern capital migrated in large amounts to finance western railroad construction. Foreign capital also provided an active source of demand for American railroad bonds during the early 1850s, and Taylor claims that by 1853 foreigners owned slightly more than one-fourth of American railroad bonds.[12] Modern institutions and techniques of capital accumulation developed largely during the railroad construction boom, and, by the 1850s, the financial market for railroad bonds was becoming increasingly concentrated in eastern seaboard cities, and speculation in railroad securities was becoming common.[13]

Despite the attractiveness of railroad investment to the private sector, there was still substantial public support behind railroad construction. During the antebellum period, the majority of public support came from state and local governments, and most of this effort was concentrated in rural areas, particularly in the South. In fact, Taylor claims that the public sector supported 50 percent of total antebellum railroad construction in that region.[14] On the contrary, private capital financed most railroad con-

---

[11] Fishlow, *American Railroads,* Chapter IV, argues that railroads were not built ahead of demand but instead chose their routes carefully and were highly motivated by profits. This proposition will be examined later in this chapter.

[12] Taylor, *Transportation Revolution,* p. 100.

[13] For an interesting discussion of railroad financial techniques see Alfred D. Chandler, *The Railroads: The Nation's First Big Business* (New York: Harcourt, Brace, and World, 1965), Part II.

[14] Taylor, *Transportation Revolution,* p. 92.

struction in the populous areas of the Northeast. The most common form of state and local support was to provide financial aid to private railroad companies. There was some direct railroad construction by state and local governments but, in almost all cases, this was confined to minor projects.[15] State and local aid to railroads was concentrated in the antebellum period; very little support was given after the Civil War.

During most of the antebellum period, federal government support for railroad construction was extremely limited. Between 1824 and 1838, federal engineers made railroad surveys at the government's expense, and, between 1830 and 1843, reduced tariffs on railroad iron were permited. Taylor says the surveys and tariff subsidy saved the railroads approximately $6 million.[16] The first federal land grant for railroad construction was made in Illinois in 1850, and after that the gift of public lands became the chief form of federal government support for railroad construction. In 1871, public outrage brought an end to the federal land grant policy, but, between 1850 and 1871, the government offered almost 200 million acres of federal land to railroads, and the companies took 131 million acres. Typically, land grants were made so that the railroads acquired alternating sections of land on each side of the proposed route. The government retained the remaining sections of land contiguous to the railroad. It was anticipated that railroad development would significantly raise the value of land, and, by retaining a share of the land with direct access to the railroads, the government could capture some of the benefits of railroad extension. Railroads receiving land grants generally were required to transport troops, mail, and government commodities at reduced rates. In addition to land grants, the federal government also made construction loans and provided railroads with free access to materials (stone, lumber, etc.) on government lands.

The federal government was particularly active during the period of transcontinental railroad development. In addition to providing liberal amounts of federal land, the government loaned approximately $65 million to railroads and agreed to take second mortgage railroad securities. This enabled the railroads to market the more secure first mortgage securities directly to the private sector. The federal government's lending policy proved to be financially sound, and, by 1900, most railroad debt obligations to the federal government, including interest, had been repaid. Despite the federal government's efforts during the period of transcontinental expansion, Fishlow claims that the public sector provided less than 10 percent of the total resources committed to late nineteenth-century railroad construction.[17]

---

[15] One exception was the state (Georgia) built railroad between Atlanta and Chattanooga; see Taylor, *Transportation Revolution*, pp. 90–92.

[16] Taylor, *Transportation Revolution*, p. 95.

[17] Davis, Easterlin, Parker, et al., *American Economic Growth*, p. 506.

The Economics of Federal Land Grants

There has been a great deal of debate concerning the appropriateness and effectiveness of federal land grants to the railroads. The debate has focused on the actual quantity and value of land grants, the benefits of the policy to the nation, and the financial returns of the policy to the land grant railroads. Colonel Robert Henry, who was employed by the railroad interests, argued in 1945 that the traditional interpretation of federal land grants overstated the amount and value of the subsidy.[18] He pointed out that much land granted to the railroads was not used but was forfeited back to the federal government. Of the total offering of almost 200 million acres, the railroads actually took and utilized only 131 million acres. (See Table 6–8 and Figure 6–2.) Henry also claimed that federal land grants supported less than 8 percent of all railroad construction. Grants were heavily concentrated in the hands of the transcontinentals, and more than 100 million acres of land were given to four railroads: Northern Pacific, 42 million; Southern Pacific, 24 million; Union Pacific, 20 million; and Santa Fe, 16 million. The nominal price of government land during the era of grants was $1.25 per acre; at this price, the government grants were worth $164 million. However, Henry claimed that the average selling price for government land at this time was less than $1.00 per acre, and, therefore, he argued that the grants were worth less than $130 million. He concluded that the return to the nation from the land grant policy was much greater than the original value of the land, and he defended the policy as a rational government subsidy to private industry.

Henry's views were criticized almost immediately by his contemporaries.[19] David Ellis argued that Henry's analysis did not present a complete picture of land subsidy to railroads, and he pointed out that the railroads used 49 million acres of state land as well as 131 million acres of federal land.[20] Henry has also been criticized for underestimating the value of federal land grants. Ellis suggested that the appropriate method to determine the value of government land grants was to use the sale value of land to the railroads rather than the average cost of land from the federal government. The federal land grants were sold for approximately $440 million, and, including state grants, the land was worth over $500 million. Although Ellis expressed concern about the magnitude of federal aid to railroads, he con-

---

[18] Robert S. Henry, "The Railroad Land Grant Legend in American History Texts," *Mississippi Valley Historical Review*, September 1945.

[19] Comments on Henry's work appeared in the *Mississippi Valley Historical Review*, March 1946, pp. 557–76.

[20] Ellis (*Mississippi Valley Historical Review*, March 1946) also pointed out that 43 million acres of federal land were granted to the railroads but were forfeited or released to the government. Henry was aware of the state land grants, but he restricted his analysis to consideration of the federal government's land subsidy.

Table 6-8 Federal Land Grants Utilized by Railroads

State	Acres
Alabama	2,747,479
Arizona	7,695,203
Arkansas	2,586,970
California	11,585,393
Colorado	3,757,673
Florida	2,218,705
Idaho	1,320,591
Illonois	2,595,133
Iowa	4,711,328
Kansas	8,234,013
Louisiana	1,375,000
Michigan	3,134,038
Minnesota	9,953,008
Mississippi	1,075,345
Missouri	2,328,674
Montana	14,736,919
Nebraska	7,272,623
Nevada	5,086,283
New Mexico	3,355,179
North Dakota	10,697,490
Oregon	3,655,390
Utah	2,230,085
Washington	9,582,878
Wisconsin	3,666,062
Wyoming	5,749,051
Total U.S.	131,350,534

Source: U.S. Department of the Interior Bureau of Land Management, *Annual Report of the Commissioner of the General Land Office,* 1943, pp. 124-28.

cluded that the land grants were an important causal factor behind the early development of the West.

Lloyd Mercer made an economic analysis of the benefits of land grants to the American economy and the railroads.[21] He argued that railroads were much more profitable than anticipated and that free land had only a marginal effect on railroad profits.[22] However, he claimed that land grants increased the pace of westward settlement and advanced the welfare of society. He concluded that a free land policy may not have been the least

[21] Lloyd J. Mercer, "Land Grants to American Railroads: Social Cost or Social Benefit," *Business History Review,* Summer 1969.

[22] Mercer, "Land Grants to American Railroads," argued that profit rates on land grant railroads would have been 13 percent without land subsidies and were only increased to 14 percent as a result of free land.

Figure 6-2 Federal Land Grants for Railroads

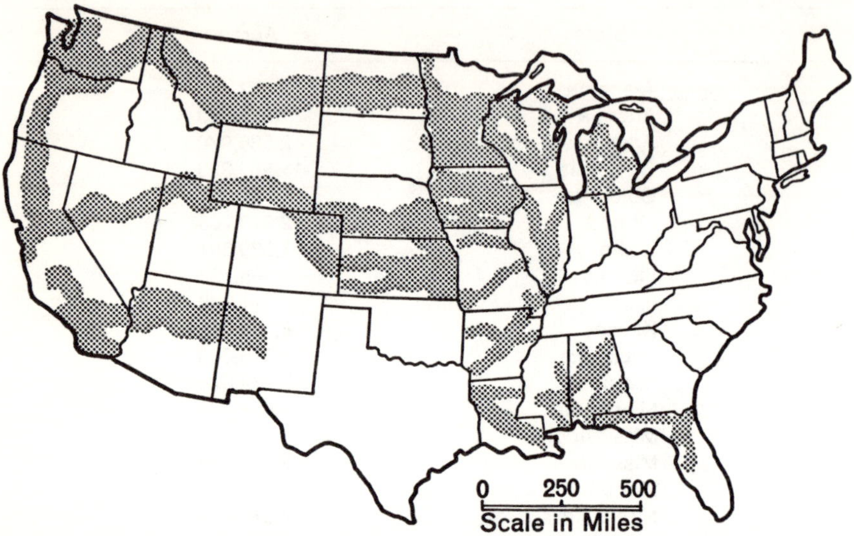

Source: Richard M. Highsmith, Jr., J. Granville Jensen, and Robert D. Rudd, *Conservation in the United States* (Chicago: Rand McNally, 1969), p. 17.

Note: The map shows the approximate areas in which the railroads received grants. Only a portion of the land covered by the shaded area actually was granted to the railroads.

expensive method of getting the railroads built, but the system did have a positive effect on economic welfare.[23]

Industry Linkage Effects of Railroads

Railroad construction required a tremendous labor force and substantial materials inputs. Fishlow has provided a convenient summary of the major expenditures in antebellum railroad development, and his figures suggest the following: roadbed construction, including rails and bridges, accounted for 65–70 percent of costs; machinery and equipment accounted for 10–15 percent; engineering for 3–4 percent; land costs for 3–7 percent; interest and discount increased from 3 percent in the 1830s to about 15 percent in the 1850s; and the residual was involved in miscellaneous fees.[24] Fishlow pointed out that labor costs were a large factor in roadbed, railroad

[23] Also see Mercer, "Rates of Return for Land Grant Railroads: The Central Pacific System," *Journal of Economic History,* September 1970.

Stanley Engerman, "Some Economic Issues Relating to Railroad Subsidies and the Evaluation of Land Grants," *Journal of Economic History,* June 1972, has recently reviewed the debate regarding the rationality of public subsidy to railroad development, and he argues that the issue deserves further analysis.

[24] Fishlow, *American Railroads,* p. 119.

car, and locomotive construction, and he estimated that labor may have accounted for two-thirds of total railroad construction costs.[25] He also suggested that many railroad demands for materials were for nonindustrial products such as firewood.[26]

Both Fishlow and Fogel have made a careful survey of the railroads' impact on the iron, coal, machinery, and lumber industries. It is generally agreed that antebellum railroad construction provided an important source of demand for pig iron. There were many other industries that also required pig iron, however, and Fishlow estimated that the railroads' share of total demand rose from less than 10 percent in the 1840s to 15 percent during 1851–55 and 19 percent during 1856–60.[27] Fogel suggested that between 1840 and 1860, 17 percent of the total domestic production of crude iron was consumed by the railroad industry for construction and maintenance.[28] He argued that the period of peak railroad demand for iron probably occurred in the early 1870s, and he estimated that in 1872 one-third of all pig iron and approximately three-fourths of all rolled steel went into rail production.[29] Peter Temin's estimates of the percentage share of total rolled iron and steel going into rails indicate the following trend: 1867, 44 percent; 1870, 46 percent; 1872, 50 percent; 1875, 40 percent; 1880, 42 percent; 1885, 33 percent; 1890, 31 percent; 1895, 21 percent; 1900, 25 percent; 1905, 20 percent; and 1910, 17 percent.[30]

Railroad construction also had a significant effect on the machinery industry. Fishlow showed that in 1860 total machinery production was equal to $52.0 million, and locomotive construction was equal to $4.9 million.[31] He argued that the railroads had an important effect on the machinery industry, but he noted that production of cotton and woolen textile machinery in 1860 also equaled $4.9 million, and, therefore, he cautioned that the railroads' impact should not be exaggerated. Fogel examined the railroads' impact on transportation equipment apart from other machinery. He argued that in 1860 railroad equipment (locomotives, railroad cars, springs, wheels, axles, brakes, and linings) accounted for one-fourth of the nation's total output of transportation equipment.[32] He estimated the percentage share of other machinery production that was geared to satisfying railroad demands at approximately 6 percent. Fogel also tried to gauge the total effect of railroads on manufacturing, and he estimated that 3.94 per-

---

25 Fishlow, *American Railroads,* pp. 120–24.

26 Fishlow, *American Railroads,* p. 129.

27 Fishlow, *American Railroads,* pp. 141–49.

28 Fogel, *Railroads,* p. 132.

29 Fogel, *Railroads,* p. 130.

30 Peter Temin, *Iron and Steel in Nineteenth Century America* (Cambridge, Mass.: M.I.T. Press, 1964).

31 Fishlow, *American Railroads,* p. 149.

32 Fogel, *Railroads,* pp. 137–40.

cent of total manufacturing value added was produced to satisfy railroad demands. However, he cautioned that this figure overstated the real contribution of railroads because in the absence of railroads there would have been greater production related to alternative forms of transportation.[33] Fishlow suggested that the wide geographic dispersion of sophisticated machinery that resulted from railroad development encouraged the railroads to institute their own nationwide system of repair and maintenance shops, and this helped to spread skilled labor throughout the nation.[34]

Coal consumption by railroads was unimportant in the antebellum period. Fishlow showed that direct railroad use of coal increased from approximately 2 percent of total output in 1860 to 20 percent during the 1880s.[35] He also estimated the value of coal consumed in the antebellum iron industry to make rails and other railroad products, but this only raised the total railroad consumption of coal to about 5 percent.[36]

Fishlow calculated that railroads consumed less than 5 percent of the nation's lumber production during the 1840s and slightly more than 10 percent during the 1850s.[37] Fogel estimated that between 1840 and 1860 the railroads consumed 5.4 percent of total lumber production.[38] In their calculations, neither Fogel nor Fishlow included consumption of firewood and Fogel also omitted consumption of lumber that was not produced by sawmills or planing mills. It does not appear, however, that these omissions substantially alter the conclusion that the railroad's impact on the lumber industry was rather small.[39]

Railroad Construction Ahead of Demand

Rostow's analysis of antebellum American economic development stressed that railroads were the leading sector of growth and were built ahead of demand.[40] Fishlow countered this argument and claimed that railroads were built for the profit motive. He demonstrated that the sequential pattern of railroad construction closely followed patterns of earlier settlement developed by water transportation.[41] To support his argument that antebellum railroad construction lagged behind the West's development, Fishlow pointed to profit rates, population density along railroad routes, and the large role of private capital. Chapter 5 demonstrated that a strong west-

---

33 Fogel, *Railroads*, pp. 140–46.

34 Fishlow, *American Railroads*, pp. 154–56.

35 Fishlow, *American Railroads*, pp. 156–57.

36 Fogel, *Railroads*, pp. 135–36, calculated a similar measure of the total impact of railroads on the coal industry for 1840–60 and estimated total railroad consumption at 6 percent.

37 Fishlow, *American Railroads*, pp. 158–59.

38 Fogel, *Railroads*, pp. 136–37.

39 Fishlow, *American Railroads*, pp. 156–59.

40 Rostow, *Stages of Economic Growth*, Chapter 4.

41 Fishlow, *American Railroads*, Chapter IV.

ward drift of population was in motion well before the western railroads were constructed. The built-in demand for railroad services created by earlier development guaranteed high profits, attracted private capital, and diminished the need for heavy government subsidy and construction. This does not deny that the antebellum railroads encouraged additional westward migration. Indeed, it is generally agreed that much settlement in the upper Midwest was due to railroads. Furthermore, railroad expansion during the post–Civil War period largely preceded the economic development of the Great Plains and Far West.

The Indispensability of the Railroad

One of the major goals of the Fogel and Fishlow studies was to estimate the quantitative contribution of railroads to American growth. Fogel attempted to estimate the social saving due to railroads in 1890. He defined social saving as the difference between the actual level of national income in 1890 and the level of national income that would have prevailed in the absence of railroads.[42] He estimated the cost of distributing the 1890 volume of output by railroads and compared this to the cost of distributing the same volume of output by alternative (generally water) means of transportation. Using this technique, he attributed a social saving to railroads of approximately 5 percent of G.N.P., and he concluded that railroads were important to American economic growth but not indispensable.

Fishlow attempted to estimate the social saving of railroads by quantifying the value of the following direct benefits: greater speed, lower risk, freedom from seasonality, more direct routing, and regularity of service.[43] He estimated the value of direct benefits in 1859 as equal to approximately 5 percent of G.N.P., and he concluded that the railroads' impact during the antebellum period was rather small. Antebellum railroads were viewed as a very expensive product whose services could have been duplicated by canals and steamboats. Fishlow extrapolated the calculation of social savings to the late nineteenth century and estimated that the direct benefits of railroads in 1890 were in excess of 10 percent of G.N.P. This is a significantly greater value than Fogel estimated (5 percent) and reflects the difference in counterfactual propositions examined by the authors. Fogel tried to gauge the cost differences between railroads and alternative transportation facilities whereas Fishlow attempted to quantify the value of the railroads' direct benefits.

Despite differences in methods and results, both Fogel and Fishlow concluded that the railroad was not indispensable to the nineteenth-century economic development of the United States. The Fogel-Fishlow conclusion

---

[42] Fogel, *Railroads,* Chapters II, III, and VI.
[43] Fishlow, *American Railroads,* Chapter II.

brought about sharp rebuttal from many economic historians, both traditional and new, and the debate persists in the literature.[44] Criticism of the Fogel-Fishlow analysis has focused on the concept of social savings, difficulties in measuring social returns, inadequate specification of the railroads' total benefits, choice of alternatives to the railroads, and use of poor data. The current state of knowledge suggests that the issue of the railroads' indispensability to nineteenth-century American economic development is still open. Railroads were the single most important source of new investment throughout the late nineteenth century, and the techniques that Fogel and Fishlow have applied do not capture many of the benefits of railroad construction.

Postscript on the Railroad

Railroads were the most important growth force in the late nineteenth-century American economy. In the antebellum period, most railroad construction duplicated the routes of alternative carriers (canals and steamboats). However, by the time of the Civil War, railroads were being extended into new areas of development, and, throughout most of the late nineteenth century, they were the major source of new investment spending in the economy. Recent studies by Robert Fogel and Albert Fishlow have greatly improved our understanding of the impact of railroads on American economic development, but the conclusion that the railroad was not indispensable to American economic development has not been widely accepted. Much research remains to be completed before an acceptable answer to the question of indispensability can be given, and perhaps such questions never can be satisfactorily answered because of difficulties in defining the notion of indispensability and in measuring social savings. In the meantime, railroads can be viewed as the most important growth force in the American economy in the last half of the nineteenth century.

Suggested Reading

Chandler, Alfred D., *The Railroads: The Nation's First Big Business.* New York: Harcourt, Brace, and World, 1965.

David, Paul A., "Transport Innovation and Economic Growth," *Economic History Review,* December 1969.

[44] Peter D. McClelland, "Railroads, American Growth, and the New Economic History: A Critique," *Journal of Economic History,* March 1968; Paul A. David, "Transport Innovation and Economic Growth," *Economic History Review,* December 1969; and Stanley Lebergott, "United States Transport Advance and Externalities," *Journal of Economic History,* December 1966.

Engerman, Stanley L., "Some Economic Issues Relating to Railroad Subsidies and the Evaluation of Land Grants," *Journal of Economic History,* June 1972.

Fishlow, Albert, *American Railroads and the Transformation of the Ante-Bellum Economy.* Cambridge, Mass.: Harvard University Press, 1965.

———, "Productivity and Technological Change in the Railroad Sector, 1846–1910," in *Output, Employment, and Productivity in the United States after 1800,* Conference on Research in Income and Wealth, Studies in Income and Wealth, National Bureau of Economic Research, Vol. 30. New York: Columbia University Press, 1966.

Fleisig, Heywood, "The Union Pacific Railroad and the Railroad Land Grant Controversy," *Explorations in Economic History,* Winter 1973–74.

Fogel, Robert W., "A Quantitative Approach to the Study of Railroads in American Economic Growth: A Report of Some Preliminary Findings," *Journal of Economic History,* June 1962.

———, *Railroads and American Economic Growth: Essay in Econometric History.* Baltimore: Johns Hopkins, 1964.

Lebergott, Stanley, "United States Transport Advance and Externalities," *Journal of Economic History,* December 1966.

McClelland, Peter D., "Railroads, American Growth, and the New Economic History: A Critique," *Journal of Economic History,* March 1968.

———, "Social Rates of Return on American Railroads in the Nineteenth Century," *Economic History Review,* August 1972.

Mercer, Lloyd J., "Building Ahead of Demand: Some Evidence for the Land Grant Railroads," *Journal of Economic History,* June 1974.

———, "Land Grants to American Railroads: Social Cost or Social Benefit," *Business History Review,* Summer 1969.

———, "Rates of Return for Land Grant Railroads: The Central Pacific System," *Journal of Economic History,* September 1970.

Royd, J. Hayden and Gary Walton, "The Social Savings from Nineteenth Century Rail Passenger Services," *Explorations in Economic History,* Spring 1972.

Schaefer, Donald and Thomas Weiss, "The Use of Simulation Techniques in Historical Analysis: Railroads versus Canals," *Journal of Economic History,* December 1971.

Taylor, George R., *The Transportation Revolution, 1815–1860.* New York: Harper & Row, 1968, Chs. V, VII, and VIII.

7
Nineteenth-Century Manufacturing Development

During the nineteenth century, a major change occurred in the structural composition of American economic activity. At the beginning of the period, most Americans were employed in agriculture, and the small amount of manufacturing that took place was almost entirely the result of household production. By the end of the nineteenth century, manufacturing had replaced agriculture as the leading source of economic growth, and the United States was the leading industrial nation in the world. Before the beginning of World War I, United States production accounted for over one-third of the world's output of manufactured goods. Obviously, a great deal of improvement in the American standard of living is rooted in this nineteenth-century industrial expansion, and, in order to more fully understand the pace and pattern of American economic development, it is necessary to survey the major features of this industrial boom. This chapter devotes specific attention to the following topics: importance of manufacturing to the economy, changes in industrial organization, mobilization of industrial capital, sources of power, the role of tariffs in encouraging industrialization, exports of manufactured goods, output trends, regional manufacturing specialization, and productivity trends.

Quantitative Significance of Manufacturing

Robert Gallman's commodity output series was cited in Table 2–4 to demonstrate the expansion of manufacturing relative to other commodity-producing sectors during the late nineteenth century. Gallman's calculations revealed that it was not until 1889 that manufacturing replaced agriculture as the leading industry in the American economy. An alternative view of the increasing importance of manufacturing to the American economy is provided in Table 7–1, which shows the major industry distribution of employment from 1840 to 1920. Because average output per worker was much lower in agriculture than in manufacturing, it was not until the 1920s that manufacturing replaced agriculture as the chief source of employment in the United States. In addition to the sharp decline in agricultural employment and expansion of manufacturing employment, Table 7–1 also shows significant late nineteenth- early twentieth-century employment expansion in transportation, utilities, trade and other service industries.

Organization of Manufacturing Enterprise

Most early nineteenth-century manufactured goods were produced by households for their own consumption. Independent craftsmen—blacksmiths, coppersmiths, coopers, tailors, cobblers, etc.—were another important source of production. By the end of the Napoleonic Wars, some craftsmen had expanded their operations into craft shops and employed other craftsmen as well as journeymen and apprentices. The household organization of manufacturing continued to expand until the 1820s and then quickly declined in the Northeast, although it continued to expand in the West. After 1830, household manufacture remained important only in food and clothing; it declined in all regions as larger scale productive units such as craft shops, the putting out system, mills, and factories were established.

The putting out system represented a combination of effort by craft shops, merchant capitalists, and households. In some cases production originated in a craft shop where certain stages of production were parceled out to households. It was also common for merchants to provide materials to households that produced manufactured goods which the merchant sold. The putting out system was most important in boots and shoes and other leather products, textiles, clothing, and hats. The system flourished for a short period in the early nineteenth century, and one of its important advantages was that it helped conserve on the scarcity of labor. Throughout most of its history, the American economy has been faced with a high degree of labor scarcity. The putting out system allowed much production to take place in the home, where labor could be supplied on a part time basis primarily by women and children who otherwise might not have been employed.

During the first several decades of the nineteenth century, manufacturing production was highly localized, and there was little concern with production for the national market. A few important exceptions in which industries were market oriented include cotton textiles, sugar, tar, rum, whiskey, and flour. Households were almost exclusively concerned with production for family use, and there was little or no market orientation in this form of organization. A great deal of production by craft shops, mills,

Table 7-1 Percentage Distribution of Employment by Major Sector, 1840-1920

Sector	1840	1850	1860	1870	1880	1890	1900	1910	1920
Agriculture, Forestry and Fisheries	68.6%	64.0%	59.5%	50.2%	50.1%	42.8%	37.6%	31.6%	27.4%
Mining	0.3	1.2	1.6	1.5	1.8	2.0	2.6	2.9	3.0
Manufacturing and Hand Trades[a]	14.6	16.4	18.3	17.4	18.2	20.0	21.8	22.4	26.2
Construction	—	—	—	5.8	4.8	6.1	5.7	6.3	5.2
Transportation and Public Utilities[b]	—[c]	5.5	7.4	5.0	4.9	6.4	7.2	8.7	10.1
Trade, Finance, and Real Estate	—	—	—	6.4	7.0	8.4	9.5	10.6	11.7
Services	—[c]	12.2	12.4	13.2	13.2	13.5	14.3	16.0	15.6
Not Allocated	16.5	0.7	0.8	0.5	0.0	0.8	1.3	1.5	0.8

Source: Computed on the basis of figures in *Historical Statistics*, Series D57-71.
[a] Includes construction through 1860.
[b] Includes trade, finance, and real estate through 1860.
[c] Unavailable.

and the putting out system was intended for sale in the domestic market, but the marketing problem was generally left to merchant capitalists.

Improved transportation during the 1820s and 1830s integrated the spatially separated markets in the East and West and stimulated the development of regional economic specialization. Regions could now specialize according to their comparative advantage and produce for the national market. The creation of a national market in America made large-scale production feasible and encouraged the development of factories. In addition to improved interregional transportation, population growth and rising income levels acted to further expand the domestic market potential and encourage large-scale production. Craft shops and mills merged into factories, and the basic industrial unit in America became the factory.

The factory system first flourished in the cotton textile industry during the Napoleonic Wars. Factory-sized units developed in woolen textiles and carpets during the 1820s and 1830s, but factory production in most other industries did not become entrenched until the 1840s and 1850s. At this time, factories developed in primary and fabricated metals, machinery, technical instruments, transportation equipment, hardware and farm implements, clothing, shoes, and food processing. The mechanized production brought about by the factory system provided greater separation of the various stages of production, and the average level of skill required was lower than was characteristic of craft shop or mill production. As a result, much employment in factories could be provided by low-skilled labor, and women and children supplied a substantial portion of the work force.

Despite the rise of factories in the pre–Civil War decades, many smaller operations such as sawmills, gristmills, distilleries, breweries, and tanneries continued to exist. During the late nineteenth century, the factory became the standard operating unit in American manufacturing and accounted for the bulk of industrial output. By modern standards, the average size of manufacturing plants throughout most of the nineteenth century was rather small. Table 7–2 contains estimates of the average output, employment, and capital stock per manufacturing establishment.[1] The data show that the significant increase in the average size of manufacturing firms began around 1880. Average output per establishment doubled between 1880 and 1900, doubled again between 1900 and 1910, and tripled between 1910 and 1930. The average number of employees per plant increased slowly during the late nineteenth century but more than quadrupled during

[1] The capital stock per establishment was calculated on the basis of the capital stock estimates in *Historical Statistics,* Series P 30–133. Capital stock tabulations were provided in the census surveys of manufacturing beginning in 1850, but the capital estimation procedures were not reliable, and I have not calculated capital per establishment prior to 1880. Capital stock estimates were eliminated from the census in 1940, and currently the census provides information regarding new capital expenditures rather than the aggregate value of the capital stock.

Table 7-2 Changes in the Average Size of Manufacturing Plants, 1850-1950

Year	Real Value Added per Establishment (1929 dollars)	Average Number of Employees per Establishment	Real Capital Stock per Establishment (1929 dollars)
1850	$ 5,654	7.8	$ –
1860	8,243	9.3	–
1870	6,458	8.2	–
1880	9,787	10.8	18,991
1890	18,197	13.3	31,392
1900	17,012	11.2	36,327
1910	38,882	24.6	117,557
1920	64,795	49.9	215,008
1930	119,956	49.0	300,020
1940	146,746	49.2	–
1950	184,147	55.3	–

Source: The figures on value added, employment, and number of establishments were taken from the following publications of the U.S. Bureau of the Census: (1850-1900) *Twelfth Census of the United States, Manufactures,* Vol. VIII, pp. 982-83; (1910) *Thirteenth Census of the United States, Manufactures,* Vol. VIII, p. 57; (1920 and 1930) *Fifteenth Census of the United States, Manufactures,* Vol. I, p. 17; (1940) *Sixteenth Census of the United States, Manufactures,* Vol. I, pp. 44-45; (1950) *Annual Survey of Manufactures,* 1951, p. 13. The value-added figures were converted to 1929 dollars by the wholesale price index for all commodities in *Historical Statistics,* Series E 1-12 and E 13-24. The capital stock figures were obtained from *Historical Statistics,* Series P 30-133.

the first two decades of the twentieth century. The average capital stock per establishment doubled between 1880 and 1900 and more than tripled between 1900 and 1910.

Mobilizing Industrial Capital

Before the Napoleonic War period, manufacturing was conducted on a small scale, and virtually all manufacturing establishments were organized as family enterprises, individual proprietorships, or partnerships. Corporations were utilized almost exclusively in banking, transportation, insurance, and government. Increased use of the corporate form in manufacturing developed after the Napoleonic Wars; however, many people viewed corporations with distrust, and it was difficult to raise capital through standard corporate techniques. By the late 1830s, a number of states had passed laws regulating incorporation of private businesses, and this legislation spawned many new industrial corporations. Even so, it remained difficult to obtain a corporate charter, and most industrial charters granted before 1860 required a special act of a state legislature. Despite the increased usage of the corporate form in American industry during the pre–Civil War decades, at the war's beginning most manufactured goods were produced by unincorporated businesses.[2] As the scale of American industry increased in the late nineteenth century, the capital requirements of manufacturing firms increased and led to greater utilization of the corporate form. By the end of the nineteenth century, the corporate form was the dominant technique for mobilizing business capital, and corporations produced approximately two-thirds of industrial output.

Power Sources

Water power was the dominant source of energy in American manufacturing until the mid-nineteenth century. During the first several decades of the 1800s, most water power facilities were rather simple and used waterwheels, cogwheels, and shafts made of wood to transmit power to machinery. Construction techniques and materials put a limit on the amount of water power that could be harnessed, and, until the 1820s, most manufacturing establishments were located on small streams. In the 1820s, technological improvements such as river damming, metal cogwheels, and leather transmission belts resulted in more effective use of the available natural water facilities. During the 1840s, some mills converted from the waterwheel to the water turbine which increased the efficiency of water power utilization.

At the same time that the water turbine was being perfected, however, steam power began to replace water power as the dominant form of energy in American manufacturing. Steam engines had been used since the early nineteenth century in inland water transportation, but the abundance of water power discouraged the use of steam in manufacturing. Steam engines were costly to build and were characterized by high maintenance and fuel expenses, and the cost advantages of water power made it the dominant energy source in American manufacturing until the Civil War. Immediately after the war, however, there was rapid conversion to steam power. In part, this reflected construction and fuel cost reductions for steam engines as well as increased scarcity of available water power facilities. Impetus to steam power was also provided by the severe locational restrictions imposed by water-power technology. Conversion to steam allowed for much more flexibility in industrial location decisions, and consumer markets, labor and capital supplies, and other factors could determine plant site apart from power considerations. By the end of the nineteenth century, very few factories used water power, and the utilization of this energy source was almost completely restricted to textile plants, paper mills, gristmills, and sawmills.

Electric power developed during the late nineteenth century. In the

[2] See Thomas C. Cochran, "Business Organization and the Development of an Industrial Discipline," in Harold F. Williamson, ed., *The Growth of the American Economy* (Englewood Cliffs, N. J.: Prentice-Hall, 1951), pp. 279–95.

formative years of the industry, most electrical energy was generated by burning coal, although some electricity was generated by harnessing water power. In addition to generating electricity, coal was also used to create steam power, and, at the end of the nineteenth century, coal accounted for 80–90 percent of all energy generated in the United States. During the first two decades of the twentieth century, electricity replaced steam power in many factories, and petroleum and natural gas began to be substituted for coal in creating electrical power.

Tariffs and American Manufacturing

Tariffs have traditionally been used to protect industries from foreign competition or to raise revenue for government. Most economists view revenue raising tariffs as an unsound method of securing funds for the public sector. The generally favored procedure is for government to rely on an equitable system of taxation. However, until the income tax amendment (1913), the tax structure in the United States was highly regressive, and tariffs were viewed as a principal means of public finance. Economists also hold suspect tariffs which protect the market position of domestic industries since they subvert the normal operation of the free market. A protective tariff raises the price of foreign goods relative to domestic goods and thereby alters consumer demand. Theoretically, it can be argued that if domestic industry needs tariff protection in order to survive, the industry is not one in which we have a comparative advantage, and we should redirect our resources into other lines of economic activity. Some exceptions to this logic are usually made for industries producing goods and services related to our national defense. Since tariff legislation in the United States is largely a political matter, with tariffs often resulting from lobbying pressures, the United States has a rich tradition of protective tariff legislation that has been aimed at preserving the market position of numerous industries such as iron and steel, textiles, and shoes.

Some economists are willing to support a special case of the protective tariff, generally referred to as an "infant industry" tariff. This type of tariff is intended to provide short-run protection to enable industries to become efficient enough to compete effectively with foreign imports. Alexander Hamilton made a classic statement of the rationale for protecting industries during their initial years of expansion in his *Report on Manufactures.* Hamilton was concerned with the creation of an industrial base in the United States and argued for government subsidization of manufacturing through tariffs, import prohibitions, and bounty payments. Hamilton's ambitious scheme of government protection for American industry was not adopted, but some protection was granted by the Tariff of 1789.

Between 1789 and 1812 tariff rates were generally low, ranging between 5 and 15 percent on dutiable items; during the War of 1812 tariff rates were doubled. Many manufacturing firms developed as a result of the trade restrictions imposed during the latter half of the Napoleonic Wars. At the end of the conflict, this self-interest group argued for increased protection, and, in 1816, there was a considerable increase in duties. Despite the increased protection, American manufacturing was still relatively inefficient compared to British industry, and most of the textile mills that had developed during the Napoleonic Wars succumbed to British competition.

Eastern manufacturing interests were supported in their agitation for higher tariffs by western farmers who assumed that increased manufacturing in the East would lead to increased demand for western agricultural products. Southerners opposed tariff protection since they depended on foreign demand for cotton and foreign supplies of manufactured goods. Protection adversely affected the region's terms of trade by raising the prices paid for manufactured goods; tariffs also limited the American demand for European manufactured goods, and therefore, limited the European demand for cotton. In 1824 and 1828, tariff rates were increased again. After 1824, the average tariff rate, calculated as the ratio of duties to dutiable imports, was approximately 50 percent, and, after 1828, the average rate exceeded 60 percent. The 1828 level of protection represented the highest average tariff rate in United States history, and the upward trend was reversed by tariff cuts in 1830 and 1832. The 1832 revisions brought a decline in the average tariff rate to approximately 40 percent. Rates continued to drift downward until 1842 at which time they approached 25 percent. In 1842, rates were raised, but they were subsequently lowered in 1846 and 1857, and, by the time of the Civil War, they had reached 20 percent.

High levels of tariff protection characterized the late nineteenth and early twentieth centuries. The Republicans came to power in 1861, and, during the Civil War, tariff rates were increased to approximately 48 percent. Modest reductions in tariff rates were made in 1870 and 1872, and, during the late 1870s, there was considerable pressure for further lowering of tariffs. However, the new tariff law passed in 1883 provided for offsetting increases and decreases, and the high levels of protection were maintained. The Democrats captured the White House in 1885 but were unsuccessful in their attempts to reduce tariff rates. The Republicans were returned to power in 1889, and, in 1890, they extended coverage of the tariff and raised the average rate to 49 percent. Rates were reduced slightly in 1894, but some of these reductions were canceled in 1897. New tariff legislation in 1909 had little effect on rates, and high protective walls were maintained for American industry. Minor reductions were made on the eve of World War I, and some goods were put on a free list, but the average tariff rates were still highly protective.[3]

---

[3] Detailed annual statistics concerning average tariff rates between 1821–1957 are available in *Historical Statistics*, Series U 15–20.

Despite the generally high levels of protection throughout the late nineteenth and early twentieth centuries, tariffs are not viewed as an important causal force in the rate of American industrialization. The fact that tariffs were a political phenomenon and subject to periodic fluctuations meant that business could not make long-range plans according to the current tariff structure. The problem of volatile tariff rates was particularly acute during the antebellum decades. It should also be made clear that in many cases tariffs not only protected the price position of finished American products but also raised the price of necessary raw materials, and the net effect may have been nil. Another aspect of tariff protection that must be considered in determining the effect on the rate of American industrialization is the impact on technology. F. W. Taussig has argued that in certain industries such as iron, tariff protection tended to perpetuate archaic techniques of production.[4]

Chapter 5 showed that improved interregional transportation widened the market and created distinct patterns of regional economic specialization. Strong linkages developed between East and West during the 1820s and 1830s and permitted the Northeast to export manufactured goods to the West in exchange for food products. The tariff certainly had some marginal effects in particular industries and on particular firms, but the broad pattern of American manufacturing development was more or less unaffected by tariff legislation.[5]

Exports of Manufactured Goods

Until the late nineteenth century, most American manufactured goods were produced for sale in the domestic United States market. Some exceptions occurred in resource processing industries such as flour, lumber, and meat and meat products, but most industries did not generate an export surplus. Late nineteenth-century expansion of American manufacturing led to a search for export markets, and the nation's export trade began to include a greater volume of manufactured goods. Table 7–3 shows the most important manufacturing export industries of the late nineteenth- early twentieth-centuries. The data indicate a steady increase in the weight of technically sophisticated manufacturing production in the composition of our export trade, and, by 1920, the leading manufacturing export industries were petroleum and coal products, machinery, iron and steel, meat and meat products, cotton manufactures, and cars, carriages, and automobiles.

---

[4] See Frank W. Taussig, *The Tariff History of the United States* (New York: Johnson Reprint Corporation, 1966), Ch. III.

[5] For a full discussion of the tariff issue see Frank W. Taussig, *Some Aspects of the Tariff Question* (Cambridge, Mass.: Harvard University Press, 1934); also see Taussig's *Tariff History of the United States.*

Table 7-3 Exports of Selected Manufactured Goods, 1880-1920 (millions of dollars)

Manufacturing Sector	1880	1890	1900	1910	1920
Wheat Flour	$ 35	$ 57	$ 68	$ 47	$224
Meat and Meat Products	114	126	176	134	471
Naval Stores	5	7	12	19	35
Lumber and Wood Products	15	27	46	74	174
Petroleum and Coal Products	—	61	105	151	953
Copper (including Manufactured items)	1	8	59	89	142
Cotton Manufactures	10	10	24	33	398
Cars, Carriages, and Automobiles	1	5	10	11	303
Iron and Steel	—	3	39	60	498
Machinery	—	20	78	117	588

Source: *Historical Statistics,* Series U 73-93.

Structural Changes in Manufacturing Between 1860–1900

The survey by Victor S. Clark stands as the most comprehensive treatment of manufacturing development in the American economy.[6] Because Clark's study is encyclopedic in scope and is organized to provide an industry by industry treatment, it is difficult to comprehend the broad structural changes which took place in the industrial base. Clark's work makes very little use of the available empirical information provided in the census, and, in places, this information is used incorrectly. Clark and other scholars have used the census tabulations of the gross value of output rather than value added to gauge structural changes in manufacturing.[7] Value added is defined as the gross value of output minus the cost of intermediate production items (materials, fuel, etc.), and it is the accepted accounting concept for final product. Use of the gross value of output to determine the structural composition of American manufacturing greatly overstates the importance of resource-processing industries that contribute little to value added but use heavy amounts of materials.

In spite of the numerous volumes which have been written about American industrialization, very little formal attention has been given to an assessment of structural developments within manufacturing. The absence of formal treatment of this important subject is due largely to deficiencies in

[6] Victor S. Clark, *History of Manufactures in the United States,* 3 vols. (New York: McGraw-Hill for the Carnegie Institution, 1929). Other standard reference works include Albert S. Bolles, *Industrial History of the United States* (Norwich, Conn.: Henry Bill Publishing, 1881) and J. Leander Bishop, *A History of American Manufactures* (Philadelphia: Edward Young, 1864).

[7] See Clark, *History of Manufactures,* Vol. 2, Ch. 16; also see Bishop, *History of American Manufactures,* Vol. 2, Ch. 7, and Gilbert C. Fite and Jim E. Reese, *An Economic History of the United States* (Boston: Houghton Mifflin, 1973), Ch. 12.

the available census data. The industry classification scheme varied with each census and was very detailed, ranging between 400 and 600 industries. There was no attempt at any aggregation by major industry groups until the early twentieth century. As a result of the industry detail and its variability over time, it is difficult to analyze changes in the structural composition of American industry. Another difficulty incorporated in the census data is that it includes many nonmanufacturing industries such as construction, mining, and hand trades (blacksmiths, tinsmiths, plumbers, etc.).

In a recent study, I have attempted to fill the void in our knowledge of late nineteenth-century American industrialization by classifying the census manufacturing value added data according to the Standard Industrial Classification (SIC) two-digit industry categories.[8] This conversion provides an aggregation of the detailed census tabulations into the twenty two-digit industry groups: food; tobacco; textiles; apparel; lumber and wood products; furniture; paper; printing and publishing; chemicals; petroleum and coal products; rubber and plastics; leather and leather products; stone, clay, and glass products; primary metals; fabricated metals; nonelectrical machinery; electrical machinery; transportation equipment; instruments; and miscellaneous manufacturing.[9] This reclassification was performed separately for all states and census regions in 1860 and 1900 and allows for treatment of the changing structural composition of late nineteenth-century American manufacturing.[10]

Table 7–4 exhibits the percentage distribution of United States manufacturing value added across the two-digit industries in 1860 and 1900. The figures indicate that much antebellum manufacturing development occurred in the resource-processing industries, particularly food and lumber and wood products, and in the light manufacturing industries, especially textiles, apparel, and leather products. However, the figures also suggest that there was more emphasis on heavy industry than is generally recognized, and, as a group, primary and fabricated metals, machinery, and transportation equipment accounted for almost one-fourth of American value added in 1860. During the late nineteenth century there was a general

---

[8] Albert W. Niemi, Jr., *State and Regional Patterns in American Manufacturing, 1860–1900* (Westport, Conn.: Greenwood Press, 1974).

[9] The definitions for converting census data to the SIC categories are fully explained in *State and Regional Patterns.*

[10] Estimates of manufacturing value added were provided for the following regions of states: New England (Maine, New Hampshire, Vermont, Massachusetts, Rhode Island, and Connecticut); Middle Atlantic (New York, New Jersey, Pennsylvania, Delaware, and Maryland); East North Central (Ohio, Indiana, Illinois, Michigan, and Wisconsin); West North Central (Minnesota, Iowa, Missouri, Kansas, Nebraska, North Dakota, and South Dakota); South Atlantic (Virginia, West Virginia, North Carolina, South Carolina, Georgia, and Florida); East South Central (Kentucky, Tennessee, Alabama, and Mississippi); and West South Central (Arkansas, Louisiana, Oklahoma, and Texas). These are the traditional geographic divisions of the United States as defined by the Bureau of the Census, with the exception that Delaware and Maryland are included in the Middle Atlantic rather than in the South Atlantic Region, and the District of Columbia is excluded from the South Atlantic.

Table 7-4 Percentage Distribution of Manufacturing Value Added, United States, 1860 and 1900

SIC Code Number and Industry		1860	1900
20	Food	12.1%	14.9%
21	Tobacco	1.9	3.6
22	Textiles	14.3	8.5
23	Apparel	7.8	9.3
24	Lumber and Wood Products	9.7	7.0
25	Furniture	2.4	2.1
26	Paper	1.5	2.0
27	Printing and Publishing	2.9	5.8
28	Chemicals	2.7	3.6
29	Petroleum and Coal Products	1.5	1.8
30	Rubber	0.4	0.8
31	Leather and Leather Products	11.4	4.2
32	Stone, Clay and Glass	3.7	5.9
33	Primary Metals	7.5	7.5
34	Fabricated Metals	4.7	4.7
35	Nonelectrical Machinery	6.4	8.9
36	Electrical Machinery	—	—[a]
37	Transportation Equipment	5.1	5.0
38	Instruments	0.4	0.6
39	Miscellaneous	3.7	3.8

Source: Albert W. Niemi, Jr., *State and Regional Patterns in American Manufacturing, 1860-1900* (Westport, Conn.: Greenwood Press, 1974), Table 1.
[a] Included in SIC 35.

decline in light industry, particularly textiles and leather products. Resource-processing industries such as food and lumber and wood products continued to be important to the nation's industrial output, and the heavy industries advanced their share of total value added from 23.7 percent to 26.1 percent. In addition to these broad movements, gains were made in printing and publishing, chemicals, paper, and stone, clay, and glass products.

Regional Manufacturing Specialization

Estimates of manufacturing value added in 1860 for seven census regions appear in Table 7–5.[11] The figures suggest that a great deal of antebellum

[11] The absolute dollar estimates and an analysis of state manufacturing developments between 1860–1900 are available in *State and Regional Patterns*.

Table 7-5 Percentage Distribution of Manufacturing Value Added Across Two-Digit Industries, by Region, 1860

SIC Code Number and Industry	New England	Middle Atlantic	East North Central	West North Central	South Atlantic	East South Central	West South Central
20 Food	3.3%	11.8%	24.6%	26.2%	12.9%	16.9%	14.7%
21 Tobacco	0.4	1.3	0.9	4.4	16.0	4.5	1.3
22 Textiles	32.4	9.5	1.8	2.9	9.1	6.7	2.6
23 Apparel	6.3	10.9	6.0	2.6	1.1	2.7	8.4
24 Lumber and Wood Products	4.6	6.8	17.8	22.5	16.2	19.6	29.8
25 Furniture	1.8	2.4	4.3	2.0	1.5	1.8	0.9
26 Paper	2.3	1.4	0.9	0.1	1.1	0.3	0.0[a]
27 Printing and Publishing	1.5	4.4	2.3	1.5	1.0	2.1	1.4
28 Chemicals	1.4	3.5	1.9	1.5	7.8	1.8	1.6
29 Petroleum and Coal Products	1.0	2.0	1.0	1.8	1.2	1.9	0.4
30 Rubber	0.6	0.6	0.0[a]	—	—	—	—
31 Leather and	2.9	4.6	1.9	1.2	2.8	4.3	1.3
Leather Products	14.1	5.3	5.9	5.5	3.6	6.0	9.0
32 Stone, Clay and Glass	2.1	4.7	3.6	5.4	3.5	2.7	4.7
33 Primary Metals	4.5	10.1	6.4	7.6	6.7	6.8	0.7
34 Fabricated Metals	5.8	4.3	4.5	4.4	2.6	4.8	6.0
35 Nonelectrical Machinery	5.4	6.0	9.4	5.1	5.0	8.0	9.7
36 Electrical Machinery	—	—	—	—	—	—	—
37 Transportation Equipment	4.1	5.2	5.1	3.9	7.5	7.8	6.7
38 Instruments	0.6	0.6	0.1	0.0[a]	—	0.0[a]	—
39 Miscellaneous Manufacturing	4.7	4.6	1.9	1.4	0.3	1.2	0.8

Source: Niemi, *State and Regional Patterns*, Table 2.
[a] Signifies values of less than .05.

manufacturing effort in New England took place in light industries, especially textiles and leather products. The Middle Atlantic region was characterized by much more diversification than New England and emphasized food, textiles, apparel, and primary metals. Antebellum manufacturing activity in the West and South was highly concentrated on resource processing industries such as food, lumber, and tobacco. Some exceptions to this general pattern include textile development in the South Atlantic and East South Central regions, chemical production in the South Atlantic region, and leather and metals, machinery, and transportation equipment in each southern and western region. Douglass North and G. R. Taylor have argued that the antebellum decades brought about some diversification away from resource-processing manufacturing activity in the South and West, and the data in Table 7–5 corroborate this view.

American manufacturing underwent significant change during the late nineteenth century; the regional manufacturing structure in 1900 is exhibited in Table 7–6. Light industries continued to provide an important share of the Northeast's industrial production, although there were significant relative declines in textiles and leather products. Heavy industry made a slight relative advance in the Northeast due to the increased importance of machinery production. Western manufacturing remained highly concentrated on processing industries, although there were sharp gains in heavy industry. By the turn of the century, the East North Central region exhibited a higher degree of specialization in heavy industry than any region in the nation. Late nineteenth-century southern manufacturing was heavily weighted toward resource-oriented manufacturing activity, and SIC 20, 21, and 24 provided between 40 and 60 percent of total manufacturing value added in each southern region. Another significant development in the South was the rise of the South Atlantic region as a major textile center during the last decade of the nineteenth century. The most significant decline in the South occurred in the heavy industry group, and, despite the late nineteenth-century development of primary metals in Alabama, SIC 33–37 declined relative to total manufacturing in each region.

Productivity Change in Manufacturing: 1850–1900

Labor productivity is the most easily calculated measure of industrial efficiency, and it examines the relationship between output and labor input.[12] Decennial rates of change in real value added per employee have been calculated, and the results appear in Table 7–7.[13] The figures for aggregate

---

[12] The two most often used measures of labor productivity are output per employee and output per manhour.

[13] See Albert W. Niemi, Jr., "Structural and Labor Productivity Patterns in United States Manufacturing, 1849–1899," *Business History Review* (Spring 1972): Table 4.

Table 7-6 Percentage Distribution of Manufacturing Value Added Across Two-Digit Industries, by Region, 1900

SIC Code Number and Industry	New England	Middle Atlantic	East North Central	West North Central	South Atlantic	East South Central	West South Central
20 Food	6.9%	11.6%	21.0%	27.5%	9.4%	18.4%	28.2%
21 Tobacco	0.7	3.4	2.5	6.7	14.0	9.0	2.0
22 Textiles	24.5	8.0	1.1	0.7	17.4	5.1	1.3
23 Apparel	5.9	13.5	7.4	7.1	2.6	5.0	5.1
24 Lumber and Products	3.8	3.3	8.5	9.9	19.3	21.2	29.8
25 Furniture	1.7	1.8	3.2	1.9	1.2	1.3	1.1
26 Paper	4.0	2.1	1.5	0.4	0.7	0.1	0.2
27 Printing and Publishing	4.5	6.4	5.5	8.2	3.0	4.3	6.7
28 Chemicals	2.0	4.2	3.0	2.9	8.7	4.4	1.6
29 Petroleum and Coal Products	1.1	2.4	1.7	1.9	0.9	1.2	1.3
30 Rubber	3.2	0.4	0.4	0.2	—	0.0	—
31 Leather and	1.0	1.3	0.7	0.2	1.1	1.2	0.0
Leather Products	8.3	2.1	2.3	3.4	1.3	1.7	2.9
32 Stone, Clay and Glass	4.6	6.9	5.8	6.2	3.8	3.9	4.0
33 Primary Metals	3.1	10.3	7.7	3.1	6.0	8.7	0.9
34 Fabricated Metals	5.0	3.8	7.2	3.9	1.2	2.1	1.9
35 Nonelectrical Machinery	9.5	9.3	10.7	5.1	3.0	5.3	3.6
36 Electrical Machinery[a]	—	—	—	—	—	—	—
37 Transportation Equipment	2.6	4.2	6.2	7.8	5.9	6.0	8.3
38 Instruments	0.8	0.8	0.4	0.4	0.0	0.1	0.2
39 Miscellaneous	6.6	4.2	3.2	2.5	0.4	1.0	0.9

Source: Niemi, *State and Regional Patterns*, Table 3.
[a] Included in SIC 35.

Table 7-7 Decennial Percentage Rates of Change in Real Manufacturing Value Added per Employee, 1849-99 (1860 prices)

SIC Code Number and Industry	1849-59	1859-69	1869-79	1879-89	1889-99
20 Food	25%	−49%	40%	41%	−31%
21 Tobacco	5	−39	4	234	28
22 Textiles	54	−28	66	13	19
23 Apparel	30	−6	40	75	20
24 Lumber	11	−34	11	0	4
25 Furniture	15	−17	52	38	−2
26 Paper	13	−10	24	33	−13
27 Printing and Publishing	11	7	16	43	−16
28 Chemicals	20	−8	46	50	−18
29 Petroleum	5	−19	—	—	−24
30 Rubber	45	—	—	−26	30
31 Leather and Leather Products	−22	24	33	38	−14
32 Stone, Clay and Glass	41	−20	2	28	11
33 Primary Metal	37	−8	31	35	48
34 Fabricated Metal	32	−13	44	35	−11
35 Nonelectrical Machinery	47	−23	35	44	−6
36 Electrical Machinery	—	—	—	—	—
37 Transportation Equipment	13	−22	55	17	−4
38 Instruments	−2	16	−12	31	−10
39 Miscellaneous	21	10	12	42	−19
Total	24	−16	33	40	1

Source: Albert W. Niemi, Jr., "Structural and Labor Productivity Patterns in United States Manufacturing, 1849-1899," *Business History Review*, Spring 1972, Table 4.

manufacturing reveal that productivity growth was rapid in 1849–59, declined sharply during the Civil War, made a very sharp recovery during the postwar decades, 1869–89, and was stagnant during the last decade of the nineteenth century. With the exception of 1889–99, the individual industries rather closely followed the growth pattern for total manufacturing. Excluding wartime disturbances, the steadiest productivity growth was shown in the primary metals industries. On the other hand, extremely volatile shifts in the decennial rate of productivity advance characterized food processing, instruments, tobacco, and chemicals.

Summary

The structure of the American economy was revolutionized in the nineteenth century as America was transformed from a nation of farmers into the world's leading industrial power. Much early manufacturing activity was stimulated by transportation developments. Initially, transportation linkages between east and west opened up the possibility of regional specialization and helped create the industrial Northeast; later, the development of the railroad created heavy demands for industrial products. However, transportation-related manufacturing development only accounted for a small portion of total industrial activity, and there were many other demands on American manufacturing. Agricultural expansion required heavy production of implements and machines; population expansion required increased production of textiles, apparel, leather products, and processed foods; and applications of new technological improvements required increased production of machinery, instruments, and chemicals. This chapter's review of structural developments in nineteenth-century American manufacturing indicates that the nation's industrial expansion was broadly based and involved heavy activity in many sectors.

Suggested Reading

Baack, Bennett D. and Edward John Ray, "Tariff Policy and Comparative Advantage in the Iron and Steel Industry: 1870–1929," *Explorations in Economic History,* Fall 1973.

Bateman, Fred, James D. Foust, and Thomas J. Weiss, "Large-Scale Manufacturing in the South and West, 1850–1860," *Business History Review,* Spring 1971.

David, Paul A., "Learning By Doing and Tariff Protection: A Reconsideration of the Case of the Ante-Bellum United States Cotton Textile Industry," *Journal of Economic History,* September 1970.

Livesay, Harold C. and Glenn Porter, "The Financial Role of Merchants in the Development of U.S. Manufacturing, 1815–1860," *Explorations in Economic History,* Fall 1971.

Niemi, Albert W., Jr., *State and Regional Patterns in American Manufacturing, 1860–1900.* Westport, Conn.: Greenwood Press, 1974.

———, "Structural Shifts in Southern Manufacturing, 1849–1899," *Business History Review,* Spring 1971.

———, "The Development of Industrial Structure in Southern New England," *Journal of Economic History,* September 1970.

Pope, Clayne, "The Impact of the Ante-Bellum Tariff on Income Distribution," *Explorations in Economic History,* Summer 1972.

Poulson, Barry W., "Estimates of the Value of Manufacturing Output in the Early Nineteenth Century," *Journal of Economic History,* September 1969.

Temin, Peter, *Iron and Steel in Nineteenth Century America: An Economic Inquiry.* Cambridge, Mass.: M.I.T. Press, 1964.

Uselding, Paul J., "Factor Substitution and Labor Productivity Growth in American Manufacturing, 1839–1899," *Journal of Economic History,* September 1972.

8
The Economic Impact of Government

Government actions affect the operation of the economy in many ways. The direct actions of government (local, state, and federal) involve the employment of individuals and the purchase and sale of goods and services. Much government employment is involved in providing services such as military protection, police and fire protection, education, health, welfare, utilities, and sanitation. A large amount of government employment is also involved in the collection and distribution of revenue to support the service functions of government. In addition to its direct service role in the economy, government also has an important regulatory function. The Employment Act of 1946 committed the federal government to pursue policies that would maintain full employment in the economy. (See Chapter 18.) Federal government regulation of the aggregate level of economic activity is administered through its fiscal and monetary policies.[1] In addition to its attempts to regulate total economic activity, the federal government also regulates and controls individual industries and organizations such as labor unions. Natural resource conservation and environmental protection also have become important areas of federal government regulation. In addition to federal supervision, state and local agencies also exert regulatory control over the operation of industries and organizations within their domain.

Until the 1930s, most economists viewed the American economy as a private enterprise system in which initiative for economic decision making resided in the private sector. The government was generally viewed as play-

[1] Chapter 18 will provide an analysis of the effectiveness of the federal government's fiscal (taxing and spending) and monetary (credit control) policies in combating the depression of 1929. For a brief review of federal fiscal actions between 1815 and 1860, see George R. Taylor, *The Transportation Revolution* (New York: Harper & Row, 1968), Ch. XVI.

ing a passive role within the economy; its main function was to respond to the actions of the private sector. Recent decades have seen a steady increase in direct market operations and interference by government, particularly at the federal level. In fact, government activity has increased to such an extent that most economists now view the American system as a mixed economy characterized by significant areas of direct economic activity by both the public and private sectors.

This chapter will provide empirical evidence of the increase in the size and scope of governmental economic activity. It is generally agreed that the government's share of gross national product during the nineteenth century was rather small by today's standards, but quantitative measures alone do not capture the entire significance of nineteenth-century government activity. For example, review of Chapters 5 and 6 establishes the strategic role of the public sector in nineteenth century transportation development, and yet, the aggregate expenditure of all levels of government for transportation expansion during the antebellum decades was probably less than 1 percent of gross national product. Nevertheless, transportation improvements were a necessary factor in the creation of regional economic specialization and the development of a national market. Therefore, in assessing the nineteenth-century economic role of government, the reader should keep in mind not only the aggregate level of government spending but also the strategic areas in which government spending was concentrated.

The following areas of government economic activity are treated elsewhere in this book: promotion of transportation (Chapters 5 and 6); nineteenth-century trends in tariff protection for manufacturing (Chapter 7); monetary developments and financial institutions (Chapter 12); immigration policy (Chapter 13); agricultural policy (Chapter 14); labor control and legislation (Chapter 15); regulation of industry (Chapter 16); fiscal and monetary policies, antidepression efforts, and wartime activity (Chapter 18); and protection of the environment (Chapter 19). This chapter will focus attention on the increasing direct role of government in the economy, government expenditure patterns, and government revenue-raising measures. In addition, the chapter will examine the distribution of public lands and the problems of land speculation, government educational spending, and literacy trends.

Government Spending in the Nineteenth Century

Our knowledge of the aggregate level of nineteenth-century government spending is far from complete, but the information that has been gathered indicates that the fiscal operations of government were rather limited. Until the time of the Civil War, state and local government activity was heavily concentrated on transportation expansion; in the postbellum period, state

Table 8-1 Percentage Distribution of Federal Expenditures, by Major Function, 1790-1860

Item	Percent of Total
Defense	48.2%
General Government	15.2
Postal Service	3.3
Indian Affairs	4.4
Pensions	4.9
Interest	10.4
Aid to Foreign Commerce	2.6
Aid to Domestic Transport	1.8
Foreign Indemnities	3.1
Miscellaneous	6.1

Source: Paul B. Trescott, "The United States Government and National Income, 1790-1860," in *Trends in the American Economy,* Conference on Research in Income and Wealth, Studies in Income and Wealth, National Bureau of Economic Research, Vol. 24 (Princeton: Princeton University Press, 1960), p. 343. Reprinted by permission of the National Bureau of Economic Research.

and local governments turned their attention to education.[2] Federal government spending during the nineteenth century was largely geared to national defense. Paul B. Trescott made a careful study of federal government economic activity between 1790 and 1860, and he found that defense accounted for approximately one-half of total federal spending.[3] (See Table 8–1.) R. A. Musgrave and J. M. Culbertson estimated the functional distribution of the combined expenditures of federal, state, and local governments, and their calculations for 1890 are shown in Table 8–2.[4] National defense and veterans benefits were funded almost exclusively by the federal government, and educational spending was supported largely by local government efforts.

Recently, Lance E. Davis and John Legler prepared estimates of the regional distribution of nineteenth-century government spending.[5] They concluded that aggregate spending by all governments was rather small com-

[2] For an analysis of nineteenth-century state government economic activity, see Charles F. Holt, "The Role of State Government in the Nineteenth Century American Economy, 1820–1902: A Quantitive Study," Ph.D. dissertation, Purdue University, 1970.

[3] Paul B. Trescott, "The United States Government and National Income, 1790–1860," in *Trends in the American Economy in the Nineteenth Century,* Conference on Research in Income and Wealth, Studies in Income and Wealth, National Bureau of Economic Research, Vol. 24 (Princeton: Princeton University Press, 1960). Also see Henry W. Broude, "The Role of the State in American Economic Development, 1820–90," in Hugh G. J. Aitken, ed., *The State and Economic Growth* (New York: Social Science Research Council, 1959).

[4] R. A. Musgrave and J. M. Culbertson, "The Growth of Public Expenditures in the United States, 1890–1948," *National Tax Journal,* June 1953.

[5] Lance E. Davis and John Legler, "The Government in the American Economy, 1815–1902: A Quantitative Study," *Journal of Economic History,* December 1966.

Table 8-2 Percentage Distribution of Federal, State, and Local Government Expenditures, 1890

Purpose	Percent of Total
National Defense	6.1%
Veteran's Benefits	13.3
Regulation and Protection	6.8
Economic Development	11.3
(Transportation)	(10.1)
Social Welfare	25.4
(Education)	(17.3)
Interest	9.8
General Government	9.9
Miscellaneous	17.4

Source: R. A. Musgrave and J. M. Culbertson, "The Growth of Public Expenditures in the United States, 1890-1948," *National Tax Journal,* June 1953, p. 114.

pared to total economic activity, but they noted that there were substantial regional differences in the level of government spending. They constructed estimates of per capita expenditures by federal, state, and local government. The results indicated that the level of federal and state spending was similar and rather small and that the bulk of government spending during the nineteenth century came from local governments. The results also showed that substantial permanent increase in per capita government spending took place during the Civil War decade.[6]

It is difficult to gauge the exact share of total nineteenth-century spending that was contributed by government. Musgrave and Culbertson estimated that in 1890 spending by the public sector (federal, state, and local) accounted for 8 percent of net national product.[7] Trescott's analysis showed that aggregate federal income payments during the antebellum period were generally less than 2 percent of national income.[8] The results of Trescott and Musgrave and Culbertson, in conjunction with Davis and Legler's demonstration of a significant post–Civil War increase in government activity, make it doubtful that government contributed more than 5 percent of total spending during the antebellum years.[9]

---

[6] Davis and Legler regard their conclusions as tentative, and they caution the reader about the estimation problems involved in their study.

[7] Musgrave and Culbertson, "The Growth of Public Expenditures," p. 98.

[8] Trescott, "The United States Government and National Income," p. 342.

[9] Robert F. Martin estimated that during the antebellum period the government's share of national income was approximately 2–3 percent; see *National Income in the United States, 1799–1938* (New York: National Industrial Conference Board, 1939), p. 87.

Table 8-3 Percentage Distribution of Federal Government Revenue Sources, 1800-1900

Year	Tariffs	Internal Revenue	Land Sales	Other
1800	83.7%	7.5%	0.0%	8.8%
1810	91.5	0.1	7.4	1.0
1820	83.9	0.6	6.3	9.2
1830	88.2	0.1	9.4	2.3
1840	69.3	0.0	16.9	13.8
1850	91.0	—	4.3	4.7
1860	94.9	—	3.2	1.9
1870	47.3	45.0	0.8	6.9
1880	55.9	37.2	0.3	6.6
1890	57.0	35.4	1.6	6.0
1900	41.1	52.1	0.5	6.3

Source: *Historical Statistics*, Series Y 258-63 and Y 264-79.

Raising Government Revenue in the Nineteenth Century

Throughout most of the first half of the nineteenth century, land sales, receipts from government enterprise (transportation), and property taxes generated state government revenues. By the time of the Civil War, state involvement in transportation had been greatly reduced, and most state lands had been sold, and the property tax became the major instrument for generating state government revenues. Throughout the nineteenth century, local governments used the property tax almost exclusively to obtain revenue.

In the antebellum period, the federal government raised most of its revenue from tariffs. (See Table 8–3.) During the 1830s and 1840s, land sales accounted for 10-15 percent of federal revenues, and, in 1835–36, almost one-half of federal revenues were obtained through the sale of public lands.[10] Internal revenue measures such as excise taxes were imposed during the late nineteenth century; by 1900, they had become the major source of federal revenues. Between 1870 and 1900, virtually all federal internal revenues were raised through excise taxes (approximately $5.5 billion), and most of this sum (more than $4.0 billion) was obtained through excises on tobacco and alcohol.[11]

[10] The factors behind the clustering of federal land sales in the middle 1830s are explained later in this chapter.

[11] See *Historical Statistics*, Series Y 258–63 and Y 264–79.

Table 8-4 Percentage Distribution of Direct Expenditures, by Level of Government, 1902-70

Year	Federal	State	Local
1902	34.0%	8.2%	57.8%
1913	29.8	9.2	61.0
1922	39.2	11.7	49.1
1927	30.4	12.9	56.7
1932	32.4	16.3	51.3
1936	49.3	14.6	36.1
1940	45.0	17.4	37.6
1946	82.4	6.2	11.4
1950	65.7	16.4	17.9
1955	67.3	15.9	16.8
1960	65.4	17.0	17.6
1965	62.1	19.2	18.7
1970	61.5	20.6	17.9

Source: *Historical Statistics,* Series Y 484-516, Y 601-47, and Y 670-82, and *Statistical Abstract,* 1968, p. 407, and 1973, p. 410.

Government Expenditures in the Twentieth Century

At the beginning of the twentieth century, local governments accounted for approximately 60 percent of total government spending. However, recent decades have witnessed a sharp relative decline in the importance of local government spending, and, in the 1960s, over 60 percent of total government spending originated at the federal level.[12] The figures in Table 8–4 show that a significant relative increase in federal expenditures occurred during the 1930s, and the trend toward increased federal spending has continued since that time. State government spending increased sharply during the past two decades, and, by the 1960s, it surpassed spending by local government. The share of gross national product accounted for by government expenditures increased from slightly more than 10 percent in 1922 to almost 35 percent in 1970. (See Table 8–5.) During this period, federal spending increased from approximately 5 percent to more than 20 percent of gross national product; at the same time, state and local government spending increased from 8 to 13 percent of G.N.P.

Table 8–6 exhibits the major functional components of federal spending. In the early twentieth century, national defense and veterans services accounted for approximately one-half of total federal spending, and, in recent decades, the federal government has allocated almost 50 percent of its total budget to defense related areas. The sharpest relative declines in federal

---

[12] The figures in Table 8–4 show direct spending and do not include intergovernmental transfers.

Table 8-5 Government Spending as a Share of Gross National Product, 1922-70

Year	Total Government	Federal Government	State and Local Government
1922	12.6	4.9	7.7
1927	11.6	3.5	8.1
1932	21.2	6.8	14.4
1936	20.3	10.0	10.3
1940	20.3	9.1	11.2
1946	37.8	31.1	6.7
1950	23.5	15.5	8.0
1955	26.9	18.1	8.8
1960	30.4	19.9	10.5
1965	29.6	18.4	11.2
1970	34.3	21.1	13.2

Source: *Historical Statistics,* Series Y 484-516, Y 601-47, Y 670-82, and F 1-5, and *Statistical Abstract,* 1968, p. 407, and 1973, p. 410.

spending occurred in postal service, veterans services, and farm support. The farm support program was born during the 1930s, and, despite the decline in farm support relative to other federal spending between 1936 and 1970, the federal allocation to farmers increased from $600 million in 1936 to $6.2 billion in 1970. Federal aid to education has been sporadic. Immediately following World War II, thousands of veterans attended school through federal support; after the early 1950s, however, the relative share of federal funds committed to education declined until the middle 1960s. At this time, there was a sharp advance in federal support to education and research, but, in the early 1970s, the federal effort in education was substantially reduced. Conservation of natural resources received tremendous federal support during the 1930s and accounted for almost 20 percent of the federal government's total spending. However, in recent decades, the effort in this area has fallen to approximately 2 percent of total federal outlays. Public welfare programs increased substantially in the 1960s and presently account for about 3 percent of the federal budget. Programs for old age and survivors insurance and other trust expenditures (unemployment compensation, employee retirement, and railroad retirement) were nonexistent in the early twentieth century but accounted for one-fourth of total federal spending in 1970.

State and local government expenditures are disaggregated by major function in Table 8–7. Since the middle nineteenth century, education has been the most important area for state and local activity, and, in 1970, this allocation accounted for 35 percent of total state and local expenditures. In addition to education support, considerable shares of state and local funds

Table 8-6 Percentage Distribution of the Federal Government's Direct Expenditures, 1902-70

Year	National Defense	Postal Service	Education	Farm Support	Public Welfare	Natural Resources	Veterans Services	Interest	Old Age and Survivors Insurance	Other Trust fund Expenditures	Other
1902	29.2%	22.3%	0.5%	–	0.7%	1.4%	25.0%	5.1%	–	–	15.8%
1913	26.1	28.2	0.5	–	0.5	3.1	18.5	2.4	–	–	20.7
1922	24.0	15.2	0.2	–	0.2	2.2	11.7	27.1	–	0.3%	19.1
1927	18.1	20.9	0.2	–	0.3	3.3	17.0	22.4	–	0.9	16.9
1932	17.9	19.7	0.3	–	0.0[a]	4.0	23.0	14.4	–	1.3	19.4
1936	11.3	9.1	2.3	7.3%	2.1	16.5	20.6	8.7	–	0.8	21.3
1940	17.3	8.8	2.1	7.6	1.7	19.8	5.5	9.8	0.2%	2.9	24.3
1946	76.9	2.1	0.5	3.1	0.0[a]	1.2	3.9	5.9	0.5	1.2	4.6
1950	43.3	5.4	5.8	6.4	0.1	3.8	6.6	10.4	1.7	8.9	7.6
1955	61.8	3.9	1.1	5.5	0.1	2.4	4.3	6.9	6.2	2.7	5.1
1960	46.7	0.5	1.4	3.6	2.4	1.8	5.4	9.5	11.4	10.9	6.4
1965	39.8	0.6	1.6	3.7	2.7	2.3	4.4	9.1	17.3	6.2	12.3
1970	40.8	0.8	3.7	3.2	2.6	1.3	4.4	9.3	13.9	11.1	8.9

Source: *Historical Statistics,* Series Y 484-516, and *Statistical Abstract,* 1967, pp. 284 and 390-91, and 1971, pp. 376-77.
[a]Less than 0.05.

Table 8-7 Percentage Distribution of State and Local Government Direct Expenditures, 1902-70

	Education	Highways	Public Welfare	Hospitals and Health	Police Fire, and Sanitation	Natural Resources[a]	General Control	Utility and Liquor Stores	Trust Expenditures	Other
1902	23.3%	16.0%	3.4%	5.5%	12.9%	3.5%	12.9%	7.5%	—	15.0%
1913	25.6	18.6	2.3	4.8	11.6	3.2	9.4	8.2	0.3%	16.0
1922	30.2	22.9	2.1	4.6	9.5	2.6	5.5	6.4	1.3	14.9
1927	28.6	23.2	1.9	4.6	10.1	3.2	5.3	6.3	1.4	15.4
1932	27.5	20.7	5.3	5.4	9.0	3.7	5.6	6.2	1.4	15.2
1936	25.6	16.8	9.7	5.5	8.5	3.5	5.9	8.3	1.8	14.4
1940	23.5	14.0	10.3	5.4	7.2	3.4	5.0	11.8	6.1	13.3
1946	23.9	11.9	10.0	5.8	8.1	3.4	5.0	12.3	9.3	10.3
1950	25.7	13.6	10.5	6.3	7.5	3.5	3.7	9.8	8.5	10.9
1955	29.5	16.0	7.9	6.3	7.6	3.2	3.6	9.6	6.9	9.4
1960	30.7	15.5	7.2	6.2	7.5	3.2	3.5	8.3	6.6	11.3
1965	33.0	14.1	7.3	6.2	7.2	3.3	3.2	8.2	5.7	11.8
1970	35.6	11.1	9.9	6.5	6.7	3.1	3.2	6.4	4.9	12.6

Source: *Historical Statistics*, Series Y 547-574, and *Statistical Abstract*, 1973, p. 419.
[a] Includes parks and recreation.

have been devoted to highway development, public welfare, utility and liquor stores, hospitals and health, and insurance trust expenditures.

Government Revenue-Raising Measures in the Twentieth Century

Tariffs and excise taxes were the major revenue sources for the federal government in the late nineteenth and early twentieth centuries. However, in 1913, the income tax amendment (16th) was passed, and direct taxes on individual and corporate income quickly became the chief source of federal revenue. By 1970, almost 50 percent of total federal revenues were garnered through taxes on individual income, and employment taxes accounted for an additional 23 percent of total government revenues. (See Table 8–8.) Taxes on corporate income have declined as a share of total federal revenues during the past decade but still provide a substantial portion of federal funds. Excise taxes and tariffs, which accounted for over 90 percent of federal revenues in 1900, accounted for approximately 10 percent in 1970. The increased use of direct taxes on income has resulted in a sharp increase in federal tax rates, and Table 8–9 depicts the changes between 1913 and 1962 in effective tax rates for selected income groups.

Property taxes accounted for most state and local government revenues in the nineteenth century, and, until the middle 1930s, property taxes generated more than half of state and local funds. (See Table 8–10.) State and local taxation has always been highly regressive, and, in 1970, property taxes and sales and gross receipts taxes accounted for 50

Table 8-8 Percentage Distribution of Federal Revenue Sources, 1900-70

Year	Individual Income Tax	Corporate Income Tax	Employment Taxes	Excise Taxes	Estate and Gift Taxes	Tariffs	Other
1900	—	—	—	50.1%	0.5%	41.1%	8.3%
1910	—	—	—	39.6	—	49.4	11.0
1920	—[a]	—[a]	—	12.2	1.6	4.8	[a]
1930	27.5%	30.2%	—	13.5	1.6	14.0	13.2
1940	16.7	19.5	14.2%	32.0	6.1	5.9	5.6
1950	41.5	26.3	6.4	18.4	1.7	1.0	4.7
1960	44.0	23.2	15.9	12.6	2.9[b]		1.4
1970	46.7	16.9	23.4	8.1	3.1		1.8

Source: *Historical Statistics*, Series Y 258-63 and Y 264-79, and *Statistical Abstract*, 1973, p. 389.

[a]Not Available.

[b]For 1960 and 1970 tariffs and estate and gift taxes are included together.

Table 8-9 Effective Rates of Individual Income Tax Liability, Selected Income Groups, 1913-62

Income Period	Income Class									
	$600	$1000	$3000	$5000	$10,000	$15,000	$25,000	$50,000	$100,000	$1,000,000
1913-15	–	–	–	0.4%	0.7%	0.8%	1.1%	1.5%	2.5%	6.0%
1916	–	–	–	0.8	1.4	1.6	2.0	2.7	3.9	10.0
1917	–	–	1.3%	2.4	4.0	5.1	7.3	10.4	16.2	47.5
1918	–	–	4.0	4.8	9.5	11.9	15.4	22.3	35.2	70.3
1919-21	–	–	2.7	3.2	6.7	8.7	11.8	18.5	31.3	66.3
1922	–	–	2.7	3.2	6.0	7.6	10.6	17.4	30.2	55.1
1923	–	–	2.0	2.4	4.5	5.7	7.9	13.1	22.7	41.3
1924	–	–	1.0	1.2	2.3	3.9	6.5	12.3	22.7	43.0
1925-27	–	–	0.6	0.8	1.5	2.6	4.9	9.9	16.1	24.1
1928	–	–	0.6	0.8	1.5	2.6	4.4	9.3	15.8	24.1
1929	–	–	0.2	0.3	0.9	1.9	3.7	8.5	14.9	23.1
1930-31	–	–	0.6	0.8	1.5	2.6	4.4	9.3	15.8	24.1
1932-33	–	–	2.7	3.2	6.0	7.6	10.6	17.4	30.2	57.1
1934-35	–	–	2.3	2.8	5.6	7.4	11.2	18.7	31.4	57.2
1936-39	–	–	2.3	2.8	5.6	7.4	11.2	18.7	33.4	68.0
1940	–	0.4%	2.8	3.4	6.9	9.8	17.0	29.4	44.3	71.8
1941	–	2.1	7.4	9.7	14.9	20.0	28.9	41.8	53.2	73.3
1942	2.5%	8.9	15.7	18.4	23.9	29.1	38.5	51.6	64.6	85.5
1943	2.8	10.7	19.1	22.1	27.8	33.1	42.6	56.1	69.7	90.0
1944-45	3.8	11.5	19.5	22.1	27.6	32.9	42.4	55.9	69.9	90.0
1946-47	3.2	9.5	16.2	18.4	23.5	28.5	37.5	50.3	63.5	84.0
1948-49	–	6.6	13.6	16.2	21.2	26.0	34.4	46.4	58.8	77.0
1950	–	7.0	14.3	16.9	22.0	26.9	35.6	48.0	60.8	80.0
1951	–	8.2	16.6	19.3	24.9	30.2	39.9	53.5	67.3	87.2
1952-53	–	8.9	18.1	21.0	27.2	33.1	43.8	56.9	69.7	88.0
1954-62	–	8.0	16.3	18.9	24.4	29.7	39.2	52.8	66.8	87.0

Source: *Historical Statistics*, Series Y 319-32.
Note: The figures show the percent of income taxed away at various income classes with one exemption.

Table 8-10 Percentage Distribution of Revenue Sources for State and Local Governments, 1902-70

Year	Individual Income Tax	Corporate Income Tax	Sales and Gross Receipts Tax	Property Tax	Other Taxes	Utility and Liquor Stores Revenue	Insurance Trust Revenue	Charges and Miscellaneous
1902	–	–	2.7%	67.8%	12.1%	6.0%	–	11.4%
1913	–	–	2.9	66.0	10.9	5.7	0.1%	14.4
1922	0.8%	1.1%	3.0	65.6	8.7	5.3	2.5	13.0
1927	0.9	1.2	6.1	61.3	9.4	5.2	2.1	13.8
1932	1.0	1.0	9.8	58.6	10.1	6.0	2.1	11.4
1936	1.8	1.3	17.6	48.7	10.2	8.9	2.6	8.9
1940	2.1	1.4	18.3	41.0	9.4	9.2	10.6	8.0
1946	2.8	3.0	19.7	33.0	8.3	13.4	10.5	9.3
1950	3.4	2.6	22.3	31.7	8.8	11.7	8.7	10.8
1955	3.6	2.2	22.2	31.1	9.1	10.7	8.3	12.8
1960	4.6	2.2	22.2	30.8	7.9	9.1	9.3	13.9
1965	5.3	2.5	22.3	29.4	7.2	8.3	9.7	15.3
1970	8.4	2.9	23.6	26.6	6.1	6.7	8.4	17.3

Source: *Historical Statistics*, Series Y 517-35, and *Statistical Abstract*, 1973, p. 419.

Table 8-11 Territorial Expansion of the United States

Year	Acquisition	Gross Area of Land and Water (square miles)
1790		888,811
1803	Louisiana Purchase	827,192
1819	Florida and other areas	72,003
1845	Texas Annexation	390,144
1846	Oregon Country	285,580
1848	Mexican Cession	529,017
1853	Gadsden Purchase	29,640
1867	Alaska	586,400
1898	Hawaii	6,423

Source: *Historical Statistics*, Series J 1-2.

percent of total state and local government revenue.[13] Progressive taxes on individual and corporate income have only recently become an important revenue source for state and local governments, and today they provide about 10 percent of state and local funds. State governments have been reluctant to impose heavy direct taxes on income because this type of taxation is not conducive to attracting industry. States compete with each other for industry, and studies of industrial location show that industries view a tax structure with little or no direct burden on individual and corporate income as a positive factor.[14] State governments are aware of this competition, and they have erected their tax structures accordingly. Trends in recent years show greater utilization of progressive measures of direct taxation, but currently these taxes account for a small share of state and local revenues.

Acquisition of Public Lands

The territorial boundaries of the United States were expanded tremendously during the first half of the nineteenth century. Between 1803 and 1853, the land acreage of the United States more than tripled, and the present continental boundaries were established with the Gadsden Purchase in 1853. (See Table 8–11.) Alaska (1867) and Hawaii (1898) were added later in the

---

[13] Progressive taxes are those which take a higher proportion of income from the rich than from the poor; regressive taxes are those which take a lower proportion of income from the rich than from the poor.

[14] See Joe. S. Floyd, *Effects of Taxation on Industrial Location* (Chapel Hill: University of North Carolina Press, 1952), and William V. Williams, "A Measure of the Impact of State and Local Taxes on Industry Location," *Journal of Regional Science*, Summer 1967.

nineteenth century and provided an additional 600,000 square miles of land. In addition to the above federal acquisitions, the eastern states relinquished their western claims early in the nineteenth century, and the federal government acquired the land areas of Ohio, Indiana, Illinois, Michigan, Wisconsin, Alabama, and Mississippi.

Distribution of the Public Lands

The large land acreage acquired by the federal government raised the issue of distribution of the public land holdings. Most individuals agreed that the land should be distributed, but question arose as to whether the land should be used to generate government revenues or to facilitate rapid settlement of the West. Liberal elements asked for a land policy that would provide family-sized plots (40 acres) free of charge to anyone who would settle the land. However, the first land policy established (1785) represented a very conservative outlook on land distribution. (See Table 8–12.) The price per acre ($1.00) seems low by today's standards, but, in conjunction with the minimum purchase size (640 acres) and lack of credit, land could only be purchased by the upper income classes. The modifications that were made in the distribution system in 1796 rendered it even more restrictive and kept land out of the hands of the low and middle income groups. It is clear from the figures in Table 8–13 that very little land was sold under the provisions of the land acts of 1785 and 1796.

Liberal demands for credit and small acreages were partially answered by the land acts of 1800 and 1804. Land was still out of the reach of many middle income families, however, and most of the demand for land between 1800 and 1820 came from speculators who were attracted to land by the low

Table 8-12 Government Land Acts Adopted, 1785-1832

Year	Minimum Purchase Unit in Acres	Minimum Auction Price/Acre	Terms of Sale
1785	640	$1.00	Cash
1796	640	2.00	½ Cash; ½ Credit for 1 year
1800	320	2.00	¼ Cash; ¼ in 2 years; ¼ in 3 years; ¼ in 4 years
1804	160	2.00	Same as in 1800
1820	80	1.25	Cash
1832	40	1.25	Cash

Source: Phillip H. Overmeyer, "Westward Expansion Before the Homestead Act," in Harold F. Williamson, ed., *Growth of the American Economy*, 2nd ed. (Englewood Cliffs, N.J.: Prentice-Hall; 1951), p. 104.

Table 8-13 Distribution of Public Lands by Selected Method, 1785-1923, (thousands of acres)

Period	Land Sales	Homesteads	Grants to Support Transportation	Grants to States
Prior to 1800	1282	—	—	—
1800-1804	1409	—	—	817
1805-09	1893	—	—	—
1810-14	2929	—	—	807
1815-19	11394	—	—	3736
1820-24	3696	—	49	1409
1825-29	4985	—	3611	71
1830-34	15684	—	—	30
1835-39	46632	—	139	2146
1840-44	7891	—	—	7807
1845-49	9847	—	1845	12648
1850-54	20967	—	8904	60988
1855-59	29103	—	20774	6518
1860-64	4678	—	33750	17427
1865-69	5517	859	68272	230
1870-74	7587	4667	3382	—
1875-79	3628	11802	—	3842
1880-84	19033	11536	—	322
1885-89	26546	15303	—	15367
1890-94	9036	17683	—	16156
1895-99	2564	14778	—	5719
1900-1904	9620	19872	—	28
1905-09	17106	18630	—	3130
1910-14	14872	32022	—	17150
1915-19	3699	37717	—	6
1920-23	2806	29000	—	—
1785-1923	284404	213869	140726	176354

Source: *Historical Statistics*, Series J 43, J 44-48, and J 10-18, and Benjamin Horace Hibbard, *A History of Public Land Policies* (Madison: University of Wisconsin Press, 1965), pp. 100-15.

cash down payment. Further liberalization was introduced in 1820, but it was not until 1832 that land was within reach of most lower and middle income families. The 1832 policy was in effect until 1862, but several modifications were made during this period. In 1841, Congress passed the Pre-emption Act, which guaranteed to squatters the right to purchase their holdings at the minimum sale price existing at the time of auction. In 1854, the Graduation Act established a system of graduated reduction in the purchase price of land that remained unsold at the normal auction price. The Homestead Act, adopted in 1862, provided that any family head or any person over twenty-one years of age could obtain 160 acres of free land if he lived on the land or cultivated it for five years.[15] If the homesteader did not meet the requirements of the agreement, he could buy the land for $1.25 per acre.[16]

In addition to the above policies governing the sale and distribution of public lands, the federal government also provided free land to veterans, granted land to states, and provided land grants to railroads, canals, and turnpikes. Table 8–13 provides a clear picture of the acreage of public land disposed of by the major distribution methods between 1785 and 1923.

Land sales were most active during the 1830s, 1850s, and 1880s, and the periods of greatest land sale coincided with the periods of most vigorous transportation development.[17] Most transportation related land grants were made during the late 1850s and 1860s, and this form of distribution was legally terminated in 1871. Grants of public lands to states represented cessions of swamp lands and grants for educational purposes. Most of these grants were made between 1845 and 1865 and during the 1880s.

The first homesteads were completed in 1868, and there was a steady rise in this form of distribution until the early 1920s. In fact, almost twice as many acres were successfully homesteaded between 1900 and 1923 than were brought to completion between 1868 and 1900. Land sales continued to be an important means of public land distribution after the homestead provisions were instituted, and, between 1870 and 1900, 76 million acres of land were homesteaded and 68 million acres of land were purchased from the federal government.

In addition to land grants to states and transportation companies and sale and homesteading of public lands, several hundred million acres of land were distributed during the nineteenth and early twentieth century for the following purposes: forest reserves, national parks, etc., 170 million; military grants to veterans, 68 million; mineral and power reservations, 48 million; timber, stone, and desert reclamations, 78 million; and Indian reservations, 36 million.[18]

---

[15] Under homesteading, the land was free, but a small fee was charged to cover the cost of transferring title to the land.

[16] Land speculation before and after the passage of the Homestead Act will be examined later in this chapter. Under the homestead provisions, an individual could acquire rights to land, improve it, buy it for $1.25 per acre, and sell it for considerably more. This practice was used by late nineteenth-century settlers to acquire capital to start a permanent farm. See Paul W. Gates, "The Homestead Act: Free Land Policy in Operation, 1862–1935," in Howard W. Ottoson, ed., *Land Use Policy and Problems in the United States* (Lincoln: University of Nebraska Press, 1963).

[17] Arthur Cole, "Cyclical and Sectional Variations in the Sale of Public Lands, 1816–1860," *Review of Economics and Statistics,* January 1927, has examined the relationship between land and transportation development for 1860, and he identified transportation expansion as a significant factor in explaining land sales. However, he also pointed to speculative demand as a major cause of cyclical variation in land sales.

[18] See Benjamin Horace Hibbard, *A History of Public Land Policies* (Madison: University of Wisconsin Press, 1965), p. 570.

Land Speculation

Throughout the nineteenth century, land speculators provided a major source of demand for government land. During the antebellum period, speculative demand for land was concentrated in 1818–19, 1835–37, and 1854–58. The land policies in effect between 1800 and 1820 allowed land to be purchased for one-quarter cash down payment. The liberal credit, in conjunction with the beginning of the East-West transportation boom, attracted speculators to land as an investment. Depression in 1819 and the elimination of credit in 1820 discouraged land speculation in the 1820s. During the 1830s, the country experienced tremendous inflation, and the real value of paper notes issued by state banks rapidly declined. However, the federal government accepted paper notes at their face value in exchange for land, and this situation promoted a tremendous speculative land boom. Paul W. Gates estimated that 38 million acres of land were sold between 1835 and 1837, and he claimed that 29 million acres were sold to speculators.[19] A major portion of the speculative demand for land was furnished by banking interests. The speculative land boom of the 1830s was brought to an end by Andrew Jackson in 1837 with the passage of the Specie Circular which required gold or silver as payment for land purchases.[20]

The peak years of antebellum speculative land purchase came between 1854 and 1858. During this period, the federal government sold 65 million acres and granted an equivalent amount to the states. Gates has argued that speculators acquired much of the land sold directly by the federal government as well as a substantial portion of the land granted to state governments.[21] Resentment against speculators led to agitation to restrict land sales to settlers. The Homestead Act developed out of this situation and was partially aimed at curbing land speculation. At the time of the Act's passage, however, speculators already held considerable acreage, and there was much land for sale outside of the public domain. States, railroads, and veterans held a vast supply of land and were willing to sell to speculators. The land acquired by speculators was generally of higher quality than land available through homesteads, and speculators played a major role in land distribution throughout the late nineteenth century.

For many years, land speculation was viewed as a negative factor in the development of the American economy. Critics asserted that land speculators resisted taxes, introduced tenant farming, bought up the best land,

---

[19] Paul W. Gates, "The Role of the Land Speculator in Western Development," in Vernon Carstensen, ed., *The Public Lands* (Madison: University of Wisconsin Press, 1963).

[20] For further discussion of the Specie Circular see Richard H. Timberlake, Jr., "The Specie Circular and Distribution of the Surplus," *Journal of Political Economy,* April 1960; and Timberlake, "The Specie Circular and Sales of Public Lands: A Comment," *Journal of Economic History,* September 1965.

[21] Gates, "The Role of the Land Speculator," p. 360.

and held land out of production.[22] It is true that speculators acquired a great deal of high quality land, but, in view of the tremendous excess supply of land that existed during most of the nineteenth century, it is difficult to accept the argument that speculative holdings retarded the nation's rate of economic progress. Tax resistance and tenant farming may have been social ills, but it does not appear that they had any negative effect on the economy's growth rate. On the positive side, speculators provided an active source of demand for western transportation development since this would bring about rapid appreciation of their land. A recent study by Robert Fogel and Jack Rutner examined the impact of land speculation on the nineteenth century growth of the American economy and concluded that the speculative purchase of land had no perceptible effect on the economy's rate of growth.[23] Fogel and Rutner stressed the tentative nature of their conclusions, but they clearly demonstrated the lack of support for the view that speculative purchase of land had a negative impact on American economic development.

Until recently, it was also argued that land speculation was generally not profitable. The first formal treatment of speculator profits was the pioneering work of Allan and Margaret Bogue.[24] They estimated returns to land speculation in Illinois and Nebraska for the middle and late nineteenth century and found that profits were normally high. However, they cautiously avoided generalizing on the basis of their small sample to the conclusion that frontier land speculation was profitable. Instead, they concluded that further area studies were needed before the issue could be settled. Recently, Robert Swierenga analyzed returns to land speculation in central Iowa, and he concluded that profits in land speculation were far greater than those that could have been expected in a normal business investment.[25] Swierenga's results, in conjunction with those of the Bogues, seriously damage the view that frontier land speculation was unprofitable.

The West as a Safety Valve

Many early studies concerned with land distribution policies and their effect on American economic development viewed the abundance of land

---

[22] See Gates, "The Role of the Land Speculator," pp. 360–365, and Hibbard, *A History of Public Land Policies*, pp. 209–27.

[23] Robert W. Fogel and Jack Rutner, "The Efficiency Effects of Federal Land Policy, 1850–1900: A Report of Some Provisional Findings," in William Aydelotte et al., eds., *Dimensions of Quantitative Research in History* (Princeton: Princeton University Press, 1972).

[24] Allan G. Bogue and Margaret B. Bogue, "Profits and the Frontier Land Speculator," *Journal of Economic History*, March 1957; the Bogues provide an excellent review of the literature regarding profits in land speculation.

[25] See Robert P. Swierenga, "Land Speculator Profits Reconsidered: Central Iowa as a Test Case," *Journal of Economic History*, March 1966, and *Pioneers and Profits: Land Speculation on the Iowa Frontier* (Ames: Iowa State University Press, 1968).

and the existence of a frontier as a positive force in creating stability in the economy. It was argued that in times of distress the poor and disenfranchised could migrate to the West and start a new life. In other words, the West acted as a safety valve and siphoned off the unemployed and dissident elements in eastern urban areas and, thereby, helped to maintain political stability.[26]

In a classic article published in 1941, Clarence H. Danhof brought damaging evidence against the safety-valve thesis.[27] Danhof examined the costs that an individual would have had to meet in order to establish a new farm in the West in the 1850s, and he concluded that the poor could not have afforded the costs of farm-making. In addition to acquiring land, the land would have to be cleared and fenced; draft animals, livestock, seed, and farm implements would have to be purchased; some means of shelter would have to be built; transportation to the West would have to be obtained; and the necessary capital to support the family until the first crop was harvested would have to be obtained. Danhof showed that a 40-acre farm with free land and the bare minimum of agricultural implements would have cost at least $1000 to begin under the conditions of the 1850s. This amount of capital could not have been raised by the poor. Danhof suggested that western migration was generally made by individuals of the middle income class who sold their property in the East to raise the capital needed to finance development of a new farm in the West.[28]

Rationality of the Government's Land Distribution Policy

Early scholarly treatments were severely critical of the federal government's methods of distributing the public domain. Land grants to railroads were viewed as a giveaway to special interests, pre-homestead land sales programs were viewed as an inducement to speculation, and the homestead provisions were viewed as an encouragement to inefficiency and fraud. Thomas Le Duc has provided an appraisal of the land policies followed up to the Homestead Act.[29] He argued that the sales policy pursued during the first half of the nineteenth century encouraged speculative purchase of land but not settlement. Land was only a small portion of the

[26] The classic statement of the safety-valve thesis is in Frederick J. Turner, *The Frontier in American History* (New York: Henry Holt, 1920), pp. 259–61.

[27] Clarence H. Danhof, "Farm-Making Costs and the Safety Valve: 1850–1860," *Journal of Political Economy*, June 1941.

[28] Several recent studies by Martin L. Primack corroborate Danhof's argument concerning the high costs of fencing and land clearing in the mid-nineteenth century; see "Land Clearing Under Nineteenth Century Techniques: Some Preliminary Calculations," *Journal of Economic History*, December 1962; and "Farm Fencing in the Nineteenth Century," *Journal of Economic History*, June 1969.

[29] Thomas Le Duc, "History and Appraisal of United States Land Policy to 1862," in Ottoson, ed., *Land Use Policy and Problems*.

cost of farm-making, and rapid land settlement required some type of long-term agricultural credit. Le Duc was also critical of federal grants to veterans, and he claimed that most veterans did not settle the land but instead sold their land rights to speculators for less than the nominal price ($1.25 per acre) of government land. In addition, federal land grants to states often were resold to speculators. Low land prices and free land grants led to concentration of land in the hands of speculators who acted as middlemen between the government and settlers. Le Duc concluded that the federal government's land program before 1862 retarded American economic development.

Paul Gates has provided careful analysis of the Homestead Act and its effects on the distribution of public lands. In 1936, he argued that the homestead provisions brought very little change in land distribution, and large estates and high-quality land continued to be bought up by speculators and other buyers.[30] (See Table 8–13 for a comparison of land sales and homesteads.) Much land available through homesteads was unproductive, and speculators could outbid settlers for the higher quality land offered for sale by railroads and state governments.

In a recent paper, Gates modified his criticism of the homestead system.[31] He reiterated the argument that the better lands were sold to speculators, and he pointed to the great deal of fraud that was encouraged by the homestead provisions.[32] He also noted the high failure rate on homesteads and pointed out that slightly less than 50 percent of the original homestead entries were brought to successful completion. Between 1880 and 1900, abuses of the system were common, and failure rates were extremely high. However, between 1862 and 1880 and after 1900, the Homestead Act was rather effective in stimulating agricultural settlement. Despite abuses and inadequacies in the homestead system, Gates argued that it did provide 1.5 million people with farm land, many of whom developed permanent farms, and he defended homesteading as a rational system for land distribution.[33]

Recent examination of the government's land program has defended the methods used to distribute the land.[34] It is acknowledged that the distribu-

---

30 Paul W. Gates, "The Homestead Law in an Incongruous Land System," *American Historical Review,* July 1936.

31 See Gates, "The Homestead Act: Free Land Policy."

32 Many large mining, cattle, and lumber companies encouraged employees to file for homesteads, make slight improvements, acquire title to the land, and then sell the land to the company.

33 Fred A. Shannon argued that the homestead system did not encourage tremendous westward migration in the nineteenth century, and he showed that four times as much land was homesteaded after 1890 than before; see "The Homestead Act and the Labor Surplus," *American Historical Review,* July 1936.

34 See Fogel and Rutner, "The Efficiency Effects of Federal Land Policy."

tion plans created problems such as concentrating productive land in the hands of speculators who held it for appreciation. It is also recognized that homestead lots (160 acres) were too small for much of the land in the Great Plains. However, Fogel and Rutner found little or no negative effect on the economy's growth resulting from the great amount of nineteenth-century land speculation. Our current state of knowledge suggests that the distribution system had no significant negative effect on the economy's rate of growth.

The Role of Education in Economic Growth

Recent research into the sources of economic growth has focused a great deal of attention on education as a causal growth force and has demonstrated the strong link between education and productivity and technological change.[35] With regard to its role as a positive growth force, education is best looked upon as an investment in human capital whereby educational spending improves the quality of the labor force. For the economy as a whole, qualitative improvements in the labor force result in increased technological growth and more efficient and productive workers.[36] Recent analysis has shown that widespread mass education developed rapidly in America, and educational improvements played a major positive role in the American economy's development.[37]

Trends in Educational Spending: 1850–1950

Until the mid-nineteenth century, education expenditures were primarily generated by the private sector. During the 1830s and 1840s, strong arguments were raised in favor of public support for education of the masses, and, by the early 1850s, all states had developed programs of public funding for common schools.[38] The late nineteenth century witnessed a steady increase in the commitment of public monies to education, and

---

[35] See the following: Gary S. Becker, "Under-Investment in College Education," *American Economic Review,* May 1960; E. F. Denison, "United States Economic Growth," *Journal of Business,* April 1962; T. W. Schultz, "Investment in Human Capital," *American Economic Review,* May 1960; and Robert M. Solow, "Technical Change and the Aggregate Production Function," *Review of Economics and Statistics,* August 1957.

[36] The human capital approach to education does not take into account the many psychic benefits that accrue to the individual as a result of his education.

[37] For a summary of the issues and the relevant literature, see Stanley L. Engerman, "Human Capital, Education, and Economic Growth," in Fogel and Engerman, eds., *The Reinterpretation of American Economic History.*

[38] For an excellent treatment of the development of a common school system, see Albert Fishlow, "The American Common School Revival: Fact or Fancy?" in Henry Rosovsky, ed., *Industrialization in Two Systems* (New York: Wiley, 1966).

Albert Fishlow's analysis suggests that the public sector's share of total educational expenditures increased as follows: 1850, 47 percent; 1860, 57 percent; 1870, 65 percent; 1880, 77 percent; 1890, 79 percent; and 1900, 79 percent.[39] In 1850, most public funds were spent on elementary education, but, during the late nineteenth century, an increasing share of public monies were funneled into secondary schools, colleges, and universities. During the twentieth century, the importance of private funding declined at the elementary level but advanced at the college and university level, and the private sector's share of total educational spending remained at approximately 21 percent between 1900 and 1960.[40] In recent decades, the greatest volume of private funds for elementary and secondary education has come from church related schools, especially Catholic.

Despite the heavy commitment of public funds to education, as late as the early twentieth century, education beyond the primary grades was considered a luxury beyond the reach of most low income groups. The direct costs of education are only a small portion of the total cost of schooling. Enrollment in school prevents an individual from earning an income, and the income foregone while enrolled in school, generally referred to as the opportunity cost of education, is a real cost to the individual. Late nineteenth-century opportunity costs were high, and only those individuals who could self-finance their education through past savings could afford to forgo income long enough to obtain a secondary education.[41] As a result of high opportunity costs, most lower income children dropped out of school at an early age, and upper income children represented a large share of the secondary school population.[42] Secondary education did not begin to be widespread before the 1920s, and the percentage share of the population 17 years old that graduated from high school showed the following trend: 1871, 2.0 percent; 1880, 2.5 percent; 1890, 3.5 percent; 1900, 6.4 percent; 1910, 8.8 percent; 1920, 16.8 percent; 1930, 29.0 percent; 1940, 50.8 percent; and 1950, 59.0 percent.[43]

Table 8–14 provides a convenient summary of late nineteenth-century education expenditures, opportunity costs, and education's share of G.N.P. and government spending. The figures show that, throughout the nineteenth century, educational expenditures accounted for a very small

---

[39] Albert Fishlow, "Levels of Nineteenth Century American Investment in Education," *Journal of Economic History,* December 1966.

[40] Fishlow, "Levels of Nineteenth Century American Investment in Education," p. 421.

[41] Imperfections in nineteenth-century capital markets made it very difficult for individuals to borrow for educational purposes.

[42] See Fishlow, "Levels of Nineteenth Century American Investment in Education," pp. 422–24. Theodore W. Schultz showed that in 1900 only 11 percent of 14–17 year olds were enrolled in secondary schools, but, by 1956, the enrollment share had risen to 75 percent; see "Capital Formation by Education," *Journal of Political Economy,* December 1960, p. 582.

[43] See *Historical Statistics,* Series H 223–33.

Table 8-14 Trends in Educational Spending, 1840-1900 (dollar figures in millions)

Year	(1) Total Direct Expenditures	(2) Public Educational Expenditures	(3) Opportunity Cost	(4) Total Cost	(5) Direct Expenditures as Percent of G.N.P.	(6) Total Cost as Percent of G.N.P.	(7) Public Educational Expenditures as Percent of Total Government Expenditures
1840	$ 9.2	–	–	–	0.6%	–	–
1850	16.2	$ 7.6	–	–	0.7	–	–
1860	34.7	19.9	24.8	$ 59.5	0.8	1.4%	13.0%
1870	95.4	61.7	–	–	1.3	–	10.0
1880	106.4	81.5	72.1	180.7	1.1	1.8	14.0
1890	187.3	147.4	–	–	1.5	–	17.0
1900	289.6	229.9	213.9	502.9	1.7	2.9	16.0

Source: Albert Fishlow, "Levels of Nineteenth Century American Investment in Education," *Journal of Economic History*, December 1966; pp. 423 and 430.

portion (less than 2 percent) of G.N.P., but recent decades have witnessed a steady rise in the share of G.N.P. devoted to schooling: 1950, 3.4 percent; 1960, 5.1 percent; and 1970, 7.6 percent.[44] A considerable share of nineteenth-century government spending (approximately 14 percent) went into education, and data for recent years suggest that the share of public spending committed to education has increased to almost 20 percent.[45]

The twentieth century has seen increased educational spending for secondary and college training. In 1900, 80 percent of all education outlays was committed to elementary schooling, and the share of funds devoted to secondary and college education (6 and 14 percent) was minor.[46] By the 1950s, elementary education accounted for approximately 50 percent of all spending, and secondary and college education each accounted for approximately 25 percent of the total.

Direct expenditures for education have originated largely from the actions of local governments, and, until the late 1920s, direct outlays by local governments accounted for 90 percent of total educational spending. During recent years, the share of funds coming from the federal and state governments has risen, but local governments still provide approximately three-fourths of total direct funding.[47]

Regional Differences in Antebellum Education

The New England states led the nation in the development of education. By 1850, 99 percent of the region's native born whites over 20 years of age were literate; correspondingly, in other regions, the following percentage shares of the native born white population were literate: Middle Atlantic, 97 percent; North Central, 90 percent; South, 80 percent; and Southwest, 83 percent.[48] A recent study by Albert Fishlow showed that substantial advances were achieved in education outside New England during the period 1840–60.[49] Impressive gains were made in mass enrollment, literacy, and educational spending in the North Central states. The South generated large increases in school expenditures but failed to develop a program of widespread education for the masses.

Table 8–15 shows changes in enrollment rates (number of pupils/white population between the ages of 5–19) between 1840 and 1860. It is clearly evident that regional differences in educational participation narrowed con-

---

[44] See *Statistical Abstract,* 1971, p. 102.

[45] See *Statistical Abstract,* 1973, pp. 391 and 419.

[46] See Schultz, "Capital Formation," pp. 578–79.

[47] See *Historical Statistics,* Series Y 412–445, Y 484–516, Y 601–647, and Y 683–714.

[48] U.S. Bureau of the Census, *A Compendium of the Seventh Census* (Washington, D.C.: Senate Printer, 1854), p. 153.

[49] Fishlow, "The American Common School Revival."

Table 8-15 Enrollment Rates by Region, 1840-60

Region	1840	1850	1860
New England	81.4%	76.1%	73.8%
Middle Atlantic	54.7	61.9	61.3
North Central	29.1	52.4	69.4
South Atlantic	16.2	29.7	31.4
South Central	13.4	31.0	38.6
Total	38.4	50.4	57.0

Source: Albert Fishlow, "The American Common School Revival: Fact or Fancy?" in Henry Rosovsky, ed., *Industrialization in Two Systems* (New York: Wiley, 1966), p. 49.
Note: The enrollment rate is defined as the ratio of the total number of pupils to the total white population between the ages of 5-19.

siderably during the antebellum decades. The enrollment rate doubled in the South Atlantic region and more than doubled in the North Central and South Central states. At the same time, there was only a slight increase in the Middle Atlantic region and a decline in New England. The decline in New England reflected the large influx of foreign migrants to the region, many of whom did not attend school.[50] By 1860, enrollment rates in the New England, Middle Atlantic, and North Central regions were quite similar, but popular participation in education in the South was still decidedly below that in the northern regions.

Despite the relatively low enrollment in formal education in the South, the region devoted considerable resources to education, and expenditures per pupil were substantially higher than those in any other region. Fishlow estimated that in 1860 the following shares of regional output were committed to educational expenditures: New England, 0.7 percent; Middle Atlantic, 0.6 percent; North Central, 1.1 percent; South Atlantic, 1.0 percent; and South Central, 0.8 percent.[51] Fishlow also calculated educational expenditures per white person and per pupil, and these figures appear in Table 8–16. It is clear from the figures that the South's per capita educational expenditures compared favorably to the average for the nation, and, because of low enrollment, the average expenditure per pupil was substantially above the national average. The relatively high expenditure per pupil in the South partly reflected the high percentage of southern students

[50] Illiteracy rates of foreign born whites were much higher than those of native born whites, and, in New England in 1850, the following illiteracy rates were reported for the population twenty years of age and older: native born whites, 0.4 percent; and foreign born whites, 24.4 percent. See *Compendium of the Seventh Census*, p. 153.

[51] Fishlow, "The American Common School Revival," p. 61.

Table 8-16 Educational Expenditures by Region, 1850 and 1860

Region	Outlay per White Person Between the Ages of 5-19		Outlay per Pupil	
	1850	1860	1850	1860
New England	$3.32	$4.60	$4.23	$ 6.25
Middle Atlantic	2.42	3.76	3.90	6.14
North Central	1.28	3.07	2.44	4.50
South Atlantic	2.48	3.69	8.34	11.60
South Central	2.63	3.86	8.46	10.00
Total	2.23	3.66	4.43	6.43

Source: Fishlow, "The American Common School Revival," p. 55.

enrolled in college; however, at each level of schooling, per pupil expenditure in the South exceeded that in any other region.[52]

Despite the South's relatively heavy educational expenditure per pupil, failure to develop widespread popular participation in schooling resulted in relatively high rates of illiteracy in the region. The figures in Table 8–17 exhibit the percentage share of the white population (native and foreign born) over twenty years of age that could not read and write. All southern states had an illiteracy rate of at least 10 percent; by comparison, outside the South only Delaware, Indiana, Michigan, and Missouri had illiteracy rates exceeding that figure.

Literacy Trends: 1870–1930

The literacy level of the American people improved substantially between 1870 and 1930. (See Table 8–18.) During this period, the percentage of the nation's population ten years of age and over that could not write fell from 20 to less than 5. The greatest improvement in literacy standards was made by Negroes where the illiterate percentage fell from 81 percent in 1870 to 16 percent in 1930. Regional differences in literacy for native whites (native parentage) and Negroes are shown in Table 8–19.[53] By 1930, literacy of native whites exceeded 99 percent in the New England, Middle Atlantic, East North Central, West North Central, and Pacific regions; literacy for

[52] Fishlow, "The American Common School Revival," p. 60.

[53] The figures in Table 8–18 for native born whites include both native and foreign parentage, whereas the figures in Table 8–19 only include native born whites with native parentage; therefore, the tables are not strictly comparable.

Table 8-17 White Literacy Rates by State, 1860

State	Percentage of White Population Unable to Read and Write
Alabama	16.6%
Arkansas	17.7
California	7.4
Connecticut	3.2
Delaware	15.0
Florida	15.4
Georgia	16.9
Illinois	7.2
Indiana	10.2
Iowa	6.6
Kansas	5.8
Kentucky	16.3
Louisiana	9.8
Maine	2.3
Maryland	6.1
Massachusetts	6.5
Michigan	17.4
Minnesota	5.7
Mississippi	9.9
Missouri	12.3
New Hampshire	2.4
New Jersey	5.7
New York	5.6
North Carolina	23.1
Ohio	5.4
Oregon	5.9
Pennsylvania	5.2
Rhode Island	6.0
South Carolina	10.8
Tennessee	19.1
Texas	9.8
Vermont	5.1
Virginia	15.1
Wisconsin	4.5
United States	8.3

Source: Calculated from the U.S. Bureau of the Census, *Compendium of the Ninth Census* Washington, 1872), p. 458, and *Eighth Census of the United States, Population,* pp. 592-93.

whites in the South was only slightly lower (96 percent). Striking improvements in Negro literacy were made in all regions between 1890 and 1930, and, by 1930, Negro literacy rates outside the South were approximately 95 percent and within the South approximately 80 percent.

Table 8-18 Percentage of Population Ten Years of Age and Over Unable to Write, by Population Group, 1870-1930

Population Group	1870	1880	1890	1900	1910	1920	1930
Total Population	20.0%	17.0%	13.3%	10.7%	7.7%	6.0%	4.3%
White Population	11.5	9.4	7.7	6.2	5.0	4.0	2.7
Native Born	—	8.7	6.2	4.6	3.0	2.0	1.5
Foreign Born	—	12.0	13.1	12.9	12.7	13.1	9.9
Negro Population	81.4	70.0	57.1	44.5	30.4	22.9	16.3

Source: U.S. Bureau of the Census, *Thirteenth Census of the United States, Population,* Vol. I, p. 1187; and *Fifteenth Census of the United States, Population,* Vol. II, p. 1223.

Postscript on Government's Role in American Economic Development

Quantitive indicators of the direct impact of government during the nineteenth century show that government activity was small relative to total economic activity, and this has helped to create the illusion that nineteenth-century American economic development was largely the result of unfettered private enterprise. It should be made clear that despite the small amount of direct government spending, the efforts of the public sector were concentrated in strategic areas which had far-reaching consequences for the pace of American economic development. The government's efforts in transportation development, manufacturing subsidies, education, land distribution, and industrial regulation admittedly did not involve a great deal of direct expenditures. However, the rate of development of the American economy would have been much slower if government had not concentrated its efforts in those areas which were exceedingly risky or unremunerative and, therefore, did not attract the private sector but had large benefits for the economy as a whole. Much research remains to be done before an accurate estimate of the government's impact in the nineteenth-century economy can be made. However, present knowledge suggests that it is impossible to discuss nineteenth-century American economic development without taking recognition of the crucial impact of government activity.

Recent decades have seen a sharp increase in the breadth and scope of direct government economic activity, particularly at the federal level. The quantitive importance of government action is no longer questioned, and, at present, over one-third of total spending originates in government. In addition to the large volume of direct spending, the importance of government economic activity is augmented by its commitment to areas of strategic importance such as economic stabilization, education, defense, health, welfare, environmental protection, industrial regulation, and equality of opportunity.

Table 8-19 Percentage of Population Ten Years of Age and Over Unable to Write, by Region and Population Group, 1890-1930

Region	Native Whites (Native Parentage)					Negroes				
	1890	1900	1910	1920	1930	1890	1900	1910	1920	1930
New England	1.1%	0.9%	0.7%	0.6%	0.6%	15.5%	11.6%	7.8%	7.1%	5.5%
Middle Atlantic	3.0	2.0	1.2	0.7	0.6	22.3	14.2	7.9	5.0	3.7
East North Central	4.1	2.8	1.7	1.0	0.7	26.7	18.5	11.0	7.3	4.7
West North Central	4.1	2.9	1.7	1.1	0.8	37.4	25.4	14.9	10.5	7.6
South Atlantic	15.4	12.0	8.0	5.4	3.9	60.1	47.1	32.5	25.2	19.7
East South Central	17.3	13.6	9.6	6.6	5.1	61.5	49.2	34.8	27.9	22.0
West South Central	12.9	9.2	5.6	3.9	2.7	60.9	48.0	33.1	25.3	17.0
Mountain	11.4	7.1	3.6	2.4	1.5	21.8	13.5	8.0	5.3	4.1
Pacific	1.7	0.8	0.4	0.4	0.3	24.6	12.7	6.3	4.6	3.1
United States	7.5	5.7	3.7	2.5	1.8	57.1	44.5	30.4	22.9	16.3

Source: U.S. Bureau of the Census, *Thirteenth Census of the United States, Population*, Vol. I, p. 1196; and *Fifteenth Census of the United States, Population*, Vol. II, p. 1231.

Suggested Reading

Bogue, Allan G., and Margaret B. Bogue, "Profits and the Frontier Land Speculator," *Journal of Economic History,* March 1957.

Bowman, Mary Jean, "The Land Grant Colleges and Universities in Human Resource Development," *Journal of Economic History,* December 1962.

Broude, Henry W., "The Role of the State in American Economic Development, 1820–90," in Hugh G. J. Aitken, ed., *The State and Economic Growth.* New York: Social Science Research Council, 1959.

Bruchey, Stuart W., *The Roots of American Economic Growth, 1607–1861: An Essay in Social Causation.* New York: Harper & Row, 1965.

Danhof, Clarence H., "Farm-Making Costs and the Safety Valve: 1850–1860," *Journal of Political Economy,* June 1941.

Davis, Lance E., and John Legler, "The Government in the American Economy, 1815–1902: A Quantitative Study," *Journal of Economic History,* December 1966.

Fishlow, Albert, "Levels of Nineteenth Century American Investment in Education," *Journal of Economic History,* December 1966.

———, "The American Common School Revival: Fact or Fancy," in Henry Rosovsky, ed., *Industrialization in Two Systems.* New York: Wiley, 1966.

Fogel, Robert W., and Jack Rutner, "The Efficiency Effects of Federal Land Policy, 1850–1900: A Report of Some Provisional Findings," in William Aydelotte et al., eds., *Dimensions of Quantitative Research in History.* Princeton: Princeton University Press, 1972.

Gates, Paul W., "The Homestead Act: Free Land Policy in Operation, 1862–1935," in Howard W. Ottoson, ed., *Land Use Policy and Problems in the United States.* Lincoln: University of Nebraska Press, 1963.

———, "The Role of the Land Speculator in Western Development," in Vernon Carstensen, ed., *The Public Lands.* Madison: University of Wisconsin Press, 1963.

Goodrich, Carter, *Government Promotion of American Canals and Railroads, 1800–1890.* New York: Columbia University Press, 1960.

———, *The Government and the Economy, 1783–1861.* Indianapolis: Bobbs-Merrill, 1967.

Landes, William M., and Lewis C. Solomon, "Compulsory Schooling Legislation: An Economic Analysis of Law and Social Change in the Nineteenth Century," *Journal of Economic History,* March 1972.

Le Duc, Thomas, "History and Appraisal of United States Land Policy to 1862," in Ottoson, ed., *Land Use Policy and Problems in the United States.*

Musgrave, R. A., and J. M. Culbertson, "The Growth of Public Expenditures in the United States, 1890–1948," *National Tax Journal,* June 1953.

Primack, Martin L., "Land Clearing Under Nineteenth Century Techniques: Some Preliminary Calculations," *Journal of Economic History,* December 1962.

———, "Farm Fencing in the Nineteenth Century," *Journal of Economic History,* June 1969.

Scheiber, Harry N., "Property Law, Expropriation, and Resource Allocation by Government: The United States, 1789–1910," *Journal of Economic History,* March 1973.

———, "State Policy and the Public Domain: The Ohio Canal Lands," *Journal of Economic History,* March 1965.

Solmon, Lewis C., "Estimates of the Costs of Schooling in 1880 and 1890," *Explorations in Economic History,* Supplement, 1970.

———, "Opportunity Costs and Models of Schooling in the Nineteenth Century," *Southern Economic Journal,* July 1970.

Swierenga, Robert P., "Land Speculator Profits Reconsidered: Central Iowa as a Test Case," *Journal of Economic History,* March 1966.

———, *Pioneers and Profits: Land Speculation on the Iowa Frontier.* Ames: Iowa State University Press, 1968.

Timberlake, Richard H., Jr., "The Specie Circular and Distribution of the Surplus," *Journal of Political Economy,* April 1960.

———, "The Specie Circular and Sales of Public Lands: A Comment," *Journal of Economic History,* September 1965.

Trescott, Paul B., "The United States Government and National Income, 1790–1860," in *Trends in the American Economy in the Nineteenth Century,* Conference on Research in Income and Wealth, Studies in Income and Wealth, National Bureau of Economic Research, Vol. 24. Princeton: Princeton University Press, 1960.

9
The Economy of the Antebellum South

With the possible exception of the economic impact of the Civil War, no issue in American economic history has undergone a more significant revision in thinking than the economics of plantation slavery. For years, slavery was viewed as an inefficient and unprofitable form of economic organization, and the new economic history's first major application of theory and statistics was aimed at testing the reliability of this assertion. The revisions suggested by the new economic history were damaging to the traditional interpretation, and the current state of knowledge suggests that slavery was a profitable and viable institution. This chapter will highlight the differences between the old and new views of plantation slavery, and it will also examine the related issues of industrial slavery and food self-sufficiency in the antebellum South.

It must be made clear at the outset that this chapter is concerned only with the *economics* of slavery. Studies of the profitability and viability of slavery should in no way be confused with the ethical issues involved. The fact that slavery was an immoral and inhumane part of American growth is undeniable. However, historical interest in the economics of the system in no way endorses the institution of slavery.

The Antebellum Southern Economy

The antebellum South was largely a rural agricultural society. Heavy emphasis on large scale plantation agriculture encouraged geographic dispersion of the population, and, as a result, there was little urban clustering. The figures in Tables 9–1 and 9–2 clearly indicate the sparse and rural character of population settlement in the antebellum South. Table 9–1 shows that population density in the South Atlantic region was markedly

Table 9-1 Average Number of People per Square Mile, 1860

Area	Population Density
New England	49.8
Maine	20.3
New Hampshire	36.1
Vermont	34.0
Massachusetts	157.3
Rhode Island	166.5
Connecticut	94.6
Middle Atlantic	73.6
New York	81.1
New Jersey	89.4
Pennsylvania	64.6
Delaware	56.6
Maryland	69.5
East North Central	28.4
Ohio	57.1
Indiana	36.5
Illinois	30.7
Michigan	13.2
Wisconsin	14.3
West North Central	6.0
Minnesota	2.2
Iowa	12.1
Missouri	17.1
Nebraska	0.4
Kansas	1.3
South Atlantic	17.6
Virginia	30.7
West Virginia	15.7
North Carolina	20.3
South Carolina	23.3
Georgia	18.2
Florida	2.6
East South Central	22.5
Kentucky	29.2
Tennessee	26.9
Alabama	19.0
Mississippi	16.7
West South Central	4.9
Arkansas	8.4
Louisiana	15.8
Texas	2.3

Source: Calculated from the population statistics in U.S. Bureau of the Census, *Eighth Census of the United States, Population.*

Table 9-2 United States Cities in 1860 with Population Exceeding 25,000

City	Population
New York, N. Y.	805,658
Philadelphia, Pa.	565,529
Brooklyn, N.Y.	266,661
Baltimore, Md.	212,418
Boston, Mass.	177,840
New Orleans, La.	168,675
Cincinnati, Ohio	161,044
St. Louis, Mo.	160,773
Chicago, Ill.	109,260
Buffalo, N.Y.	81,129
Newark, N. J.	71,941
Louisville, Ky.	68,033
Albany, N.Y.	62,367
San Francisco, Cal.	56,802
Providence, R. I.	50,666
Pittsburgh, Pa.	49,217
Rochester, N.Y.	48,204
Detroit, Mich.	45,619
Milwaukee, Wis.	45,246
Cleveland, Ohio	43,417
Charleston, S.C.	40,578
Troy, N. Y.	39,235
Richmond, Va.	37,910
Lowell, Mass.	36,827
Mobile, Ala.	29,258
Jersey City, N. J.	29,226
Hartford, Conn.	29,152
Allegheny, Pa.	28,702
Syracuse, N. Y.	28,119
Portland, Me.	26,341
Cambridge, Mass.	26,060
Roxbury, Mass.	25,137
Charlestown, Mass.	25,065

Source: U.S. Bureau of the Census, *Eighth Census of the United States, Population.*

below that in other eastern seaboard areas, and the only region in the nation with a lower population density was the frontier. Table 9–2 shows the 1860 rank ordering of cities with population in excess of 25,000. Only one southern city, New Orleans, exceeded 100,000 population, and only one other, Louisville, exceeded 50,000.

The most important staple crop produced in the antebellum South was cotton. In the early nineteenth century, the cotton industry was concentrated in Virginia, the Carolinas, and Georgia; during the pre–Civil War decades, due to soil exhaustion in the old South, the industry moved westward into Alabama, Mississippi, Louisiana, Arkansas, and Texas. (See Figures

Figure 9-1 Cotton Production, 1839

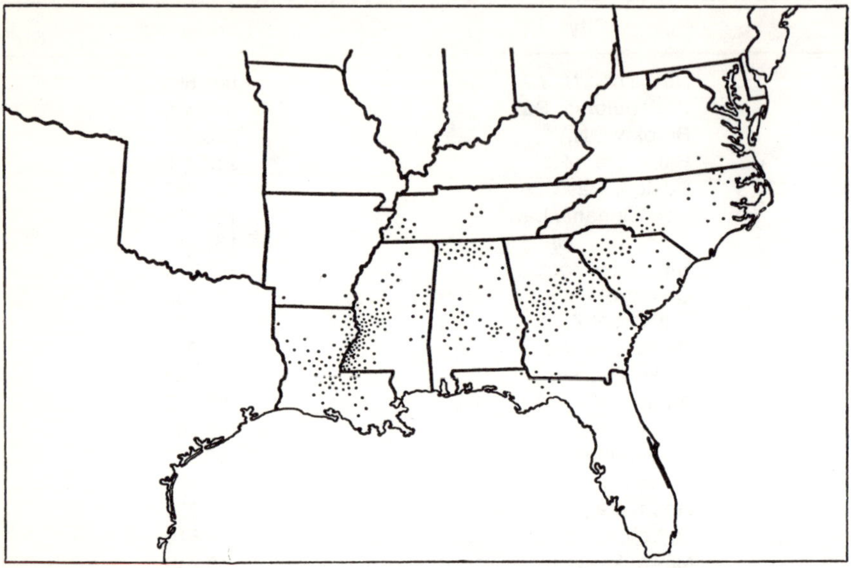

Source: Charles O. Paullin, *Atlas of the Historical Geography of the United States* (Washington, D.C.: The Carnegie Institution of Washington and the American Geographical Society of New York, 1932), Plate 142B.
Note: Each dot represents 4,000 bales.

9–1 and 9–2 and Table 9–3.) Other leading staple crops in the antebellum South included tobacco, sugar, corn, and rice. In 1860, tobacco production was especially important in Virginia (124 million pounds), Kentucky (108 million pounds), Tennessee (43 million pounds), Maryland (38 million pounds), and North Carolina (33 million pounds). Louisiana dominated cane sugar and molasses production and accounted for over 90 percent of the nation's output of each commodity.[1]

Large amounts of grain and other staple food products were also produced in the antebellum South. Later in this chapter, we will look specifically at the issue of southern self-sufficiency in basic food products. However, it is clear from the data in Table 9–4 that the South was heavily involved in food production, and substantial shares of the nation's output of wheat, corn, rice, peas and beans, and sweet potatoes were produced in the region.

---

[1] See U.S. Bureau of the Census, *Eighth Census of the United States, Agriculture* (Washington, D.C.: U.S. Government Printing Office, 1864), pp. 184–87.

Figure 9-2 Cotton Production, 1859

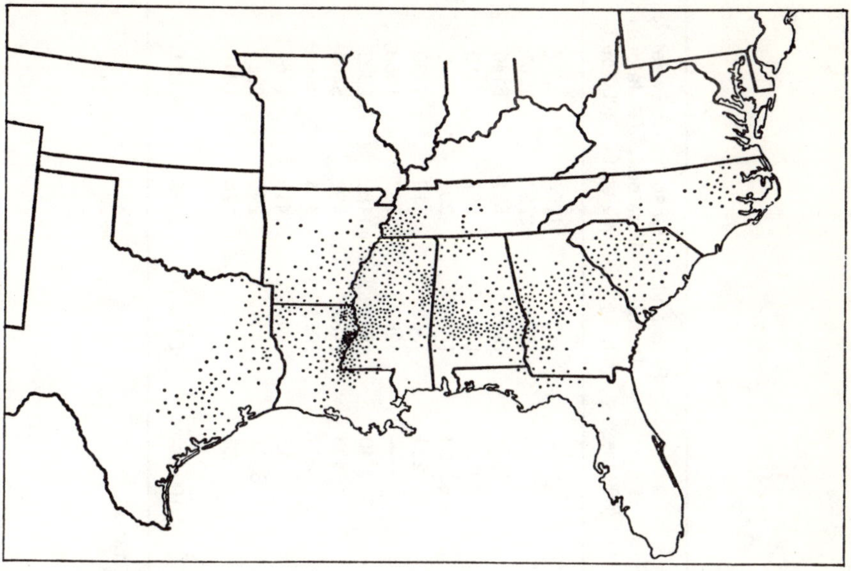

Source: Charles O. Paullin, *Atlas of the Historical Geography of the United States* (Washington, D.C.: The Carnegie Institution of Washington and the American Geographical Society of New York, 1932), Plate 142C.
Note: Each dot represents 4,000 bales.

Table 9-3 Leading Cotton Producing States in 1860

State	Bales of 400 Pounds Each
Mississippi	1,202,507
Alabama	989,955
Louisiana	777,738
Georgia	701,840
Texas	431,463
Arkansas	367,393
South Carolina	353,412
Tennessee	296,464
North Carolina	145,514
Florida	65,153
Missouri	41,188
Virginia	12,727

Source: U.S. Bureau of the Census, *Eighth Census of the United States, Agriculture*, p. 185.

Table 9-4 Southern Production of Selected Agricultural Commodities, 1860

State	Wheat (000 bu.)	Rye (000 bu.)	Corn (Million bu.)	Oats (000 bu.)	Rice (000 lbs.)	Peas and Beans (000 bu.)	Irish Potatoes (000 bu.)	Sweet Potatoes (000 bu.)
Maryland	6103	519	13.4	3959	—	34	1264	237
Virginia	13131	944	38.3	10187	8	515	2292	1961
North Carolina	4744	437	30.1	2782	7594	1932	831	6140
South Carolina	1286	89	15.1	937	119101	1728	227	4116
Georgia	2545	116	30.8	1232	52508	1765	304	6509
Florida	3	21	2.8	47	224	363	19	1130
Kentucky	7395	1055	64.0	4617	—	288	1757	1058
Tennessee	5459	258	52.1	2268	40	548	1182	2605
Alabama	1218	72	33.2	682	493	1482	492	5440
Mississippi	588	39	29.1	221	809	1955	414	4564
Arkansas	958	78	17.8	475	17	440	418	1567
Louisiana	32	36	16.9	89	6331	431	295	2061
Texas	1478	112	16.5	986	26	342	174	1847
Percent of National Production	26.0%	17.9%	42.9%	16.5%	100.0%	78.5%	8.7%	93.2%

Source: U.S. Bureau of the Census, *Eighth Census of the United States, Agriculture*, pp. 184-85.

In large part, the labor force utilized to produce these staples consisted of slaves. Importation of slaves was officially closed at the beginning of the nineteenth century, but, throughout the antebellum decades, slave owners encouraged high slave birth rates in order to take advantage of the high and rising prices offered in the interstate slave market.[2] Ulrich B. Phillips cited a rise in the average price paid for a male field hand from $700 in 1828 to $1800 in 1860.[3] The high slave birth rate resulted in a steady increase in the number of slaves relative to the total southern population, and, by 1860, the region's population of almost 10 million consisted of 4 million slaves. (See Table 9–5.) The majority of southerners did not own slaves, and the 4 million slaves in the antebellum South were owned by approximately 385,000 individuals. (See Table 9–6.) Most slaveholders (72 percent) owned fewer than 10 slaves, and there were only slightly more than 10,000 slaveholders who owned more than 200. Slave ownership was concentrated, and the majority of slaves were owned by 12 percent of the slaveholders.

The Traditional View of the Economics of Southern Slavery

Perhaps no single issue has received as much attention from new economic historians as the economics of antebellum plantation slavery. Stanley Engerman has provided an excellent summary of the old and new views concerning the profitability of slavery to the planter, the viability of the institution, and the effects of slavery on southern economic development.[4] The old view is generally associated with the work of Ulrich B. Phillips, who argued that the slave system was unprofitable to the slave owner, was a dying institution, and was the major factor retarding the growth of the southern economy.[5] To support his argument concerning the unprofitability and dying nature of the institution, Phillips pointed to a rise in the ratio of slave prices (male field hands) to cotton prices (price per pound) of ten to twelve times during 1800–1860. He stated, without empirical verification, that the pace of this rising price differential could not be explained by rising slave productivity.

---

[2] See Alfred H. Conrad and John R. Meyer, "The Economics of Slavery in the Antebellum South," *Journal of Political Economy,* April 1958. Conrad and Meyer claim that the average female slave produced between five and ten marketable children. For an assessment of the interstate slave trade see William L. Miller, "A Note on the Importance of the Interstate Slave Trade of the Ante Bellum South," *Journal of Political Economy,* April 1965.

[3] Ulrich B. Phillips, "The Economic Cost of Slaveholding in the Cotton Belt," *Political Science Quarterly,* June 1905, p. 267.

[4] Stanley L. Engerman, "The Effects of Slavery upon the Southern Economy: A Review of the Recent Debate," *Explorations in Entrepreneurial History,* Winter 1967.

[5] Ulrich B. Phillips, "The Economic Cost of Slaveholding," and *American Negro Slavery* (London: D. Appleton, 1918).

Table 9-5 Slave Population of the Major Slave States, 1810, 1840, and 1860

State	1810	1840	1860
Maryland	111,502	89,737	87,189
Virginia	392,518	449,087	490,865
North Carolina	168,824	245,817	331,059
South Carolina	196,365	327,038	402,406
Georgia	105,218	280,944	462,198
Florida	—	25,717	61,745
Kentucky	80,561	182,258	225,483
Tennessee	44,535	183,059	275,719
Alabama	—	253,532	435,080
Mississippi	17,088	195,211	436,631
Louisiana	34,660	168,452	331,726
Arkansas	—	19,935	111,115
Texas	—	—	182,566

Source: U.S. Bureau of the Census, *Eighth Census of the United States, Population,* pp. 594-603.

Phillips suggested that the following factors were responsible for the rise in slave prices: increases in the cost of maintaining slaves (food, clothing, shelter), increases in demand for slaves from large plantations concerned with economies of scale, and prestige demand for slaves.[6] According to Phillips, prestige demand for slaves had an adverse effect on southern capital formation and economic growth because funds were wasted in conspicuous displays of consumer purchasing power instead of being placed in productive investments. Another offset to southern growth mentioned by Phillips was the overconcentration on agriculture which he claimed put the South in a chronic debtor relationship to northern capitalists and merchants.

Charles W. Ramsdell was another important voice in the old view of the economics of slavery.[7] Ramsdell's argument, commonly referred to as the natural limits hypothesis, suggested that slavery had reached its natural geographic limits by 1860. After that time, the institution would have become unprofitable and nonviable and ceased to exist before the end of the nineteenth century. The high slave birth rate, coupled with the fixed supply of land, would result in a steady rise in the ratio of slave labor to land, and the maintenance costs of slaves would soon exceed their earnings. In other words, Ramsdell argued that diminishing returns would set in, and that this would lead to falling profits and result in the death of slavery.

---

[6] Prestige demand, or conspicuous consumption, generally refers to lavish consumption intended to enhance one's stature or prestige.

[7] Charles W. Ramsdell, "The Natural Limits of Slavery Expansion," *Mississippi Valley Historical Review,* September 1929.

Table 9-6 Number of Slaveholders Owning Various Numbers of Slaves, by State, 1860

Area	Number of Slaves									
	1	2-4	5-9	10-20	20-50	50-100	100-200	200-500	500-1000	1000+
District of Columbia	654	409	131	27	7	1	–	–	–	–
Delaware	237	239	86	25	–	–	–	–	–	–
Maryland	4119	4254	2830	1718	747	99	15	1	–	–
Virginia	11085	14270	12222	8774	4917	746	105	9	–	–
North Carolina	6440	9631	8449	6073	3321	611	118	15	–	–
South Carolina	3763	6254	6182	5210	3646	1197	363	78	7	1
Georgia	6713	10821	9657	7530	5049	1102	181	30	1	–
Florida	863	1370	1135	976	603	158	45	2	–	–
Kentucky	9306	12720	9793	5271	1485	63	6	1	–	–
Tennessee	7820	11359	9210	5523	2555	335	40	7	–	–
Alabama	5607	8797	7389	5906	4344	1341	312	34	–	–
Mississippi	4856	7833	6870	5489	4220	1359	279	36	1	–
Arkansas	281	378	282	142	56	10	–	–	–	–
Louisiana	4092	6143	4651	3222	2349	1029	460	83	4	–
Texas	4593	6749	4950	3423	1827	282	52	2	–	–
Kansas	2	–	–	–	–	–	–	–	–	–
Nebraska	1	4	1	–	–	–	–	–	–	–
Missouri	6893	8770	5717	2400	502	34	4	–	–	–
Utah	8	2	1	1	–	–	–	–	–	–
Total	77333	110003	89556	61710	35623	8367	1980	298	13	1

Source: U.S. Bureau of the Census, *Eighth Census of the United States, Agriculture*, p. 247.

Eugene D. Genovese put forth the argument that slavery retarded the overall economic development of the South.[8] In examining the antebellum southern consumer market, Genovese argued that slavery created a great degree of inequality in the income distribution which resulted in low levels of demand for mass-produced goods. He suggested that the southern consumer market consisted primarily of planters, low-income white farmers, and slaves; the absence of a large middle-class consumer demand resulted in a relatively low stimulus to southern industrialization. Because of the insufficient demand for standardized products, Genovese concluded that the South developed into a rural agricultural society dependent on the North for industrial goods. Genovese also argued that the unequal distribution of southern income encouraged conspicuous consumption and acted as an offset to capital formation.

New Views of the Economics of Southern Slavery

Recent empirical investigation by new economic historians has resulted in a revised view of the economics of plantation slavery. Ramsdell's argument concerning the natural limits to slavery expansion is more appropriately viewed as an argument concerning the natural limits to cotton production. In order to accept Ramsdell's conclusion that the geographic containment of slavery would have led to manumission of slaves, one must assume that slaves could only be used productively in cotton growing.[9] On the eve of the Civil War there was very little cotton production in Virginia and North Carolina, but substantial numbers of slaves were located in this area and used productively in other occupations.[10] If diminishing returns to cotton production had set in, perhaps slave owners would have followed the example set in the old South and turned their slaves to other tasks instead of freeing them.

A revision of the traditional view of the profitability of slavery was provided in an important paper by Alfred H. Conrad and John R. Meyer.[11] Conrad and Meyer estimated the rate of return earned in plantation slave

---

[8] Eugene D. Genovese, "The Significance of the Slave Plantation for Southern Economic Development," *Journal of Southern History*, November 1962.

[9] Engerman, "Effects of Slavery," p. 74, points out that Ramsdell's argument is poorly supported by empirical evidence. Engerman also raises the question of using fertilization to increase land acreage suitable for cotton growing in the old South. Also see Robert W. Fogel and Stanley L. Engerman, "The Economics of Slavery," in Fogel and Engerman, eds., *The Reinterpretation of American Economic History* (New York: Harper & Row, 1971) for further comment on defects in Ramsdell's argument.

[10] Compare the cotton production figures in Table 9–3 with the slave population figures in Table 9–5. Also see Victor Clark, *History of Manufactures of the United Sattes,* Vol. 1 (New York: McGraw-Hill for the Carnegie Institution of Washington, 1929), pp. 399, 553–55, for an indication of the use of slaves in manufacturing.

[11] Conrad and Meyer, "The Economics of Slavery."

agriculture and compared this to returns in alternative investments. Their results suggest that, in the average case, profits earned in slavery compared favorably to profits on alternative investments. Using 6 percent as the average rate of return for all business investment, Conrad and Meyer estimated the following rates of return to utilization of male slaves in plantation agriculture: majority of plantations, 4.5-8.0 percent; poorest quality plantations, 2.2–5.4 percent; and the best plantations, 10.0–13.0 percent. Returns to ownership of female slaves required a separate estimation procedure because a portion of the return resulted from the sale of offspring. The average rate of return to female slave ownership was estimated at 7.1-8.1 percent. For both males and females, Conrad and Meyer's results suggest that slavery was a very profitable form of business enterprise in the antebellum South.

Conrad and Meyer's study encouraged further debate concerning the profitability of slavery, and there has been some question concerning the accuracy of their estimates.[12] However, the weight of the evidence is with the Conrad and Meyer position, and most economic historians now view slavery as profitable to the planter. The high slave prices cited by Phillips appear to have been warranted by the high profits being earned by slave owners, and one does not have to resort to conspicuous consumption to explain the high demand for slaves and the inflated slave prices.

Several studies have been directed at the issue of slavery's viability.[13] The most direct measure of the institution's viability is provided by comparing the market price of slaves to the cost of raising a slave. As long as the market price exceeded the total sum of rearing costs invested in the slave, the institution would continue to exist. In a detailed study of slavery's viability Yasukichi Yasuba showed that the surplus between slave prices and rearing costs widened during the antebellum period. This surplus, or capitalized rent, was measured for the case of a male slave marketed at age 18. Table 9–7 exhibits the capitalized rent in constant (1846–50) dollars under two assumptions: Variant I assumes that the slave was not used

---

[12] See the following: Yasukichi Yasuba, "The Profitability and Viability of Plantation Slavery in the United States," *The Economic Studies Quarterly,* September 1961; Robert Evans, Jr., "The Economics of American Negro Slavery," in *Aspects of Labor Economics,* National Bureau of Economic Research (Princeton: Princeton University Press, 1962); Edward Saraydar, "A Note on the Profitability of Ante Bellum Slavery," *Southern Economic Journal,* April 1964; Richard Sutch, "The Profitability of Ante Bellum Slavery—Revisited," *Southern Economic Journal,* April 1965 (see also Saraydar's reply to Sutch in the same issue); James D. Foust and Dale E. Swan, "Productivity and Profitability of Antebellum Slave Labor: A Micro-Approach," in William N. Parker, ed., *The Structure of the Cotton Economy of the Antebellum South,* special issue of *Agricultural History,* January 1970; William N. Parker, "Slavery and Southern Economic Development: An Hypothesis and Some Evidence," in *The Structure of the Cotton Economy of the Antebellum South;* and Fogel and Engerman, "The Economics of Slavery."

[13] See Sutch, "The Profitability of Ante Bellum Slavery," and Yasuba, "The Profitability and Viability of Plantation Slavery."

Table 9-7 Capitalized Rent in the Price of a Male Slave, Age 18

Date	Average Price of a Slave	Rearing Costs	Net Income from Children	Capitalized Rent (1846-50 Dollars) Variant I[a]	Variant II[a]
1821-25	$ 736	$657	$349	$ 62	$ 334
1826-30	792	614	286	170	442
1831-35	974	671	431	268	650
1836-40	1206	848	497	280	668
1841-45	744	591	379	168	585
1846-50	936	737	546	199	745
1851-55	1252	807	600	412	968
1856-60	1596	938	922	544	1306

Source: Yasukichi Yasuba, "The Profitability and Viability of Plantation Slavery in the United States," *The Economic Studies Quarterly*, September 1961, p. 65.

[a] Variant I represents the deflated value of the difference between the average price of slaves and the rearing costs; Variant II represents the deflated value of the difference between the average price of slaves and the rearing costs plus the net income from child labor.

in the field before being sold, and Variant II assumes that the slave was used in the field.[14] Yasuba's calculations suggest that, on the eve of the Civil War, plantation slavery was viable and showed no signs of dying.

The traditional view of slavery as a retarding force in antebellum southern economic development emphasized the low rate of capital formation and inadequate demand for industrial products that resulted from the high degree of inequality in southern income distribution. Historians frequently pointed to low levels of industrialization and urbanization and heavy specialization on the production of agricultural staples, especially cotton, as indicators of backwardness in the antebellum southern economy. Urbanization and industrialization statistics are not appropriate indicators of the level of economic development, but, in the absence of per capita income figures, this type of information was used.

The empirical basis for studying regional disparities in antebellum standards of living was substantially improved by Richard A. Easterlin's presentation of regional per capita income estimates. [15] (See Table 9–8.)

[14] See Fogel and Engerman, "The Economics of Slavery," for a critical discussion of Yasuba's techniques; they suggest that the Variant I calculations should eliminate any bias and yield a lower-bound estimate of capitalized rent. Also see Stanley L. Engerman, "The Effects of Slavery," pp. 82–85, for a discussion of the issue of viability.

[15] Richard A. Easterlin, "Regional Income Trends, 1840–1950," in Seymour Harris, ed., *American Economic History* (New York: McGraw Hill, 1961); see also Richard A. Easterlin, "Interregional Differences in Per Capita Income, Population, and Total Income, 1840–1950," in *Trends in the American Economy in the Nineteenth Century* (Princeton: Princeton University Press, 1960).

Table 9-8 Per Capita Income Relatives, by Region, 1840, 1860, 1880, and 1900 (U.S. = 100)

Region	1840	1860	1880	1900
United States	100	100	100	100
Northeast	135	139	141	137
New England	132	143	141	134
Middle Atlantic	136	137	141	139
North Central	68	68	98	103
East North Central	67	69	102	106
West North Central	75	66	90	97
South	76	72	51	51
South Atlantic	70	65	45	45
East South Central	73	68	51	49
West South Central	144	115	60	61
West	–	–	190	163
Mountain	–	–	168	139
Pacific	–	–	204	163

Source: Richard A. Easterlin, "Regional Income Trends, 1840-1950," in Seymour Harris, ed., *American Economic History* (New York: McGraw Hill, 1961), p. 528. Used with permission of McGraw-Hill Book Company.

Easterlin's data indicate that the per capita income level in the antebellum South was significantly below the national average. To many observers, this might suggest that slavery was a retarding force in the South and resulted in relatively low standards of consumer welfare, but Engerman has pointed out that Easterlin's calculations include slaves in the southern population and an estimate of slave maintenance costs in the southern income. If slaves are excluded from the analysis and viewed as intermediate goods or part of the expenses of running southern agriculture, the per capita income of the free South can be calculated. Clearly, it can be argued that this latter view of slaves provides a more valuable measure, since per capita income figures are used as indicators of economic welfare, and the welfare of slaves was held at a subsistence level. Engerman has provided a recalculation of Easterlin's figures, viewing slaves as intermediate goods, and these appear in Table 9–9. The figures show the welfare of the free population, and they do not suggest that the antebellum southern economy was stagnating. On the contrary, the 1860 standard of welfare in the free South exceeded the national average, and the rate of growth in southern per capita income during 1840–60, 1.8 percent, was substantially greater that the national average, 1.3 percent.

Other traditional views concerning the retarding influence of slavery on southern economic development can be questioned. The South's high concentration on the production of agricultural staples need not have resulted in a stagnant economy. If the South's staple products were selling at a high price, and there were favorable terms of trade, there is no reason

Table 9-9 Per Capita Income, by Region, 1840 and 1860 (1860 dollars)

Region	Slaves as Consumers		Slaves as Intermediate Goods	
	1840	1860	1840	1860
United States	$ 96	$128	$109	$144
North	109	141	110	142
Northeast	129	181	130	183
North Central	65	89	66	90
South	74	103	105	150
South Atlantic	66	84	96	124
East South Central	69	89	92	124
West South Central	151	184	238	274

Source: Stanley L. Engerman, "The Effects of Slavery upon the Southern Economy: A Review of the Recent Debate," *Explorations in Entrepreneurial History*, Winter 1967, p. 87.

why it could not have prospered. The West concentrated on the production of staple food products, and no one has suggested that this high degree of specialization was inconsistent with western development. It is commonly argued that southern income distribution was characterized by more inequality than that in the rest of the nation, but this did not have to lead to low rates of capital formation.[16] Our current knowledge of income distribution and its effects on savings suggests that increases in inequality generally lead to increases in savings. These savings may be siphoned off into conspicuous consumption, but they also may lead to productive investment. If southern income were distributed unequally and savings were funneled into conspicuous consumption, the South still could have prospered. The southern concentration on agricultural staples did not require any great degree of capital formation since these goods were produced most efficiently with labor-intensive techniques. Arguments concerning the exhaustion of the soil in the old South have been presented to demonstrate the absence of dynamic entrepreneurship in the South. Engerman has countered these arguments by pointing out that least cost production, given the availability of cheap land in the South, called for movement to new farms rather than refurbishing the soil in the old South, and the westward drift of plantation agriculture was consistent with a profit-motivated business spirit.[17]

---

[16] Fogel and Engerman, "The Economics of Slavery," indicate that the issue of southern income inequality is still under debate. See Fabian Linden, "Economic Democracy in the Slave South: An Appraisal of Some Recent Views," *Journal of Negro History*, April 1946; and Frank L. Owsley, *Plain Folk of the Old South* (Baton Rouge: Louisiana State University Press, 1949).

[17] See Engerman, "The Effects of Slavery," p. 88.

The revisions provided by the new economic history suggest the following view of the economics of plantation slavery on the eve of the Civil War: slavery was profitable to the slave owner; slavery was viable and not about to disappear; and slavery was not inconsistent with the achievement of a level of per capita income in the South comparable with that of northern agricultural areas.[18]

Industrial Slavery

Plantation agriculture employed most slaves during the antebellum period, but Robert S. Starobin has concluded that at the time of the Civil War, industrial slavery employed 160,000–200,000 slaves.[19] About 80 percent of the slaves employed in industry were owned by industrialists; the remaining 20 percent were generally rented from slaveowners for a specified time period. Starobin argues that antebellum textile development in the South was tied to industrial slavery, and, by 1860, southern cotton and woolen textile mills employed more than 5,000 slaves. The iron industry was also heavily dependent on slave labor, and it has been argued that slaves were the chief source of labor for Upper South iron works in 1860. The major iron works in the antebellum South, Tredegar Iron Company of Richmond, had the third largest iron-manufacturing labor force in the nation in 1860 (900), and one-half of these workers were slaves. By 1860, approximately 10,000 slaves were employed in antebellum southern iron works.[20]

Slave labor provided virtually the entire labor force for southern tobacco manufacturers, and, by 1860, almost 15,000 slaves were employed in this industry. The antebellum hemp industry was concentrated in New York, Massachusetts, Missouri, and Kentucky, and Kentucky and Missouri both employed a substantial number of slaves (5,000 and 2,500 respectively). In 1860, approximately 30,000 slaves worked in the agricultural processing industries of sugar refining, rice milling, and gristmilling, and another 30,000 slaves were employed in lumber and naval-stores production.[21] At the time of the war, fisheries and related industries employed approximately 20,000 slaves. Slaves were also used extensively in hand trades (blacksmiths, tanners, coopers, cobblers, carpenters, wheelwrights), cotton ginning and cotton pressing, and mining (coal, iron, gold, lead, salt).[22]

---

[18] The most concise statement of the new view is available in Fogel and Engerman, "The Economics of Slavery"; for a more complete treatment, see Fogel and Engerman, *Time on the Cross* (Boston: Little, Brown and Co., Inc. 1974).

[19] Robert S. Starobin, *Industrial Slavery in the Old South* (New York: Oxford University Press, 1970).

[20] Starobin, *Industrial Slavery,* pp. 13–15.

[21] Starobin, *Industrial Slavery,* pp. 17–28.

[22] Starobin, *Industrial Slavery,* pp. 28–31.

Food Self-Sufficiency in the Antebellum South

The generally accepted view of regional production patterns in antebellum America suggests that a high degree of regional specialization existed; the Northeast concentrated on manufactured goods, the West on foodstuffs, and the South on agricultural staples (cotton, sugar, tobacco, rice). It has been argued that these regional specialization patterns resulted in a great amount of interregional trade; one of the important features of this trade was the dependence of the South on western food products.[23]

Recently, a great deal of question has been raised concerning southern dependence on western foodstuffs. Albert Fishlow argued that many western food products shipped to New Orleans were re-exported outside the South.[24] He concluded that the antebellum South did not have to depend on the West for its food supplies and that prior to the Civil War commercial ties between the West and South became increasingly unimportant. Robert W. Fogel challenged Fishlow's analysis because it concentrated on an examination of New Orleans trade flows. Fogel argued that many of the agricultural staples that were exported from the West to the East were re-exported to South Atlantic ports. He claimed that it was cheaper for the South Atlantic states to purchase food products from New York than from New Orleans. Fishlow countered Fogel's criticism by arguing that many of the re-exports from eastern cities went to the Northeast rather than the South. The exchange between Fogel and Fishlow served to raise doubts concerning the degree of antebellum interdependence between the South and West. It is obvious from census production records that the South did produce significant quantities of many foodstuffs, but whether the region was self-sufficient in food is another question.

Robert E. Gallman has examined the issue of food self-sufficiency in the antebellum South.[25] Restricting his analysis to large plantations in the cotton South, Gallman estimated the supply of and demand for grain and meat, in order to determine the need for external supplies.[26] He concluded

---

[23] A summary of the traditional view is provided by Louis B. Schmidt, "Internal Commerce and the Development of a National Economy Before 1860," *Journal of Political Economy*, December 1939. Recently, Douglass C. North, *The Economic Growth of the United States, 1790–1860* (New York: W. W. Norton, 1966), has provided a restatement of this traditional view.

[24] A full presentation of the Fogel-Fishlow debate concerning the directions of antebellum interregional trade is contained in Ralph Andreano, ed., *New Views on American Economic Development*, (Cambridge, Mass.: Schenkman Publishing, 1965), pp. 187–225.

[25] Robert E. Gallman, "Self Sufficiency in the Cotton Economy of the Antebellum South," in *The Structure of the Cotton Economy of the Antebellum South*. Of related interest in the same volume are the following papers: Raymond C. Battalio and John Kagel, "The Structure of Antebellum Southern Agriculture: South Carolina, A Case Study"; Diane L. Lindstrom, "Southern Dependence Upon Interregional Grain Supplies: A Review of the Trade Flows, 1840–1860"; and Stanley L. Engerman, "The Antebellum South: What Probably Was and What Should Have Been."

[26] Gallman's cotton South included the region that produced 98 percent of the southern cotton crop in 1860.

that the large plantations in the antebellum South were attempting to be self-sufficient in the production of meat and grain and normally were successful in achieving their goal. He argued that cotton production required a concentration of effort at picking time, but during the remainder of the year the planters had a labor surplus. It is suggested that the combination of cheap land and surplus labor encouraged southern food production, and in most cases, grains could be produced without any negative effect on cotton production.

Gallman's efforts to determine whether the cotton South was self-sufficient in meat and grain have been subjected to a great deal of scrutiny by Stanley Engerman.[27] Although Engerman raised many questions concerning Gallman's procedures and suggested directions for future research concerning southern food self-sufficiency, he left Gallman's basic conclusion intact. A recent study by William K. Hutchinson and Samuel H. Williamson corroborated Gallman's findings and concluded that the antebellum South as a whole was generally self-sufficient in the basic foods.[28]

Summary

Recent research has suggested than antebellum plantation slavery was a profitable and viable institution, and the South's expenditure on slaves can be defended as a rational business investment. Most slaves were used in plantation agriculture, but they also were used extensively in other types of agriculture and in industry. Research has also shown that slavery was not inconsistent with southern economic development, and, on the eve of the Civil War, the average standard of living of free southerners was approximately the same as the national average. The old view of a stagnating South, dominated by one crop, and employing an unprofitable and inefficient system of agricultural organization, is inconsistent with all the available empirical evidence.

Suggested Reading

Conrad, Alfred H., and John R. Meyer, "The Economics of Slavery in the Antebellum South," *Journal of Political Economy,* April 1958.

Engerman, Stanley L., "The Effects of Slavery Upon the Southern Economy: A Review of the Recent Debate," *Explorations in Entrepreneurial History,* Winter 1967.

---

[27] Stanley L. Engerman, "The Antebellum South: What Probably Was"; in the same volume, see Eugene Genovese, "Commentary: A Historian's View," pp. 143–47.

[28] William K. Hutchinson and Samuel H. Williamson, "The Self Sufficiency of the Antebellum South: Estimates of the Food Supply," *Journal of Economic History,* September 1971.

Fischbaum, Marvin, and Julius Rubin, "Slavery and the Economic Development of the American South," *Explorations in Entrepreneurial* History, Fall 1968.

Fishlow, Albert, "Antebellum Interregional Trade Reconsidered," in Ralph L. Andreano, ed., *New Views on American Economic Development.* Cambridge, Mass.: Schenkman Publishing, 1965.

———, "Postscript on Antebellum Interregional Trade," in Andreano, ed., *New Views on American Economic Development.*

Fogel, Robert W., "A Provisional View of the 'New Economic History,'" in Andreano, ed., *New Views on American Economic Development.*

———, "American Interregional Trade in the Nineteenth Century," in Andreano, ed., *New Views on American Economic Development.*

——— and Stanley L. Engerman, *Time on the Cross.* Boston: Little, Brown, 1974.

———, "The Economics of Slavery," in Robert W. Fogel and Stanley L. Engerman, eds., *The Reinterpretation of American Economic History.* New York: Harper & Row, 1971.

Foust, James D., and Dale E. Swan, "Productivity and Profitability of Antebellum Slave Labor: A Micro Approach," in William N. Parker, ed., *The Structure of the Cotton Economy of the Antebellum South,* special issue of *Agricultural History,* January 1970.

Gallman, Robert E., "Self Sufficiency in the Cotton Economy of the Antebellum South," in Parker, ed., *The Structure of the Cotton Economy of the Antebellum South.*

Genovese, Eugene D., "The Significance of the Slave Plantation for Southern Economic Development," *Journal of Southern History,* November 1962.

Gunderson, Gerald, "Southern Ante-Bellum Income Reconsidered," *Explorations in Economic History,* Winter 1973.

Hutchinson, William K., and Samuel H. Williamson, "The Self Sufficiency of the Antebellum South: Estimates of the Food Supply," *Journal of Economic History,* September 1971.

Lindstrom, Diane L., "Southern Dependence Upon Interregional Grain Supplies: A Review of the Trade Flows, 1840–1860," in Parker, ed., *The Structure of the Cotton Economy of the Antebellum South.*

Parker, William N., "Slavery and Southern Economic Development: An Hypothesis and Some Evidence," in Parker, ed., *The Structure of the Cotton Economy of the Antebellum South.*

Passell, Peter, "The Impact of Cotton Land Distribution on the Antebellum Economy," *Journal of Economic History,* December 1971.

Phillips, Ulrich B., "The Economic Cost of Slaveholding in the Cotton Belt," *Political Science Quarterly,* June 1905.

Starobin, Robert S., *Industrial Slavery in the Old South.* New York: Oxford University Press, 1970.

Sutch, Richard, and Roger Ransom, "The Ex-Slave in the Post-Bellum South: A Study of the Economic Impact of Racism in a Market Environment," *Journal of Economic History,* March 1973.

Wright, Gavin, "New and Old Views on the Economics of Slavery," *Journal of Economic History,* June 1973.

10
The Economic Impact of the American Civil War

The debate among economic historians over the issue of the economic impact of the Civil War has been especially heated. Traditionally, the war was regarded as a major turning point in American economic history because it insured the successful industrialization of the American economy. Recent investigation by both old and new economic historians has focused attention on the disruptions caused by the conflict, and most economic historians view the war as a major negative disturbance to the economy's long-run growth path. This chapter highlights the major arguments on both sides of this issue.

The Traditional View: The Beard-Hacker Thesis

Traditionally, the Civil War was viewed as a major positive force in the political, social, and economic development of the American economy.[1] Charles A. Beard and Louis M. Hacker are most closely identified with this interpretation, and they argued that American capitalism owed a large part of its development to the Civil War.[2] During the conflict, national political power shifted from southern agrarians to northern industrialists, and the traditional argument held that this shift in control of national politics produced legislation that stimulated industrial growth. The demise of slavery was the significant social change associated with the war. Beard and Hacker

---

[1] An excellent summary of the economic impact of the Civil War is provided by Stanley L. Engerman, "The Economic Impact of the Civil War," *Explorations in Entrepreneurial History,* Spring 1966.

[2] Charles A. Beard and Mary R. Beard, *The Rise of American Capitalism* (New York: Macmillan, 1930); Louis M. Hacker, *The Triumph of American Capitalism* (New York: Columbia University Press, 1940).

argued that the southern economy was stagnating in the antebellum era, and they attributed this stagnation to the inefficient allocation of labor provided by the slave system. The overthrow of slavery created a free labor force that, according to Beard and Hacker, was more conducive to southern industrialization and growth. On the economic side, Beard and Hacker argued that the Civil War had the stimulating effects of other wars; they cited rising business profits, rapid technological development, and a shift within manufacturing to heavy industry to support their assertion of positive war-associated economic growth.

The Beard-Hacker hypothesis that the Civil War represented a major watershed in American economic development has come under severe attack by both old and new economic historians. Nevertheless, the Beard-Hacker thesis is still argued, and Hacker's latest book contains a clear statement reiterating his earlier views concerning the significance of the war.[3]

New Views on the Civil War's Impact on Long-Run Growth Trends

Robert E. Gallman's study of commodity output provides a useful empirical base for assessing the significance of the Civil War to the American economy.[4] Gallman's estimates of the decennial rate of change during 1839–99 in real output, employment, and real output per employee appear in Tables 10–1, 10–2, and 10–3, and it is apparent from the figures that the Civil War decade did not represent a major period of growth for the American economy. On the contrary, the performance of the economy during the war was relatively low. In agriculture and manufacturing, during the period 1839–99, the lowest rate of increase in real value added occurred in the decade 1859–69. The decennial rate of increase in real manufacturing value added during the war decade was especially low (26 percent) compared to the average rate of growth in manufacturing for the nineteenth century (79 percent). Manufacturing employment also increased at a below average rate during the war decade. Gallman's measure of technical efficiency—real value added per worker—showed that during the War there was a negative movement in mining, manufacturing, and construction. After contrasting the Civil War decade to trends during the middle and late nineteenth century, the suggested conclusion is that the period was not conducive to aggregate economic growth, industrialization, or technological development.

However, there are dangers in focusing entirely on the Civil War decade.

[3] Louis M. Hacker, *The Course of American Economic Growth and Development* (New York: Wiley, 1970), Ch. IX.

[4] Robert Gallman, "Commodity Output, 1839–1899," in *Trends in the American Economy in the Nineteenth Century* (Princeton: Princeton University Press, 1960).

Table 10-1 Decennial Rates of Change in Real Value Added, by Commodity Producing Sector, 1839-99 (1879 prices)

End of Decade	Agriculture	Mining	Manufacturing	Construction[a]
1849	26%	138%	152%	48%
1859	51	88	76	85
1869	15	114	26	33
1879	51	118	82	46
1889	25	126	112	56
1899	21	59	51	11
Averages				
1839-99	31	106	79	45
1839-59	38	112	113	66
1869-99	32	99	80	36

Source: Robert E. Gallman, "Commodity Output, 1839-1899," in *Trends in the American Economy in the Nineteenth Century* (Princeton: Princeton University Press, 1960), p. 24. Reprinted by permission of the National Bureau of Economic Research.

[a]In Tables 10-1, 10-2, and 10-3 Gallmans' Variant A has been used for construction.

Table 10-2 Decennial Rates of Change in Employment, by Commodity Producing Sector, 1839-99

End of Decade	Agriculture	Mining and Manufacturing	Construction
1849	32%	88%	33%
1859	27	58	27
1869	10	47	48
1879	27	56	21
1889	19	46	65
1899	8	38	17
Averages			
1839-99	19	55	35
1839-59	29	73	30
1869-99	18	46	33

Source: Gallman, "Commodity Output," p. 30. Reprinted by permission of the National Bureau of Economic Research.

It is possible that the War brought significant benefits to the American economy that would not show up in the decade of wartime disturbances. For this reason, it is useful to compare the average decennial growth rates for the periods 1839–59 and 1869–99 in order to capture the long-run impact of the conflict. (See Tables 10–1, 10–2, and 10–3.) Once again, it is difficult to derive empirical support for the Beard-Hacker proposition that the American economy's growth, especially industrial growth, was positively affected by the war. In most instances, the economy's antebellum

Table 10-3 Decennial Rates of Change in Real Value Added per Worker, by Commodity Producing Sector, 1839-99

End of Decade	Agriculture	Mining and Manufacturing	Construction
1849	–5	36	11
1859	19	12	46
1869	5	–13	–10
1879	19	18	21
1889	5	46	–5
1899	12	9	–5
Averages			
1839-99	9	16	7
1839-59	7	25	27
1869-99	12	24	5

Source: Gallman, "Commodity Output," p. 31. Reprinted by permission of the National Bureau of Economic Research.

growth was significantly greater than postwar growth. Manufacturing output and employment experienced especially rapid relative growth before the Civil War, and the rate of increase in technical efficiency was similar in the antebellum and postwar decades.

Engerman cites the following average annual rates of increase in total commodity output: 1840–60, 4.6 percent; 1860–70, 2.0 percent; and 1870–1900, 4.4 percent.[5] He estimates that manufacturing value added grew at the following annual rates: 1840–60, 7.8 percent; 1860–70, 2.3 percent; and 1870–1900, 6.0 percent. These results suggest that the rate of increase in manufacturing declined in the postwar period, and the postwar growth rate in manufacturing declined relative to the growth of total commodity output.

The Regional Impact of the War

It is generally agreed that the burden of the war fell heavily on the South. Engerman has prepared a regional breakdown of Gallman's commodity output series, and it is apparent from the figures that the war decade brought slow growth to the non-South and heavy absolute losses to the South. (See Table 10–4.) It is estimated that real commodity output in the South declined by 25 percent during 1860–70 and by 1880 was not appreciably higher than the prewar level. Per capita commodity output figures, also prepared by Engerman, bear further testimony to the war's heavy burden on the South. (See Table 10–5.) Before the war, the South had a slight edge over the non-South in per capita commodity output; by 1880,

[5] See Engerman, "The Economic Impact of the Civil War," pp. 178–79.

Table 10-4 Commodity Output, by Region and Sector, 1860-80 (1879 prices; millions of dollars)

Year	Total[a]	Agriculture	Mining and Manufacturing
Non-South			
1860	$1674	$ 853	$ 821
1870	2337	1246	1091
1880	3876	1861	2015
South			
1860	$ 710	$ 639	$ 71
1870	534	477	57
1880	838	738	100

Source: Stanley L. Engerman, "The Economic Impact of the Civil War," *Exploration in Entrepreneurial History,* Spring 1966, p. 180.
[a] Engerman's calculations exclude construction.

Table 10-5 Per Capita Commodity Output, by Region, 1860-80 (1879 prices)

Year	Non-South	South
1860	$ 75	$78
1870	82	48
1880	106	62

Source: Stanley L. Engerman, "The Economic Impact of the Civil War," p. 181.

the South's per capita commodity output was 40 percent below the non-South's average. Real per capita commodity output in the South in 1880 is estimated at 20 percent below the prewar level.

A study by James L. Sellers provided several additional indicators of the war's regional impact.[6] During the war years, the total assessed property valuation of the confederate states declined from $4.4 billion to $1.6 billion. Sellers points out that over $1.6 billion of the decline was due to the emancipation of slaves, and over $1.1 billion was due to declines in property values or actual losses. During the Civil War decade, the total wealth of the South declined by 30 percent; conversely, the total wealth of the North increased by 50 percent during the same period. Sellers argues that a large part of this decline in wealth reflected the declining value of southern real estate.

[6] James L. Sellers, "The Economic Incidence of the Civil War in the South," in Ralph Andreano, ed., *The Economic Impact of the American Civil War* (Cambridge, Mass.: Schenkman Publishing, 1967).

Southern agriculture also suffered heavy wartime destruction. According to Sellers, the following percentage declines occurred between 1860 and 66 in southern livestock: horses, 32 percent; mules, 30 percent; cattle, 35 percent; sheep, 20 percent; and swine, 42 percent. During the decade of the conflict, the value of farm implements declined by 45 percent, and the value of farms declined by almost 50 percent. Sellers indicates that, at the beginning of the twentieth century, southern farm values had just attained their antebellum level; during the same period, northern farm values had more than doubled. More recent evidence concerning the decline of southern agriculture during the postwar decades is provided in a study by Eugene M. Lerner.[7] Lerner presents estimates of the average annual output of major commodities in the South and non-South for 1859, 1866–70, and 1876–80. A summary of his results is found in Table 10–6, and the South's relative decline is clearly documented.

The war also seriously disturbed banking and credit conditions in the South. Sellers indicates that the war decade witnessed a decline in banking capital from $61 million to $17 million and in currency from $51 million to $15 million. Further disruption in the southern capital market was created because many northern capitalists avoided direct investments in the South during the period of Reconstruction.

Southern manufacturing structure was significantly affected by the war. I have argued that there was a great degree of similarity between manufacturing structure in the South and non-South during the antebellum decades, but this similarity ended with the Civil War.[8] During the antebellum period, the South showed significant activity in the metals and machinery industries, and the region's relative degree of concentration in these industries compared favorably with national trends. The destruction of tangible and human capital, the disruption of financial and capital markets, and other factors related to the war's influence worked to encourage southern concentration on resource-intensive manufacturing industries. The relative shift in emphasis in the South is clearly shown by the industry shares of national production exhibited in Table 10–7. The only significant relative gains made by the South during the late nineteenth century came in textiles and lumber; considerable relative declines occurred in the metals and machinery industries (SIC 33–35).

The new labor market situation created by the manumission of slaves and the federal government's war debt policy which put a high share of the burden on the South caused further problems of adjustment. The incidence

[7] Eugene M. Lerner, "Southern Output and Agricultural Income, 1860–80," *Agricultural History*, July 1959. (Also appeared in Andreano, ed., *Economic Impact of the American Civil War.)*

[8] See Albert W. Niemi, Jr., "Structural Shifts in Southern Manufacturing, 1849–1899," *Business History Review*, Spring 1971.

Table 10-6 Average Annual Output of Selected Commodities in the South and Non-South in 1859, 1866-70, and 1876-80

Commodity	South[a]			Non-South		
	1859	1866-70	1876-80	1859	1866-70	1876-80
Cotton (000,000 lbs.)	2373	1213	2395	–	–	–
Barley (000 bu.)	22	121	166	15605	24574	40827
Potatoes (000 bu.)	6600	4969	7158	104500	111840	147696
Corn (000,000 bu.)	283	188	293	556	682	1310
Oats (000,000 bu.)	20	19	40	152	228	367
Wheat (000,000 bu.)	31	18	28	142	216	395
Sweet Potatoes (000,000 bu.)	38	24	32	4	3	5
Rye (000 bu.)	2201	1199	983	18900	16398	19421
Buckwheat (000 bu.)	572	209	219	17000	10442	11024
Tobacco (000,000 lb.)	204	89	133	231	205	364
Sugar Cane (000 short tons)	116	42	107	–	–	–
Rice (000,000 bu.)	7	2	3	–	–	–

Source: Eugene M. Lerner, "Southern Output and Agricultural Income, 1860-80," *Agricultural History*, July 1959.
[a] The South includes the eleven states that seceded from the Union; the non-South includes all other states.

Table 10-7 Southern Shares of National Manufacturing Value Added, by Two Digit Industry, 1860 and 1900

SIC Code Number and Industry	1860	1900
20 Food	12.7%	10.1%
21 Tobacco	50.1	25.8
22 Textiles	5.2	10.9
23 Apparel	3.9	4.0
24 Lumber and Wood Products	21.5	29.9
25 Furniture	6.6	5.5
26 Paper	4.2	1.8
27 Printing and Publishing	5.4	6.8
28 Chemicals	17.2	15.2
29 Petroleum and Coal Products	9.1	5.2
30 Rubber and Plastics	0.0	0.1
31 Leather and Leather Products	8.0	7.0
32 Stone, Clay and Glass Products	9.6	6.2
33 Primary Metals	8.1	7.4
34 Fabricated Metals	8.9	3.3
35 Nonelectrical Machinery	11.4	4.2
36 Electrical Machinery[a]	—	—
37 Transportation Equipment	15.5	12.2
38 Instruments	0.0	1.8
39 Miscellaneous	2.1	1.6
Total	10.5	9.5

Source: The figures were computed from estimates of manufacturing value added, provided by this author in *State and Regional Patterns in American Manufacturing: 1860-1900* (Westport, Conn.: Greenwood Press, 1974).

[a] All machinery is included in SIC 35.

of the war fell most heavily on the states of the old South, and the burdens imposed by the conflict were carried into the twentieth century.

The Impact of the Civil War on Industrialization

The work of Thomas C. Cochran and Stephen Salsbury provides an exchange of views concerning the impact of the Civil War on American industrialization.[9] Cochran attempted to show that the Civil War decade was a period of relatively slow growth. He provided many comparisons of growth in leading industrial indicators (pig iron and copper production, railroad

[9] Thomas C. Cochran, "Did the Civil War Retard Industrialization," *Mississippi Valley Historical Review,* September 1961 (also reprinted in the Andreano, ed., *The Economic Impact of the American Civil War;* Stephen Salsbury, "The Effects of the Civil War on American Industrial Development," in Andreano, ed., *The Economic Impact of the American Civil War.*

construction, cotton consumption, immigration, etc.) for the antebellum period, the war decade, and the postwar period and concluded that the war retarded the growth of industrialization. Salsbury attacked Cochran's analysis and argued that it was too short run, focusing almost exclusively on changes during the Civil War decade. Salsbury argued that the Beard-Hacker proposition was concerned with the long-run stimulus to American industrialization and not with immediate wartime disturbances. Using the same indicators as Cochran, Salsbury compared growth in the pre–Civil War decade, 1850–60, with growth in the postwar decade, 1865–75, and concluded that expansion during the latter period was much more important. If there were immediate negative wartime disturbances, however, the use of 1865 as a base period would provide an artificially low starting point for measuring the war's economic impact; consequently, the value of Salsbury's results must be questioned.

Within manufacturing, it was commonly argued by Beard, Hacker, and others that the Civil War stimulated growth in the heavy industries such as metals and machinery.[10] Harry N. Scheiber has surveyed much of the recent work concerning the economic impact of the Civil War and has resurrected this argument.[11] I have analyzed the war's long-run effects on heavy industry and concluded that it had little or no influence on the basic structure of American manufacturing.[12] Structural movements in American manufacturing show a clear trend toward increased concentration in the metals and machinery industries during the antebellum and war decades. The percentage share of aggregate manufacturing output contributed by the primary and fabricated metals and machinery industries increased as follows: 1849, 15.2 percent; 1859, 18.4 percent; and 1869, 22.1 percent. During the late nineteenth century, the structural shift toward heavy industry subsided, and the metals and machinery share of total manufacturing output fell to 21.9 percent in 1879 and 20.4 percent in 1889.

It should be made clear that the relative shift toward heavy industry during the Civil War decade was, in large part, due to the very low growth in light industry, especially textiles, and was not the result of exceptionally high positive growth in the metals and machinery industries. During 1859–69, real output in the heavy industries increased at a decennial rate of 64.1 percent; for the same period, the following decennial rates of change were recorded: food, 22 percent; apparel, 7 percent; and textiles, 5 percent. Furthermore, the wartime growth in heavy industry was low compared to

[10] See Louis Hacker, *The Triumph of American Capitalism,* pp. 437–38.

[11] Harry N. Scheiber, "Economic Change in the Civil War Era: An Analysis of Recent studies," *Civil War History,* December, 1965, p. 409.

[12] Albert W. Niemi, Jr., "Structural and Labor Productivity Patterns in United States Manufacturing, 1849–1899," *Business History Review,* Spring 1972.

other decades: 1849–59, 103.0 percent; 1869–79, 85.3 percent; and 1879–89, 108.5 percent. The available evidence suggests that the nineteenth-century shift toward heavy industry began apart from the war's influence, and long-run structural developments within manufacturing were relatively unaffected by the conflict.[13]

Summary

At present, most economic historians view the Civil War as a major disruption in the economic progress of the United States. It must be admitted that there were significant changes wrought in American political life, and northerners were able to assume control over national politics. However, this political change does not appear to have resulted in any major change in the structure of the American economy, and postwar economic trends represented a continuation of trends set in motion several decades before the conflict.[14] The disintegration of slavery in the South represented a fundamental change in American social institutions, but, during the postwar period, blacks continued to live at the poverty level and work in low paid unskilled jobs. In all respects, the weight of the empirical evidence gathered by the new economic history runs counter to the Beard-Hacker proposition that the Civil War insured the triumph of American capitalism.

Suggested Reading

Andreano, Ralph L., ed., *The Economic Impact of the American Civil War,* 2nd ed. Cambridge, Mass.: Schenkman Publishing, 1967.

Cochran, Thomas C., "Did the Civil War Retard Industrialization?" *Mississippi Valley Historical Review,* September 1961.

Engerman, Stanley L., "The Economic Impact of the Civil War," *Explorations in Entrepreneurial History,* Spring 1966.

Lerner, Eugene M., "Southern Output and Agricultural Income, 1860–80," *Agricultural History,* July 1959.

Niemi, Albert W., Jr., "Structural and Labor Productivity Patterns in United States Manufacturing, 1849–1899," *Business History Review,* Spring 1972.

---

[13] A full discussion of late nineteenth-century structural developments in American manufacturing is provided in Chapter 7.

[14] See Engerman, "The Economic Impact of the Civil War," pp. 189–90, for a summary of the economic effects of postwar legislation.

Salsbury, Stephen, "The Effects of the Civil War on American Industrial Development," in Andreano, ed., *The Economic Impact of the American Civil War.*

Scheiber, Harry N., "Economic Change in the Civil War Era: An Analysis of Recent Studies," *Civil War History,* December 1965.

Sellers, James L., "The Economic Incidence of the Civil War in the South," in Andreano, ed., *The Economic Impact of the American Civil War.*

11
Technology and American Economic Development

The level and rate of economic progress is a function of the efficiency with which the fundamental economic problem of scarcity is handled. The scarcity problem involves the allocation of scarce resources to unlimited demands in order to produce goods and services. In any society, the level and rate of economic development is largely determined by the efficiency of the resource allocation system; efficiency depends heavily on the current level of technology and its rate of application.[1] Technology refers to the current stock of knowledge regarding the industrial arts, and improvement in technology, or technological change, takes place through the introduction of new products, new methods of production, new techniques of organization, and in many other ways.[2] Technological change allows a greater volume of goods and services to be produced from a given stock of resources; in other words, it permits a more efficient solution to the scarcity problem.

The level of technology existing at any given time places a limit on the output that can be produced with a given factor input. (See Figure 11–1.) For simplification, the diagrammatic treatment in Figure 11–1 assumes that there are only two factors of production, capital and labor. The isoquant Q represents a fixed level of output, and it shows the various combinations

---

[1] Recent studies of the American experience suggest that improvements in technology have been a major factor in the advance of economic growth and welfare; see the discussion at the end of this chapter and in Chapter 17.

[2] The most concise statement of technological change is found in Edwin Mansfield, *Technological Change* (New York: W. W. Norton, 1971); see also Mansfield, *The Economics of Technological Change* (New York: W. W. Norton, 1968).

Figure 11-1 Demonstration of Fixed Technology with Varying Factor Proportions

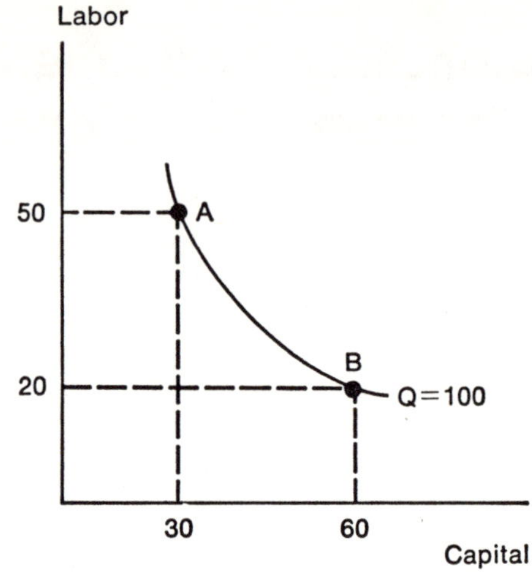

of capital and labor that can be used to produce $Q = 100$.[3] For example, at point *A*, the output level $Q = 100$ is produced by using 50 units of labor and 30 units of capital; at point *B*, the output level $Q = 100$ is produced by using 20 units of labor and 60 units of capital. Along the isoquant, there are an infinite number of possible factor combinations that will each yield an output of $Q = 100$, and the decision to use a particular factor combination will depend on the relative prices of capital and labor. If labor is inexpensive relative to capital, a factor combination such as *A* will be chosen; if labor is expensive relative to capital, a factor combination such as *B* will be chosen.

Figure 11–1 shows the situation with a fixed state of technology. An advance in technology brings about more efficient resource allocation and permits the previous output level to be produced with fewer inputs. In the diagram, technological change can be shown by a shift to the left in the isoquant. For example, in Figure 11–2, technological change is shown by a shift from Q_1 to Q_2, where Q_1 and Q_2 represent the same level of output. For all factor combinations, the technology of Q_2 exhausts fewer resources than the technology of Q_1 to produce the same volume of output. Technological change not only improves the efficiency of utilization of the current stock of resources, but it can introduce new resources into the production function.

In the two-factor world shown in the diagrams, technological change may be neutral, labor-saving, or capital-saving. If technological change

[3] The shape of the isoquant *Q* shows the rate at which capital can be substituted for labor at a constant output level.

Figure 11-2 Demonstration of Technological Change

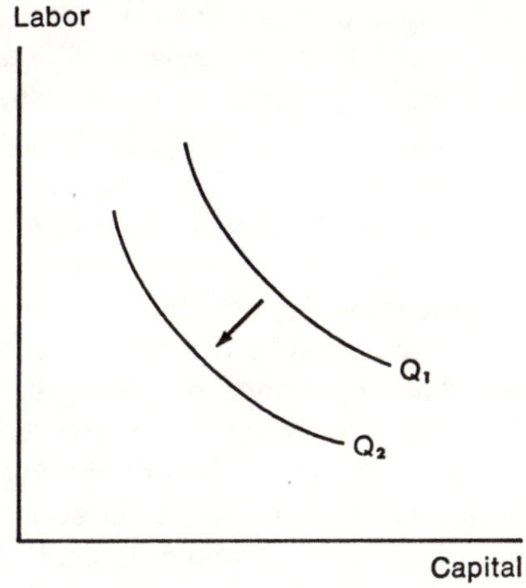

results in an equal percentage reduction in capital and labor, it is neutral; if the percentage reduction in capital is greater than the percentage reduction in labor, it is capital-saving; if the percentage reduction in labor is greater than the percentage reduction in capital, it is labor-saving.[4]

The simplified diagrammatic treatment of technology shows only the substitutability between capital and labor. For the nineteenth-century American economy, the standard argument is that the economy was both labor and capital scarce and resource abundant. Given this factor supply situation, it is argued that America conserved on both capital and labor and concentrated on resource intensive economic activities.[5] The relationship between factor supply conditions and technology has been given formal treatment by H. J. Habakkuk, and this issue will be considered later in this chapter.[6]

The level and rate of change in technology is largely a function of demand factors and supply constraints. The current level of technology is limited by the stock of known resources and the state of knowledge. Demand patterns indicate the needed directions for future research and exploration, and they also show the spectrum of current needs and desires in the marketplace. Nathan Rosenberg and H. J. Habakkuk have argued that consumer demand was an important factor in establishing the bound-

---

[4] See Mansfield, *Technological Change,* pp. 20–21, for a discussion and diagrammatic treatment of the factor intensity of technological change.

[5] See Nathan Rosenberg, *Technology and American Economic Growth* (New York: Harper & Row, 1972), pp. 25–31.

[6] See H. J. Habakkuk, *American and British Technology in the Nineteenth Century* (Cambridge: At the University Press, 1967).

aries of acceptable techniques in nineteenth-century America and Britain.[7] American consumers were willing to purchase mass-produced standardized products, and British consumers were not. This sharp dichotomy in consumer preference was partially responsible for the dominance of handicraft skills in nineteenth-century British industry and mass production techniques in American industry. In addition to supply and demand forces, the rate of development and diffusion of new techniques is also affected by institutional factors such as changes in market structure, legal structure, and social and cultural attitudes toward change.

The above survey of technological change provides a convenient and necessary background for analyzing the role of technology in American economic development. The remainder of this chapter will provide an overview of nineteenth- and twentieth-century trends in American technology and will also include a brief analysis of the following issues: nineteenth- and twentieth-century energy and power sources, the relationship between factor supply conditions and technological change, and the impact of technological change on American economic growth.

Nineteenth- and Twentieth-Century Trends in American Technology

Improvements in American technology in the nineteenth century were made at a very rapid rate and reflected a high level of domestic inventive activity as well as a great deal of adoption of techniques perfected in Britain.[8] America's high educational attainment, foreign in-migration, and late-coming to economic development allowed it to borrow heavily from the technical expertise of the British; American borrowing was especially rapid during the early nineteenth century. The nation quickly developed its own expertise in steam engine construction but lagged behind the British in the railroad and iron industries. By the late 1830s, the large majority of locomotives in operation in America were domestically produced, and, by the late 1850s, American rail production exceeded imports.[9] American railroad technology was structured to fit the needs and conditions of the American economy; for example, wood was used extensively as fuel and was substituted for metal in many areas of construction.[10] The utilization of steam power poses another clear example of adaptation of technology to fit the conditions of the American economy. Steam engines were rapidly

---

[7] See Rosenberg, *Technology and American Economic Growth,* pp. 39–51, and Habakkuk, *American and British Technology,* pp. 123–24 and pp. 208–11.

[8] Throughout this section I have relied heavily on Rosenberg's treatment in *Technology and American Economic Growth.*

[9] British rails continued to play a significant role in American railroad development in the late nineteenth century; see Rosenberg, *Technology and American Economic Growth,* p. 73.

[10] Unlike the Americans, the British tried to conserve on the use of wood in the railroad industry.

applied to river transportation because of the need for improved means of internal trade; however, steam applications in manufacturing came slowly as a result of the abundance of natural water power, and, as late as 1869, 48 percent of the power generated in American manufacturing was produced by water power and 52 percent by steam power.[11]

American technology in the iron industry lagged behind British technology throughout most of the nineteenth century. For most of the antebellum period, the British technology used bituminous coal as fuel whereas the American technology used charcoal. The use of the technologically old charcoal process in the United States was rational given the abundance of wood and the isolation of known deposits of bituminous coal west of the Alleghenies.[12] The problems associated with bituminous coal were eliminated by the British hot blast technique which permitted the use of anthracite coal. This technique was quickly adopted (1850s) in America because it utilized the anthracite coal deposits in eastern Pennsylvania. Anthracite iron production rapidly gave way to coke during the immediate post–Civil War years, and, in the 1870s and 1880s, steel production sharply increased with the rapid diffusion of the Bessemer process. In the late nineteenth century, the open hearth process began to replace the Bessemer process because of its ability to produce high quality steel from phosphorous ores which could not be used by the Bessemer process.[13] (See Tables 11–1 and 11–2.)

The above examples of American adoption of British techniques indicate that the borrowing process displayed a great deal of selectivity. In situations where demand and supply conditions in the American economy were consistent with new technological developments, new techniques were adopted rapidly; where market factors were at odds with the new technology, new techniques were adopted at a slow rate. The clearest examples of the individuality of American technology were shown by the charcoal process in iron making and water-power technology in manufacturing.

In addition to borrowing techniques from abroad, Americans made many significant contributions to nineteenth-century technology. The most characteristic feature of American technology was the principle of inter-

---

[11] See Rosenberg, *Technology and American Economic Growth*, pp. 62–72.

[12] In addition to being isolated, the deposits of bituminous coal contained high amounts of sulfur and produced a low-quality pig iron. For an excellent review of nineteenth-century American technology in the iron industry, see Peter Temin, "A New Look at Hunter's Hypothesis About the Ante-Bellum Iron Industry," *American Economic Review*, May 1964, pp. 344–51.

[13] For a more complete discussion of developments in iron and steel technology, see Rosenberg, *Technology and American Economic Growth*, pp. 75–83. The most comprehensive analysis of the iron and steel industry is Peter Temin, *Iron and Steel in Nineteenth Century America* (Cambridge, Mass.: M.I.T. Press, 1964).

Table 11-1 Percentage Share of Pig Iron Produced with Various Fuels, 1855-1910

Year	Bituminous Coal and Coke	Anthracite Coal and Coke	Charcoal
1855	8%	46%	47%
1860	13	57	30
1865	20	52	28
1870	31	50	20
1875	42	40	18
1880	45	42	13
1885	59	32	9
1890	69	24	7
1895	84	14	2
1900	85	12	3
1905	91	7	2
1910	96	2	1

Source: Peter Temin, *Iron and Steel in Nineteenth Century America: An Economic Inquiry* (Cambridge, Mass.: M.I.T. Press, 1964), pp. 268-69.

Table 11-2 Percentage of Steel Ingots and Castings Produced by Various Methods, 1870-1940

Year	Bessemer	Open Hearth	Crucible	Electric and All Other
1870	54.5%	1.9%	43.6%	
1875	86.0	2.1	9.0%	2.9%
1880	86.1	8.1	5.2	0.6
1885	88.8	7.8	3.4	0.0[a]
1890	86.2	12.0	1.7	0.1
1895	80.3	18.6	1.1	0.0[a]
1900	65.6	33.4	1.0	0.0[a]
1905	54.6	44.8	0.5	0.1
1910	36.1	63.2	0.5	0.2
1915	25.8	73.6	0.4	0.2
1920	21.1	77.5	0.2	1.2
1925	14.8	83.8	0.0[a]	1.4
1930	12.4	86.1	0.0[a]	1.5
1935	8.3	90.1	0.0[a]	1.6
1940	5.5	91.9	0.0[a]	2.6

Source: *Historical Statistics*, Series P 187-232.
[a] Less than 0.05.

changeable parts. The American system, as this practice came to be called, began in the firearms industry but quickly spread to clocks, watches, sewing machines, agricultural implements, locomotives, locks, hardware, ammunition, and bicycles.[14] The basic principle involved in the American system was the substitution of highly sophisticated machinery for handicraft skills. Instead of utilizing expensive handicraft labor to assemble final products, the American technology developed machines that could produce interchangeable parts which could easily be assembled without the expensive finishing touches of handicraft labor. The initial growth of the machine tool industry was largely a response to the demand for machinery to produce interchangeable parts. By the late nineteenth century, machine tool production was a highly specialized operation, and most firms concentrated on the production of a narrow range of products.[15] The American system of standardized production was further refined in the early twentieth century by the introduction of the assembly line (automobiles); more recently, automation of production has carried the American system to higher levels of mechanization.

Rosenberg has argued that a fundamental change in the source of a new technology occurred in the late nineteenth century.[16] Most technological breakthroughs in the nineteenth century, especially before the Civil War, originated from empirical testing; since the late nineteenth century, many new techniques have resulted from advancements in scientific knowledge.[17] Advancements in electricity, electronics, physics, and nuclear energy have revolutionized power and energy technology; advancements in chemistry and biology have created new materials, new combinations of materials, and new plant and animal varieties. These advances in knowledge have extended technology far beyond the limits of an empirically based system. Alloyed steels, plastics, hybrid crops, and synthetic fibers are only a few of the major breakthroughs of the past decades that have resulted from improved scientific knowledge. These advances have extended man's control over the natural resource base and have led to the following decline in the natural resource/G.N.P. ratio: 1870, 36 percent; 1900, 27 percent; 1930, 17 percent; and 1954, 12 percent.[18]

The scientific approach to inventiveness has brought an increasing bureaucratization of technological change and has stimulated increased

---

[14] The principle of interchangeable parts was later applied in the production of automobiles and consumer and producer durables.

[15] See Rosenberg, *Technology and American Economic Growth,* pp. 99–101. For further treatment of the machine tool industry, see the following: Duncan McDougall, "Machine Tool Output, 1861–1910," in *Output, Employment, and Productivity in the United States After 1800,* Conference on Research in Income and Wealth, Studies in Income and Wealth, National Bureau of Economic Research, Vol. 30 (New York: Columbia University Press, 1966); Ross M. Robertson, "Changing Production of Metalworking Machinery, 1860–1920," in *Output, Employment, and Productivity.*

[16] See Rosenberg, *Technology and American Economic Growth,* Chapter V.

[17] For an excellent statement of the practical nature of nineteenth-century American technology, see Alexis de Tocqueville, *Democracy in America* (New York: Century, 1898), Vol. 2, pp. 40–53.

[18] See Rosenberg, *Technology and American Economic Growth,* pp. 145–46.

Table 11-3 Percentage of Patents Issued to Individuals, United States Corporations, Foreign Corporations, and the United States Government, 1901-62

Year	Individuals	United States Corporations	Foreign Corporations	United States Government
1901	81.8%	17.1%	1.1%	—
1906	79.4	19.4	1.2	—
1911	75.4	23.1	1.5	—
1916	72.3	26.3	1.4	—
1921	71.7	26.1	2.2	—
1925	65.3	31.9	2.8	—
1930	52.5	43.6	3.9	—
1935	43.7	51.3	5.0	0.0[a]
1940	41.7	52.5	5.7	0.1
1945	35.5	61.9	2.3	0.3
1950	44.1	50.6	3.9	1.4
1955	39.2	52.9	5.7	2.2
1960	27.7	59.8	9.9	2.6
1962	27.8	58.5	11.5	2.2

Source: *Historical Statistics,* Series W 66-76.
[a] Less than 0.05.

expenditure for research and development. Table 11–3 shows the percentage distribution of patents by major source, and the sharp decline in individual initiative is clear.[19] At the beginning of the twentieth century, individuals received 80 percent of all patents; by the 1960s, individuals received less than 30 percent. A recent study by Yale Brozen showed that industrial research and development expenditures increased from 0.2 percent of G.N.P. in 1929 to 2.0 percent in 1960.[20] Brozen's study also revealed that research and development expenditures increased from 2 percent of total firm expenditures in 1929 to over 20 percent in 1960. Table 11–4 shows that most research and development is funded by the federal government (55–65 percent) and private industry (30–40 percent). Universities, colleges, and other nonprofit institutions have generally contributed 5 percent or less of total research and development expenditures. National defense has been an important area for research and development spending, and, during the period 1955–70, approximately 50 percent of total research and development spending by all sources went into defense and space related projects.[21]

[19] For an excellent treatment of patents and American economic growth, see Jacob Schmookler, *Invention and Economic Growth* (Cambridge, Mass.: Harvard University Press, 1966).

[20] Yale Brozen, "The Future of Industrial Research," *Journal of Business,* October 1961, p. 437.

[21] *Statistical Abstract,* 1971, p. 508.

Table 11-4 Percentage Distribution of Funding of Research and Development Expenditures, by Sector, 1955-70

Sector	1955	1960	1965	1970
Federal Government	55.9%	63.7%	63.8%	55.6%
Industry	40.0	32.8	32.0	39.3
University and College	3.0	2.4	3.0	3.7
Other Nonprofit Institutions	1.1	1.1	1.2	1.4

Source: *Statistical Abstract,* 1971, p. 509, and 1973, p. 523.

Energy and Power Sources in the Nineteenth and Twentieth Centuries

Antebellum American industry depended heavily on natural sources of power and energy. The transition from water power to steam occurred slowly in American manufacturing, and Allen H. Fenichel has shown that steam power did not exceed water power in manufacturing until the late 1860s.[22] However, the shift from water to steam came quickly in the 1880s and 1890s, and, by 1899, steam generated over 80 percent of power capacity in American manufacturing. During the early twentieth century, electricity replaced steam power in most industries. Sam H. Schurr and Bruce C. Netschert showed that electricity accounted for 5 percent of total horsepower generation in manufacturing in 1899 and over 80 percent in 1929.[23] Rosenberg argued that electrification of American industry played a significant role in increasing productivity because the flexible nature of electric power permitted more efficient plant design.[24]

Schurr and Netschert showed that, in 1850, 90 percent of American energy consumption (excluding wind, water, animal, and human power) was generated by wood. (See Table 11–5.) Between 1850 and 1910, there was a steady decline in the use of wood as a fuel and a steady rise in the use of coal, and, by 1910, coal accounted for over 75 percent of all energy consumption, and wood accounted for approximately 10 percent. The importance of coal has declined in the twentieth century, and, by 1955, coal produced less than 30 percent of the energy consumed in the United States. Recent decades have seen a sharp increase in the share of energy derived from oil and natural gas. By 1955, oil (40 percent) and natural gas (25 per-

---

[22] Allen H. Fenichel, "Growth and Diffusion of Power in Manufacturing, 1838–1919," in *Output, Employment, and Productivity,* p. 476.

[23] Sam H. Schurr and Bruce C. Netschert, *Energy in the American Economy, 1850–1975* (Baltimore: Johns Hopkins, 1960), p. 187.

[24] Rosenberg, *Technology and American Economic Growth,* p. 162.

Table 11-5 Specific Energy Sources as Percentages of Aggregate Energy Consumption, 1850-1955

Year	Bituminous Coal	Anthracite	Oil	Natural Gas	Natural Gas Liquids	Hydro-Power	Fuel Wood
1850	4.7%	4.6%	—	—	—	—	90.7%
1855	7.3	7.7	—	—	—	—	85.0
1860	7.7	8.7	.1%	—[a]	—	—	83.5
1865	9.6	8.9	.3	—[a]	—	—	81.2
1870	13.8	12.7	.3	—[a]	—	—	73.2
1875	19.9	13.4	.3	—[a]	—	—	66.4
1880	26.7	14.3	1.9	—[a]	—	—	57.0
1885	33.4	16.9	.7	1.5%	—	—	47.5
1890	41.4	16.5	2.2	3.7	—	.3%	35.9
1895	45.8	18.8	2.2	1.9	—	1.2	30.1
1900	56.6	14.7	2.4	2.6	—	2.6	21.0
1905	61.2	14.5	4.6	2.8	—	2.9	13.9
1910	64.3	12.4	6.1	3.3	—	3.3	10.7
1915	62.7	12.2	7.9	3.8	—	3.9	9.5
1920	62.3	10.2	12.3	3.8	.2%	3.6	7.5
1925	58.4	7.3	18.5	5.3	.6	3.1	6.8
1930	50.3	7.3	23.8	8.1	1.0	3.3	6.1
1935	45.6	6.3	26.9	9.4	0.9	4.1	6.8
1940	44.7	4.9	29.6	10.6	1.1	3.6	5.4
1945	44.8	4.0	29.4	11.8	1.5	4.5	3.9
1950	33.9	2.9	36.2	17.0	2.2	4.6	3.3
1955	27.2	1.5	40.0	22.1	2.9	3.7	2.6

Source: Sam H. Schurr and Bruce C. Netschert, *Energy in the American Economy, 1850-1975* (Baltimore: Johns Hopkins, 1960), p. 36.
[a] Not available.

cent) accounted for major shares of America's energy consumption, and petroleum's importance has increased in recent years.[25] Political events in the early 1970s raised questions about the rationality of a petroleum based energy system in a nation such as the United States which has limited petroleum reserves. This situation has spawned a search for alternative power sources such as nuclear and solar energy and has raised the issue of making more adequate use of the nation's large coal reserves.

Factor Proportions and Technological Change: The Habakkuk Thesis

A recent study by H. J. Habakkuk argued that America adopted new technology at a more rapid rate than England in the nineteenth century because of its factor supply conditions.[26] Whereas the American economy was characterized by an extreme shortage of labor relative to capital and natural resources, England's economy was characterized by a surplus of labor relative to capital and natural resources. Habakkuk argued that the scarcity of labor in America encouraged rapid adoption and invention of new techniques and led to capital intensive production.[27] On the contrary, the large elastic supply of cheap labor available in England did not promote the adoption and invention of labor-saving techniques. Habakkuk recognized that capital also was scarce in America, but he pointed out that the mobility of capital allowed the United States to attract foreign investment and partially overcome the shortage of domestic savings.

As a result of factor proportions differences, Habakkuk claimed that the Americans and British developed differing views concerning the time horizon for scrapping machines. Americans were willing to scrap machines at an early age, and they built nondurable machinery so that they could afford to scrap it early and install a new machine that incorporated the most recent advances in knowledge. The British, on the other hand, built durable, heavy equipment that could not be scrapped economically at an early age, and, instead, they maintained and repaired the old machines. Habakkuk argued that the Americans were concerned with maximizing the productivity of labor, and, therefore, they wanted labor to have access to

---

[25] By 1971, 72 percent of total energy consumption (mineral fuels and hydropower) was provided by crude petroleum and natural gas, and 23 percent was provided by coal; see *Statistical Abstract,* 1972, p. 506.

[26] Habakkuk, *American and British Technology.*

[27] For further treatment of the issue of labor scarcity and American technology in the nineteenth century, see the following: Peter Temin, "Labor Scarcity and the Problem of American Industrial Efficiency in the 1850's," *Journal of Economic History,* September 1966; Temin, "Labor Scarcity in America," *Journal of Interdisciplinary History,* Winter 1971; and Robert W. Fogel, "The Specification Problem in Economic History," *Journal of Economic History,* September 1967.

machinery that embodied the most recent advances in technology. On the contrary, since the British could obtain a virtually unlimited supply of labor at a constant wage, they were concerned with maximizing profit on the capital investment. Another factor encouraging the Americans to scrap equipment rather than repair it were the high labor costs involved in maintaining and repairing old machines.

Habakkuk also pointed to several sociological and demand factors that may have influenced the rate of adoption of new technology in the United States and Britain. He claimed that English society was antimechanistic, and this attitude may have mitigated against the adoption of new methods of production. American society was more open and free from preconceptions and traditions, and, therefore, it was better suited to the new technology. Furthermore, the political consequences of technological unemployment in England were much more serious than in the United States. Finally, Habakkuk argued that American industry was faced by a large middle class demand for low-quality standardized products that could be produced by mechanized techniques; consumer demand in England was much more diverse and was not conducive to mass-production technology.

The Impact of Technological Change on American Economic Growth

Recent research into the sources of economic growth has focused attention on the crucial importance of improvements in the techniques of production.[28] Although efficiency improvements were important, quantitative increases in the factors of production accounted for the bulk of our nineteenth-century growth.[29] Since the turn of the century, improvements in the quality of inputs and increases in the efficiency of input utilization have accounted for an increasing share of American economic growth, and Edward F. Denison's estimates show that by the 1930s qualitative improvements were a more important source of growth than quantitive increases in factors of production.[30] (See Table 11–6.) Denison's calculations show the portion of growth due to the increase in total input and the increase in output per unit of input. The latter factor represents growth achieved through advances in knowledge, improved application of knowledge, and economies of scale.[31] Denison included the following qualitative

---

[28] See Edward F. Denison, *The Sources of Economic Growth in the United States and the Alternatives Before Us* (New York: Committee for Economic Development, 1962), and Solow, "Technical Change and the Aggregate Production Function."

[29] See Robert E. Gallman, "Commodity Output, 1839–1899," in *Trends in the American Economy in the Nineteenth Century* (Princeton: Princeton University Press, 1960), p. 34.

[30] Denison, *The Sources of Economic Growth*, p. 266.

[31] Scale refers to the size of the firm's operation. Economies of scale are achieved when expansion of the size of operation (increase in inputs) results in a more than proportionate increase in output.

Table 11-6 Percentage of Growth in Total Real National Income Explained by Selected Factors, 1909-57

Factor	1909-29	1929-57
Real National Income	100%	100%
Increase in Total Inputs	80	68
Labor (adjusted for quality change)	54	54
Employment and hours	39	27
Education	12	23
Increased experience and better utilization of female workers	2	4
Changes in age-sex composition	0	0
Land	0	0
Capital	26	15
Increase in Output Per Unit of Input	20	32
Advance of knowledge and its application	—[a]	20
Economies of scale	10	11

Source: Edward F. Denison, *The Sources of Economic Growth in the United States and the Alternatives Before Us* (New York: Committee for Economic Development, 1962), p. 266.
[a] Not available.

improvements in the labor supply in his calculation of growth due to increased labor input: increased educational attainment, increased experience, and better utilization of female workers. Each of these factors results in improved efficiency of labor, and, in order to fully demonstrate the significant relationship between efficiency improvements and recent American economic growth, I have separated the qualitative improvements in labor from the pure quantitative increases in employment and hours.

With this reconstruction, it can be argued that quantitative increases in capital and labor accounted for 65 percent of American growth between 1909 and 29 and 42 percent between 1929 and 57. Over 50 percent of the total increase in real national income between 1929 and 57 was due to increased education, advances in knowledge and its application, and economies of scale. Table 11–7 shows the relationship between quantitative and qualitative changes in productive factors and growth in real national income per employed person. The results show that qualitative improvements accounted for approximately 80 percent of the increased real income per employee between 1909 and 29 and for virtually the entire increase between 1929 and 57.

Denison's results dramatize the strong linkage between advances in knowledge and education and economic growth; the relationship between per capita growth and qualitative improvements is particularly striking. It is clear that improvements in economic welfare in the modern American economy are heavily dependent on technological advance. Denison's re-

Table 11-7 Percentage of Growth in Real National Income Per Employed Person Explained by Selected Factors, 1909-57

Factor	1909-29	1929-57
Real National Income Per Person	100%	100%
Increase in Total Inputs Per Person	54	42
Labor	34	36
Effect of shorter hours on quality of a man-years work	0	−12
Annual hours	−19	−33
Effect of shorter hours on quality of a man-hours work	19	21
Education	29	42
Increased experience and better utilization of female workers	5	7
Changes in age-sex composition	1	−1
Land	−9	−3
Capital	29	9
Increase in Output Per Unit of Input	46	58
Advance of Knowledge and Its Application	—[a]	36
Economies of scale	23	21

Source: Denison, *The Sources of Economic Growth,* p. 270.
[a] Not available.

sults have been corroborated by other research, and more attention will be given to the role of efficiency changes in American economic progress in Chapter 17.[32]

Summary

Technological change has been a major force underlying the steady improvement in the American standard of living. In the nineteenth and early twentieth centuries, new technology was developed primarily through individual initiative and empirical testing; in recent decades, new technology has been developed through basic research conducted by corporate research teams. In both instances, the rate of technological change has been rapid, and technology has demonstrated a high degree of adaptability to

[32] See Solow, "Technical Change and the Aggregate Production Function;" John W. Kendrick, "Productivity Trends: Capital and Labor," *Review of Economics and Statistics,* August 1956; F. C. Mills, "The Role of Productivity in Economic Growth," *American Economic Review,* May 1952; Jacob Schmookler, "Changing Efficiency of the American Economy, 1869–1938," *Review of Economics and Statistics,* August 1952; and Moses Abramovitz, "Resource and Output Trends in the United States Since 1870," *American Economic Review,* May 1956.

existing economic conditions. Currently, the development of severe shortages in conventional energy supplies is stimulating research and development into nuclear and solar power. In addition to the energy shortage, air and water pollution will make technology a crucial factor in future growth and development.

Suggested Reading

Brozen, Yale, "The Future of Industrial Research," *Journal of Business,* October 1961.

Denison, Edward F., *The Sources of Economic Growth in the United States and the Alternatives Before Us.* New York: Committee for Economic Development, 1962.

DuBoff, Richard B., "The Introduction of Electric Power in American Manufacturing," *Economic History Review,* December 1967.

Feller, Irwin, "The Urban Location of United States Invention, 1860–1910," *Explorations in Economic History,* Spring 1971.

Fenichel, Allen H., "Growth and Diffusion of Power in Manufacturing, 1838–1919," in *Output, Employment, and Productivity in the United States after 1800,* Conference on Research in Income and Wealth, Studies in Income and Wealth, National Bureau of Economic Research, Vol. 30. New York: Columbia University Press, 1966.

Fogel, Robert W., "The Specification Problem in Economic History," *Journal of Economic History,* September 1967.

Habakkuk, H. J., *American and British Technology in the Nineteenth Century.* Cambridge: At the University Press, 1967.

Higgs, Robert, "American Inventiveness, 1870–1920," *Journal of Political Economy,* May/June 1971.

Mansfield, Edwin, *Technological Change.* New York: W. W. Norton, 1971.

McDougall, Duncan, "Machine Tool Output, 1861–1910," in *Output, Employment, and Productivity in the United States.*

Rosenberg, Nathan, "Factors Affecting the Diffusion of Technology," *Explorations in Economic History,* Fall 1972.

———, "Technological Change in the Machine Tool Industry, 1840–1910," *Journal of Economic History,* December 1963.

———, *Technology and American Economic Growth.* New York: Harper & Row, 1972.

Strassman, W. Paul, *Risk and Technological Innovation: American Manufacturing Methods During the Nineteenth Century.* Ithaca, N.Y.: Cornell University Press, 1959.

Temin, Peter, "A New Look at Hunter's Hypothesis About the Ante-Bellum Iron Industry," *American Economic Review,* May 1964.

———, "Labor Scarcity and the Problem of American Industrial Efficiency in the 1850's," *Journal of Economic History,* September 1966.

———, "Labor Scarcity in America," *Journal of Interdisciplinary History,* Winter 1971.

———, "Steam and Waterpower in the Early Nineteenth Century," *Journal of Economic History,* June 1966.

12
Banking and the Money Supply

Financial institutions play a crucial role in the process of economic growth. The essential function provided by banks and other financial institutions is to serve as intermediaries between savings and investment. (See Chapter 1, Figure 1–1.) Individuals who save are generally not those who invest, and financial institutions collect the surplus funds of savers and make them available through loans to entrepreneurs for investment purposes. In addition to performing this function of credit creation, financial institutions—especially banks—stimulate the rate of economic growth by monetizing economic activity through the establishment of a system of money and prices. The development of a sound money and price system encourages production for the market and discourages production for self-sufficiency. Market orientation promotes specialization in production and results in an overall improvement in efficiency.

This chapter is concerned with the institutional structure and operation of American banks in the nineteenth and twentieth centuries. Throughout most of the period from the Constitutional Convention to the establishment of the Federal Reserve system (1913), the nation operated without a formal central bank. There were several abortive attempts at central banking in the antebellum period, and the United States Treasury provided some of the functions of a central bank in the middle and late nineteenth century. However, throughout much of this period, especially before the Civil War, the creation of credit and the issuance of paper currency were largely determined by the initiative and decision of individual bankers. All commercial banks chartered during the antebellum decades and a large number of banks chartered in the post–Civil War period were chartered by state governments, and the restrictions and conditions of bank operation were as varied as the state legislatures granting bank charters. Despite this heterogeneity in nineteenth-century banking institutions, the nation developed a workable mechanism of credit creation and an acceptable means of exchange.

The institutional structure and credit creation and money issuing functions of banks will be examined in this chapter. Attention will be given to the following topics: antebellum state commercial banking activity, antebellum experiments in central banking, post–Civil War developments in national banking, the Federal Reserve system, changes in the composition of the money supply, greenbacks, the monetization of silver, and nineteenth-century price trends.

Operation of State Commercial Banks

The first commercial banks in the United States were established in Philadelphia (1781), New York (1784), and Boston (1784). Bank chartering was substantial in the late eighteenth and early nineteenth centuries, and, by 1811, there were eighty-eight commercial banks in the United States which, with two exceptions, had been chartered by state legislatures. Some bank charters contained rigid specifications concerning the minimum capital stock and the maximum ratio of notes to specie; however, bank charters generally were not restrictive, and there was a great deal of variation between state regulations regarding banking operation.

State-chartered commercial banks performed the traditional functions of receiving deposits and making loans. Loans could be made by issuing state bank notes directly to the borrower or by crediting the borrower's account by the amount of the loan. During most of the antebellum period, bank loans were usually made by issuing notes to borrowers, but, by the middle nineteenth century, an increasing percentage of loans was made by crediting the borrower's account with deposits which could be tapped by check.

State restrictions allowed a great deal of flexibility in bank operation. Banks in large eastern cities generally operated according to sound banking principles and restricted their loans and note issue to conform to the specie base.[1] Banks in the South and West generally were not as conservative as eastern banks, and many issued liberal quantities of notes relative to their available specie.[2] Within regions, urban banks were usually more conservative than rural banks, and the overall quality of banks deteriorated as the distance from major financial centers increased.

Because of the quality differences between banks, a discounted price mechanism existed for commercial bank notes. Notes that were easily con-

---

[1] It was in a bank's interest to maintain convertibility between its notes and specie. If a bank were to issue too many notes and did not meet customers' demands for specie, the value of its notes would decline and so would its ability to lend.

[2] There are many stories about rural banks in the West and South that issued thousands of dollars in notes with little or no specie backing; however, despite these abuses, there were many sound banks in the West and South, particularly in the larger urban areas.

vertible into specie generally circulated at par; notes without specie backing circulated at a discount ranging from 1 percent to an excess of 50 percent. The discount on notes increased with the distance of note circulation from the bank of issue, although, on notes of poorly managed banks, the discount was heavy even in local markets. The heterogeneity of the money supply created numerous problems in exchange and tended to restrict the usage of many bank notes to local trade. The absence of uniform state banking regulations precluded the establishment of a national currency, and, instead, the banking policies of the early nineteenth century created a heterogeneous supply of paper money whose quality was as variable as the operating procedures of banks.

The First Bank of the United States

Alexander Hamilton argued that the United States needed a central type bank that would act as the fiscal agent for the federal government, and, in 1791, Congress chartered the First Bank of the United States for twenty years.[3] Hamilton wanted a bank that was independent of executive authority but that would help the government and the economy by serving as depository for federal funds, stimulating economic growth, stabilizing monetary conditions, and lending money to the government during emergencies. The Bank was successful in performing its function as fiscal agent for the federal government, and it also was actively engaged in lending money to business and government.

In addition to performing its fiscal function, the Bank brought about monetary stability by curtailing the note issue of state commercial banks. The Bank's control over the operation of commercial banks stemmed from its conservative lending policy. The Bank made loans and issued high-quality notes that circulated at par; however, these notes represented a small share of the total volume of paper money. Because of its smaller volume of note circulation, the Bank became a net holder of state commercial bank notes. The Bank would present its net holdings of state bank notes and demand payment in specie. The threat of periodic specie demands by the Bank of the United States forced state banks to adopt some meaningful note/specie ratio, and this automatically forced them to reduce their note issue. As all banks adopted a somewhat uniform note/specie ratio, the money supply became relatively homogeneous, and the discount between various paper currencies was drastically reduced.

The Bank did not view its control function as a means for driving state banks out of business. State banks were providing many useful functions, and they were the most important and often the only source of credit in rural

---

[3] The Bank of Philadelphia, the largest private bank in the nation, became the First Bank of the United States and was capitalized for $10 million with 80 percent of the capital subscribed by the private sector and 20 percent by the federal government.

areas. The Bank was merely trying to impose sound banking principles on the state banks. If all banks adhered to a reasonable note/specie ratio, the wild fluctuations in the amount of currency in circulation that resulted from periodic specie demands would be partially overcome, and the supply of paper money would be more or less homogeneous. Those banks which could not redeem all of their notes but showed signs of bringing their note/specie ratio to manageable proportions were allowed to stay in operation, and, in some cases, they obtained short-term specie loans from the Bank.

The Second Bank of the United States

The charter for the First Bank of the United States expired in 1811, and the Bank was not rechartered. The Bank had performed effectively and had provided many of the services of a central bank; however, its control of state commercial bank operations created a great deal of opposition from state bankers, particularly in rural areas. Other opposing groups objected to the Bank's power, the English control of its stock, and its restrictive credit policies. The termination of the First Bank was followed by a tremendous increase in state banking activity which reflected the need for additional banking services and the opportunity to operate without restrictions. Between 1811 and 1816, the number of state banks increased from 88 to 246, and the issue of bank notes expanded at a rapid rate and caused a tremendous inflation.[4] (See Table 12–1.) By 1814, specie payments had been suspended by most banks outside New England and New York, and, by 1816, specie payments had been suspended by all banks. The homogeneity of the money supply had been destroyed, and monetary conditions were more unstable than they had been in the early days of the First Bank of the United States.

The chaotic monetary situation was coupled with financial difficulties in funding the War of 1812, and these conditions provided the stimulus needed to charter the Second Bank of the United States. This bank, similar to the First, represented a combination of public and private funding and direction and was given a twenty year charter (1816–36).[5] The Bank was poorly run and ineffective between 1816 and 1819, but the situation was reversed during 1819–23, and, between 1823 and 1832, the Bank operated as an effective government fiscal agent and brought a high degree of monetary stability to the economy.[6]

---

[4] George R. Taylor, *The Transportation Revolution* (New York: Harper & Row, 1968), p. 331, concluded that the inflation in 1811 was the worst in the nineteenth century. An examination of wholesale prices is provided later in this chapter, and it reveals that the highest price levels in the nineteenth century were reached in 1815 and 1865; see George F. Warren and Frank A. Pearson, *Prices* (New York: Wiley, 1933), pp. 25–27.

[5] The Second Bank was capitalized for $35 million ($28 million private and $7 million federal government) and had twenty-five directors (twenty private and five federal government).

[6] For a careful treatment of the Second Bank's operations, see Ralph C. H. Catterall, *The Second Bank of the United States* (Chicago: University of Chicago Press, 1902).

Table 12-1 Number of State-Chartered Banks, 1811-65

Year	Number of Banks
1811	88
1815	208
1816	246
1820	307
1830	329
1834	506
1835	704
1836	713
1837	788
1838	829
1839	840
1840	901
1841	784
1842	692
1843	691
1844	696
1845	707
1846	707
1847	715
1848	751
1849	782
1850	824
1851	879
1852	815
1853	750
1854	1208
1855	1307
1856	1398
1857	1416
1858	1422
1859	1476
1860	1562
1861	1601
1862	1492
1863	1466
1864	1089
1865	349

Source: The 1811-30 figures were obtained from *Historical Statistics,* Series X 1-5; the 1834-65 figures were obtained from *Banking Studies,* Board of Governors of the Federal Reserve System, Second Reprint, 1948, p. 418.

The Second Bank operated very much like its predecessor. It accumulated large amounts of state bank notes and redeemed its net holdings for specie payment. This policy forced state banks to restrict their note issue, and it brought a sharp reduction in inflation and greatly reduced the discount between paper currencies. Despite these improvements, throughout the Second Bank's tenure many rural bank notes had a narrow geographic market and suffered large discounts when circulated outside the local trading area. By the late 1820s, however, the money supply was relatively homogeneous, and the Bank had effectively created monetary stability.

The Bank's achievements were substantial, but there were many who still opposed the concept of a single powerful financial institution. Andrew Jackson was elected President in 1828 and made it clear that he would lead the fight against recharter in 1836 if re-elected in 1832. The Bank president, Nicholas Biddle, raised the issue of rechartering the Bank during the election campaign of 1832, and, in that year, Congress passed a bank rechartering bill which Jackson vetoed. In 1833, Jackson began withdrawing funds and depositing them in state banks, and the Bank's power was eroded well before its charter ran out in 1836.[7] The Treasury performed some central bank functions during the middle and late nineteenth century, but it was not until the establishment of the Federal Reserve system in 1913 that the United States had a formal central banking structure.[8]

Developments in Money and Banking Prior to the Civil War

When it became clear that the Second Bank of the United States would not be rechartered, there was a sharp increase in the number of state banks. (See Table 12–1.) However, the experience of the First and Second Banks had demonstrated the benefits of banking regulation, and many states imposed restrictions regarding note issues, minimum capital requirements, and bank examinations.[9] State reforms were not strong enough to create a homogeneous money supply, and, by 1860, there were over 1,500 banks issuing notes in a variety of denominations. Most notes were circulated at a discount, although, for large city banks, the discount was generally small. By the 1850s, the heterogeneity of the money supply was so great that reporting services developed which provided quotations regarding the current discount on individual bank currency. The issue of over 9,000 different types of notes by over 1,500 banks also created immense problems of

---

[7] For an excellent discussion of the battle between Biddle and Jackson concerning the Second Bank, see Jacob Meerman, "The Climax of the Bank War: Biddle's Contraction, 1833–34," *Journal of Political Economy,* August 1963, and Peter Temin, "The Economic Consequences of the Bank War," *Journal of Political Economy,* March/April 1968. For further discussion of this period, see Peter Temin, *The Jacksonian Economy* (New York: W. W. Norton, 1969), and Hugh Rockoff, "Money, Prices, and Banks in the Jacksonian Era," in Robert W. Fogel and Stanley L. Engerman, eds., *The Reinterpretation of American Economic History,* (New York: Harper & Row, 1971).

[8] Taylor has argued that the organization of the Second Bank of the United States was not a suitable format for central banking in the United States; see *Transportation Revolution,* pp. 310–11. For further discussion of central banking during the antebellum period, see Richard H. Timberlake, Jr., "The Specie Standard and Central Banking in the United States Before 1860," *Journal of Economic History,* September 1961.

[9] See Taylor, *Transportation Revolution,* pp. 313–18, for an excellent review of state banking reforms.

Table 12-2 State Bank Notes in Circulation, 1800-1863 (millions of dollars)

Year	Outstanding State Bank Notes
1800	$ 10.5
1810	28.0
1820	44.8
1830	61.0
1832	91.5
1835	103.7
1837	149.2
1840	107.0
1843	58.6
1845	89.6
1847	105.5
1850	131.4
1852	171.7
1854	204.7
1858	155.2
1860	207.1
1862	183.8
1863	238.7

Source: *Annual Report of the Comptroller of the Currency*, 1919, Vol. II, p. 35.

counterfeiting, and financial guides also provided information on counterfeit money.

State banking reforms not only failed to produce homogeneity in the money supply, but they also failed to stabilize the amount of currency in circulation. Demands for specie caused sharp fluctuations in the volume of circulating currency. (See Table 12–2.) The amount of circulating currency and monetary stability were dependent on the collective decisions and actions of individual bankers, and, despite attempts at state reform, bankers maintained a great deal of autonomy and independence.

A significant change took place in bank lending operations during the antebellum period. In the early nineteenth century, banks had made loans by issuing bank notes directly to the borrower. By the 1830s, it was common to make loans in large eastern cities by crediting the borrowers account with demand deposits. During the middle nineteenth century, checking grew rapidly in importance in large cities everywhere, but it was not until the late nineteenth century that checking became common in rural areas.[10]

[10] Another reason for the rapid decline of notes relative to deposits was the tax the National Bank Act put on outstanding state bank notes; see the discussion later in this chapter. The ratio of notes/deposits moved as follows: 1835, 1.25; 1845, 1.02; 1860, .81; 1870, .43; 1880, .29; 1890, .07. See the Board of Governors of the Federal Reserve System, *Banking Studies*, Second Reprint, 1948, p. 417.

In addition to the paper instruments that circulated as money, gold and silver coins were a major component of American currency in the antebellum period. Data from the *Annual Report of the Comptroller of the Currency* indicate that before the 1840s state bank notes generally comprised 65–75 percent of the currency in circulation.[11] By the 1840s, however, the value of state bank notes and specie in circulation was about equal, and, by the late 1850s, state bank notes represented approximately 40 percent of circulating currency.[12]

The Development of National Banking

Proponents of national banking argued that the establishment of uniform federal chartering regulations would provide a homogenous paper currency to replace state bank notes. The uncoordinated efforts of state governments had not promoted a suitable monetary system, and, in many cases, the actions of state banks were inconsistent with the public welfare. To correct this long-standing deficiency, Congress passed the National Bank Act (1864), which established the requirements for obtaining a federal bank charter. The legislation carefully specified minimum capital requirements, conditions of note issue, and required reserves. However, state bank chartering was unaffected by the National Bank Act, and, since state restrictions generally allowed much more flexibility of operation than the national provisions, very few state banks gave up their charters to join the national banking system. The goal of a uniform currency could not be achieved as long as state bank notes enjoyed wide circulation. To encourage membership in the national bank system and to discourage the circulation of state bank notes, the federal government (1865) established an annual tax of 10 percent on all outstanding state bank notes.

The tax proved to be an effective instrument, and the majority of state banks joined the national banking system. With the spread of checking throughout the nation, however, banks began to make most of their loans by creating deposits rather than by issuing notes, and, therefore, the tax on notes no longer forced state banks to join the federal system. During the late nineteenth century, the number of state chartered banks increased rapidly, and, by the early twentieth century, there were over 10,000 state banks in operation. (See Table 12–3.) The joint expansion of state and national banks reflected the different advantages of each type of charter. National bank charters carried a certain amount of prestige which was important in extending operations beyond the local area; however, state bank

---

[11] In the reports, currency is defined as the value of notes and specie; see *Annual Report of the Comptroller of the Currency*, 1919, Vol. II, p. 35.

[12] The rise of specie circulation in the 1850s largely reflected the California gold discoveries.

Table 12-3 Number and Total Assets of National, Non-National, and State Banks, 1863-1940

	National Banks		Non-National Banks[a]		State Banks
Year	Number	Assets (millions of dollars)	Number	Assets (millions of dollars)	Number
1863	66	$ 17	1466	$ 1192	1466
1865	1294	1127	349	231	349
1870	1612	1566	325	215	325
1875	2076	1913	1260	1291	586
1880	2076	2036	1279	1364	650
1885	2689	2422	1661	2005	1015
1890	3484	3062	4717	3296	2250
1895	3715	3471	6103	4139	4369
1900	3731	4944	9322	6444	5007
1905	5664	7325	13103	10186	9018
1910	7138	9892	18013	13030	14348
1915	7597	11790	20420	16573	17748
1920	8024	23267	22885	29827	20635
1925	8066	24252	20986	37980	19573
1930	7247	28828	17026	45462	15798
1935	5425	26009	10622	33942	9752
1940	5164	36816	9912	42913	9238

Source: The national and non-national statistics were obtained from *Historical Statistics,* Series X 42-63 and X 64-85; the number of state banks were obtained from the Board of Governors of the Federal Reserve System, *Banking Studies,* Second Reprint, 1948, p. 418.
[a]Non-national banks include state commercial banks, mutual, and stock savings banks, private banks, and loan and trust companies.

charters imposed fewer restrictions and allowed greater flexibility of operation. A bank's goals largely determined the choice of state or national chartering.

Greenbacks

The Civil War was partially financed by issuing noninterest-bearing notes that were not redeemable in specie. These notes were called greenbacks, and they circulated widely but generally at a substantial discount.[13] Davis Dewey placed a great deal of blame on the federal government for the low

[13] For further discussion of greenbacks and Civil War finance, see Bray Hammond, "The North's Empty Purse, 1861–62," *American Historical Review,* October 1961; Wesley C. Mitchell, *A History of the Greenbacks: With Special Reference to the Economic Consequences of Their Issue, 1862–65* (Chicago: University of Chicago Press, 1903); and Mitchell, *Gold, Prices, and Wages Under the Greenback Standard* (Berkeley: University of California Press, 1908).

esteem with which greenbacks were held.[14] He claimed that greenbacks were created as second-class money, and, as evidence, he noted that the government would not accept greenbacks in payment for customs. The discount on greenbacks increased steadily during the war, and, by July 1864, \$100 of greenbacks was worth \$39 in gold on the New York money market; however, the discount fell sharply in 1865, and, by the end of the war, \$100 in greenbacks was worth \$68 in gold.[15] Greenbacks were scheduled for retirement at the end of the conflict, but, because of the inadequate supply of money, approximately \$350 million were allowed to remain in circulation.

The Monetization of Silver

Bimetallism caused problems in United States coinage in the first half of the nineteenth century due to temporary variations between the mint and market ratios of gold and silver.[16] The mint ratio indicates the relative value of silver to gold at the mint; the market ratio indicates the relative value of silver to gold in the marketplace. The conversion rate between silver and gold was generally around 16:1; that is, 16 ounces of silver equaled 1 ounce of gold. If the government offered a mint ratio of 15:1 and the market ratio was 16:1, silver would flow to the mint to take advantage of the higher value. The gold obtained at the mint would be used to buy more silver at the market price, and the silver would be taken to the mint, etc. The mint would become glutted with silver, and gold would be driven out of circulation. Temporary disequilibrium between the mint and market ratios was not uncommon in the antebellum decades, and, during the California gold discoveries of the 1850s, silver was driven out of circulation.

During the middle 1870s, the world output of silver increased substantially, and several countries in western Europe went on the gold standard.[17] Both of these factors promoted a decline in the market price of silver, and silver began to flow to the mint to take advantage of the favorable mint ratio. However, the government had revised its coinage standards in the early 1870s and eliminated coinage of the silver dollar; as a result, the government no longer required much silver and bought only what it needed. This situation sparked a great uproar from the silver interests and inflationists, and it resulted in passage of several pieces of legislation which required the federal government to purchase and coin a stipulated amount of silver at

---

[14] Davis Dewey, *Financial History of the United States* (New York: Augustus M. Kelley, 1968).

[15] Dewey, *Financial History of the United States*, p. 293.

[16] For an argument that bimetallism ended with the Coinage Act of 1853, see David A. Martin, "1853: The End of Bimetallism in the United States," *Journal of Economic History*, December 1973.

[17] For an excellent discussion of the silver issue, see Milton Friedman and Anna Jacobson Schwartz, *A Monetary History of the United States, 1867–1960* (New York: National Bureau of Economic Research, 1963), pp. 113–19.

the prevailing market price.[18] Government silver purchases were used to mint silver dollars and to underwrite the issuance of silver certificates and treasury notes. The burden of compulsory silver purchase was removed in 1893, but, in 1898, compulsory coinage of silver was once again required by legislation. The silver question was more or less put to rest in 1900 with the official adoption of the gold standard which required that all money be convertible into gold.[19]

Nineteenth-Century Price Trends

Throughout much of the nineteenth century there was a downward trend in prices. (See Figure 12–1.) The highest price levels in the nineteenth century were reached in 1815 and in 1864–65, and the lowest level was reached in 1843. During the antebellum period 1815–60, the trend was downward, but this largely reflected the high price level in 1815. With the exception of a decline in the early 1840s, price trends between 1820 and 60 were rather stable. Following the tremendous inflation during the Civil War years, prices drifted down rather steadily for the last three decades of the nineteenth century.

The long-run decline in American prices was part of a worldwide phenomenon. Inflationists argued that the long-term American price decline was due to a shortage of money. Their argument was rooted in the quantity theory of money, which viewed prices as a function of the supply of money and the velocity with which money is spent.[20] Data on the per capita amount of currency show that there was a fairly steady and substantial increase in circulating currency during the nineteenth century. (See Table 12–4.) Furthermore, bank deposits grew much more rapidly than circulating currency, and the results in Table 12–4 do not support the view that there was a shortage of money in the nineteenth century.[21]

The majority of demand deposits were concentrated in the Northeast, however, and there may have been money shortages in the West and South. In addition, money may have been concentrated among individuals with a

[18] The term inflationists refers to those who argued that the late nineteenth-century American economy suffered from a shortage of money. The first silver purchase requirement was instituted in 1878, and the conditions of the agreement were modified several times in the 1880s and 1890s.

[19] Davis Dewey claimed that, for all meaningful purposes, the United States was on a gold standard beginning in 1879. He showed that the federal government's policy to eliminate the premium on gold was successful, and, by 1879, paper currency was quoted at par with gold. See Dewey, *Financial History of the United States*, pp. 374–76.

[20] The quantity theory of money and prices can be represented as follows:

$$P = \frac{MV}{Q}$$

where P price level, $M =$ money supply, $V =$ velocity, and $Q =$ output. According to the quantity theory, for a given output level and constant velocity of circulation, increases in the money supply are transmitted directly into increases in the price level.

[21] The figures in Table 12–4 are not deflated, but, in view of the long-term price decline, deflation would only accentuate the increase in currency.

Figure 12-1 Wholesale Price Trends, All Commodities, 1800-1900
(5-year moving averages; 1910-14 = 100)

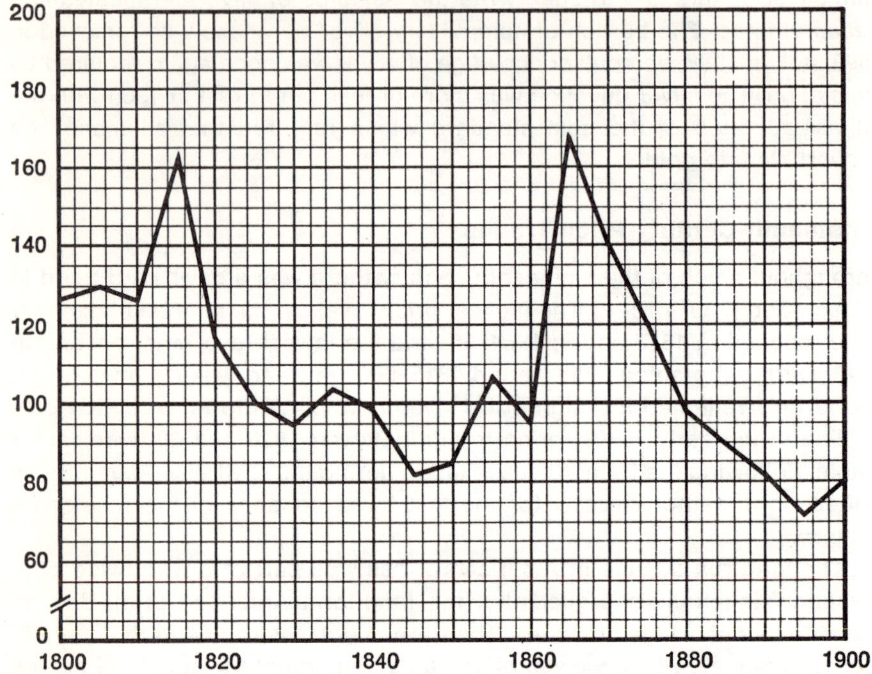

Source: George F. Warren and Frank A. Pearson, *Prices* (New York: Wiley, 1933), pp. 25-26.

low propensity to consume, and, therefore, it may not have put pressure on prices. Furthermore, the velocity of circulation decreased substantially during the late nineteenth century, and this may have contributed to the deflationary bias.[22] Technological advance and sharp increases in aggregate production act to depress prices, and this may have been an important factor throughout the nineteenth century.[23] It also should be stressed that, during most of the nineteenth century, American price trends were very similar to those in western Europe, and European economic conditions had some influence on American price levels.[24] Further research needs to be com-

---

[22] Friedman and Schwartz showed that between 1879 and 1897 velocity declined at an average rate of almost 3 percent per year; see *A Monetary History of the United States*, p. 96.

[23] Friedman and Schwartz suggested that the deflationary trend between 1879 and 1897 was due to rapid increases in aggregate production, slow increases in the world's stock of gold, and adoption of a gold standard by a number of countries; see *A Monetary History of the United States*, p. 91.

[24] For discussion of the effect of outside influences on American monetary stability in the antebellum period, see the following: George Macesich, "Sources of Monetary Disturbances in the United States, 1834–1845," *Journal of Economic History*, September 1960; Jeffrey Williamson, "International Trade and United States Economic Development, 1827–1843," *Journal of Economic History*, September 1961; George Macesich, "International Trade and

Table 12-4 Per Capita Deposits in All Banks and per Capita Currency in Circulation, 1835-1910

Year	Per Capita Deposits	Per Capita Currency
1835	$ 8.13	$ 9.72
1840	7.01	10.88
1845	5.65	8.82
1850	6.28	11.99
1855	8.62	15.26
1860	9.84	13.82
1865	19.30	30.34
1870	19.42	19.42
1875	44.57	18.50
1880	44.20	19.37
1885	54.32	22.81
1890	72.57	22.66
1895	79.60	23.02
1900	117.24	27.35
1905	164.30	31.29
1910	194.20	34.07

Source: *Historical Statistics,* Series X 20-41 and X 281-84.

pleted before the exact sources of nineteenth-century deflation can be determined; however, it does seem clear that the American price deflation involved much more than a shortage of domestic currency.

The Establishment of the Federal Reserve System

With the exception of two brief experiments with central type banks in the late eighteenth and early nineteenth centuries, the United States was without a formal central bank until the Federal Reserve system was established in 1913. Central bank operations have occupied a crucial role in western economic development, and the absence of a central bank during most of the nineteenth century was certainly not consistent with maximizing the economy's rate of progress.[25] Despite this institutional deficiency, the American economy grew at a rapid rate in the nineteenth century, and the Treasury performed some of the central bank functions.

The basic defect in nineteenth-century American banking structure was an inability to adjust the money supply and credit conditions to conform to

United States Economic Development Revisited," *Journal of Economic History,* September 1961; and Thomas D. Willett, "International Specie Flows and American Monetary Stability, 1834–60," *Journal of Economic History,* March 1968.

[25] See Rondo Cameron, *Banking in the Early Stages of Industrialization* (New York: Oxford University Press, 1967).

sudden changes in economic conditions. The highly individual character of nineteenth-century banks and banking mitigated against swift collective action. The Federal Reserve system was designed to provide the institutional framework needed to achieve flexibility in money and credit, and it replaced individual decisions with collective decisions of monetary experts. Federal Reserve legislation divided the country into twelve districts, each with a district bank, and the system was headed by a Federal Reserve Board. Initially, the Federal Reserve Board was composed of the Secretary of the Treasury, Comptroller of the Currency, and five members appointed by the President; in 1935, the name was changed to the Board of Governors and all seven members were appointed by the President. All national banks were required to join the system, and state banks could become members if they met certain conditions. Member banks were required to maintain cash reserves on deposit with district banks. The original act required the majority of reserves to be deposited with the district banks, but in 1917, this requirement was extended to cover all reserves.

Pooling member bank reserves in the district banks created the means for adjusting money and credit conditions to fit short-term fluctuations in demand. For example, in times of need, a member bank could obtain additional currency or expand its credit operations by simply increasing its deposits with the Fed, selling bonds or commercial paper, or borrowing from the Fed.[26] The speed and flexibility introduced in the adjustment of money and credit conditions to business conditions was a hallmark of the Federal Reserve system. In addition to creating a flexible money and credit system, the Fed provided a national clearinghouse for checks and greatly increased the speed of business transactions.

Congress gave the Federal Reserve several strong powers to influence and control the member banks' credit operations.[27] One of its important powers was the authority to determine the interest rate (rediscount rate) charged on loans to member banks. By setting the rediscount rate, the Fed could control the ability and willingness of banks to lend money, and, in this way, it could achieve some control over the economy's rate of expansion. The Fed also exerted control over the money supply by buying and selling government bonds in the open market; purchase of bonds would increase the money supply, and sale of bonds would reduce it. A third major power given to the Fed was the authority to change legal reserve requirements of member banks. This latter power has rarely been used, however, and most Fed policies have been administered through the rediscount rate and open market operations.

---

[26] For a detailed statement of Federal Reserve operation, see *The Federal Reserve System*, Board of Governors of the Federal Reserve System, 1961. For a more concise treatment, see Paul A. Samuelson, *Economics*, 9th edition (New York: McGraw-Hill, 1973), Chapter 17.

[27] See Samuelson, *Economics*, pp. 318–25.

Table 12-5 Composition of Currency in Circulation, by Kind, 1865-1955 (millions of dollars)

Year	Gold Coin and Gold Certificates	Subsidiary Silver, Silver Dollars, and Silver Certificates	Federal Reserve Notes	United States Notes	National Bank Notes	Other[a]
1865	$ 148.6	$ 8.7	–	$378.9	$146.1	$401.2
1870	113.3	9.0	–	325.0	288.6	39.1
1875	81.9	22.1	–	349.7	340.5	39.5
1880	233.7	74.4	–	327.9	337.4	0.0
1885	468.4	184.3	–	331.2	308.6	0.0
1890	505.1	407.9	–	334.7	181.6	0.0
1895	528.0	432.0	–	319.1	207.0	115.9
1900	811.5	550.6	–	317.7	300.1	101.4
1905	1136.3	629.9	–	332.4	480.0	44.8
1910	1393.7	686.6	–	334.8	683.7	50.0
1915	1409.4	686.6	$ 70.8	309.8	782.1	60.7
1920	733.8	423.2	3064.7	278.1	689.6	278.0
1925	1407.1	699.1	1636.1	282.6	681.7	108.6
1930	1352.0	706.7	1402.1	288.4	650.8	121.9
1935	117.2	1029.6	3222.9	285.4	704.3	207.8
1940	66.8	2011.9	5163.3	247.9	165.2	192.6
1945	52.1	2564.2	22867.5	322.6	120.0	820.2
1950	40.8	3312.2	22760.3	320.8	86.5	635.8
1955	34.5	3594.9	25617.8	319.1	66.8	596.2

Source: *Historical Statistics,* Series X 285-298.

[a]Between 1865 and 1880, other includes state bank notes, fractional currency, and other U.S. currency; between 1885 and 1955, other includes treasury notes of 1890, minor coin, and Federal Reserve banknotes.

Late Nineteenth- and Twentieth-Century Changes in the Money Supply

Table 12–5 shows the composition of the money supply between 1865 and 1955. The circulation of hard money increased sharply in the last two decades of the nineteenth century, and, by 1900, two-thirds of the currency in circulation consisted of gold and silver coins or certificates. Silver's circulation increased sharply throughout the twentieth century, but legislation in 1933 withdrew gold coins and certificates from circulation. The circulation of United States notes (greenbacks) was fixed by Congress at $347 million in 1878. National bank notes were an important form of paper currency in the late nineteenth and early twentieth centuries, but the issue of national notes leveled off during the 1920s and early 1930s, and the power to issue notes was legislated away by Congress in 1935. Federal Reserve notes became the chief form of paper currency in the twentieth century, and, by 1955, they accounted for 85 percent of all currency in circulation.

Summary

In most societies that have achieved a high level of economic progress, the establishment of sound banking and financial institutions has been an important force in the early stages of development. Generally, an economy's banking and financial structure has been organized around a central or national bank whose function has been to maintain monetary stability. The United States did not develop a formal central banking system until the second decade of the twentieth century, and the late development of modern banking structure was in sharp contrast to the economy's progress in other areas. Of course, as this chapter has shown, there were numerous attempts to achieve monetary stability throughout the nineteenth century, and, in some degree, each of these attempts was successful. In addition to tracing the development of American banking structure from the First Bank of the United States (1791) to the establishment of the Federal Reserve system (1913), this chapter has also surveyed the issuing of greenbacks, the monetization of silver, and long-term trends in the money supply and prices.

Suggested Reading

Cameron, Rondo, *Banking in the Early Stages of Industrialization.* New York: Oxford University Press, 1967.

Davis, Lance E., "The Investment Market, 1870–1914: The Evolution of a National Market," *Journal of Economic History,* September 1965.

Friedman, Milton, and Anna Jacobson Schwartz, *A Monetary History of the United States, 1867–1960.* New York: National Bureau of Economic Research, 1963.

Martin, David A., "Metallism, Small Notes, and Jackson's War with the Bank of the United States," *Explorations in Economic History,* Spring 1974.

———, "1853: The End of Bimetallism in the United States," *Journal of Economic History,* December 1973.

Meerman, Jacob, "The Climax of the Bank War: Biddle's Contraction, 1833–34," *Journal of Political Economy,* August 1963.

Olmstead, Alan L., "Investment Constraints and New York City Mutual Savings Bank Financing of Antebellum Development," *Journal of Economic History,* December 1972.

Rockoff, Hugh, "Money, Prices, and Banks in the Jacksonian Era," in Robert W. Fogel and Stanley L. Engerman, eds., *The Reinterpretation of American Economic History.* New York: Harper & Row, 1971.

Sylla, Richard, "American Banking and Growth in the Nineteenth Century: A Partial View of the Terrain," *Explorations in Economic History,* Winter 1971–72.

———,"Federal Policy, Banking Market Structure, and Capital Mobilization in the United States, 1863–1913," *Journal of Economic History,* December 1969.

Taylor, George R., *The Transportation Revolution, 1815–1860.* New York: Holt, Rinehart and Winston, 1951, Ch. XIV.

Temin, Peter, "The Economic Consequences of the Bank War," *Journal of Political Economy,* March/April 1968.

———, *The Jacksonian Economy.* New York: W. W. Norton, 1969.

Timberlake, Richard H., Jr., "The Specie Standard and Central Banking in the United States Before 1860," *Journal of Economic History,* September 1961.

13
Immigration and American Economic Development

A unique feature of American economic development was the heavy inflow of foreign-born labor in the nineteenth and early twentieth centuries. Between 1845 and 1915, over 30 million individuals, mostly from Europe, migrated to the United States. The flow of foreign-born labor was partially stimulated by political, social, and economic conditions in Europe, but the bulk of the immigrants were attracted by economic opportunities in the United States. The majority of migrants were males in their most productive years, and they saved the United States a considerable sum of human capital investment by providing a labor force whose rearing, education, and training costs had been met elsewhere. This chapter will review the following aspects of nineteenth- and twentieth-century immigration: legislation regarding the influx of immigrants; trends in migration flows; national origins of immigrants; geographic distribution of immigrants; age, sex, skill, and occupational composition of immigrants; discriminaton against immigrants; and the impact of immigration on American population and labor force growth.

Control of Immigration and Establishment of Quotas

Before 1882, there were no federal regulations regarding immigration, and state controls were very limited.[1] Several eastern seaboard states had imposed light restrictions, but midwestern and western states actively

---

[1] For a fuller treatment of immigration controls, see Carl Wittke, "Immigration Policy Prior to World War I," *Annals of the American Academy of Political and Social Science*, March 1949, and Edward P. Hutchinson, "Immigration Policy Since World War I," *Annals of the American Academy of Political and Social Science*, March 1949.

recruited immigrants. The federal government entered the area of immigrant restriction in 1882 by imposing on immigrants a head tax which rose over time from fifty cents to eight dollars. In addition, the federal government initiated attempts to exclude undesirables, and it prohibited Chinese immigration. In 1891, health standards were established and the solicitation of foreign labor was prohibited. In the late nineteenth and early twentieth centuries, Congress passed several bills establishing a literacy test for permanent admission, but, in each case, the President vetoed the bill, and it was not until 1917 that a literacy test was formally adopted.[2] It was generally acknowledged that the purpose of the literacy test was to discriminate against the new migration from eastern and southern Europe. The Act of 1917 also doubled the head tax, denied entry as immigrants to people from Southeast Asia, and gave immigration officials the power to exclude and deport aliens.

Restrictions were tightened in 1921 with the establishment of annual quotas for the various nationalities. The quotas were set at 3 percent of the number of each nationality in residence in the United States according to the census of 1910. In 1924, the base for establishing the annual allotment for each nationality was shifted to 1890, and the percentage was reduced to 2 percent.[3] In 1929, the quotas were reapportioned according to the national origins of the white population in 1920. The purpose of the quotas was to restrict the absolute number of immigrants and to exclude the non-English-speaking migration from eastern and southern Europe.[4] For the decade before World War I, the average annual immigration was approximately 1 million. The 1921 quotas reduced the maximum inflow to 358,000; in 1924, this was reduced to 165,000 and, in 1929, to 154,000.[5] The 1921 quotas allowed 198,000 individuals from northwest Europe and 156,000 from eastern and southern Europe; in 1924, the allocation was 141,000 from northwest Europe and 20,000 from eastern and southern Europe and, in 1929, 127,000 from northwest Europe and 23,000 from eastern and

[2] Satisfactory performance on the literacy test was a requirement for permanent residence for individuals over age 16.

[3] Japanese immigration was excluded by the Immigration Act of 1924.

[4] Brinley Thomas claims that the literacy test alone would have been enough to exclude many immigrants from eastern and southern Europe since one-third of the migrants from this region were illiterate; see *Migration and Economic Growth* (Cambridge: At the University Press, 1954), pp. 190–91.

[5] There were many reasons behind the restrictionist movement of the early twentieth century. Contemporary arguments for restriction stressed the low wages accepted by the new immigrants from eastern and southern Europe, the negative effect of the immigration on American culture and institutions, crime and pauperism associated with immigration, rise of nationalism stemming from World War I, and dangers of unemployment. For a full treatment of these issues, see Isaac A. Hourwich, *Immigration and Labor* (New York: G. P. Putnam's, 1912), and Jeremiah W. Jenks and W. Jett Lauck, *The Immigration Problem* (New York: Funk and Wagnalls, 1926).

southern Europe.[6] The quotas gave large allotments to nations which did not use their allocation, and, between 1924 and 1946, only 38.4 percent of the total quota was used. However, there were exemptions to the quotas such as relatives, residents of other western hemisphere countries, and war refugees, and, in many years, the exemptions exceeded the number arriving by quota. There was very little change in policy between 1924 and 1939, and, in 1940, the Alien Registration Act was passed which required an annual registration of all noncitizens.

Flow of Immigrants to the United States

The flow of immigrants to the United States was quite slow before the middle 1840s, and, between 1820 and 1844, slightly more than one million immigrants arrived in the United States. (See Table 13–1.) The pace of immigration accelerated sharply in the 1840s, and over one million immigrants arrived during 1845–49 and almost 2 million during 1850–54. The rate of immigration slowed in the late 1850s and early 1860s but increased sharply in the late 1860s and early 1870s. Immigration continued to increase in the late nineteenth century and reached an annual flow of 1 million individuals between 1905 and 1914. The imposition of restrictions on immigration after World War I brought about a sharp decline, and, during the depression decade of the 1930s, the annual inflow was less than 100,000.

In the post–Civil War period, the annual flow of immigrants to the United States was largely controlled by economic conditions in the United States.[7] During the earlier years, the abundance of land and opportunities in agriculture allowed immigrants to move somewhat independently of American business conditions. In the late nineteenth century, however, most job opportunities for immigrants were in manufacturing, and the annual flow of immigration was heavily controlled by the overall pace of expansion in the American economy.[8]

The majority of immigrants became permanent residents in the United States, but a large number, especially in the late nineteenth and early twentieth centuries, emigrated back to their native lands after spending a short period in the United States. Simon Kuznets and Ernest Rubin estimated that the ratio of alien departures to arrivals moved as follows: 1870–80, .243; 1880–90, .188; 1890–1900, .386; 1900–1910, .448; 1910–15, .505;

---

[6] See William S. Bernard, ed., *American Immigration Policy* (New York: Harper and Row, 1950), p. 27. The major effect of the 1929 quotas was to give a greater allocation of the northwest Europe total to the British.

[7] See Harry Jerome, *Migration and Business Cycles* (New York: National Bureau of Economic Research, 1926).

[8] See Thomas, *Migration and Economic Growth*, p. 113.

Table 13-1 Immigration to the United States, 1820-1939

Period	Number of Immigrants
1820-24	38,689
1825-29	89,813
1830-34	230,442
1835-39	307,939
1840-44	400,031
1845-49	1,027,306
1850-54	1,917,527
1855-59	897,027
1860-64	707,243
1865-69	1,374,018
1870-74	1,886,501
1875-79	855,636
1880-84	3,037,594
1885-89	2,210,974
1890-94	2,320,645
1895-99	1,373,649
1900-04	3,255,149
1905-09	4,947,239
1910-14	5,174,701
1915-19	1,172,679
1920-24	2,774,600
1925-29	1,520,910
1930-34	426,953
1935-39	272,422

Source: *Historical Statistics,* Series C 88-114.

1915–20, .692; 1920–30, .276; and 1930–40, .818.[9] Emigration was especially heavy between 1908 and 1914, averaging almost 300,000 individuals per year.[10]

National Origin of Immigrants

Until the 1890s, 70 percent or more of American immigration came from northwest Europe.[11] Within that region, the bulk of American immigration came from Ireland and Germany. The Irish contributed 45 percent of total immigration between 1820 and 1850, and the Germans contributed 40 percent between 1852 and 1860 and 30 percent between 1866 and 1885.[12] Dur-

[9] Simon Kuznets and Ernest Rubin, *Immigration and the Foreign Born,* National Bureau of Economic Research, Occasional Paper 46, 1954, pp. 38–40.

[10] The ratio of emigrants to immigrants was especially high for eastern and southern Europeans; see Jenks and Lauck, *The Immigration Problem,* p. 38.

[11] For an excellent summary of major sources of immigration to the United States, see Bernard, *American Immigration Policy,* p. 40.

[12] See *Historical Statistics,* Series C 88–114.

ing the decade of the 1890s, immigration from eastern and southern Europe slightly exceeded that from northwest Europe; between 1900 and 1915, this new source provided approximately 70 percent of total immigration, and Italians (23 percent) and Russians (19 percent) were the major contributors. The relative share of eastern and southern European immigration decreased sharply after World War I, and this was offset by relative increases from northwest Europe and Canada.

Geographic Distribution of Immigrants

The foreign-born proportion of America's population reached a peak in 1890 and 1910 at 14.7 percent. Immigrants represented a large percentage of total population in the New England, Middle Atlantic, North Central, Mountain, and Pacific regions of the United States.[13] In absolute terms, however, the heaviest concentration of immigrants was in the New England, Middle Atlantic, and East North Central regions, and, in 1920, over 10 million immigrants, out of a national total of 13.9 million, resided in these regions. The South was not attractive to immigrants because of its large supply of cheap black labor and its lack of an industrial base, and, throughout the period of heavy immigration, approximately 97 percent of the region's total population was native-born.[14] In all regions, a high percentage of immigrants were concentrated in cities. In the Northeast, most immigrants were employed in industry, and urban concentration was especially heavy; outside the Northeast, immigrant employment was diversified across manufacturing, mining, construction, and agriculture, and a greater percentage of immigrants lived in rural areas.[15]

Age-Sex Composition of Immigrants

Migration studies reveal that a selective type of individual tends to migrate, and the age and sex characteristics of the American immigration reflect the standard pattern. For the period 1820–1940, males represented almost two-thirds of total immigration, and the 15–44 age group accounted for 70–80 percent of all migrants.[16] The selective age-sex composition of Amer-

---

[13] In the early twentieth century, over 25 percent of total population in New England and the Middle Atlantic regions was foreign born, and approximately 15 percent of the population in the North Central regions was foreign born. The foreign-born share of total population in the Mountain and Pacific regions reached a peak in the 1870s at approximately 30 percent. See *Fifteenth Census of the United States: 1930, Population,* Vol. II, p. 39.

[14] Within the South, there was a heavy clustering of immigrants in New Orleans.

[15] See Walter F. Wilcox, "The Distribution of Immigrants in the United States," *Quarterly Journal of Economics,* August 1906.

[16] See A. Ross Eckler and Jack Zlotnick, "Immigration and the Labor Force," *Annals of the American Academy of Political and Social Science,* March 1949, p. 93. In addition, see *Historical Statistics,* Series C 133–38.

ican immigration yielded a foreign-born labor force with a very high rate of labor force participation.[17] The figures in Table 13–2 reveal that foreign-born males had a significantly higher participation rate than native white males; the difference in participation habits between native white and foreign-born females was slight.

Immigrant Skills and Occupational Distribution

Immigrant skills are difficult to measure, but they are reflected in the ability to speak English, literacy rates, and occupational structure. With the large influx of eastern and southern Europeans, the percentage of the foreign-born population that could not speak English increased sharply and reached a peak in 1910 at almost 25 percent.[18] The inability to speak English was a handicap to immigrants and excluded them from many jobs where this was a critical skill. The foreign-born labor force was less literate than native whites, and illiteracy was especially high among the new immigrants from eastern and southern Europe. (See Table 13–3.) During the decade 1899–1909, 26.7 percent of all immigrants fourteen years of age and older were illiterate; the illiterate group included 35.8 percent of all immigrants from eastern and southern Europe and 2.7 percent of all immigrants from northwest Europe.[19] School enrollment of foreign-born children

Table 13-2 Percentage of Persons 10 Years of Age and Older Engaged in Gainful Occupations, 1910, 1920, and 1930

Sex Group and Year	Native White	Foreign-Born White
Males		
1910	77.9%	90.0%
1920	75.1	89.3
1930	73.4	88.4
Females		
1910	19.2	21.7
1920	19.3	18.4
1930	20.5	18.8

Source: *Fifteenth Census of the United States: 1930, Population,* Vol. V, p. 74.

17 There are several different ways of calculating labor force participation rates; in this chapter, the participation rate for each nativity group refers to the ratio of the number gainfully employed to the total population 10 years of age and older.

18 The percentage of the American foreign-born population that could not speak English changed as follows: 1890, 15.6 percent; 1900, 12.2 percent; 1910, 22.8 percent; 1920, 11.0 percent; and 1930, 6.6 percent. See the *Fifteenth Census of the United States: 1930, Population,* Vol. II, p. 1349.

19 Jenks and Lauck, *The Immigration Problem,* p. 36.

Table 13-3 Percentage of Native- and Foreign-Born White Population 10 Years of Age and Older That Was Illiterate, 1850-1930

Year	Native White[a]	Foreign-Born White
1850	4.1%[b]	8.7%[b]
1860	3.2[b]	8.4[b]
1870	14.8	14.0
1880	8.7	12.0
1890	6.2	13.1
1900	4.6	12.9
1910	3.0	12.7
1920	2.0	13.1
1930	1.5	9.9

Source: *Ninth Census of the United States: 1870, Population, pp. 396-97*, and *Fifteenth Census of the United States: 1930, Population*, Vol. II, p. 1223.

[a] Figures for 1850-70 are for all native-born, white and nonwhite.

[b] Figures for 1850 and 1860 are for population twenty years and older.

was very high, and the literacy of young immigrants was substantially improved upon arrival in the United States. However, this improvement was continually offset by large inflows of illiterate immigrants, and, throughout the late nineteenth and early twentieth centuries, approximately 13 percent of the foreign-born labor force was illiterate. On the other hand, literacy of the native white population improved substantially during the late nineteenth and early twentieth centuries, and the relative gap between native and foreign-born labor increased.

Throughout the period of heavy immigration, the majority of immigrant labor was relatively unskilled. (See Table 13–4.) During the antebellum decades, many immigrants were artisans or farmers, and, until the Civil War, these groups accounted for 50 percent or more of total immigration.[20] By the 1860s, however, unspecified general labor dominated the occupational structure of immigrants and, during most of the late nineteenth century, accounted for almost 50 percent of total foreign-born labor. While many late nineteenth-century immigrants were specified as general labor, a large number had had experience in the European industrial labor force, and they greatly aided American industrialization. It often has been argued that the immigration from eastern and southern Europe was less skilled than the earlier immigration from northwest Europe. It is true that a higher percentage of the migrants from northwest Europe were literate and able to speak English; however, the figures in Table 13–4 clearly show that the

[20] For a good survey of immigrant occupations in the antebellum period, see William J. Bromwell, *History of Immigration to the United States* (New York: Augustus M. Kelley, 1969), and *Eighth Census of the United States: 1860, Population*, p. xxii.

Table 13-4 Percentage Distribution of Immigrants by Major Occupation Group, 1820-1930

Occupation Group	Time Period							
	1820-29	1830-39	1840-49	1850-59	1860-69	1870-79	1880-89	1890-98
Professional	3.2%	1.7%	0.9%	0.5%	1.4%	1.6%	1.0%	1.1%
Commercial	28.1	16.3	6.3	8.7	10.5	4.3	3.1	2.8
Skilled	30.5	31.5	23.2	18.1	13.1	24.0	21.2	22.0
Farmers	21.2	30.5	32.7	31.1	20.4	18.5	15.0	13.3
Servants	2.1	1.0	3.1	1.7	7.3	7.8	9.3	13.8
Laborers	14.9	19.0	33.8	39.9	47.3	43.8	50.4	47.1

Occupation Group	Time Period		
	1899-1910	1911-20	1921-30
Professional, technical and kindred workers	1.3%	2.4%	4.5%
Farmers and farm managers	1.5	2.1	4.9
Managers, officials, and proprietors, excluding farm	2.7	2.9	3.5
Clerical and sales	1.4	2.9	7.0
Craftsmen, foremen, operatives etc.	17.9	18.3	23.7
Private household	14.2	16.4	17.2
Service workers, excluding private household	1.3	3.3	6.0
Laborers[a]	59.7	51.8	33.2

Source: *Historical Statistics,* Series C 115-32.

[a] For years before 1899, farm laborers were included under the category farmers; from 1899 onward, the category laborers includes all farm and nonfarm labor.

occupational structure of both old and new immigration was heavily weighted toward unskilled occupations.

Foreign-born labor was heavily concentrated in mining and manufacturing, and Table 13–5 shows the industries with the greatest concentration in 1910. Over one-half of the nation's labor force in copper and iron mines, clothing factories, woolen and worsted mills, blast furnaces and steel rolling mills, bakeries, and tanneries was foreign-born; over 40 percent of total employment in all other industries shown in Table 13–5 was supplied by immigrants. The heavy concentration of immigrants in particular industries was partially a function of the imperfect knowledge about existing job opportunities. The only knowledge available to many immigrants came from relatives or friends who were already employed in the United States, and, as a result, new arrivals often were attracted into the same areas and industries.

Table 13-5 Foreign-Born Whites Among Male Workers in Selected Industries, 1910

Industry	Percentage of Foreign-Born
Coal Mines	48.3%
Copper Mines	65.4
Iron Mines	66.8
Quarries	45.2
Lime, Cement, and Gypsum Factories	40.0
Marble and Stone Yards	44.2
Clothing Factories (suits, coats, etc.)	75.9
Clothing Factories (other)	72.2
Hat Factories (wool and felt)	42.4
Bakeries	50.5
Slaughter and Packing Houses	45.8
Car and Railroad Shops	45.6
Tanneries	52.9
Breweries	49.2
Piano and Organ Factories	43.2
Brass Mills	45.8
Blast Furnaces and Steel Rolling Mills	51.1
Carpet Mills	48.3
Silk Mills	46.5
Textile Dyeing, Finishing, and Printing Mills	48.7
Woolen and Worsted Mills	50.2
Rubber Factories	40.3
Construction and Maintenance of Streets, Bridges, etc.	46.0
All Industries	20.5

Source: A. Eckler and Jack Zlotnick, "Immigration and the Labor Force," *Annals of the American Academy of Political and Social Science #262*, March 1949: 100.

A detailed view of immigrant occupational structure in 1920 is shown in Table 13–6. The figures reveal that foreign-born labor accounted for 16 percent of total United States employment with particularly heavy concentration in mining (34.5 percent) and manufacturing (25.1 percent) and light concentration in agriculture (8.1 percent), professional service (7.5 percent), domestic and personal service (10.8 percent), and clerical occupations (5.6 percent). The figures indicate that the unspecified nature of much immigrant labor did not block employment in many jobs requiring high skills.[21] One-fourth or more of the nation's blacksmiths, boilermakers,

[21] The category "laborers" was rather broadly defined and may have included many semi-skilled individuals.

Table 13-6 Foreign-Born Share of Employment in Selected Occupations, 1920

Occupation	Percentage of Foreign-Born
Agriculture	8.1%
Mining	34.5
Foremen, etc.	23.6
Officials, Managers, etc.	11.4
Operatives	35.7
Manufacturing	25.1
Blacksmiths	26.0
Boilermakers	23.6
Masons	35.8
Cabinetmakers	53.2
Carpenters	24.9
Electricians	11.9
Engineers	19.0
Foremen and Overseers	20.2
Jewelers, Watchmakers, etc.	32.5
Laborers (general)	24.0
Machinists	24.4
Managers and Superintendents	13.7
Mechanics	14.1
Molders, Founders, and Casters	40.7
Plasterers and Cement Finishers	28.3
Plumbers and Gas and Steam Fitters	16.0
Semi-skilled Operatives	21.6
Transportation	17.5
Railroad Foremen	21.7
Railroad Laborers	32.9
Trade	18.2
Bankers, Brokers, etc.	9.5
Clerks	8.9
Retail Dealers	30.0
Salesmen	10.3
Wholesale Dealers, Importers and Exporters	30.9
Public Service	16.4
Policemen	16.9
Professional Service	7.5
Chemists	14.1
Designers, Draftsmen, etc.	17.4
Lawyers and Judges	6.1
Musicians	13.1
Doctors	10.1
Technical Engineers	11.7
Domestic and Personal Service	10.8
Clerical	5.6
All Occupations	15.9

Source: *Fourteenth Census of the United States: 1920, Population*, Vol. IV, pp. 342-59.

masons, cabinetmakers, carpenters, jewelers and watchmakers, and plasterers and cement finishers were born overseas. In manufacturing, immigrants provided 24.0 percent of general manufacturing labor, 21.6 percent of semi-skilled operatives, and over 25 percent of skilled manufacturing labor. In mining, immigrants provided 35.7 percent of the operatives and 23.6 percent of the foremen; in railroads, immigrants provided 32.9 percent of the laborers and 21.7 percent of the foremen. The overall picture suggested by Table 13–6 is one of a rather diversified contribution by immigrants to American industry.[22] To be sure, immigrants were concentrated in skilled, semi-skilled, and unskilled blue collar occupations, and their contribution in many areas of professional service was limited. However, even in the professional area, there was evidence of significant participation, and immigrants accounted for 14 percent of chemists, 17 percent of designers and draftsmen, 13 percent of musicians, 12 percent of technical engineers, and 10 percent of doctors.[23]

Discrimination Against Immigrants

It is well documented that immigrants earned less than native-born Americans, but, given that immigrants were concentrated in blue collar occupations, this should not be surprising.[24] Even within particular industries, data show that immigrants earned less than native whites; however, since the managerial functions of industry were dominated by the native-born, and immigrants were concentrated in operative functions of varying skills, this result, again, should not be surprising.

The fact that immigrants earned less than native whites does not mean that there was discrimination against immigrants. In order for discrimination to have existed, immigrants would have had to receive lower pay than native-born workers for the same quantity and quality of work, or they would have had to be excluded from jobs for which they were suitably trained.[25] In a recent study, Robert Higgs examined earnings differentials between native- and foreign-born workers in 1909, and he concluded that earnings differences largely reflected real skill differences, namely literacy

---

[22] Within the foreign born labor force, the majority of the skilled jobs went to immigrants from northwest Europe, and the majority of the unskilled jobs went to immigrants from eastern and southern Europe.

[23] For a detailed view of immigrant occupational structure in 1930, see W. S. Woytinsky, *Labor in the United States* (Washington, D.C.: Committee on Social Security, Social Science Research Council, 1938), pp. 257–59.

[24] Data for children aged 14–18 and adult females suggest that there was no significant earnings differential between native- and foreign-born laborers; see Jenks and Lauck, *The Immigration Problem,* pp. 160–61.

[25] Differential pay for equal work is generally referred to as wage discrimination; job exclusion is generally referred to as occupational discrimination. An analysis of both types of discrimination, with particular reference to blacks and females, is provided in Chapter 19.

Table 13-7 Percentage Change in Population and Labor Force Due to Immigration, by Decade, 1850-1940

Decade	Percentage Change in Population	Percentage Change in Labor Force
1850-60	22.9%	
1860-70	17.1	
1870-80	10.8	16.2%
1880-90	20.1	30.1
1890-1900	8.4	10.1
1900-10	19.9	24.9
1910-20	2.9	−1.2
1920-30	1.7	−5.3
1930-40	−29.3	−40.7

Source: Simon Kuznets and Ernest Rubin, *Immigration and the Foreign Born,* National Bureau of Economic Research, Occasional Paper 46, 1954, p. 45. Reprinted by permission of the National Bureau of Economic Research.

and the ability to speak English.[26] He found little evidence of discrimination and claimed that the newer immigrants from eastern and southern Europe earned less because they had fewer skills.[27] These results do not mean that prejudice against foreigners was not strong and widespread; however, they do suggest that the earnings variation between natives and immigrants reflected a real skill difference and not blind prejudice.

Impact of Immigration on Population and the Labor Force

The heavy immigration flow represented a major source of growth for America's population and labor force in the late nineteenth and early twentieth centuries. (See Table 13–7.) The calculations of Kuznets and Rubin show the net increases in population and the labor force due to immigration, taking into account deaths and emigration. By the second decade of the twentieth century, the net contribution of immigrants had disappeared, and this means that the large inflow of migration during this decade was offset by losses through death and emigration.[28] After World War I, the contribution of immigration declined sharply and became negative as deaths and emigration greatly outweighed new inflows.

[26] Robert Higgs, "Race, Skills, and Earnings: American Immigrants in 1909," *Journal of Economic History,* June 1971.

[27] Using multiple regression analysis, Higgs found that 80 percent of the earnings variation between natives and immigrants was explained by differences in literacy and the ability to speak English.

[28] The method of calculation used by Kuznets and Rubin only shows the quantitative differences between inflows and outflows of migrants. If there was a significant difference between immigrants and emigrants in age-sex composition, a simple quantity index might be misleading.

In another study, Kuznets estimated the effects on the American economy of cessation of immigration in 1870.[29] He calculated that the 1940 population would have been only approximately 75 percent of its actual level, 102 million instead of 132 million; he also estimated that the 1940 labor force would have been only 70 percent of its actual level and would have been equal in size to the 1910 labor force.

Recent Trends in Immigration

Quota restrictions were revised in 1952, and they maintained the heavy allocation for northwest Europeans. In fact, Great Britain (42.3 percent), Germany (16.7 percent), and Ireland (11.5 percent) accounted for 70 percent of the total quota allotment.[30] Between 1965 and 1968, the rigidity of the quotas was relaxed; if the allocation to a country were not used, this was put into a pool, and these slots were made available to immigrants from countries whose quotas were filled. In 1968, a ceiling of 120,000 was established for all western hemisphere countries, with no limits on any one country; a ceiling of 170,000 was established for all eastern hemisphere countries, with a maximum of 20,000 from any one country. In addition, throughout the post–World War II period, there have been numerous provisions covering special circumstances such as wars and natural disasters.

The national origins of immigrants to the United States have changed sharply in recent years. Disruptions caused by World War II promoted a heavy outflow from western Europe in the late 1940s and 1950s, especially from Germany, England, and Poland. By the 1960s, the flow from Europe had subsided, and, in recent years, the greatest source of migration to the United States has been from our neighbors to the north and south. In the 1960s, 40 percent of all United States immigration originated in Canada, Mexico, the West Indies, and Central America. South America and Asian migration to the United States has also increased sharply in recent decades, and, by 1970, approximately two-thirds of the immigration was non-European.[31]

Summary

The American economy often has been referred to as the "melting pot" because of its heterogeneous mixture of races achieved through immigration. In recent years, restrictions have been placed on the free flow of migrants into the United States, but, even today, the economy annually

---

[29] Simon Kuznets, ed., *Income and Wealth of the United States, Trends and Structure* (Cambridge, Mass.: Bowes and Bowes, 1952), pp. 199–201.

[30] See *Statistical Abstract,* 1973, p. 94, for quota allotments by country.

[31] See *Statistical Abstract,* 1973, p. 96.

assimilates 350,000–400,000 immigrants. The previous pages have shown the selective age-sex-occupational characteristics of the migrant population, and the great impact of immigration on the course of American economic development has been made clear. The analysis here has been restricted to the economic aspects of immigration, but the social and cultural effects of immigration also have been far-reaching and have had a profound impact on the American character.

Suggested Reading

Eckler, A. Ross, and Jack Zlotnick, "Immigration and the Labor Force," *Annals of the American Academy of Political and Social Science,* March 1949.

Gallaway, Lowell E., and Richard K. Vedder, "Emigration from the United Kingdom to the United States: 1860–1913," *Journal of Economic History,* December 1971.

———, and Vishwa Shukla, "The Distribution of the Immigrant Population in the United States: An Economic Analysis," *Explorations in Economic History,* Spring 1974.

Gilboy, Elizabeth W., and Edgar M. Hoover, "Population and Immigration," in Seymour Harris, ed., *American Economic History.* New York: McGraw-Hill, 1961.

Handlin, Oscar, and Mary F. Handlin, "The United States," in *The Positive Contribution by Immigrants,* International Sociological Association. Paris: Unesco, 1955.

Higgs, Robert, "Race, Skills, and Earnings: American Immigrants in 1909," *Journal of Economic History,* June 1971.

Hutchinson, Edward P., "Immigration Policy Since World War I," *Annals of the American Academy of Political and Social Science,* March 1949.

Kuznets, Simon, and Ernest Rubin, *Immigration and the Foreign Born,* Occasional Paper 46. New York: National Bureau of Economic Research, 1954.

Niemi, Albert W., Jr., "The Role of Immigration in United States Commodity Production, 1869–1929," *Social Science Quarterly,* June 1971.

Uselding, Paul, "Conjectural Estimates of Gross Human Capital Inflows to the American Economy: 1790–1860," *Explorations in Economic History,* Fall 1971.

Wittke, Carl, "Immigration Policy Prior to World War I," *Annals of the American Academy of Political and Social Science,* March 1949.

14

Late Nineteenth- and Twentieth-Century Agricultural Developments

The crucial role of agriculture in America's nineteenth-century economic development has been evident in earlier chapters. The nation's abundance of productive land encouraged resource-oriented economic activity. Until the last decade of the nineteenth century, agriculture was the leading source of production in the nation, and, until the 1920s, farming was the nation's leading occupation.[1] This chapter begins with a brief survey of nineteenth- and twentieth-century trends in agricultural output and includes an assessment of growth in farm output, the number of farms, farm acreage, and the regional distribution of agricultural activity. Technological changes and improvements in agricultural productivity resulting from mechanization and scientific management of farms are also analyzed. Agrarian unrest in the late nineteenth century is treated, and the traditional arguments concerning the causes of agricultural distress are viewed in relation to the relevant empirical evidence. The chapter closes with a brief examination of twentieth-century trends in agricultural purchasing power.

Trends in Agricultural Output

Mid-nineteenth-century transportation improvements brought about a fundamental change in American agriculture. American farmers always had produced cash crops for sale in foreign markets; however, because of

[1] The following aspects of agriculture are treated in other chapters: quantitative importance of agriculture, Chapters 2 and 7; antebellum southern agriculture, Chapter 9; the impact of the Civil War on agriculture, Chapter 10; distribution of public land, land speculation, and the rise of western agriculture, Chapter 8; the impact of transportation on agriculture, Chapters 5 and 6.

Table 14-1 Decennial Rates of Change and Levels of Real Net Farm Output, 1800-1900

Year	Real Net Farm Output (millions of 1910-14 dollars)	Decennial Rate of Change[a]
1800	$ 323	
1810	433	34.1%
1820	571	31.9
1830	784	37.3
1840	1100	40.3
1850	1363	23.9
1860	1932	41.8
1870	2264	17.2
1880	3411	50.7
1890	4064	19.1
1900	5071	24.8

Source: *Historical Statistics,* Series K 139-49.
[a] The decennial rate of change is for the decade ending in the designated year.

inadequate internal transportation facilities, food production was characterized by a high degree of self-sufficiency.[2] (See Chapter 5.) The improved means of distribution offered by canals, steamboats, and railroads encouraged production for the market, and, by the middle nineteenth century, many farmers concentrated on particular food crops, and regions developed specialized patterns of production.

Between 1800 and 1900, real agricultural output increased at an average annual rate of 2.8 percent, and the decennial rates of change shown in Table 14–1 suggest that the nineteenth-century expansion of agriculture was rather smooth; only two decades, the 1860s and 1880s, showed decennial increases significantly below 25 percent. Farm output advanced at an average annual rate of 0.8 percent during 1899–1953, and John W. Kendrick's estimates of real net farm output (1929 prices) suggest the following percentage increases for specified time periods: 1899–1910, 10.1 percent; 1910–19, 2.8 percent; 1919–29, 10.9 percent; 1929–37, 1.9 percent; 1937–48, 16.9 percent; and 1948–53, 2.2 percent.[3] The figures in Table 14–2 show that the number of farms remained rather constant be-

[2] The share of gross farm income generated by agricultural exports remained rather stable between 1870 and 1930 and ranged from 19.3 percent in 1881–85 to 14.7 percent in 1926–30; see J. Frederick Dewhurst and Associates, *America's Needs and Resources* (New York: The Twentieth Century Fund, 1947), p. 605.

[3] See John W. Kendrick, *Productivity Trends in the United States* (Princeton: Princeton University Press, 1961), p. 347.

Table 14-2 Number of Farms, Land in Farms, and Average Size of Farms, 1850-1950

Year	Number of Farms (000)	Land in Farms (millions of acres)	Average Size of Farms (acres)
1850	1449	293.5	202.6
1860	2044	407.2	199.2
1870	2660	407.7	153.3
1880	4009	536.1	133.7
1890	4565	623.2	136.5
1900	5737	838.6	146.2
1910	6406	878.8	137.2
1920	6518	955.9	146.7
1930	6546	986.8	150.8
1940	6350	1060.9	167.1
1950	5648	1158.6	205.1
1960	3963	1176.0	297.0
1970	2954	1103.0	373.0

Source: *Historical Statistics,* Series K 1-7, and *Statistical Abstract,* 1973, p. 585.

tween 1910 and 1940 and declined sharply after World War II. Farm acreage doubled between 1870 and 1900, increased by 38 percent between 1900 and 1950, and remained roughly constant between 1950 and 1970. The increase in farm acreage coupled with the decline in the number of farms resulted in a sharp increase in average farm size, and, between 1940 and 1970, average unit size more than doubled.

Regional Concentration of Agriculture

Distinct patterns of regional specialization and concentration developed in American agriculture by the end of the nineteenth century. During the latter part of the century, agriculture became spatially concentrated in the Midwest, and the westward drift of agricultural activity is shown in Figures 14–1, 14–2, and 14–3. In 1850, the bulk of American farm acreage was in the eastern seaboard states; by 1870, Ohio, Indiana, and Illinois were leading agricultural states; and, by the end of the nineteenth century, the North Central region dominated American agriculture. In 1900, 50 percent of the nation's total value of agricultural output was produced in the North Central states, and production was heavily concentrated on grains. The region produced three-fourths of the nation's output of cereals and provided the following shares of grain output: oats, 81 percent; buckwheat, 79 percent; corn, 73 percent; barley, 68 percent; wheat, 67 per-

Figure 14-1 Improved Land, 1850

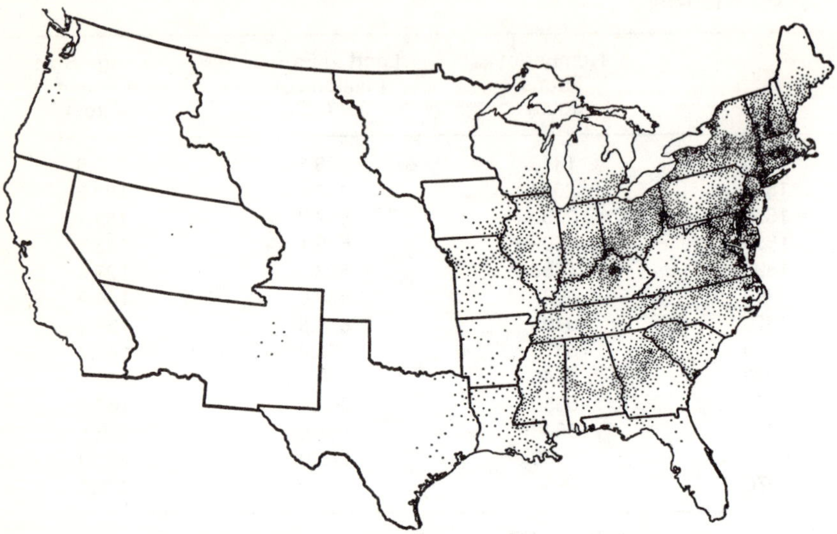

Source: Charles O. Paullin, *Atlas of the Historical Geography of the United States* (Washington, D.C.: The Carnegie Institution of Washington and the American Geographical Society of New York, 1932), Plate 144C.
Note: Each dot represents 25,000 acres.

cent; and rye, 63 percent.[4] The livestock industry was also heavily concentrated in the North Central states, and, in 1900, the region accounted for 51.2 percent of the nation's livestock valuation. (See Table 14–3.) In addition to the concentration of agricultural activity in the Midwest, the late nineteenth century also was characterized by a sharp increase in cotton production in the South, especially in Texas, Georgia, South Carolina, Alabama, and Mississippi.[5] (See Table 14–4.)

Mechanization of Agriculture

Chapter 11 showed that many early and middle nineteenth-century technological changes attempted to conserve on labor requirements and were developed as a result of practical application and empirical testing. In the late nineteenth and twentieth centuries, technological change became much more scientific and involved the application of new knowledge.

---

[4] See the *Twelfth Census of the United States: 1900, Agriculture,* Part I, pp. cxxii–cxlviii, and Part II, pp. 62–92, 214, and 342.

[5] Cotton production increased from 3.0 million bales in 1870 to 9.5 million bales in 1900; see the *Census of Agriculture: 1959, General Report,* Vol. II, *Statistics by Subject*, pp. 680–90.

Figure 14-2 Improved Land, 1870

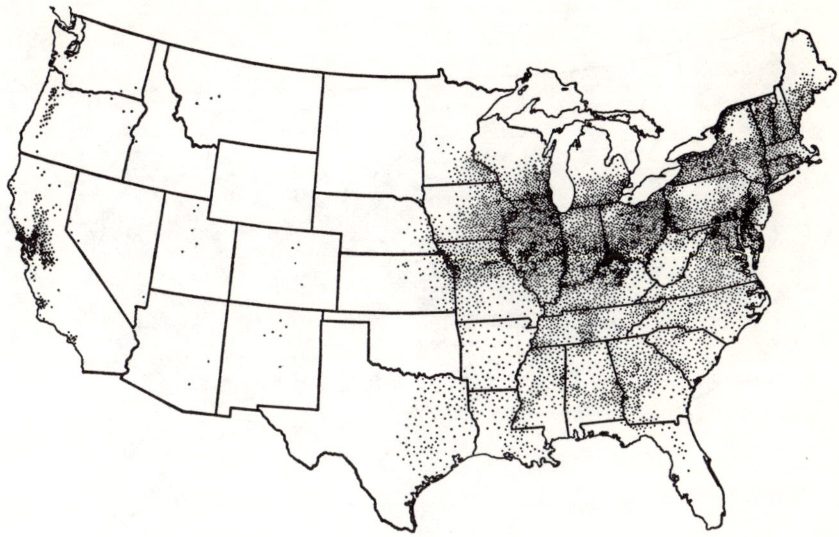

Source: Charles O. Paullin, *Atlas of the Historical Geography of the United States* (Washington, D.C.: The Carnegie Institution of Washington and the American Geographical Society of New York, 1932), Plate 144E.
Note: Each dot represents 25,000 acres.

Agricultural technology developed according to this general pattern, and, in the antebellum decades, the major thrust of technology involved the replacement of manpower with animal power. Reapers, improved plows, seed drills, cultivators, mowers, and threshers had all been developed and were in widespread use by the time of the Civil War; in the 1880s, the reaping and threshing operations were integrated in the combine.[6] Each of these inventions improved labor productivity by substituting animal input for labor input.[7] Until the early twentieth century, most farm ma-

---

[6] Wayne Rasmussen has concluded that the mechanical reaper was the single most important invention of the 1830–60 period; see, "The Impact of Technological Change on American Agriculture, 1862–1962," *Journal of Economic History,* December 1962. For further discussion, see Paul A. David, "The Mechanization of Reaping in the Antebellum Midwest," in Henry Rosovsky, ed., *Industrialization in Two Systems* (New York: Wiley, 1966).

[7] William N. Parker and Judith Klein have suggested that approximately 50 percent of the productivity improvement in wheat and oats was due to the mechanization of the reaping and threshing operations; see "Productivity Growth in Grain Production in the United States, 1840–60 and 1900–10," in *Output, Employment, and Productivity in the United States after 1800,* Conference on Research in Income and Wealth, Studies in Income and Wealth, National Bureau of Economic Research, Vol. 30 (New York: Columbia University Press, 1966), p. 544.

Figure 14-3 Improved Land, 1900

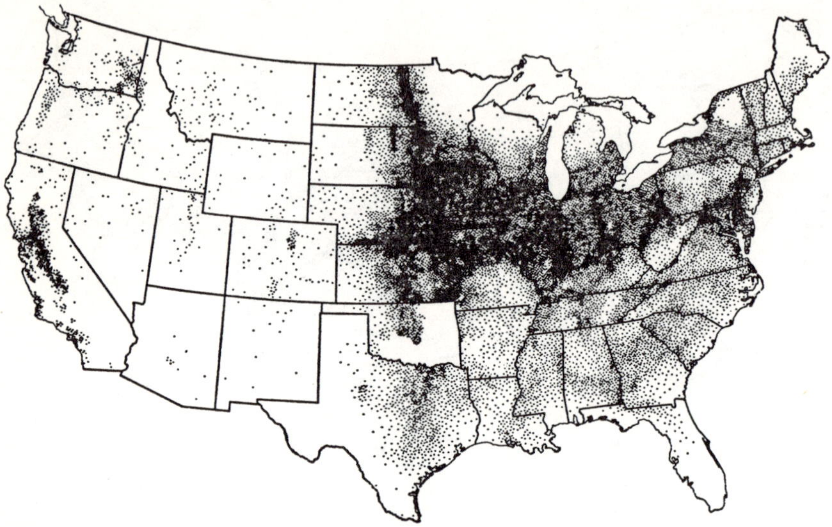

Source: Charles O. Paullin, *Atlas of the Historical Geography of the United States* (Washington, D.C.: The Carnegie Institution of Washington and the American Geographical Society of New York, 1932), Plate 144H.
Note: Each dot represents 25,000 acres.

Table 14-3 Value of Livestock on Farms, 1900

State or Region	Millions of Dollars
Regions	
North Atlantic	$ 320.5
South Atlantic	194.4
North Central	1577.0
South Central	616.5
West	367.2
Ten Leading States	
Iowa	278.8
Texas	240.6
Illinois	193.8
Kansas	191.0
Missouri	160.5
Nebraska	145.3
Ohio	126.0
New York	125.6
Indiana	109.6
Pennsylvania	102.4

Source: *Twelfth Census of the United States: 1900, Agriculture* Vol. V, p. xxxii.

Table 14-4 Total Cotton Production in Commercial Bales, 1880, 1890, and 1900

State or Region	1880	1890	1900
Virginia	19,595	5,375	10,789
North Carolina	389,598	336,261	459,707
South Carolina	522,548	747,190	881,422
Georgia	814,441	1,191,846	1,287,992
Florida	54,997	57,928	61,856
Kentucky	1,367	873	1,369
Tennessee	330,621	190,579	234,592
Alabama	699,654	915,210	1,106,840
Mississippi	963,111	1,154,725	1,313,798
Arkansas	608,256	691,494	709,880
Louisiana	508,569	659,180	709,041
Oklahoma	—	425	70,675
Texas	805,284	1,471,242	2,506,212
Missouri	20,318	15,856	25,576
Indian Territory	17,000	34,115	154,850
Other	—	212	108
United States	5,755,359	7,472,511	9,534,707

Source: *Twelfth Census of the United States: 1900, Agriculture,* Vol. V, p. 425.

chinery was drawn by work animals, and it was not until the 1920s that horsepower generated by work animals showed an absolute decline.[8]

The development of the internal combustion engine at the turn of the century resulted in rapid replacement of animal power, and, between 1910 and 1930, almost one million tractors were introduced into American farming, and the use of combines increased rapidly.[9] Nineteenth-century improvements in agricultural technology were generally dependent on animal power, and the absolute dollar investment in agricultural machinery was relatively low. With the development of flexible inanimate power available in the internal combustion engine, machines were rapidly substituted for work animals, and farm expenditures for machinery increased sharply.[10]

[8] It should be pointed out that many agricultural activities such as cotton picking and tobacco and corn harvesting were not mechanized in the late nineteenth century. In addition, Fred Bateman has demonstrated that the mechanization of dairy farming proceeded very slowly; see "Labor Inputs and Productivity in American Dairy Agriculture, 1850–1910," *Journal of Economic History,* June 1969.

[9] The number of tractors on farms increased as follows: 1910, 1000; 1930, 920,000; and 1950, 3.4 million. The number of grain combines increased as follows: 1910, 1000; 1930, 61,000; and 1950, 714,000. See *Historical Statistics,* Series K 150–158.

[10] The aggregate value of farm implements and machinery (millions of dollars) increased as follows: 1850, $152; 1860, $246; 1870, $271; 1880, $407; 1890, $494; 1900, $750; 1910, $1265; 1920, $3595. See *Census of Agriculture: 1940, General Report, Statistics by Subject,* p. 37.

Scientific Advances in Agricultural Technology

Applications of scientific advances to agricultural problems did not become important until the third decade of the twentieth century. There were some empirically based improvements in fertilization, crop selection, and animal feeding practices in the late nineteenth century, but it was not until the 1930s and 1940s that scientific advances in biochemistry resulted in substantial improvement in plant and animal varieties.[11] Twentieth-century advances in chemistry led to widespread application of insecticides, herbicides, and fertilizers and were a major force behind the sharp improvement in agricultural productivity.[12]

Agricultural research became institutionalized in the late nineteenth century with the passage of the Morrill Act (1862) and the Hatch Act (1887). The Morrill Act led to the establishment of land grant colleges in each state; the Hatch Act created a statewide system of agricultural experiment stations. The Department of Agriculture, created in 1862, provided further stimulation to agricultural research, as did the numerous farm organizations, extension services, and journals that arose in the late nineteenth century. Each of these institutions provided a source of inquiry and information dissemination which aided in the advance and diffusion of agricultural technology.

Trends in Agricultural Productivity

Nineteenth- and twentieth-century improvements in agricultural technology brought about some increase in crop yields per acre, but their most important effect was to raise labor productivity.[13] Labor requirements declined sharply throughout the nineteenth and twentieth centuries, and the figures in Table 14–5 suggest that labor productivity in wheat and corn increased by approximately ten times between 1800 and 1950.[14] Land pro-

---

[11] For an interesting discussion of the diffusion of hybrid corn varieties, see Zvi Griliches, "Hybrid Corn and the Economics of Innovation," in Robert W. Fogel and Stanley L. Engerman, eds., *The Reinterpretation of American Economic History* (New York: Harper & Row, 1971).

[12] Nathan Rosenberg claimed that the application of new chemicals was the most important factor behind twentieth-century productivity increases in agriculture; see *Technology and American Economic Growth* (New York: Harper & Row, 1972), pp. 127–38. Data from *Historical Statistics,* Series K 159–161, show the following increase in fertilizer and lime consumption (000 short tons): 1850, 53; 1860, 164; 1870, 321; 1880, 753; 1890, 1,390; 1900, 2,730; 1910, 6,493; 1920, 9,829; 1930, 11,759; 1940, 22,742; and 1950, 49,158.

[13] A detailed explanation of the various productivity concepts is provided in Chapter 17. Productivity refers to the ratio of output to input, and it is a measure of the economy's efficiency. The most common productivity measures are total factor productivity (total output/total input), labor productivity (total output/labor input), and capital productivity (total output/capital input).

[14] The number of acres farmed per agricultural worker doubled between 1870 and 1930, increasing from 17.9 to 34.2; see Dewhurst and Associates, *America's Needs and Resources,* p. 623.

Table 14-5 Man-Hours per Acre, Yield per Acre, and Man-Hours Used to Produce Specified Amount of Wheat, Corn, and Cotton, 1800-1950

Crop and Productivity Indicator	1800	1840	1880	1900	1920	1940	1950
Wheat							
Man-hours/Acre	56	35	20	15	12.0	7.5	4.6
Yield/Acre (bushels)	15	15	13.2	13.9	13.8	15.9	16.6
Man-hours/100 bushels	373	233	152	108	87	47	28
Corn							
Man-hours/Acre	86	69	46	38	32	25	15.2
Yield/Acre (bushels)	25	25	25.6	25.9	28.4	30.3	39.0
Man-hours/100 bushels	344	276	180	147	113	83	39
Cotton							
Man-hours/Acre	185	135	119	112	90	98	74
Yield/Acre (lbs. of lint)	147	147	179	191	160	245	283
Man-hours/Bale	601	439	318	280	269	191	126

Source: *Historical Statistics*, Series K 83-97.

ductivity, as measured by yield per acre, showed no significant trend for wheat but increased substantially for corn and cotton.[15] The long-term trend (1869–1954) in total factor productivity in agriculture is shown in Figure 14–4, and the chart suggests that agricultural productivity was rather stagnant between 1899 and 1924. Sharp productivity increases were made in the 1870s and late 1890s, but the long-term trend between 1869 and 1924 was erratic; since 1934, agricultural productivity has increased steadily at a sharp rate.

Agrarian Unrest in the Late Nineteenth Century

The period from the end of the Civil War to 1896 traditionally has been regarded as an era of agricultural distress. The severity of farm problems was reflected by the creation of various agricultural organizations (Grange, Greenback Party, Alliances, Leagues, and the Populists) whose major goals were government protection for farmers, establishment of farm cooperatives, and increased circulation of money. Farmers argued that they were discriminated against by the monopoly power of railroads, milling companies, commodity buyers, meat packers, and other middlemen. They contended that monopoly power acted to depress farm prices

[15] Griliches, "Hybrid Corn and the Economics of Innovation," concluded that hybrid corn varieties were 15–20 percent more productive than open pollinated varieties and were rapidly adopted during the 1940s.

Figure 14-4 Total Factor Productivity in Agriculture, 1869-1954 (decade intervals 1869-89; 5-year moving averages 1894-1954; 1929 = 100)

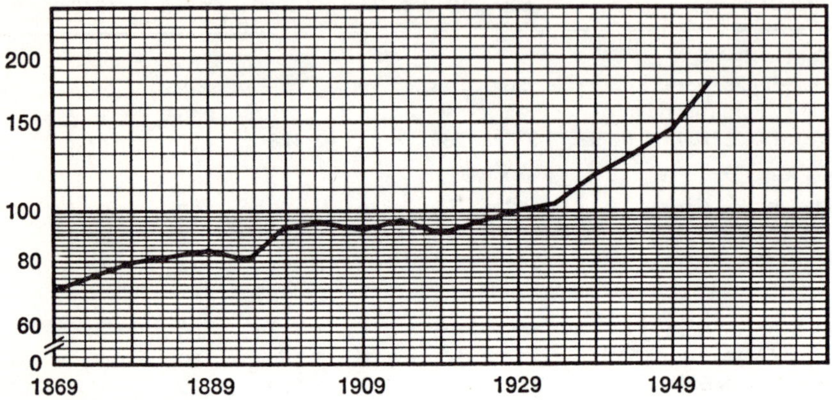

Source: John W. Kendrick, *Productivity Trends in the United States* (Princeton: Princeton University Press, 1961), pp. 362-64. Reprinted by permission of the National Bureau of Economic Research.

relative to other prices and, thereby, reduced farmers' purchasing power. Farmers also complained about the high interest rates they had to pay on mortgage loans and the high incidence of tenant farming.

Recent study of late nineteenth-century agrarian unrest suggests that farmers' complaints may have overstated the severity of farm distress and ignored several fundamental agricultural problems. The complaint regarding railroad rates does not seem justified in view of Robert Higgs' recent results which showed that railroad rates declined at about the same rate as farm prices throughout the late nineteenth century.[16] Mortgage rates were relatively high in agricultural areas, but this reflected imperfections in the capital market rather than discrimination against farmers.[17] (See Table 14–6.) Western states had to import a large portion of their capital from the East, and rural areas, both agricultural and nonagricultural, paid a premium for mortgage loans. High mortgage rates were a heavy burden to many farmers, and the burden was accentuated by the long-term deflation of the late nineteenth century.[18] However, since the majority of farms were not mortgaged and the average mortgage life was 3–5 years, the mortgage burden should not be viewed as a source of

---

16 Robert Higgs, "Railroad Rates and the Populist Uprising," *Agricultural History,* July 1970.

17 See Lance E. Davis, "The Investment Market, 1870–1914: The Evolution of a National Market," *Journal of Economic History,* September 1965.

18 Debtors suffer during deflation because they are forced to pay off their debts with appreciated currency.

Table 14-6 Average Rate of Interest on Real Estate Mortgages, by States and Regions, 1890

State or Region	Interest Rate	State or Region	Interest Rate
North Atlantic	5.55%	Minnesota	7.66%
South Atlantic	6.66	Mississippi	9.50
North Central	7.43	Missouri	7.68
South Central	8.08	Montana	10.61
West	8.89	Nebraska	8.30
		Nevada	9.48
Alabama	7.98	New Hampshire	5.98
Arizona	10.90	New Jersey	5.73
Arkansas	9.06	New Mexico	8.19
California	8.81	New York	5.49
Colorado	8.57	North Carolina	7.72
Connecticut	5.64	North Dakota	9.35
Delaware	5.71	Ohio	6.56
District of Columbia	5.93	Oregon	9.45
Florida	9.78	Pennsylvania	5.61
Georgia	8.09	Rhode Island	5.72
Idaho	10.60	South Carolina	8.37
Illinois	6.70	South Dakota	9.46
Indiana	6.84	Tennessee	6.00
Iowa	7.63	Texas	9.60
Kansas	8.68	Utah	9.70
Kentucky	6.25	Vermont	5.97
Louisiana	7.67	Virginia	6.02
Maine	6.15	Washington	8.84
Maryland	5.86	West Virginia	6.06
Massachusetts	5.44	Wisconsin	6.84
Michigan	7.13	Wyoming	10.22

Source: *Eleventh Census of the United States: 1890, Report on Real Estate Mortgages,* p. 259.

distress for all western agriculture.[19] Furthermore, the mortgage burden was lightened significantly during the late nineteenth century as a result of sharp declines in interest rates which reflected increased competition in lending and the development of a national capital market.[20]

[19] The percentage of farms mortgaged in 1890 was as follows: North Atlantic, 36.7 percent; South Atlantic, 17.6 percent; North Central, 38.7 percent; South Central, 20.9 percent; and West, 27.3 percent. See *Eleventh Census, Mortgages,* pp. 109 and 123.

[20] Allan G. Bogue has argued that there was competition in the mortgage lending industry by 1870 in Illinois and Iowa and by the late 1880s in Texas; see *Money at Interest* (Ithaca, N.Y.: Cornell University Press, 1955), p. 160; and *From Prairie to Corn Belt* (Chicago: University of Chicago Press, 1963), p. 174. Using data for Illinois, Wisconsin, Iowa, and Nebraska, John Bowman has shown that the average rate of interest on farm mortgages fell from 8–10 percent in 1870 to approximately 5–6 percent in 1900; see "An Economic Analysis of Midwestern Farm Land Values," p. 335.

Figure 14-5 Ratio of Wholesale Prices of Farm Products to Wholesale Prices of All Commodities, 1869-1919
(5-year moving averages; 1910-14 = 100)

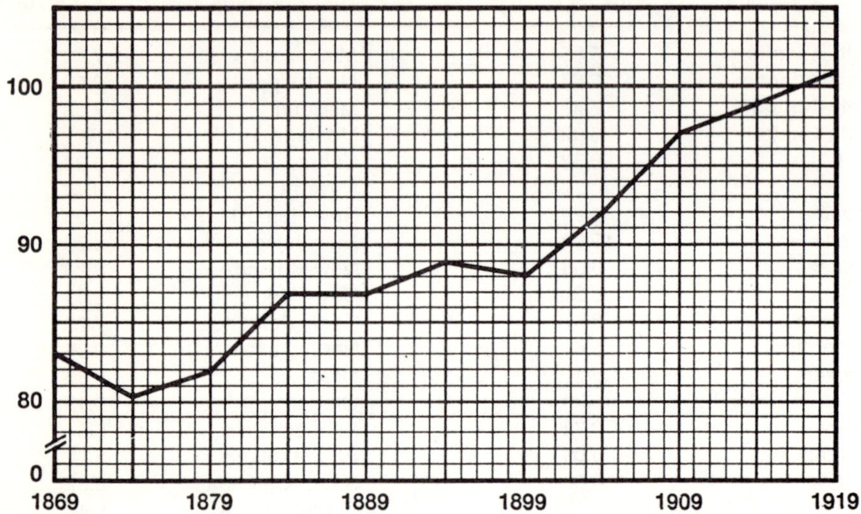

Source: George F. Warren and Frank A. Pearson, *Prices* (New York: Wiley, 1933), pp. 26-27.

Many farmers worked as tenants, either by paying rent for the use of land or by sharing output with the landowner. Tenant farming has been viewed with disfavor by many economic historians because of its social implications, but there is no *a priori* reason to believe that tenant farms were less productive than owner operated farms. There was a high degree of tenant farming in the late nineteenth-century American agriculture, especially in the Midwest and South, and there was a steady increase in tenancy between 1880 and 1930. (See Table 14–7). Tenancy declined rapidly in the 1930s, and, in recent years, the share of all farms operated by tenants has declined to less than 15 percent. Tenancy was especially high in the South, and, between 1900 and 1940, approximately one-half of all southern farms were tenant operated, and 75 percent or more of all black farms in the South were tenant operated.[21]

Farm prices declined during the late nineteenth century, but, in order to interpret the significance of this downward trend, it is necessary to view the movement in farm prices relative to nonfarm prices. Figure 14–5 shows the ratio of farm prices to all commodity prices, and it appears that farmers' terms of trade improved slightly between 1869 and 1894 and improved sharply between 1899 and 1919. Precise data on relative changes

[21] See *Historical Statistics,* Series K 8–52.

Table 14-7 Percentage of Total Farms Operated by Tenants, by Region, 1880-1969

Region	1880	1890	1900	1910	1920	1930	1940	1950	1964	1969
United States	25.6%	28.4%	35.3%	37.0%	38.1%	41.3%	38.7%	26.8%	17.1%	12.9%
New England	8.7	9.5	9.4	7.9	7.6	6.4	7.4	3.9	3.5	4.6
Middle Atlantic	19.2	22.0	25.4	21.4	20.7	14.6	14.7	7.7	6.9	6.8
East North Central	20.4	22.9	26.2	27.1	28.0	27.3	27.8	19.8	15.7	13.2
West North Central	20.5	23.9	29.6	30.9	34.2	39.9	42.4	28.2	21.2	16.9
South Atlantic	36.2	38.5	44.3	45.9	46.8	48.2	42.2	32.1	18.5	10.9
East South Central	36.7	38.3	48.2	50.8	49.6	55.9	50.2	36.6	19.0	8.8
West South Central	35.3	38.5	49.1	52.8	52.9	62.3	52.6	33.7	17.8	15.3
Mountain	7.2	7.1	12.2	10.7	15.4	24.5	24.5	15.9	12.5	12.3
Pacific	16.9	14.6	19.7	17.4	20.1	17.6	18.5	10.5	10.7	11.4

Source: U.S. Bureau of the Census, *U.S. Census of Agriculture: 1950*, Vol. II, *General Report*, pp. 992-93, and *U.S. Census of Agriculture: 1969*, Vol. II, *General Report*, Ch. 3, *Farm Management, Farm Operators*, pp. 23-24.

in farm and nonfarm income are not available, but an approximation can be made by viewing productivity trends and farm land values.[22] Agricultural productivity grew at a slightly lower rate than nonagricultural productivity in the late nineteenth century, and this suggests that farm income probably grew at a slightly lower rate.[23] John Bowman's estimates of farm land values suggest that farm incomes rose in the 1860s and 1880s, remained constant in the 1890s, and declined in the 1870s.[24] In light of the available evidence, it appears that the farmers' complaints about monopoly pressures and declining purchasing power in the late nineteenth century were overstated.[25]

If the most recent evidence is accurate and farmers' complaints about monopoly pressures, railroad rates, mortgage rates, indebtedness, tenant farming, and purchasing power were exaggerated, why was farm protest so active in the late nineteenth century, and why did it begin at that time? Anne Mayhew has hypothesized that farmers' complaints were rooted in their reaction to the commercialization of agriculture in which production for the market replaced self-sufficiency.[26] Commercial agriculture brought many new problems. Production was now geared to markets in other parts of the nation and world, and often there was no relationship between local production conditions and market prices for agricultural goods. For example, local production might be curbed by drought, leading farmers to expect high prices because of the reduced supply; however, the market price might be depressed because of bumper crops in other parts of the world, and farmers' expectations would not be met. Foreign demand for American commodities, especially food, was highly unstable, and variations in foreign demand and domestic supply conditions resulted in wild fluctuations in the volume of exports.[27]

---

22 Farm income is a function of farm prices and output; productivity shows the relationship between output and input. An examination of farm prices and productivity relative to prices and productivity in the nonfarm sector or in the total economy can provide a crude index of relative trends in farm income. Farm land values tend to be a direct reflection of farm income trends; during periods of rising income, farm values rise, and, during periods of declining income, farm values decline.

23 For productivity changes, see Kendrick, *Productivity Trends,* pp. 328 and 362. It is generally acknowledged that during the late nineteenth century the quality of industrial goods improved more rapidly than the quality of agricultural goods, and this suggests that the farmer was getting more for his dollar than is shown by relative prices.

24 See John Bowman, "Trends in Midwestern Farm Values, 1860–1914." Ph.D. dissertation, Yale University, 1964. For further information, see the *Thirteenth Census of the United States: 1910, Agriculture,* pp. 54–64.

25 For an excellent review of agrarian unrest, see Robert Higgs, *The Transformation of the American Economy, 1865–1914* (New York: Wiley, 1971), Chapter IV.

26 Anne Mayhew, "A Reappraisal of the Causes of Farm Protest in the United States, 1870–1900," *Journal of Economic History,* June 1972.

27 For example, between 1898 and 1903, wheat exports averaged approximately 130 million bushels; between 1904 and 1906, they averaged less than 30 million bushels; between 1907 and 1909, they averaged over 80 million bushels; between 1910 and 1912, they averaged slightly more than 30 million bushels; and during World War I they hit a peak of 260 million bushels. See *Historical Statistics,* Series U 73–93.

In addition to the problems associated with market orientation and internationally determined prices, late nineteenth-century agriculture was faced by problems of oversupply. Technological improvements increased productivity on American farms, and there were sharp advances in production in other parts of the world. As a result, there was a persistent tendency toward overproduction, and the problem could only be cured by a sharp decline in the number of farmers. To be sure, there were problems in agriculture that originated from the standard areas of complaint, but it seems that late nineteenth-century agricultural distress was rooted in a fundamental change in the organization of agriculture and an oversupply of farmers.[28]

Twentieth-Century Developments in Farm Prices

Figure 14–5 showed that agricultural prices improved substantially in the late nineteenth and early twentieth centuries, and, by World War I, they had reached parity with nonfarm prices. In 1910, the U.S. Department of Agriculture began collecting data on prices received and prices paid by farmers, and these figures can be used to construct an index of relative purchasing power of farmers in the twentieth century. (See Figure 14–6.) The chart shows deviations away from parity, where parity is defined as the ratio of farm prices received to prices paid in 1910–14. The figures indicate that farm purchasing power fell steadily after World War I and reached a low point during the trough of the depression of the 1930s. World War II brought sharp improvement to agriculture, but, since the war, farm prices have suffered a sharp relative decline.

The decline in farm purchasing power brought heavy pressure on the federal government to subsidize farmers, either through pegging farm prices at an artificially high level or through buying agricultural commodities.[29] Initially, the goal of federal farm support programs was to return farm prices to the position of parity reached in 1910–14; recently, support programs have allowed market forces to exert greater control on farm prices, and aid has included a combination of loans, subsidies, and crop reductions. The farm program has received much criticism, and many economists have argued that farm support mechanisms subvert the normal operations of a market economy and interrupt the flow of resources into their most productive uses.[30]

---

[28] Bowman, "An Economic Analysis of Midwestern Farm Land Values," urged caution in generalizing about nineteenth-century agrarian distress, and he argued that agricultural problems varied substantially by region, crop, and time.

[29] Farm subsidies began in 1929 during the Hoover administration; prior to this date, government aid to agriculture was largely passive and involved dissemination of information and distribution of public land.

[30] For further discussion of the federal government's farm support program, see Paul A. Samuelson, *Economics*, 9th ed. (New York: McGraw-Hill, 1973), Chapter 21.

Figure 14-6 Ratio of Prices Received by Farmers to Prices Paid by Farmers, 1914-69
(5-year moving averages; 1910-14 = 100)

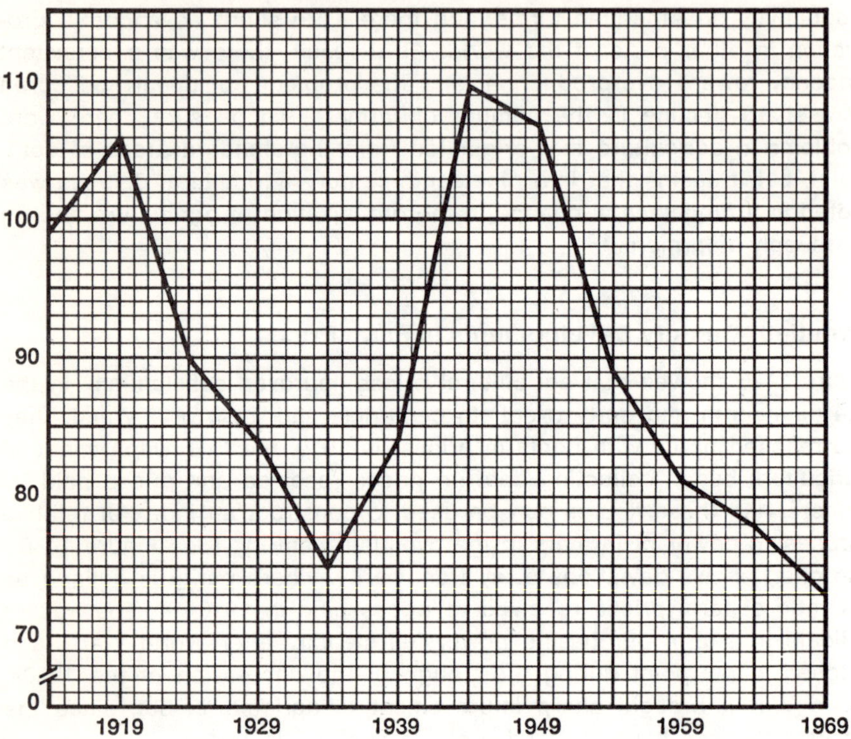

Source: *Historical Statistics*, Series K 122-38, and U.S. Department of Agriculture, *Agricultural Statistics*, 1971, p. 478.

Summary

The relative importance of agriculture in the United States economy has been declining since the late antebellum period, and, since then, there have been serious problems of farmer dislocation. In the late nineteenth century, farm problems were intensified by a change in farmer orientation from production for self-sufficiency toward production for the market. The changing fortunes of agriculture brought a loud protest from farmers. They complained about depressed prices, monopoly power of railroads and commodity buyers, mortgage rates, indebtedness, and tenant farming. This chapter's review of the most recent research into the farm protest movement suggests that the farmers' complaints were overstated and misdirected. It is true that there were many grounds for agrarian discontent, but the basic problems in agriculture resulted from an oversupply of farmers and a changed marketing structure that gave farmers very little control over final prices of their products.

Suggested Reading

Bateman, Fred, "Improvements in American Dairy Farming, 1850–1910: A Quantitative Analysis," *Journal of Economic History,* June 1968.

———, "Labor Inputs and Productivity in American Dairy Agriculture, 1850–1910," *Journal of Economic History,* June 1969.

Bogue, Allan G., *From Prairie to Corn Belt. Chicago:* University of Chicago Press, 1963.

———, *Money at Interest.* Ithaca, N.Y.: Cornell University Press, 1955.

Bowman, John, "An Economic Analysis of Midwestern Farm Land Values and Farm Land Income, 1860 to 1900," *Yale Economic Essays* 5, Fall 1965.

David, Paul A., "The Mechanization of Reaping in the Antebellum Midwest," in Henry Rosovsky, ed., *Industrialization in Two Systems.* New York: Wiley, 1966.

Griliches, Zvi, "Hybrid Corn and the Economics of Innovation," in Robert W. Fogel and Stanley L. Engerman, eds., *The Reinterpretation of American Economic History.* New York: Harper & Row, 1971.

Higgs, Robert, "Railroad Rates and the Populist Uprising," *Agricultural History,* July 1970.

———, *The Transformation of the American Economy, 1865–1914.* New York: Wiley, 1971.

Mayhew, Anne, "A Reappraisal of the Causes of Farm Protest in the United States, 1870–1900," *Journal of Economic History,* June 1972.

Parker, William N., "Sources of Agricultural Productivity in the Nineteenth Century," *Journal of Farm Economics,* December 1967.

———, and Judith Klein, "Productivity Growth in Grain Production in the United States, 1840–60 and 1900–10," in *Output, Employment, and Productivity in the United States after 1800,* Conference on Research in Income and Wealth, Studies in Income and Wealth, National Bureau of Economic Research, Vol. 30. New York: Columbia University Press, 1966.

Primack, Martin L., "Farm Capital Formation as a Use of Farm Labor in the United States, 1850–1910," *Journal of Economic History,* September 1966.

Rasmussen, Wayne, "The Impact of Technological Change on American Agriculture, 1862–1962," *Journal of Economic History,* December 1962.

Rothstein, Morton, "America in the International Rivalry for the British Wheat Market," *Mississippi Valley Historical Review,* December 1960.

Tostlebe, Alvin S., *Capital in Agriculture: Its Formation and Financing since 1870.* Princeton: Princeton University Press, 1957.

Towne, Marvin W., and Wayne Rasmussen, "Farm Gross Product and Gross Investment in the Nineteenth Century," in *Trends in the American Economy in the Nineteenth Century,* Conference on Research in Income and Wealth, Studies in Income and Wealth, National Bureau of Economic Research, Vol. 24. Princeton: Princeton University Press, 1960.

15
The Labor Movement

During the late nineteenth and early twentieth centuries, the occupational and industrial composition of the American labor force changed dramatically. The change reflected the sharp rise of manufacturing and the relative decline of agriculture. (See Figure 15–1.)

Post–Civil War industrial expansion was characterized by large-scale units whose production was geared to national and international markets, and, as a consequence, employer-employee relationships became highly depersonalized. In most instances, individual workers were unable to bargain effectively with employers, and, in order to create solidarity and enhance their bargaining strength, workers formed unions. Labor unionization did not occur smoothly; management, government, and the general public viewed it with disfavor. Many critics considered the organization of labor a threat to the capitalist system; indeed, several early labor leaders espoused socialism and revolutionary change. Because the weight of public opinion was against any form of labor organization, especially organization identified with socialism, the labor movement was forced to operate within the existing system for such pragmatic goals as shorter hours, higher wages, and better working conditions.

Despite strong opposition from outside and sharp disagreement among labor leaders on the most appropriate form of organization, skilled laborers had achieved strong organization by the early twentieth century. By the late 1930s, both skilled and unskilled workers were organized, and, since that time, unions have been effective in bargaining with management.

The following pages will review labor's accomplishments during the nineteenth and twentieth centuries, and specific attention will be focused on trends in organization, earnings, length of workday, and unemploy-

Figure 15-1 Percentage Distribution of Gainful Workers, by Major Sector, by Decade, 1870-1930

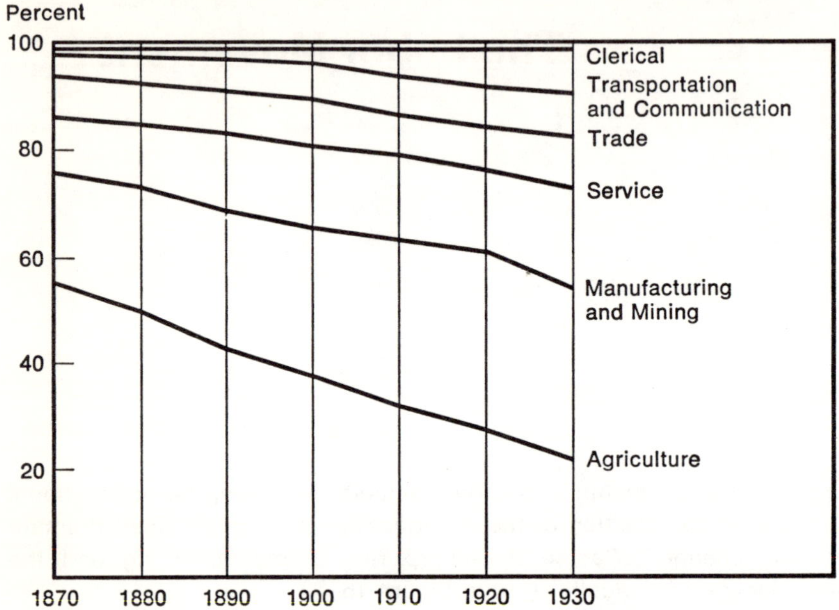

Source: U.S. Bureau of the Census, *Sixteenth Census of the United States: 1940, Population, Comparative Occupation Statistics for the United States, 1870 to 1940,* p. 101.

ment. In addition, this chapter will assess the impact of unions on wages and trends in work stoppages.

Trends in the Organization of Labor

Unions were not an important force in the antebellum economy, and the only significant union activity occurred in the skilled crafts. By the time of the Civil War, craft unions had been formed in most skilled occupations, and printers, locomotive engineers, machinists, and members of several other skilled trades had formed national federations. In contrast to the rapid spread of craft unions in the 1840s and 1850s, there was no serious attempt to organize unskilled labor; consequently, unions represented a very small portion of the nation's total labor force. Antebellum union activities were restricted to practical issues such as higher wages, shorter hours, and publicly supported education, and, in each of these areas, some modest advances were made.

The conditions of American industrial life changed rapidly in the late nineteenth century. Factory size increased sharply, and this augmented employers' bargaining strength *vis-à-vis* employees and depersonalized the employer-employee relationship. Large-scale corporate enterprises, production for national and international markets, large flows of immigration, increased mechanization of production, and technological unemployment were all facts of American industrial life in the postbellum decades, and, in order to protect its self-interest, labor was forced to organize and present a united front to management. However, there were many barriers to labor organization. Unions were viewed as an artificial interference in the market, and public opinion and government actions were hostile to labor organization throughout the late nineteenth and early twentieth centuries. The courts frequently imposed injunctions to break strikes, and they viewed unions as organizations denying due process to management. In addition to government hostility, unions were also faced by hostile management that discouraged union membership by discriminating against union members. Even within the laboring classes, a schism existed between skilled and unskilled workers, and there were many debates regarding who should be organized. There was also a fundamental dispute among labor leaders regarding the goals of the labor movement. Some idealistic leaders wanted to change the capitalist system and establish cooperatives; other pragmatic leaders worked within the system to achieve higher wages, shorter hours, and better working conditions. The bulk of the labor movement adopted a rather conservative attitude, and this made labor organization more palatable to the general public; however, public acceptance of labor unions did not become widespread until the depression of the 1930s.

The craft type of organization that had developed in the antebellum decades continued to prosper during the Civil War and immediate postwar years, and, by the middle 1870s, there were more than 300,000 craft union members, and many crafts had developed national federations.[1] Craft unions remained conservative and pragmatic and aimed most of their efforts at shortening the workday, increasing wages, and improving working conditions. The craft type of union failed to provide any significant means of organizing the large body of unskilled labor, however, and, throughout most of the nineteenth century, the American labor movement was a phenomenon of the elite.

There were two late nineteenth-century attempts to organize all labor, skilled and unskilled, into a single national union: the National Labor Union and the Knights of Labor. The National Labor Union (1866–72) was a political type of organization that tried to bring laborers of all skills together to muster support for higher wages, shorter hours, free land for

[1] National organization of craft unions was essential; without national organization, management could import laborers from outside the local labor market and circumvent the union's bargaining position.

settlers, and increased money and credit. It never received strong support from the craft unions, and, consequently, it had a very short life. The Knights of Labor also tried to unite labor of all skills, and its goals were similar to those of the National Labor Union. The Knights grew slowly during the 1870s, and, by the end of the decade, they had approximately 10,000 members. They won several key strikes in 1884–85, and membership soared to approximately 700,000; the strike successes were soon reversed, however, and membership fell to about 100,000 in 1890. In general, the Knights were not effective in negotiating with management, and they lost the support of skilled laborers who formed the American Federation of Labor (AFL) in the late 1880s.

The AFL grew slowly but steadily, and, in 1897, its membership totaled about 250,000. Membership increased sharply thereafter, rising to 1.0 million in 1902 and 1.7 million in 1904. Between 1904 and 1912, there were no significant increases in the AFL's membership, but, between 1912–20, membership more than doubled, increasing from 1.8 million to 4.1 million. In 1920, 80 percent of all union members in the United States belonged to the AFL. Union membership declined during the 1920s, and, during most of the decade, there were approximately 3.0 million AFL members and approximately 3.6 million total union members in the United States. (See Table 15–1.)

The AFL was a federation of independent national craft unions, and individual workers were not members of the AFL but, instead, belonged to a local craft union. Some semiskilled workers were brought into the AFL through the creation of amalgamated unions that combined workers of various skills who worked in similar areas, such as meat cutters, glass workers, and others. The AFL members' goals were simple and pragmatic; they demanded higher wages, shorter hours, and better working conditions. To attain these goals, they attempted to bargain with management; when bargaining failed, they resorted to strikes and boycotts.[2] The AFL members were not politically oriented, and they made no attempt to revolutionize the American capitalist system. Members accepted their position in the economy; they simply wanted to improve their economic standing and working conditions.

Most of labor's gains up until the Great Depression were made by the AFL, and, until this time, the American labor movement had largely been a union of the elite. Throughout the 1920s, only 7–8 percent of the total civilian labor force was organized into unions, and organization of unskilled workers was uncommon. Despite the small union membership,

[2] Collective bargaining did not become a regular feature of American industrial life until the 1930s. However, the need for labor-management negotiations was clearly demonstrated in the late nineteenth century by a series of violent strikes: Railroad Strikes (1877), Haymarket Riot (1886), Carnegie Steel Works (1892), and the Pullman Strike (1894).

however, labor prospered during the twenties, and there was no great drive toward unionization. The depressed economic conditions of the 1930s brought public sentiment and government action to a pro-union position, and, between 1934 and 1939, labor union membership almost tripled. (See Table 15–1.) Union membership continued to increase during the 1940s and early 1950s and then leveled off. By 1939, over 18 percent of the labor force was unionized, and, throughout the late 1940s and 1950s, 25–27 percent of the labor force was unionized. In recent years, the union share of the total labor force has declined to just below 25 percent.[3]

The sharp increase in union activity in the late 1930s reflected many factors, but most important was the federal government's new posture toward unions. Congress passed several significant pieces of legislation in the 1930s (Norris-La Guardia Act—1932, National Industrial Recovery Act—1933, and the Wagner Act—1935) which firmly established the right of unions to organize and bargain collectively.[4] The government's positive attitude encouraged union activity, and, in 1935, the Committee for Industrial Organization (CIO) was formed as a subgroup of the AFL, and its activity was directed at unionization of mass production workers. In 1939, the CIO separated from the AFL, and, during the 1940s and early 1950s, competition between these unions was great and brought about a sharp increase in union membership. In 1955, the two groups were reunited as the AFL-CIO.

Union membership has not grown relative to the total labor force in the past two decades, and this partially reflects a change in government policy and a shift in public sentiment. Management complained bitterly about federal legislation passed in the 1930s, and, in the Taft-Hartley Act (1947) and Landrum Griffin Act (1959), many restrictions were placed on union activities. The new legislation prohibited the closed shop, which allowed only union members to be employed, and it also allowed states to prohibit the union shop, which required all employees to join the union within a stipulated time period. It also provided for a presidential injunction postponing strikes for eighty days, imposed restrictions on union boycotting and picketing, required detailed reporting of union financial conditions, and established secret ballot elections for union officers. Public support for unions has been eroded by recent inflationary pressures that have resulted, in part, from union wage demands. Another factor that has helped tarnish big labor's image has been a number of highly

---

[3] See H. G. Lewis, *Unionism and Relative Wages in the United States* (Chicago: University of Chicago Press, 1963), p. 244. The slight relative decline in union membership that has occurred in the past decade partially reflects the relative increase in white collar occupations where unions traditionally have not been strong.

[4] In addition to the pro-union legislation passed in the 1930s, government also passed minimum wage laws and protective legislation regarding the employment of women and children.

Table 15-1 Labor Union Membership, 1898-1970 (thousands)

Year	Members
1898	467
1900	791
1902	1335
1904	2067
1906	1892
1908	2092
1910	2116
1912	2405
1914	2647
1916	2722
1918	3368
1920	5034
1922	3950
1924	3549
1926	3592
1928	3567
1930	3632
1932	3226
1934	3249
1936	4164
1938	8265
1940	8944
1942	10762
1944	14621
1946	14974
1948	15000
1950	15000
1952	16750
1954	17955
1956	18477
1958	18081
1960	18117
1962	17630
1964	17976
1966	19181
1968	20258
1970	20752

Source: *Historical Statistics,* Series D 741-45, and recent issues of the *Statistical Abstract.*

visible strikes by teachers, policemen, firemen, postal workers, printers, and airline workers. At the present time, union organizational activity is strong in the white collar service industries, but, in the early 1970s, over 75 percent of all union members were employed in the traditional union strongholds of manufacturing, mining, construction, transportation, and public utilities.

Trends in Hours and Earnings

Throughout the late nineteenth century, craft unions tried to reduce the length of the workday and raise wages. Clarence D. Long's classic study of wages, earnings, and hours in American manufacturing shows that the average workday declined slightly between 1860 and 1890 from 10.9 hours to 10.1.[5] Long also estimated that between 1860 and 1890 real daily wages increased by approximately 50 percent in manufacturing and by approximately 60 percent in the building trades.[6] The percentage gains in real wages may seem high, but, compared to twentieth-century wage increases, labor's gains between 1860 and 1890 were modest. During the late nineteenth century, such factors as large immigration flows, displaced agricultural workers, and the weak bargaining position of unions worked against real wage advances.

The length of the average workday declined steadily throughout the late nineteenth and first half of the twentieth centuries. Albert Rees has estimated that between 1890 and 1914 the average workday in manufacturing fell from 10 to 9.28 hours.[7] Some manufacturing plants had reduced the average workday to eight hours by the beginning of World War I; however, the forty-eight-hour week did not become common in most industries and occupations until the early 1930s, and this partially was due to the depressed economic conditions. The Fair Labor Standards Act (1938) set a maximum standard workweek of forty hours for industries engaged in interstate commerce; work in excess of forty hours was to be remunerated at the rate of one and one-half times the standard hourly rate.[8] By the early 1950s, the forty-hour workweek was standard in most industries, and, in recent years, several industries have adopted a thirty-five-hour week. The forty-hour week is still typical of most industries, however, and little change has taken place in the workweek during the past two decades. (See Table 15–2.)

Twentieth-century real wage increases were much greater than those attained in the nineteenth century. Between 1890 and 1914, wages increased at approximately the same rate that was achieved in the post–Civil War decades; for this period, Rees estimated that real hourly earnings in manufacturing rose 40 percent.[9] Between 1909 and 1940, real wages (1947–49 dollars) of manufacturing production workers doubled, increasing from

---

[5] Clarence D. Long, *Wages and Earnings in the United States, 1860–1890* (Princeton: Princeton University Press, 1960), p. 37.

[6] Real annual earnings in manufacturing increased by slightly less than 50 percent ($297 in 1860 to $434 in 1890) because of the fall in the average workday.

[7] Albert Rees, *Real Wages in Manufacturing, 1890–1914* (Princeton: Princeton University Press, 1961), p. 33.

[8] The Fair Labor Standards Act initially established a maximum standard workweek of forty-four hours, but this was scheduled for reduction to forty hours.

[9] See Rees, *Real Wages*, p. 120.

Table 15-2 Average Hourly Earnings and Average Weekly Hours, Production Workers in Manufacturing, 1909-70

Year	Average Hourly Earnings (current dollars)	Average Hourly Earnings (1947-49 dollars)	Average Weekly Hours
1909	$0.19	$0.55	51.0
1914	0.22	0.52	49.4
1920	0.56	0.65	47.4
1925	0.55	0.73	44.5
1930	0.55	0.77	42.1
1935	0.55	0.94	36.6
1940	0.66	1.10	38.1
1945	1.02	1.33	43.4
1950	1.47	1.43	40.5
1955	1.88	1.64	40.7
1960	2.26	1.79	39.7
1965	2.61	1.93	41.2
1970	3.36	2.02	39.8

Source: *Historical Statistics*, Series D 626-34, and U.S. Department of Labor, *Manpower Report of the President, 1973*, pp. 190-91.

$0.55 to $1.10 per hour; between 1940 and 1970, real wages almost doubled again, increasing from $1.10 to $2.02. (See Table 15–2.) Leo Wolman's estimates of post–World War I wages in the United States suggest that real hourly earnings in manufacturing, mining, building trades, and steam railroads doubled between 1914 and 1939.[10] In recent decades, the rate of wage increases has declined, and the figures in Table 15–2 show the following percentage changes in real hourly earnings for manufacturing production workers: 1930–40, 42.9 percent; 1940–50, 30.0 percent; 1950–60, 25.2 percent; and 1960–70, 12.9 percent.

Trends in Unemployment

Unemployment has been a chronic problem in the United States economy throughout most of the twentieth century. There is always some unemployment related to worker changes in location, technological change, seasonality, and other short-run factors, but most of this is temporary and of no great concern.[11] The economy's goal is to maintain full employment, and an unemployment rate of 4 percent or less is generally viewed

---

[10] Leo Wolman, "Wages in the United States Since 1914," *Proceedings of the Sixth Annual Meeting*, Industrial Relations Research Association, 1953, p. 45.

[11] Short-run temporary unemployment is commonly referred to as frictional unemployment.

Table 15-3 Percentage of Civilian Labor Force Unemployed, 1900-1972

Year	Percent Unemployed	Year	Percent Unemployed
1900	5.0%	1937	14.3%
1901	2.4	1938	19.0
1902	2.7	1939	17.2
1903	2.6	1940	14.6
1904	4.8	1941	9.9
1905	3.1	1942	4.7
1906	0.8	1943	1.9
1907	1.8	1944	1.2
1908	8.5	1945	1.9
1909	5.2	1946	3.9
1910	5.9	1947	3.6
1911	6.2	1948	3.4
1912	5.2	1949	5.5
1913	4.4	1950	5.0
1914	8.0	1951	3.0
1915	9.7	1952	2.7
1916	4.8	1953	2.5
1917	4.8	1954	5.0
1918	1.4	1955	4.0
1919	2.3	1956	3.8
1920	4.0	1957	4.3
1921	11.9	1958	6.8
1922	7.6	1959	5.5
1923	3.2	1960	5.5
1924	5.5	1961	6.7
1925	4.0	1962	5.5
1926	1.9	1963	5.7
1927	4.1	1964	5.2
1928	4.4	1965	4.5
1929	3.2	1966	3.8
1930	8.7	1967	3.8
1931	15.9	1968	3.6
1932	23.6	1969	3.5
1933	24.9	1970	4.9
1934	21.7	1971	5.9
1935	20.1	1972	5.6
1936	16.9		

Source: *Historical Statistics*, Series D 46-47, and *Manpower Report of the President, 1973*, p. 127.

as full employment.[12] Table 15–3 shows that the unemployment rate exceeded 4 percent in forty-five out of the last seventy-three years and in fifteen of the last twenty-four years. The most severe unemployment in our history occurred in the depression of the 1930s; on an average, about 20 percent of the labor force was unemployed during this decade. Consider-

[12] The unemployment rate is defined to include workers seeking employment but unable to find a job.

able unemployment was also experienced during 1914–15, 1921–22, and 1958–64. There are several difficulties involved in making long-run comparisons of unemployment rates, however, and these should be pointed out. Unemployment varies sharply by age, sex, and race, and changes in the composition of the labor force may have a significant effect on the unemployment rate. For example, in 1972, the following unemployment rates were reported: all males, 4.9 percent; all females, 6.6 percent; white males, 4.5 percent; black males, 8.9 percent; all males aged 16–17, 18.2 percent; all males aged 18–19, 14.0 percent; all males aged 20–24, 9.2 percent; all males aged 25–34, 3.7 percent; and all males aged 35–44, 2.7 percent. Another difficulty is that unemployment figures mask underemployment.[13] For example, unemployment rates for the 1930s do not reflect the reduced workweek or the many instances of laborers working at jobs below their skill level, and, therefore, the figures in Table 15–3 understate the impact of the depression on employment.

The Impact of Unions on Wages and Work Stoppages

Unions were not a major factor in wage negotiations until the early twentieth century. Clarence Long examined the wage gap between skilled and unskilled labor during the late nineteenth century, and he found no significant increase in the size of the differential.[14] However, Long cautioned that more research needs to be completed before the exact degree of the union impact can be determined. For the twentieth century, H. G. Lewis has examined the effect of unions on wages of union labor relative to nonunion labor, and his results suggest that unions have had a large positive impact.[15] He found that unions generally created a spread between union and nonunion wages of at least 10 percent. Between 1923 and 1929, he estimated that unions created a 15–20 percent differential, and he estimated that during 1931–33 the union effect exceeded 25 percent. The differential created by unions declined during the late 1930s, and, by 1939–41, it was between 10 and 20 percent. In the late 1940s, the union impact was at its lowest point and was less than 5 percent; unions quickly recovered, however, and, by the 1950s, the union impact had increased to 10–15 percent.

---

[13] Underemployment is defined to include those who work part time but would work full time if a suitable job developed, those who are working at jobs below their education or skill level, and those who have dropped out of the job search because they could not find acceptable employment. According to the standard definition of unemployment (footnote 12), none of the above would be considered unemployed.

[14] See Long, *Wages and Earnings*, pp. 116–17. Long did not have wage figures for unionized and nonunionized labor; therefore, he compared wages of a partially unionized group (skilled labor) to a nonunionized group (unskilled labor).

[15] See Lewis, *Unionism and Relative Wages*. It should be made clear that Lewis was only concerned with the impact of unions on wages of union members relative to wages of nonunion members. The role of unions in advancing the welfare of all workers is an area for future research.

Table 15-4 Work Stoppages, Number of Workers Involved, and Percentage of Annual Working Time Lost Due to Stoppages, 1881-1970

Year	Stoppages	Workers (000)	Percent Working Time Lost
1881	477	130	
1882	476	159	
1883	506	170	
1884	485	165	
1885	695	258	
1886	1572	610	
1887	1503	439	
1888	946	163	
1889	1111	260	
1890	1897	373	
1891	1786	330	
1892	1359	239	
1893	1375	288	
1894	1404	690	
1895	1255	407	
1896	1066	249	
1897	1110	416	
1898	1098	263	
1899	1838	432	
1900	1839	568	
1901	3012	564	
1902	3240	692	
1903	3648	788	
1904	2419	574	
1905	2186	302	
1906-13	—	—	
1914	1204	—	
1915	1593	—	
1916	3789	—	
1917	4450	—	
1918	3353	—	
1919	3630	—	
1920	3411	—	
1921	2385	—	
1922	1112	—	
1923	1553	—	
1924	1249	—	
1925	1301	—	
1926	1035	—	
1927	707	330	0.37%
1928	604	314	0.17
1929	921	289	0.07
1930	637	183	0.05
1931	810	342	0.11
1932	841	324	0.23
1933	1695	1170	0.36
1934	1856	1470	0.38
1935	2014	1120	0.29
1936	2172	789	0.21
1937	4740	1860	0.43
1938	2772	688	0.15
1939	2613	1170	0.28
1940	2508	577	0.10
1941	4288	2360	0.32
1942	2968	840	0.05
1943	3752	1980	0.15
1944	4956	2120	0.09
1945	4750	3470	0.47
1946	4985	4600	1.43
1947	3693	2170	0.47
1948	3419	1960	0.37
1949	3606	3030	0.59
1950	4843	2410	0.44
1951	4737	2220	0.23
1952	5117	3540	0.57
1953	5091	2400	0.26
1954	3468	1530	0.21
1955	4320	2650	0.26
1956	3825	1900	0.29
1957	3673	1390	0.14
1958	3694	2060	0.22
1959	3708	1880	0.61
1960	3333	1320	0.17
1961	3367	1450	0.14
1962	3614	1230	0.16
1963	3362	941	0.13
1964	3655	1640	0.15
1965	3963	1550	0.15
1966	4495	1960	0.15
1967	4595	2870	0.25
1968	5045	2649	0.28
1969	5700	2481	0.24
1970	5716	3305	0.37

Source: *Historical Statistics*, Series D 764-78.

When union bargaining for higher wages or improved working conditions has been unsuccessful, union members have generally resorted to strikes and boycotts. The historical pattern of work stoppages between 1881 and 1971 is shown in Table 15–4. The number of workers involved in stoppages increased sharply in the late 1880s and, between 1886 and 1900, averaged almost 400,000 workers per year. The number of work stoppages continued to be heavy in the first two decades of the twentieth century, but, in the 1920s, the annual number of stoppages declined from around 3,000 to less than 1,000. The number of stoppages increased moderately in the 1930s and sharply in the 1940s; since 1950, the annual number has exceeded 3,000 in all years and has exceeded 4,000 in one-half of the years. Despite the great number of work stoppages, the annual loss in working time resulting from shutdowns has been amazingly low, and, in all years except 1946 (1.43 percent), 1949 (0.59 percent), 1952 (0.57 percent), and 1959 (0.61 percent), the annual time lost during stoppages was less than one-half of 1 percent of the total annual work time.

Summary

This chapter has traced the pattern of union organization of American labor from the antebellum years to the present day. Until the 1930s, the union movement was an elitist phenomenon and was largely restricted to the skilled trades. Government action and public acceptance stimulated union activity in the 1930s, and, since that time, union membership has increased sharply, especially among low-skilled workers. Currently, about one-fourth of the total labor force and about one-half of the industrial labor force are represented by unions.[16] Unions have been very effective in raising wages, shortening hours, and improving working conditions for their members. However, as the strength of unions has increased, there has been increasing public concern about union activity. Recent strikes by teachers, firemen, and policemen and demands for higher wages in the face of inflation have raised concern over the strength of big labor. Union leaders are aware of the loss of public sentiment, and they have attempted to defend their actions and restore public support.

Suggested Reading

Adams, Donald R., Jr., "Wage Rates in the Early National Period: Philadelphia, 1785–1830," *Journal of Economic History,* September 1968.

Gitelman, H. M., "Perspectives on American Industrial Violence," *Business History Review,* Spring 1973.

[16] In 1970, the union share was 60 percent in mining and 75 percent in construction, transportation, and public utilities.

Lebergott, Stanley, *Manpower in Economic Growth: The American Record Since 1800.* New York: McGraw-Hill, 1964.

———, "Wage Trends, 1800–1900," in *Trends in the American Economy in the Nineteenth Century,* Conference on Research in Income and Wealth, Studies in Income and Wealth, National Bureau of Economic Research, Vol. 24. Princeton: Princeton University Press, 1960.

Lewis, H. G., *Unionism and Relative Wages in the United States.* Chicago: University of Chicago Press, 1963.

Long, Clarence D., *Wages and Earnings in the United States, 1860–1890.* Princeton: Princeton University Press, 1960.

Rees, Albert, *Real Wages in Manufacturing, 1890–1914.* Princeton: Princeton University Press, 1961.

Weiss, Thomas, "The Industrial Distribution of the Urban and Rural Workforces: Estimates for the United States, 1870–1910," *Journal of Economic History,* December 1972.

Wolman, Leo, "Wages in the United States Since 1914," *Proceedings of the Sixth Annual Meeting,* Industrial Relations Research Association, 1953.

Woytinsky, W. S., *Employment and Wages in the United States.* New York: Twentieth Century Fund, 1953.

16
Changes in the Organization of Business

Since the late nineteenth century, there has been a marked increase in the scale of American business. Between 1850 and 1950, real value added per manufacturing plant increased from $5,654 to $184,147, and the average employment per establishment increased from 7.8 workers to 55.3. In large part, the increase in scale of American industry has been achieved by consolidation of existing plants through merger. The merger movement began in the late nineteenth century and, with several exceptions, has continued strongly to the present day. Merger activity has occurred most heavily during periods of economic expansion, and three periods of particularly high activity can be singled out: the late 1890s–early 1900s, the 1920s, and the post-World War II years.[1] In the first merger movement, consolidation was aimed primarily at achieving monopoly control over markets for final products (horizontal integration).[2] However, there were also several attempts to achieve monopoly power by controlling all stages of production in particular industries (vertical integration).[3] The second

[1] Recent research has suggested that there is a close relationship between mergers and stock market prices; see Jesse W. Markham, "Survey of the Evidence and Findings on Mergers," in *Business Concentration and Price Policy,* National Bureau of Economic Research (Princeton: Princeton University Press, 1955), pp. 152–54, and Ralph L. Nelson, *Merger Movements in American Industry, 1895–1956* (Princeton: Princeton University Press, 1959), pp. 106–26.

[2] A monopoly is strictly defined as a market or industry with only one firm selling a product with no close substitutes. Monopoly power is used here to describe the attempts by firms to gain control of a substantial share of the market. Horizontal integration refers to mergers that join firms producing similar products and selling in similar markets.

[3] Vertical integration refers to mergers that join firms involved in different stages of production; it represents an attempt to control all aspects of an industry's production from raw materials to distribution of final products.

major wave of mergers was characterized by heavy amounts of both horizontal and vertical combination, and, in most instances, it brought about oligopoly rather than monopoly.[4] In the post–World War II period, the merger movement has involved the creation of conglomerates which have combined firms in diverse industries under a central management.[5]

This chapter will survey the major features of the merger movement during the three periods of most active consolidation. Attention will be focused primarily on the number of mergers, purpose of consolidation, government attempts to control big business, and the concentration of American industry that has resulted from consolidation.

Late Nineteenth- Early Twentieth-Century Mergers

Many late nineteenth century business combinations took the form of pools and trusts. Pools were a rather loose form of business organization and were written agreements concerning market areas, prices, production quotas, or profit shares. The simplest pools merely agreed on market areas for particular firms; more formal arrangements involved pooling all output, selling it, and distributing the profits on some predetermined basis. Pools were very popular in the 1880s and early 1890s. However, the informal nature of pooling agreements made them difficult to enforce, and their legality was questionable; consequently, they gave way to more formal types of business organization. Trusts were also popular in the 1880s and early 1890s, and, unlike pools, they represented a rigid form of business organization. Generally, trusts were formed by several companies in a particular industry by granting control of their stock to a group of trustees. Since the trustees had voting control of several companies, they usually were able to achieve monopoly control of the industry. Public resentment against trusts ran very high, and, in the early 1890s, several suits were brought against trusts, and their legality was questioned. Trust formations and pooling agreements declined sharply in the 1890s, and they were followed by a wave of direct consolidation by outright purchase of firms or by purchase of stocks to acquire a firm's voting rights.[6] This latter type of combination was termed a holding company and was made possible by liberalization

---

[4] Oligopoly refers to a market or industry with a small number of dominant firms, each of which is sufficiently powerful to exert a great deal of control on the total market or industry; for example, the automobile industry is oligopolistic. For an analysis of the change in merger activity from monopoly creation to oligopoly creation, see George J. Stigler, "Monopoly and Oligopoly by Merger," *American Economic Review*, May 1950.

[5] Most conglomerates have been formed in order to achieve product diversification; diversification allows a firm to spread its risk.

[6] The Sherman Act (1890) made pooling agreements and trusts illegal, and the passage of this legislation is viewed as a major factor behind the sharp rise in direct consolidations in the late nineteenth and twentieth centuries; see Markham, "Survey of the Evidence and Findings on Mergers," p. 167.

of state incorporation laws in the late 1880s and early 1890s. Since the late nineteenth century, most consolidation of business enterprise has taken place through these direct forms of merger.

Merger activity in the late nineteenth and early twentieth centuries was concentrated between 1898 and 1902. (See Table 16–1.) A great deal of

Table 16-1 Annual Number of Mergers in Manufacturing and Mining, 1895-1969

Nelson Series[a]		Thorp Series		FTC Series	
Year	Mergers	Year	Mergers	Year	Mergers
1895	43	1919	438	1940	140
1896	26	1920	760	1941	111
1897	69	1921	487	1942	118
1898	303	1922	309	1943	213
1899	1208	1923	311	1944	324
1900	340	1924	368	1945	333
1901	423	1925	554	1946	419
1902	379	1926	856	1947	404
1903	142	1927	870	1948	223
1904	79	1928	1058	1949	126
1905	226	1929	1245	1950	219
1906	128	1930	799	1951	235
1907	87	1931	464	1952	288
1908	50	1932	203	1953	295
1909	49	1933	120	1954	387
1910	142	1934	101	1955	683
1911	103	1935	130	1956	673
1912	82	1936	126	1957	585
1913	85	1937	124	1958	589
1914	39	1938	110	1959	835
1915	71	1939	87	1960	844
1916	117			1961	954
1917	195			1962	853
1918	71			1963	861
1919	171			1964	854
1920	206			1965	1008
				1966	995
				1967	1496
				1968	2407
				1969	2307
				1970	1357
				1971	1011

Source: Ralph L. Nelson, *Merger Movements in American Industry, 1895-1956* (Princeton: Princeton University Press, 1959), p. 37; Willard L. Thorp and Walter Crowder, *The Structure of American Industry*, Temporary National Economic Committee Monograph 27, 1941, pp. 231-34; Bureau of Economics, Federal Trade Commission, *Economic Papers, 1966-69*, p. 77; and recent issues of the *Statistical Abstract*.

[a] The Nelson series only includes large mergers; the Thorp and Federal Trade Commission (FTC) series include large and small mergers.

merger activity during this period resulted from stock market speculation, and the collapse of the stock market in 1903–4 and the Northern Securities decision (1904) brought to an end the conditions favoring merger.[7] Most of the trusts and pools formed in the 1880s and early 1890s were concerned with achieving monopoly power over final product markets, and this continued to be the most important objective behind the mergers of the late 1890s and early 1900s. Solid data on market control and degree of concentration are not available for this period, but there is wide agreement that market power was heavily concentrated in the steel, petroleum, tobacco, sugar refining, nonferrous metal, and shoe machinery industries. In addition, substantial vertical integration was achieved by John D. Rockefeller in the petroleum industry and Andrew Carnegie in the steel industry.

The consolidation of business enterprise in the late nineteenth and early twentieth centuries caused a great deal of public resentment, and pressure was put on the federal government to control the trend toward combination and to preserve competition. The government responded with the Sherman Act (1890); the Act was ambiguously written and was not used effectively until 1911 when the Standard Oil and American Tobacco companies were dissolved. However, dissolution of monopoly power in the tobacco and oil industries did not result in competition but rather substituted the oligopoly power of several large firms for the monopoly power of a single large firm. In 1914, Congress passed two new pieces of antitrust legislation, the Clayton Act and the Federal Trade Commission Act; with the beginning of World War I, however, trust-busting activity declined, and little immediate use was made of these new tools. There were several important Supreme Court cases in the first two decades of the twentieth century, but the Court's decisions were often conflicting and demonstrated the absence of a clear-cut policy toward big business. By 1920, the only action consistently viewed as illegal by the Court was overt collusion between firms to exclude competition.[8]

The Merger Movement in the 1920s

The government's modest attempt to curb business consolidation, as well as several brief periods of depressed business conditions and stock market prices (1903–4, 1907–8, and 1913–14), discouraged merger activity between 1903 and 1918. (See Table 16–1.) However, the 1920s were a period of

---

[7] The Northern Securities case made it clear that holding companies were not immune from prosecution under the Sherman Act.

[8] In 1920, in *United States* v. *United States Steel Corporation,* the Supreme Court determined that size alone was not sufficient to prove monopoly. In order to violate the law, a firm had to have monopoly power and show a willingness to use it to exclude competition. This decision has been viewed by most business historians as providing a stimulus to the merger movement of the 1920s.

high growth, and the government's attitude toward business consolidation was relaxed and nonantagonistic. As a result of these favorable circumstances, the pace of the merger movement increased sharply in the 1920s, especially between 1926 and 1929. (See Table 16–1.) In absolute numbers, merger activity was probably more active in the late twenties than it had been between 1898 and 1902, but the attitude of government and the general public toward consolidation was generally one of passive acceptance.[9] This attitude partially resulted from the fact that in the 1920s mergers generally created oligopolistic markets rather than monopolistic markets, and the effect of combination on competition was not clear. Merger activity was also more diversified than in earlier years and involved several new industries (banking and public utilities) and consisted of a combination of horizontal integration, vertical integration, and conglomerates.[10] The general prosperity of the 1920s, with rising wages and declining prices, was an additional factor favoring public and government acceptance of big business.

Merger activity in the late 1920s brought about a sharp increase in concentration of industrial power among large firms. Table 16–2 shows the large firms' share of total manufacturing assets, and, between 1925 and 1931, the asset share of the 100 largest firms increased from 34.5 percent to 42.2 percent. The twenties brought about a sharp reduction of competition in the traditional sense, and, in many industries, the competition between many small firms was replaced by oligopolistic competition between several large firms.

Post–World War II Mergers

The heavy merger activity of the 1920s was not resumed again in continuous fashion until the middle 1950s. The depressed economic conditions of the 1930s did not encourage new business ventures, and the temporary suspension of anti-trust laws by the National Recovery Administration in the early 1930s could not offset the unfavorable economic conditions. Franklin D. Roosevelt vigorously prosecuted the anti-trust laws in the late 1930s, but the figures in Table 16–1 suggest that his action had little effect. The entrance of the United States into World War II brought a sharp de-

[9] In Table 16–1, the Nelson series only shows mergers of large corporations, while the Thorp and Federal Trade Commission series show mergers of small and large corporations. As a result, it is very difficult to make accurate comparisons between the degree of merger activity in the late nineteenth-early twentieth centuries and later periods.

[10] Despite the diversified nature of mergers in the 1920s, horizontal combinations continued to be the most important type of merger until the end of World War II. Markham, "Survey of the Evidence and Findings on Mergers," p. 169, claims that one-third of the mergers in the 1920s took place in banking and public utilities, and he argues that consolidation in these industries did not arouse public attention.

Table 16-2 Share of Manufacturing Assets Held by the 200 Largest Corporations, 1925-71

Year	100 Largest Corporations	200 Largest Corporations
1925	34.5%	—
1927	34.4	—
1929	38.2	45.8%
1931	42.2	49.4
1933	42.5	49.5
1935	40.8	47.7
1937	42.1	49.1
1939	41.9	48.7
1941	38.2	45.1
1947	37.5	45.0
1950	38.4	46.1
1952	39.3	47.7
1954	41.9	50.4
1956	43.9	52.8
1958	46.0	55.2
1960	45.5	55.2
1962	45.5	55.1
1964	45.8	55.8
1966	45.8	56.1
1968	48.8	60.4
1971	48.9	61.0

Source: Federal Trade Commission, *Economic Papers, 1966-69,* p. 288, and *Statistical Abstract,* 1973, p. 483.

cline in the government's anti-consolidation effort, but economic conditions were highly uncertain, and it was not until the last stages of the war that merger activity increased. The pace of the merger movement quickened in the late 1950s, and an unparalleled wave of consolidation took place in the 1960s. (See Table 16–1.)

The large majority of recent mergers has been achieved through the formation of conglomerates; in fact, between 1967 and 1970, conglomerates accounted for over 80 percent of all consolidations. (See Table 16–3.) Horizontal combinations, which accounted for the majority of mergers throughout the period from the late nineteenth century until World War II, have declined sharply in the past two decades, and they accounted for less than 10 percent of all mergers between 1967 and 1970. Most conglomerates have been stimulated by a desire to achieve product diversification rather than to extend control over a particular market.[11] Conglomerates have also

[11] According to the Federal Trade Commission, over 75 percent of all conglomerates formed between 1951 and 1966 were created to achieve product diversification and less than 10 percent were created for market extension; see Bureau of Economics, Federal Trade Commission, *Economic Papers, 1966–69,* p. 80.

Table 16-3 Percentage Distribution of Large Acquisitions in Manufacturing and Mining, by Type of Merger, 1951-70

Period	Horizontal	Vertical	Conglomerate
1951-54			
Number of Mergers	37%	12%	51%
Assets Involved in Mergers	40	9	51
1955-58			
Number of Mergers	28	16	56
Assets Involved in Mergers	34	20	46
1959-62			
Number of Mergers	17	18	65
Assets Involved in Mergers	19	24	57
1963-66			
Number of Mergers	15	15	70
Assets Involved in Mergers	14	15	71
1967-70			
Number of Mergers	8	8	84
Assets Involved in Mergers	9	9	82

Source: Federal Trade Commission, *Economic Papers, 1966-69*, p. 45, and *Statistical Abstract*, 1973, p. 486.

been formed as a by-product of normal stock accumulation and business investment.

Recent business consolidation has taken place wtihout any strong resistance by the public or government. Between 1951 and 1966, only 4 percent of all mergers were formally challenged by anti-trust agencies, and only 10 percent of all large mergers were challenged.[12] Since most conglomerates have been formed to achieve product diversification rather than market control, it is very difficult to make a case that this type of merger limits competition and restrains trade.

Even so, conglomerates have brought about a sharp increase in concentration of American industry among large firms, and federal regulatory agencies have shown a great deal of concern over conglomerate growth.[13] Between 1950 and 1971, the total manufacturing assets held by the 100 largest firms increased from 38 percent to 49 percent, and this concentration of assets took place despite the entrance of over fifty thousand new

[12] Large mergers were defined to include those where the acquired firm had assets of $10 million or more; see Federal Trade Commission, *Economic Papers, 1966–69*, p. 36.

[13] See Federal Trade Commission, *Economic Papers, 1966–69*, pp. 264–87.

industrial corporations.[14] However, the concentration of economic activity among large firms is not inconsistent with competition within particular industries. Few conglomerates have been formed to achieve market control in specific industries, and, if one examines recent changes in the degree of competition within individual industries, it appears that conglomerates have not reduced the amount of competition. A common measure of the degree of monopoly power in particular industries is the percentage of the industry's total market controlled by the leading four firms.[15] Changes in concentration between 1947 and 1967 are shown in Table 16–4.[16] Out of the sample of fifty-four industries, there were thirty declines in market concentration and twenty-four advances; on balance, it appears that the consolidation of economic activity into large firms has not reduced the amount of competition in individual industries.[17] This result should not be surprising since conglomerates have largely been formed to attain diversification rather than market domination.[18]

Postscript on Concentration of American Business Enterprise

The above pages have traced the trends in business organization from the late nineteenth century to the present. It has been shown that there has been an almost steady increase in the concentration of economic activity among large firms. Three main waves of consolidation were singled out: 1898–1902, the 1920s, and 1955 to the present. During the interim periods, there was a slowdown in merger activity, but there was not any significant reversal of the consolidation movement. In the first two periods of heavy merger activity, consolidation generally involved firms in similar or related industries, but, in recent years, consolidation has taken the form of conglomerates which have merged firms in diverse areas of activity under one management. The large number of conglomerates that have been

---

[14] An alternative measure of concentration is yielded by value added shares; between 1947 and 1967, the share of aggregate manufacturing value added contributed by the fifty largest firms increased from 17 percent to 25 percent; see *Statistical Abstract*, 1973, p. 483. For an excellent review of concentration measures and trends, see F. M. Scherer, *Industrial Market Structure and Economic Performance* (Chicago: Rand McNally, 1970), Ch. 3.

[15] Some studies of concentration use the eight largest firms, but the choice of four or eight firms has no effect on the results shown here. Concentration ratios were published for 1935 in *The Structure of the American Economy*, U.S. National Resources Committee, 1939. The Federal Trade Commission reviewed trends in industrial concentration between 1935 and 1950 and found no significant change; see *Report of the Federal Trade Commission on Changes in Concentration in Manufacturing, 1935 to 1947 and 1950*. A summary of trends in concentration ratios between 1935 and 1967 can be found in the U.S. Department of Commerce, *1967 Census of Manufactures*, Vol. I, pp. 9-9—9-40.

[16] The industries shown in Table 16–4 were those for which data were available for both 1947 and 1967, and the annual value of shipments in 1967 was greater than $1 billion.

[17] A great deal of research must be completed before the impact of conglomerates on competition in the economy as a whole can be determined.

[18] The heterogeneous nature of the conglomerate has been a major factor in the small number of anti-trust suits that have been brought against conglomerate mergers.

Table 16-4 Percentage of Total Value of Shipments Accounted for by Four Largest Companies, by Selected Manufacturing Industries, 1947 and 1967

Industry	1947	1967	Industry	1947	1967
Meat packing	41%	26%	Fertilizers	36%	35%
Ice cream	40	33	Petroleum refining	37	33
Flour and other grain	29	30	Shoes, except rubber	28	27
Prepared feeds	19	23	Glass containers	63	60
Bread	16	26	Cement	30	29
Confectionery	17	25	Blast furnaces and steel mills	50	48
Malt liquors	21	40			
Distilled liquor	75	54	Gray iron foundries	16	27
Soft drinks	10	13	Steel foundries	23	20
Flavorings	50	67	Primary zinc	53	59
Soybean oil	44	55	Iron and steel forgings	24	30
Cigarettes	90	81	Metal cans	78	73
Tobacco stemming	88	63	Sheet metalwork	21	10
Weaving mills (synthetics)	31	46	Screw machine products	17	6
Knit outerwear	8	15	Bolts, nuts, rivets, and washers	20	18
Knit fabric mills	27	15			
Men's and boys' suits and coats	9	17	Fabricated wire products	20	11
			Valves and pipe fittings	24	14
Men's dress shirts and nightwear	19	23	Machine tools, metal cutting	20	21
Men's and boys' trousers	12	20	Ball and roller bearings	62	54
Women and children's underwear	6	15	Transformers	73	65
			Motors and generators	59	48
Wooden furniture	7	12	Lighting fixtures	18	19
Newspapers	21	16	Electrical engine equipment	67	66
Periodicals	34	24	Aircraft engines	72	64
Books	18	20	Shipbuilding	43	42
Plastic materials	44	27	Railroad and street cars	56	53
Pharmaceutical preparations	28	24	Photographic equipment	61	69
Toilet preparations	24	38	Games and toys	20	25

Source: U.S. Department of Commerce, *1967 Census of Manufactures*, Vol. I, pp. 9-9—9-40.

formed has resulted in a sharp concentration of economic activity among firms, but, because of the heterogeneous nature of conglomerates, the creation of large firms has been achieved without any apparent loss of competition in individual industries. However, economic activity is more heavily controlled by large firms than ever before, and the net effects of the conglomerate movement on competition in the economy as a whole remains a topic for further research.

John Kenneth Galbraith has recently surveyed the current state of competition in the American economy, and he has argued that competitive markets have been replaced by the planning of large firms.[19] The large-

[19] John Kenneth Galbraith, *The New Industrial State* (Boston: Houghton Mifflin, 1967).

scale production and heavy capital expenditures associated with modern industry encourage firms to plan, and, in order to guarantee that their plans will be successful, firms try to control the market to conform to their expectations. In consumer goods industries, planning often involves an attempt to dictate consumer taste. Galbraith's ideas are speculative and provocative, and they have been debated and rejected by many economists. However, in view of the sharp increase in concentration in recent years, his ideas are worthy of careful attention and should not be dismissed without further research.

Suggested Reading

Adams, Walter, "The Military-Industrial Complex and the New Industrial State," *American Economic Review,* May 1968.

Arnould, Richard J., "Changing Patterns of Concentration in American Meat Packing, 1880–1963," *Business History Review,* Spring 1971.

Chandler, Alfred D., Jr., "The Beginnings of 'Big Business' in American Industry," *Business History Review,* Spring 1959.

———, "The Structure of American Industry in the Twentieth Century: An Historical Overview," *Business History Review,* Autumn 1969.

Galambos, Louis, "The Agrarian Image of the Large Corporation, 1879–1920: A Study in Social Accommodation," *Journal of Economic History,* September 1968.

Galbraith, John Kenneth, *The New Industrial State.* Boston: Houghton Mifflin, 1967.

Harbeson, Robert W., "Railroads and Regulation, 1877–1916: Conspiracy or Public Interest," *Journal of Economic History,* June 1967.

Kolko, Gabriel, *Railroads and Regulation, 1877–1916.* New York: W. W. Norton, 1970.

Livesay, Harold C., and Patrick G. Porter, "Vertical Integration in American Manufacturing, 1899–1948," *Journal of Economic History,* September 1969.

Macavoy, Paul W., *The Economic Effects of Regulation: The Trunk Line Railroad Cartels and the Interstate Commerce Commission Before 1900.* Cambridge, Mass.: M.I.T. Press, 1965.

Markham, Jesse W., "Survey of the Evidence and Findings on Mergers," in *Business Concentration and Price Policy,* National Bureau of Economic Research. Princeton: Princeton University Press, 1955.

Nelson, Ralph L., *Merger Movements in American Industry, 1895–1956.* Princeton: Princeton University Press, 1959.

Nutter, G. Warren, and Henry Adler Einhorn, *Enterprise Monopoly in the United States: 1899–1958.* New York: Columbia University Press, 1969.

Porter, Patrick G., and Harold C. Livesay, "Oligopoly in Small Manufacturing Industries," *Explorations in Economic History,* Spring 1970.

Scherer, F. M., *Industrial Market Structure and Economic Performance.* Chicago: Rand McNally, 1970, Ch. 3.

Stigler, George J., "Monopoly and Oligopoly by Merger," *American Economic Review,* May 1950.

17
Productivity Trends in the American Economy

This chapter examines productivity trends in the American economy in the late nineteenth and twentieth centuries and borrows heavily from the path-breaking work of John W. Kendrick.[1] The chapter includes a brief survey of the concept of productivity, a summary of historical trends in productivity advance, and an assessment of the impact of productivity change on American economic growth and welfare.

The Concept of Productivity

Productivity refers to the relationship between output of final products and input of productive factors, and it is closely related to technology. Productivity is a measure of efficiency with which resources are converted into final products, and the level of productivity is defined as the ratio of output to input. Productivity advance is defined as the change in the output/input ratio, and, in large part, it results from the application of technological change.[2]

The most reliable index of efficiency change is the total factor productivity measure which shows the relationship between total output and all inputs. Due to problems in obtaining accurate data on capital inputs, however, many productivity studies have used a partial productivity mea-

[1] John W. Kendrick, *Productivity Trends in the United States* (Princeton: Princeton University Press, 1961).

[2] If technology is broadly defined, virtually everything that influences the efficiency of converting inputs into output can be attributed to technological change.

sure such as output per employee or output per manhour. Labor productivity measures are useful indicators of labor efficiency, but they are not appropriate indexes of efficiency in the economy as a whole because they are affected by factor substitution. Substitution of capital for labor in the productive process may raise labor productivity because it reduces labor input, but it may have no positive effect on efficiency in the economy as a whole because the increased capital input may simply offset the reduced labor input. Partial productivity indicators such as output per manhour and output per unit of capital are useful tools of analysis, but, in order to interpret their significance, they must be provided in conjunction with a total factor productivity index. Recent trends in the American economy have shown a rather sharp substitution of capital for labor. In fact, John W. Kendrick has estimated that, between 1899 and 1953, capital was substituted for labor at an annual rate of 0.8 percent;[3] however, given that the labor share accounted for almost 80 percent of total factor input, the ratio of total input/labor input only increased by approximately 0.25 percent per year. Kendrick concluded that substitution of capital for labor has not been a major factor in labor saving, and most of the increase in labor productivity between 1899 and 1953 was due to the adoption of more efficient techniques of production.[4]

The basic forces underlying productivity change are advances in technology, economic conditions, the institutional framework, and social and cultural attitudes. The factors that stimulate technological breakthroughs, such as increased education and research and development, create the possibility for productivity advance. However, in order for new technology to be successfully applied, the institutional framework must encourage efficiency. Despite recent advances in the government's role in the American economy, competition for markets and profits encourages efficiency and forces producers to search for the lowest-cost methods of producing and distributing their products. Social and cultural values in the United States have always stressed individual initiative and acquisitiveness, and they have encouraged rapid adoption of efficiency improvements. Finally, in any given time period, the rate of productivity advance will also reflect current and anticipated economic conditions. Available statistics show that productivity advance has occurred at a high rate during periods of economic expansion and at a slow rate or negatively during periods of economic contraction.[5]

---

[3] John W. Kendrick, "Productivity Trends: Capital and Labor," *Review of Economics and Statistics*, August 1956.

[4] Robert M. Solow, "Technical Change and the Aggregate Production Function," claimed that between 1909 and 1949 gross output per manhour doubled, and 87.5 percent of the increase was due to technical change, and 12.5 percent was due to increased use of capital.

[5] See Kendrick, *Productivity Trends*, p. 73.

Table 17-1 Private Domestic Economy: Average Annual Percentage Rates of Change in Real Output and Productivity Indicators, 1889-1957

Indicator	1889-1957	1889-1919	1919-57
Real Output	3.5%	3.9%	3.1%
Real Output Per Unit of Total Factor Input	1.7	1.3	2.1
Real Output Per Unit of Labor Input	2.0	1.6	2.3
Real Output Per Unit of Capital Input	1.0	0.5	1.3

Source: John W. Kendrick, *Productivity Trends in the United States* (Princeton: Princeton University Press, 1961), p. 60. Reprinted by permission of the National Bureau of Economic Research.

Productivity Trends

Average annual percentage rates of increase in real output, total factor productivity, labor productivity, and capital productivity are shown in Table 17–1.[6] The figures reveal that between 1889 and 1957 labor productivity (2.0 percent) increased at twice the annual rate of capital productivity (1.0 percent), and total factor productivity increased at an annual rate of 1.7 percent.[7] The positive increase in both labor and capital efficiency suggests that productivity has been both labor and capital saving. Disaggregation of productivity trends into subperiods shows that a significant break in trend occurred sometime around World War 1. (See Figure 17–1.) The annual rate of increase in total factor productivity between 1919 and 1957 (2.1 percent) was 60 percent greater than the rate of increase between 1889–1919 (1.3 percent); the sharp upward trend in capital productivity was especially marked.[8] A closer look at temporal changes in the rate of productivity advance is shown in Table 17–2. The results show that, since 1919, total factor productivity has increased at an annual rate of at least 2.0 percent except during the depressed years of the 1930s, and, even in this era, the annual rate of 1.6 percent matched the highest pre-1919 subperiod rate of growth.

[6] In Tables 17–1, 17–2, and 17–3, productivity growth is shown for the private domestic economy which is defined as the national economy minus government and the foreign sector. In Tables 17–5 and 17–6, the impact of productivity on economic growth and welfare is shown for the national economy.

[7] The relatively high rate of increase in labor productivity is due in part to the substitution of capital for labor.

[8] Solomon Fabricant claimed that the break in trend around World War I was not sensitive to the choice of 1919 as a base year; see *Basic Facts on Productivity Change,* Occasional Paper 63, National Bureau of Economic Research, 1959.

Figure 17-1 Private Domestic Economy: Trends in Total Factor Productivity, 1889-1957

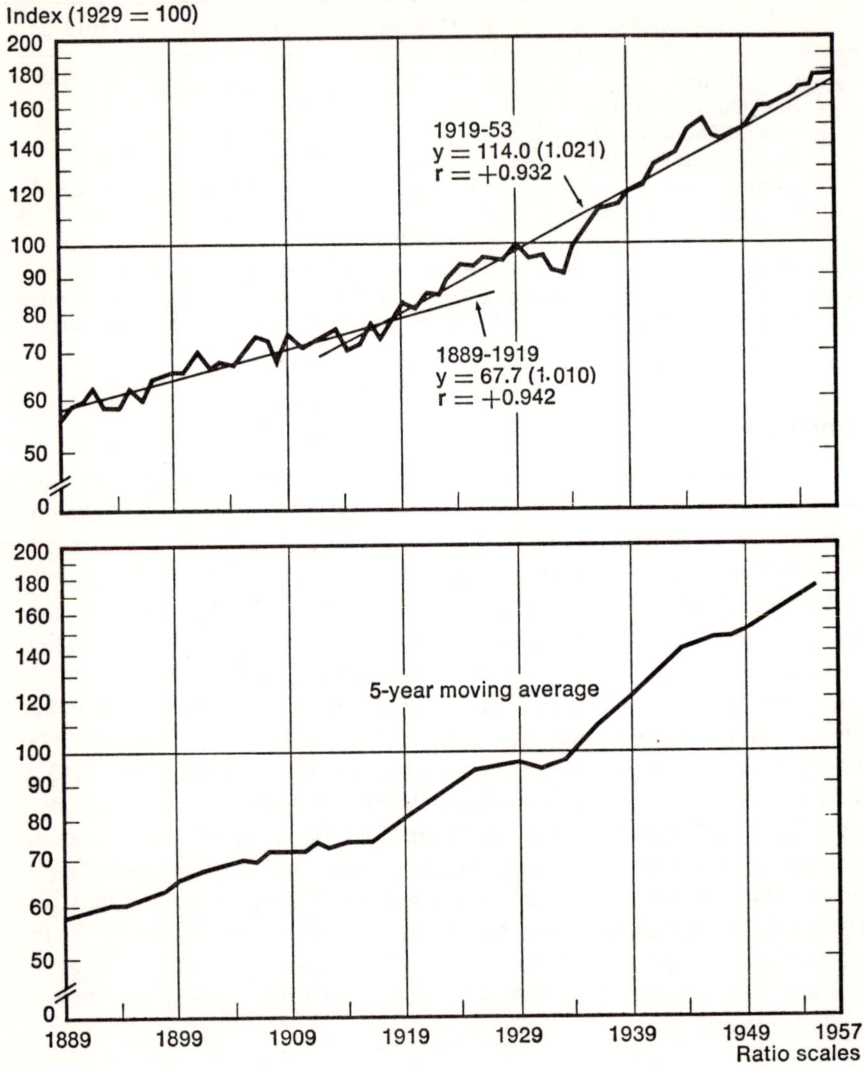

Source: John W. Kendrick, *Productivity Trends in the United States* (Princeton: Princeton University Press, 1961). Reprinted by permission of the National Bureau of Economic Research.

Kendrick's analysis of productivity trends indicated that a strong relationship existed between productivity change and the business cycle, and he argued that the major cause of annual fluctuations in productivity was

Table 17-2 Average Annual Percentage Rates of Change in Real Output and Productivity Indicators, by Subperiod, 1889-1957

Subperiod	Real Output	Real Output per Unit of Total Factor Input	Real Output per Unit of Labor Input	Real Output per Unit of Capital Input
1889-99	4.5%	1.6%	2.0%	0.4%
1899-1909	4.2	1.2	1.3	0.8
1909-19	3.0	1.1	1.5	0.3
1919-29	3.7	2.0	2.2	1.4
1929-37	0.1	1.6	1.8	0.9
1937-48	4.5	2.3	2.2	2.7
1948-57	3.6	2.3	3.1	−0.2

Source: Kendrick, *Productivity Trends,* p. 72. Reprinted by permission of the National Bureau of Economic Research.

Table 17-3 Private Domestic Economy: Average Annual Percentage Rates of Change in Real Output and Productivity Indicators, During Years of Expansion and Contraction, 1889-1957

Period	Real Output	Real Output per Unit of Total Factor Input	Real Output per Unit of Labor Input	Real Output per Unit of Capital Input
Years of Expansion				
1889-1957	6.7%	2.8%	2.4%	4.0%
1889-1919	2.8	2.8	2.5	2.5
1919-57	6.7	2.9	2.3	4.4
Years of Contraction				
1889-1957	−2.9	−0.5	1.3	−5.2
1889-1919	−1.5	−1.5	0.0	−4.9
1919-57	−4.1	0.3	2.5	−5.5

Source: Kendrick, *Productivity Trends,* p. 73. Reprinted by permission of the National Bureau of Economic Research.

fluctuations in the level of production.[9] Table 17–3 shows the average annual rates of productivity change, by subperiod, for years of expansion and contraction. The calculations demonstrate that total factor productivity was sharply affected by business conditions, and this largely reflected the significant declines that occurred in capital productivity. During contractions, labor can be laid off, and the average productivity per unit

[9] Kendrick, *Productivity Trends*, p. 73.

of labor input may be maintained at a high level. However, it is difficult to lay off unused capital, and, therefore, capital productivity generally suffers during contractions.

Trends in productivity for selected industries are shown in Table 17–4.[10] Between 1899 and 1953, the largest productivity growth occurred in the transportation and communication industries. The rate of productivity increase in mining and manufacturing was slightly above the average for the private domestic economy, and the rate in agriculture was below average.[11] Within each subperiod, there was a great deal of industry dispersion, and, in some periods, industry productivity growth ranged between 7 and 8 percent to 0 percent. However, for the period 1899–1953, the industry dispersion was much lower, and most industries showed annual growth rates from 1–3 percent. It appears that productivity advance has had a rather broad industrial base and has been a significant factor in advancing real output in all sectors.

The Impact of Productivity Change on Economic Growth and Welfare

Table 17–5 shows the percentage increase in real output due to increased total factor input and increased total factor productivity. Kendrick found that before 1919 the majority of real output growth resulted from increases in factor input; since 1919, however, productivity improvements have contributed as much to growth as factor increases. Independent of Kendrick, Jacob Schmookler found that, between 1869 and 1938, approximately 50 percent of the increase in real G.N.P. was due to an increase in resources, and approximately 50 percent was due to an increase in efficiency.[12] Kendricks' calculations of the welfare aspects of productivity growth are shown in Table 17–6, and the figures indicate that productivity advance has been responsible for the bulk of the increase in United States per capita output levels, especially since 1919.[13] In view of the crucial role that productivity has played in the nation's past achievement of improved standards of economic welfare, it is difficult to overstate the importance of efficiency improvements as a source of economic progress.

---

[10] Separate treatment is not given to the trade, finance, service, and construction industries.

[11] Kendrick found a positive correlation between high growth in real output and high growth in productivity; see *Productivity Trends*, pp. 177–88.

[12] Jacob Schmookler, "Tne Changing Efficiency of the American Economy, 1869–1938," *Review of Economics and Statistics*, August 1952.

[13] Frederick C. Mills concluded that productivity change was the major factor behind the significant increase in consumer welfare in the twentieth century; see "The Role of Productivity in Economic Growth," *American Economic Review*, May 1952.

Table 17-4 Average Annual Percentage Rates of Change in Total Factor Productivity, by Selected Industry, 1899-1953

Industry	1899-1909	1909-19	1919-29	1929-37	1937-48	1948-53	1899-1953
Farming	−0.2%	−0.3%	1.2%	0.8%	2.7%	3.7%	1.1%
Mining	0.8	1.4	3.5	4.3	1.0	2.9	2.2
Manufacturing	0.7	0.3	5.3	1.9	1.6	2.5	2.0
Food	0.3	−0.4	5.3	1.5	1.5	2.2	1.7
Textiles	1.1	0.9	2.9	4.6	2.5	2.6	2.4
Apparel	0.7	2.7	4.0	2.5	−0.7	1.3	1.7
Lumber	−0.4	−1.2	2.5	0.4	2.2	3.8	1.0
Chemicals	0.7	−0.7	7.4	3.0	3.7	4.1	2.9
Rubber Products	2.3	7.4	7.7	4.0	0.7	2.1	4.1
Leather and Leather Products	0.1	0.5	2.9	3.6	0.4	0.0	1.2
Primary Metals	2.7	−0.5	5.5	−1.3	3.2	0.5	1.9
Fabricated Metals	2.3	1.8	4.6	1.0	1.6	5.1	2.6
Nonelectrical Machinery	1.0	0.7	2.9	2.3	1.2	2.6	1.7
Electrical Machinery	0.6	0.3	3.5	3.2	2.1	5.0	2.2
Transportation	0.9	3.2	3.1	4.1	4.7	3.3	3.2
Railroads	1.8	3.4	1.9	1.7	3.6	2.7	2.6
Communications and Public Utilities	4.6	3.7	2.5	3.3	4.3	2.7	3.6
Telephone	4.8	1.9	1.6	2.4	0.9	0.5	2.0
Electric Utilities	5.2	8.2	2.5	5.0	6.6	5.0	5.5
Manufactured Gas	4.1	5.0	3.2	1.6	6.7	8.8	4.7
Natural Gas	0.0	1.1	0.2	3.7	5.5	1.6	2.0
Total Private Domestic Economy	1.2	1.1	2.0	1.6	2.3	2.7	1.7

Source: Kendrick, *Productivity Trends*, pp. 136-37. Reprinted by permission of the National Bureau of Economic Research.

Table 17-5 National Economy: Percentage Share of Growth in Real Net National Product Due to Increases in Total Factor Input and Total Factor Productivity, 1889-1953

Subperiod	Total Factor Input	Total Factor Productivity
1889-1953	55.6%	44.4%
1889-1919	66.7	33.3
1919-53	43.3	56.7
1889-99	65.9	34.1
1899-1909	73.8	26.2
1909-19	60.5	39.5
1919-29	53.3	46.7
1929-37	0.0[a]	100.0
1937-48	50.0	50.0
1948-53	47.8	52.2

Source: Kendrick, *Productivity Trends*, p. 79. Reprinted by permission of the National Bureau of Economic Research.
[a] Factor input was negative.

Table 17-6 National Economy: Percentage Share of Growth in Real Net National Product per Capita Due to Increases in Total Factor Productivity and Total Factor Input per Capita, 1889-1953

Subperiod	Total Factor Productivity	Total Factor Input per Capita
1889-1953	76.2%	23.8%
1889-1919	58.3	41.7
1919-53	94.4	5.6
1889-99	57.7	42.3
1899-1909	47.8	52.2
1909-19	65.2	34.8
1919-29	93.3	6.7
1929-37	100.0	0.0[a]
1937-48	68.8	31.2
1948-53	80.0	20.0

Source: Kendrick, *Productivity Trends*, p. 84. Reprinted by permission of the National Bureau of Economic Research.
[a] Per capita factor input was negative.

Summary

Productivity change largely reflects the development and adoption of new technology. This chapter's survey of productivity trends in the American economy has demonstrated the crucial role of efficiency improvements in advancing the standard of living. Productivity improvements have characterized all sectors of the economy, and the long-run trend in the rate of productivity advance has accelerated since World War I.

Suggested Reading

Fabricant, Solomon, *Basic Facts on Productivity Change,* Occasional Paper 63, National Bureau of Economic Research, 1959.

Kendrick, John W., "Productivity Trends: Capital and Labor," *Review of Economics and Statistics,* August 1956.

———, *Productivity Trends in the United States.* Princeton: Princeton University Press, 1961.

Mills, Frederick C., "The Role of Productivity in Economic Growth," *American Economic Review,* May 1952.

Schmookler, Jacob, "The Changing Efficiency of the American Economy, 1869–1938," *Review of Economics and Statistics,* August 1952.

Solow, Robert M., "Technical Change and the Aggregate Production Function," *Review of Economics and Statistics,* August 1957.

18
The Great Depression and World War II

By the 1920s the American economy had achieved a high degree of mass prosperity, and, during this decade, automobiles, stoves, refrigerators, and radios were purchased by most Americans. Optimism pervaded the economy, and there seemed to be no end in sight to the prosperity.[1] However, the country's most severe depression struck in late 1929 and continued for more than a decade. At the depth of the depression, one-fourth of the nation's labor force was unemployed, and 28 million people were on some type of public relief or assistance. Many revolutionary anti-depression policies were tried by President Franklin D. Roosevelt, but they did not bring about recovery, and it was not until the economy mobilized for World War II that unemployment and public assistance were eliminated.

This chapter will highlight the length and depth of the depression by surveying trends between 1920 and 1945 in G.N.P., per capita output, unemployment, and wholesale prices. The causes of the depression will be outlined, and the attempts by the Hoover and Roosevelt administrations to promote recovery will be examined. It will be shown that the recovery policies of government were not expansionary enough to overcome the full extent of the depression, and the entrance of the United States into World War II finally returned the economy to full employment.

Growth Trends During the 1920s

The 1920s were a decade of prosperity for virtually everyone except farmers. Between 1920 and 1929, real G.N.P. increased by 30 percent, and real

[1] Agriculture did not share in the prosperity of the 1920s, and, during most of the decade, agricultural prices declined relative to nonagricultural prices.

Figure 18-1 Index of Real Gross National Product, 1920-45 (1929 = 100)

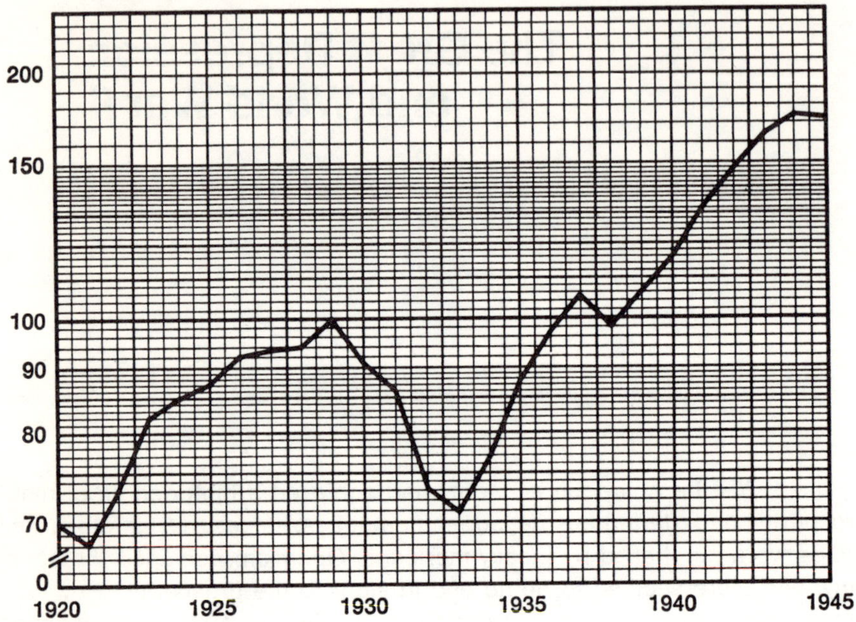

Source: *Historical Statistics,* Series F 1-5.

per capita output (1929 dollars) increased by 25 percent. (See Figures 18–1 and 18–2.) During World War I, farm output had expanded tremendously in response to European demand for American food products. With the close of the war, however, foreign markets for American commodities were greatly reduced, and the excess productive capacity in the farm sector drove farm prices downward.[2] The sharp decline in farm income and exports, coupled with cutbacks in government spending, created a short-lived but sharp recession in 1921. During the recession, the unemployment rate reached almost 12 percent, but the economy recovered quickly, and full employment was maintained throughout most of the 1920s.[3] (See Figure 18–3.) After an initial decline from the inflationary levels of World War I, prices remained relatively stable in the 1920s. (See Figure 18–4.)

---

[2] The parity index (prices received/prices paid) of farm prices (1910–14=100) declined from 99 in 1920 to 92 in 1929.

[3] The unemployment rate is defined to include those workers looking for work and unable to find it.

Figure 18-2 Real per Capita Output, 1920-45
(1929 Dollars)

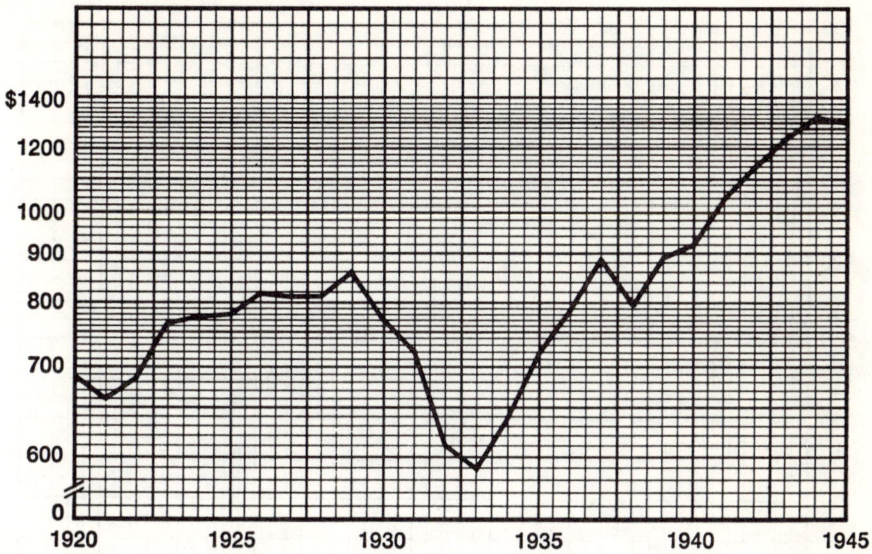

Source: *Historical Statistics*, Series F 1-5.

Figure 18-3 Percentage of Labor Force Unemployed, 1920-45

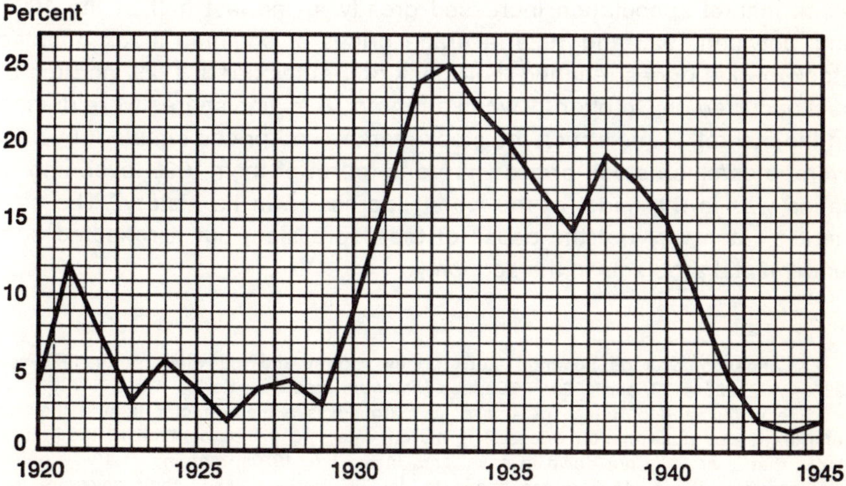

Source: *Historical Statistics*, Series D 46-47.

Figure 18-4 Wholesale Price Trends, All Commodities, 1920-45 (1929 = 100)

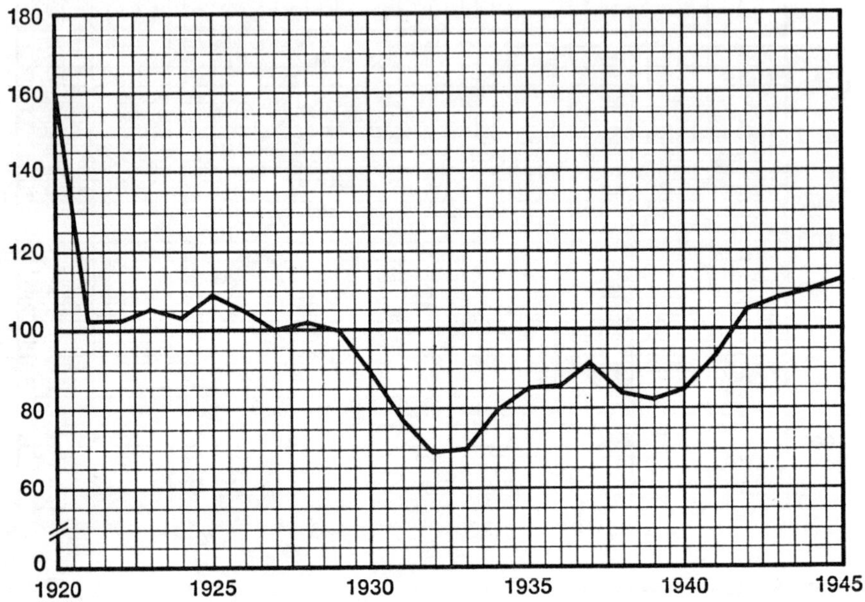

Source: *Historical Statistics,* Series E 13-24.

The Depression and its Causes

Stock market speculation increased greatly in the last half of the 1920s, and, between 1926 and 1929, average prices of common stock doubled.[4] Stock market prices reached their peak on September 3, 1929, and the big bust occurred on October 29 when a record 16 million shares were dumped on the market. Panic struck the stock market, and prices tumbled; by 1932, average common stock prices were one-fourth of their 1929 level, and the nation was in the midst of the worst depression in its history.[5] The stock market crash was not the cause of the depression, but it reflected some fundamental problems in the economy.

[4] An index of average common stock prices showed the following trend: 1926 = 48, 1927 = 59, 1928 = 77, and 1929 = 100; see *Historical Statistics,* Series X 348–54.

[5] The widespread purchase of stocks on margin was a major factor behind the rapid deterioration of stock market prices. The margin refers to the percentage of the value of stocks that is actually put down in cash, and, in the late 1920s, margins of 10–20 percent were common. When stock prices began to decline, brokers asked their investors for a greater margin, and investors who had entered the stock market with a limited amount of cash were forced to sell, driving stock prices down further.

Perhaps the most serious of these problems was the failure of consumer demand to keep pace with industrial output. Productivity increased sharply in the post–World War I period, and the nation's capacity to produce increased much faster than real wages.[6] In addition, in the late 1920s, consumer demand became sensitive to credit conditions as installment buying became popular. Consumption of large items such as housing, automobiles, and consumer durables peaked in the middle and late 1920s, and production in these industries had leveled off before 1929.[7] The failure of consumption to keep up with production partially reflected the increased in equality that developed in the nation's income distribution during the prosperity of the 1920s.[8] The relative concentration of income in the hands of the rich tended to encourage savings relative to consumption, and, in the late 1920s, many of these surplus funds were applied to stock market speculation.

In conjunction with the basic problem of underconsumption, there were several other forces at work that accentuated the initial decline. The pyramiding of credit that resulted from margin purchases of stocks and installment buying by consumers intensified short-run fluctuations in credit availability. In addition, the severity magnitude of the stock market crash and the failure of over five thousand banks destroyed confidence in the nation's financial system and prolonged the recovery. Furthermore, the Federal Reserve's actions in the early years of the depression were inconsistent with recovery and may have aggravated the unfavorable economic conditions.[9] Between 1929 and 1931, the Fed remained quite passive,

---

[6] Manufacturing employment leveled off around 1923, and the increases in industrial output in the middle and late 1920s largely were achieved through productivity increases. The most rapidly expanding area of employment in the 1920s was in the low-paying service industries, especially wholesale and retail trade; see *Historical Statistics*, Series D 48–56.

[7] The purchase of durable goods is subject to sharp swings, since expenditures on durables can be postponed until periods of prosperity. In the middle 1920s, the wave of prosperity brought a sharp increase in consumption of automobiles, household appliances, and houses; however, by the late 1920s, demand for these items had declined and production began to taper off. Automobile production reached $2.5 billion in 1926, declined sharply in 1927 and 1928, and then rose to $2.6 billion in 1929. Between 1922 and 1927, the output of electric household appliances rose from $59 million to $146 million; by 1929, output had risen to $177 million. New housing starts rose from 247,000 in 1920 to 937,000 in 1925; after 1925, there was a steady decline, and, by 1929, new starts were only 509,000. See *Historical Statistics*, Series N 106–15 and P 250–306.

[8] The inequality of income distribution refers to the concentration of income among various population groups. During the 1920s, the share of income controlled by the very rich increased, i.e., the inequality of income distribution increased. During the 1920s, the share of disposable income (income after taxes) controlled by the top 1 percent increased from 11.8 percent in 1920 to 18.9 percent in 1929; the income share of the top 5 percent increased from 24.0 percent in 1920 to 33.5 percent in 1929. See *Historical Statistics*, Series G 131–46.

[9] For an excellent account of the monetary side of the depression, see Milton Friedman and Anna Jacobson Schwartz, *The Great Contraction, 1929–1933* (Princeton: Princeton University Press, 1965).

but, in late 1931, it became concerned over the United States gold drain, and, in order to stop this outflow, it raised the rediscount rate in an attempt to raise interest rates.[10] Many banks failed as a result of the increase in the cost of lending, and the net effect of the Fed's policy between 1929 and 1933 was at best nonexpansionary, and, most likely, it intensified existing economic conditions.[11]

The magnitude of the depression is clearly evident in Figures 18–1 to 18–4. Between 1929 and 1933, real G.N.P., real per capita output, and wholesale prices declined by approximately 30 percent. The unemployment rate increased from 3.2 percent in 1929 to 24.9 percent in 1933, and those laborers who could find jobs were often forced to work reduced hours and at jobs below their skill level. The economy was in the worst depression in its history, and the knowledge and understanding of recovery measures was limited and confused. The fuzziness of thinking regarding contracyclical economic policy is reflected in the recovery policies that were adopted by the Hoover and Roosevelt administrations. The 1930s witnessed a number of revolutionary attempts to combat depression, but, at times, the policies were conflicting, and, in the aggregate, they were not sufficient to cure the nation's economic problems.

Hoover's Recovery Policy

Hoover was a firm believer in the private enterprise system, and, in the early stages of the depression, he opposed government relief programs. The economy had never been faced by such a severe economic setback, and there was no precedent for the type of massive government effort that was needed to overcome the depression. However, as conditions worsened, Hoover became involved in a positive anti-depression program. Before the depression, in 1929, he had established the Federal Farm Board which was intended to support farm prices and help farmers recover from the agricultural problems of the 1920s. This farm support program was maintained during the depression. In January, 1932, Congress established the Reconstruction Finance Corporation which was intended to make loans to encourage business investment. In addition, Hoover committed a small amount of federal funds to construction of dams, roads, and buildings. The modest anti-depression effort, coupled with reduced federal tax revenues due to the decline in economic activity, created a budget deficit,

---

[10] The rediscount rate is the interest rate charged to member banks on loans. On two other occasions, 1933 and 1937, the Federal Reserve pursued a tight money policy which was inconsistent with an anti-depression policy.

[11] See Elmus R. Wicker, "Federal Reserve Monetary Policy, 1922–33: A Reinterpretation," *Journal of Political Economy,* August 1965.

and Hoover, being a firm believer in a balanced budget, signed the Revenue Act of 1932 which virtually doubled full-employment tax yields.[12] The increase in tax rates was the highest peacetime increase that has ever been instituted, and it is indicative of the unwillingness of Hoover to fully commit the federal government's resources to the recovery effort.[13]

Roosevelt's Recovery Policies: The New Deal

In the presidential campaign of 1932, Roosevelt criticized Hoover for engaging in deficit spending, and he promised to balance the budget if elected. Roosevelt was elected in a landslide and was inaugurated in March, 1933, but the promise of a balanced federal budget was never kept. Immediately, he declared a banking holiday and closed all banks. Roosevelt wanted to reestablish confidence in the banking system, and he instituted bank examinations; the sound institutions were allowed to reopen almost immediately, but financially insecure banks remained closed until they satisfied federal regulations. Roosevelt also established the Federal Deposit Insurance Corporation.[14] In an effort to stimulate inflation and stop the hoarding of gold, he took the United States off the gold standard and made it illegal to hold gold; to encourage farm exports, he devalued the dollar. Stock market reforms were introduced in 1934 with the creation of the Securities and Exchange Commission.[15]

In addition to banking and monetary reforms, Roosevelt committed federal funds to relief for the unemployed. Throughout the depression, Roosevelt's relief program emphasized public assistance through government employment rather than direct relief payments to the unemployed.[16] The initial program, Federal Emergency Relief Administration (May, 1933), combined direct relief with federal employment, and this program was supplemented by the Civil Works Administration (November, 1933) which was primarily concerned with job relief. In the initial year of Roosevelt's

---

[12] See E. Cary Brown, "Fiscal Policy in the Thirties: A Reappraisal," *American Economic Review*, December 1956.

[13] Hoover's attempts to balance the federal budget were unsuccessful, and the deficit increased from $462 million in 1931 to $2,735 million in 1932; see *Historical Statistics*, Series Y 254–57.

[14] The Federal Deposit Insurance Corporation (FDIC) established a system of bank supervision and insured bank deposits.

[15] The Securities and Exchange Commission (SEC) required all stock exchanges to register, and it required all companies offering stock for sale to provide information concerning their financial condition.

[16] Direct relief was generally provided by state and local governments, although the federal government provided many grants to state and local governments to help underwrite the cost of direct relief; see Lester V. Chandler, *America's Greatest Depression, 1929–41* (New York: Harper & Row, 1970), pp. 191–207.

relief program, over four million people received public assistance from the federal government.[17]

By 1935, the number of individuals on federal relief had begun to decline, and Roosevelt had replaced the Federal Emergency Relief Administration and Civil Works Administration with the Works Progress Administration (WPA). Roosevelt was now strongly opposed to direct relief for those who could work, and the WPA provided jobs constructing schools, roads, bridges, dams, parks, and other public projects. Several programs for young adults were also instituted by Roosevelt. The Civilian Conservation Corps provided jobs for young males in conservation work, and the National Youth Administration provided a means for financing high school, college, and post-college education.

The economy began to recover almost immediately, and, between 1935 and 1937, the number of recipients of federal assistance declined from 4.0 million to 2.7 million.[18] Economic improvement brought a decline in public spending, and the Federal Reserve, concerned with inflation, raised the rediscount rate in 1937. As a result, the economy suffered a sharp temporary setback in 1938. Roosevelt responded with a sharp increase in federal relief, and the number of recipients of federal assistance in 1938 was as high as in 1933–34; over 3 million individuals were employed by the WPA. The number of individuals supported by federal relief programs declined steadily from the 1938 level, but, in 1941, there were still 1.8 million individuals, including slightly more than 1.0 million in the WPA, on federal aid.[19]

Agriculture received a great deal of attention from Roosevelt, and, in 1933, the Agricultural Adjustment Act established the Agricultural Adjustment Administration (AAA), which undertook a policy of raising farm prices by restricting farm output. Acreage allotments were set for major crops, and farmers who signed agreements with the federal government stating their intention of curtailing output could qualify for direct benefit payments. The Supreme Court declared the AAA unconstitutional in 1936, and Congress replaced it with the Soil Conservation and Domestic Allotment Act (1936). Under this new legislation, the federal government continued to make payments to farmers planting soil-conserving crops rather than soil-depleting crops, where soil-depleting crops included those characterized by overproduction. A new Agricultural Adjustment Act was

---

[17] Most of the four million individuals receiving federal aid were involved in work relief, and many women and children were also supported through federal programs. Chandler, *America's Greatest Depression*, p. 195, showed that the number of individuals on all forms of public assistance (federal, state, and local) reached a peak in 1934 at 28 million, and, by 1937, the number had declined to 13 million. However, as late as 1941, there were 12 million individuals receiving support through some form of public assistance or work relief.

[18] See *Historical Statistics*, Series H 199–206.

[19] See *Historical Statistics*, Series H 199–206.

passed in 1938, and it established quotas for major crops, provided for payments to cooperating farmers, and expanded the power of the Commodity Credit Corporation to make loans to farmers who withheld their commodities from the market. In addition, the Roosevelt administration helped farmers obtain mortgage loans and other forms of credit. In spite of Roosevelt's vigorous farm policy, the attempts to restrict agricultural output and raise prices were not successful; throughout the 1930s, farm prices remained well below parity (1910–14 prices), and the farm sector was plagued by overproduction.

The Roosevelt recovery effort offered something for everyone, and both labor and business were covered by the National Industrial Recovery Act (1933). The NIRA required each industry to establish a code of fair practice in which firms agreed to set minimum prices, limit output, and guarantee labor the right to organize and bargain collectively. Many codes also specified a guaranteed minimum wage and a maximum workweek. The NIRA represented a temporary suspension of anti-trust action, and it required outright collusion on the part of firms. The Supreme Court declared the Act unconstitutional in 1935, and, shortly thereafter, Roosevelt began a vigorous prosecution of the anti-trust laws.

In addition to encouraging business collusion, the NIRA gave strong encouragement to unionization and collective bargaining. When the NIRA was declared unconstitutional, Congress replaced the labor clause with the National Labor Relations Act of 1935 (Wagner Act), which guaranteed labor the right to unionize and bargain collectively. The Fair Labor Standards Act (1938) established a minimum wage of 25 cents per hour and a maximum workweek of 44 hours in industries engaged in interstate commerce; the minimum wage was scheduled to increase to 40 cents, and the workweek was scheduled to fall to 40 hours. The Act also put restrictions on child labor. In addition to the federal government's support of unionization, minimum wages, and maximum hours, labor was aided by the adoption of the Social Security Act (1935). This piece of legislation represented a fundamental break with the past and established federal aid programs for retirement pensions, old age and unemployment insurance, care of the blind, dependent children, and other needy individuals.

Conservation measures were a major element in Roosevelt's recovery program, not only through the activities of the WPA and Civilian Conservation Corps, but also through the creation of government enterprises such as the Tennessee Valley Authority. The TVA was created to control floods, improve agriculture, and provide electricity for the Tennessee Valley region. The entrance of the federal government into the production and sale of electrical power brought outrage from private utility companies. By offering cheap electrical power to industry, however, the TVA stimulated the economy of the Tennessee Valley and benefited the region as a whole.

Expansionary Fiscal Policy in Roosevelt's New Deal

The Roosevelt recovery effort consisted of a broad package of policies that extended some degree of federal control, assistance, or support to virtually every sector of the economy. At times the policies seemed inconsistent, and they were subject to sharp reversals. For example, between 1933 and 1935, the NIRA encouraged both labor and management to organize; after 1935, Roosevelt engaged in sharp prosecution of the antitrust laws. However, throughout the period 1933–41, the federal government was heavily and directly involved in the recovery effort.

Folklore has conferred upon Roosevelt the image of a fiscal liberal who engaged in heavy amount of deficit spending ("pump priming") in order to pull the economy from the depths of depression.[20] In part, this image is correct; Roosevelt ran an unbalanced budget and engaged in expansionary fiscal policy throughout the 1930s. Yet, it also should be pointed out, that throughout the 1930s, Roosevelt remained a confirmed believer in the merits of a balanced budget, and he viewed the deficit as a short-term consequence of the depression. By modern standards, the federal deficit was not large in absolute amount, but, relative to the federal budget of the 1930s, the deficit was considerable. (See Table 18–1.)

The expansionary fiscal policy of the New Deal was partially offset by a failure of state and local governments to join in the recovery effort and by federal tax increases in 1932.[21] Federal tax rates were doubled by Hoover in 1932, and Roosevelt, by increasing corporate income and estate taxes, introduced some progressivity into the tax structure in 1935 and 1936. However, Roosevelt failed to pursue the full limits of expansionary fiscal policy, and he did not reduce the tax burden on low and middle income individuals. Between 1929 and 1933, state and local governments generally ran deficits, and their net impact was expansionary; however, most states raised taxes in the early 1930s, and, after 1934, the net impact of state and local governments was neutral or slightly negative.

Success of Roosevelt's Recovery Program

A brief review of Figures 18–1 through 18–4 illustrates that Roosevelt's New Deal policies were successful in moving the economy out of the severe depression of the early 1930s, but the stimulating effects of World War II were required to achieve complete recovery. Between 1933 and 1940, real G.N.P. increased by 63 percent and real per capita output increased by

---

20 Expansionary fiscal policy or "pump priming" refers to the creation of a deliberate imbalance in the federal budget so that expenditures exceed receipts.

21 The 1932 change in federal tax rates doubled full employment tax yields. In addition, most state governments increased taxes during the early 1930s. See Brown, "Fiscal Policy in the Thirties," and *Historical Statistics*, Series Y 517–35 and Y 536–46.

Table 18-1 Federal Government Receipts and Expenditures, 1928-40 (millions of dollars)

Year	Receipts	Expenditures	Surplus or Deficit (−)
1928	$4042.3	$3103.3	$ 939.0
1929	4033.3	3298.9	734.4
1930	4177.9	3440.3	737.6
1931	3115.6	3577.4	−461.8
1932	1923.9	4659.2	−2735.3
1933	2021.2	4622.9	−2601.7
1934	3064.3	6693.9	−3629.6
1935	3729.9	6521.0	−2791.1
1936	4068.9	8493.5	−4424.6
1937	4978.6	7756.0	−2777.4
1938	5615.2	6791.8	−1176.6
1939	4996.3	8858.5	−3862.2
1940	5144.0	9062.0	−3918.0

Source: *Historical Statistics,* Series Y 254-57.

55 percent; as early as 1937, aggregate and per capita output had reached the pre-depression level. However, despite these gains in output, unemployment remained a major national problem, and, in 1940, 15 percent of the labor force was still unemployed, and more than 12 million people were still supported by some type of public assistance or work relief.[22] (See Figure 18–3.) The New Deal policies were an essential element in the economy's recovery from the depression, but they were not expansionary enough to bring the economy back to full employment.

World War II and Economic Recovery

The United States did not enter World War II until the very end of 1941, but, in 1940, Roosevelt requested funds from Congress to support a buildup of the Air Force, and the Selective Service System began drafting men. By 1941, the military buildup in the United States was quickening, and, by 1942, it was in full swing. The total military personnel increased as follows: 1940, 0.5 million; 1941, 1.8 million; 1942, 3.9 million; 1943, 9.0 million; 1944, 11.5 million; and 1945, 12.1 million.[23] Unemployment in the economy was rapidly eliminated, and labor became scarce. To overcome the labor shortage, women and retirees entered the labor force in large numbers, and the average workweek was increased from 39 to 46 hours.

[22] For a detailed statement of the number of individuals supported by all forms of public aid, see Chandler, *America's Greatest Depression,* p. 195.

[23] See *Historical Statistics,* Series Y 763–75.

Real G.N.P. increased by 50 percent between 1940 and 1945, and real per capita output increased by 41 percent. Spending by the federal government increased sharply from $9.1 billion in 1940 to $95.1 billion in 1944; by 1944, federal spending account for 45 percent of G.N.P.[24] Most of the government expenditures were tied to the war effort, and this was a high price to pay for a return to full employment; nevertheless, the sharp increase in demand created by wartime mobilization accomplished what the New Deal policies had been unable to achieve.

Summary

The depression of the 1930s was the most severe setback in the economy's history. At the bottom of the depression in 1933, one-fourth of the nation's labor force was unemployed, and approximately 28 million people were supported by some type of public relief. The depression brought huge financial losses and shook business confidence, and the responsibility for leadership in the recovery effort fell upon the government. There was no precedent for the large-scale effort that was required to achieve full recovery, however, and Hoover was too conservative to get heavily involved in recovery activities. Roosevelt tried a wide range of experimental policies involving banking reform, monetary reform, public employment, unemployment relief, farm price supports, pegged industrial prices, quotas for farm and industrial output, mortgage and credit relief, unionization and collective bargaining, minimum wage legislation, social insurance, and conservation. The New Deal extended the influence of the federal government into many areas of the economy, and many of Roosevelt's reforms became permanent features in the American economy. Roosevelt was not successful in achieving full recovery from the depression, but his efforts at expansionary fiscal policy cleared the way for future government contracyclical activity. The Employment Act of 1964 charged the federal government with the responsibility of maintaining full employment and cyclical stability. This legislation, along with the New Deal reforms, ushered in a new era of government responsibility in the American economy.

Suggested Reading

Brown, E. Cary, "Fiscal Policy in the Thirties: A Reappraisal," *American Economic Review,* December 1956.

---

[24] See *Historical Statistics,* Series Y 254–57.

Chandler, Lester V., *America's Greatest Depression, 1929–1941*. New York: Harper & Row, 1970.

Friedman, Milton, and Anna Jacobson Schwartz, *The Great Contraction, 1929–1933.* Princeton: Princeton University Press, 1965.

Galbraith, John Kenneth, *The Great Crash, 1929.* Boston: Houghton Mifflin, 1954.

Leuchtenburg, William E., *Franklin D. Roosevelt and the New Deal, 1932–1940.* New York: Harper & Row, 1963.

Reading, Don C., "New Deal Activity and the States, 1933 to 1939," *Journal of Economic History,* December 1973.

Wicker, Elmus R., *Federal Reserve Monetary Policy, 1917–1933.* New York: Random House, 1966.

———, "Federal Reserve Monetary Policy, 1922–33: A Reinterpretation," *Journal of Political Economy,* August 1965.

19
Current Economic Problems

The previous chapters have surveyed the major features of American economic development, and they have shown that no single theory or isolated event can explain the amazing economic success of the United States. From the beginning, the economy was favored with many growth-producing forces such as a rich resource base, a favorable land-labor ratio, and a tradition of individual freedom and initiative. During the past two hundred years, the economy has undergone many significant changes such as an increasingly direct role for government; a relative decline of agriculture and rise of industry; institutional and organizational changes in banking, business, and labor; rapid technological change; wars; and depressions. Throughout these changes, the economy has maintained a strong drive toward improvement in the standard of living, and the potential for further improvement in the quality of life in the United States is tremendous.

However, the economy is currently faced with many pressing socio-economic problems that demand immediate attention if progress is to be continued into the future. Among the more severe problems are the following: environmental decay, especially energy shortages and air and water pollution; discrimination and inequality of opportunity for nonwhites and females; poverty; the decline of cities; spiraling inflation; population pressure; and rising crime. It would be impossible to do justice to each of these problem areas in a single chapter, and no attempt is made here to analyze all of the economy's ills. Instead, this chapter will focus attention on three pressing environmental concerns (energy conservation, air pollution, and water pollution), and it will survey the economic problems related to discrimination and crime.

Environmental Issues: Energy Resources and Air and Water Pollution

The economy's past growth has made great demands on the nation's resource base, and the costs of economic progress have been reflected recently in dwindling energy reserves and in air and water pollution. The deterioration of the environment is not a new phenomenon; it has been occurring since the beginning of man's exploitation of nature's resources. However, the pressures on the resource base have increased with the demands of the population, and, in recent years, smoggy skies, polluted rivers, and energy shortages have brought home the reality of environmental decay.

The American economy's energy demands are tremendous; 6 percent of the world's population consumes 34 percent of the world's energy production. The United States obtains 95 percent of its energy from fossil fuels (coal, oil, natural gas) which are fixed in supply and are nonrenewable.[1] The domestic supply of coal is very large, but oil and natural gas supplies are being exhausted rapidly. Of course, the presently available supply of any resource is a function of price and technology, and, as prices rise or technology improves, marginal resources become recoverable. However, the known United States supplies of oil and natural gas, including both those recoverable (reserves) and not recoverable (resources) under current cost and revenue conditions, are very limited.[2] (See Table 19–1.) Under present market conditions, our coal reserves are adequate for 73 years at the 1969 production rate. If the price of coal was to rise, many additional coal resources would become recoverable. Oil reserves (including the Alaska reserves) are adequate for 10.6 years at the 1972 production rate, and natural gas (dry) reserves are adequate for 12 years at the 1971 production rate.[3]

Nuclear and solar energy will undoubtedly provide power in the future. However, a great deal of technological change will be required to make these energy sources usable, and, therefore, it seems that the near future will see increased usage of fossil fuels. Recent price increases have encouraged experiments to determine the feasibility of recovering shale oil; even if shale proves to be recoverable, however, its supply is limited, and it has serious environmental side-effects. The nation's large coal reserves (approximately 50 percent of the world's total) offer another possible

---

[1] Walter J. Mead has provided an excellent survey article on the energy problem, and I have drawn liberally from his work; see "Oil, Energy, and Environmental Concern," in Llad Phillips and Harold L. Votey, Jr., eds., *Economic Analysis of Pressing Social Problems* (Chicago: Rand McNally College Publishing, 1974).

[2] Reserves are recoverable under present cost and revenue conditions; resources are known supplies where recovery cost is presently greater than current market value.

[3] See Mead, "Oil, Energy, and Environmental Concern," p. 40.

Table 19-1 Domestic Energy Reserves and Resources (quadrillion BTUs)

Commodity	1969 Domestic Production	Cumulative Production Through 1969	Reserves Proved Recoverable at End of 1969[a]	Estimated Remaining Recoverable Resources
Coal	14.951	1,040	1,087	33,000-47,000
Petroleum (crude oil)	18.883	501	219.5	590-1920
Natural Gas (liquid)	2.378	49	33	168-201
Natural Gas (dry)	20.447	382	310	870-1500
Oil Shale	Neg.	Neg.	112	1053
Uranium ($/lb. cut-off price)				
$8/lb.	754	12,194	16,340	43,880
$10/lb.	—	—	25,300	64,234
$15/lb.	—	—	37,400	97,279
$30/lb.	—	—	48,000	144,000
$50/lb.	—	—	287,000	503,000
$100/lb.	—	—	527,000	1,042,000
Thorium ($10/lb.)	Neg.	Neg.	3,900	24,000

Source: Associated Universities, Inc., *An Assessment of New Options in Energy Research and Development* (Upton, N.Y.: Brookhaven National Laboratory, November 1973), p. 16.

[a] Does not include Prudhoe Bay, Alaska, estimated to contain 54 quadrillion BTUs of reserves.

Table 19-2 Percentage Distribution of Air Pollutant Emissions, by Source, 1970 (millions of tons per year)

Source	Percent of Total
Transportation	54.5%
Road vehicles	46.6
Fuel Combustion	17.0
Steam and electric	10.6
Industrial Processes	13.8
Agricultural Burning	7.3
Solid Waste Disposal	4.2
Miscellaneous	3.2

Source: *Statistical Abstract*, 1973, p. 178.

short-run solution to the energy shortage, but coal production frequently rapes the land and causes ecological problems, and, like other fossil fuels, it is a terrible air pollutant.

Projections of energy consumption over the next three decades have led the Department of the Interior to predict that although the use of fossil fuels will decline, they will still account for over 70 percent of all United States energy consumption in the year 2000.[4] If this forecast is correct, the United States, in the future, will be forced to rely heavily on imports of petroleum, and, indeed, the Interior Department's projection estimated that petroleum imports would account for over 25 percent of American energy consumption in the year 2000.[5] The fact that worldwide supplies of fossil fuels are limited and that they do pollute the air will encourage the development of nuclear and solar energy. The power available from these sources is virtually limitless, but their development will require a great deal of new technology, and most likely they will bring their own set of environmental problems.

The air pollution problem has been created largely by the burning of fossil fuels. Automobiles are the major source of air pollution, and, in 1970, they accounted for 46.6 percent of all air pollutant emissions. (See Table 19–2.) As a result, the federal government has established automobile emission standards, and this has forced auto-makers to consider alternatives to the internal combustion engine. At present, however, the air pollution standards have been successful only in developing methods for making fossil fuel consumption more acceptable, and, in the long run, it seems that a new energy source will have to be developed for automobiles.

---

[4] See *Statistical Abstract*, 1973, p. 508.

[5] In 1971, petroleum imports accounted for 11 percent of United States energy consumption.

Table 19-3 Water Pollution, by Major Drainage Area, 1971

Drainage Area	Stream Miles	Percent Polluted
United States	260,324	29.3%
Ohio	28,992	82.9
Southeast	11,726	38.3
Great Lakes	21,374	41.0
Northeast	32,431	18.0
Middle Atlantic	31,914	17.6
California	28,277	29.8
Gulf	64,719	17.9
Missouri	10,448	17.6
Columbia	30,443	18.7

Source: *Statistical Abstract,* 1973, p. 178.

Water pollution has been another consequence of American economic development. In 1971, 29.3 percent of all internal water in the United States was polluted. Table 19–3 shows the major drainage areas in the United States and the percentage of each which the Environmental Protection Agency considers polluted. Most water pollution is caused by industrial wastes, and, despite a decade of nationwide concern for clean water, federal regulations have been ineffective, and the overall quality of water has not improved.

Discrimination and Inequality

The benefits of American economic growth have not been distributed equally, and, in the past decade, there has been an enormous volume of research into the economics of discrimination.[6] Initially, most research into discrimination was concerned with racial differences in income, employment, education, and other indicators of inequality; recent research also has focused attention on sexist discrimination. Table 19–4 exhibits median earnings in major occupations for Negroes and the total population, by sex.[7] For the total labor force, female earnings were only 55 percent of male earnings, and, in each occupation, females earned sub-

[6] The pathbreaking study of Gary S. Becker, *The Economics of Discrimination,* 2nd ed. (Chicago: University of Chicago Press, 1971), has provided the conceptual framework followed in most empirical studies of discrimination.

[7] The occupational categories in Table 19–4 are very broad, and the results do not suggest that different wages were paid to males and females and whites and nonwhites for doing the same work. For example, in the professional and technical category, doctors, lawyers, teachers, nurses, social workers, and many others are included.

Table 19-4 Median Earnings of Full-Time Workers in Major Occupations, by Race and Sex, 1970

Occupation Group	Total		Negro	
	Male	Female	Male	Female
Professional, technical and kindred workers	$11,752	$6,872	$8,526	$6,520
Managers and administrators, except farm	11,747	6,102	7,899	5,899
Sales workers	9,454	3,498	6,392	3,550
Clerical and kindred workers	7,973	5,110	6,861	5,129
Craftsmen and kindred workers	8,730	5,277	6,546	4,620
Operatives, except transport	7,439	4,284	6,118	3,882
Transportation equipment operatives	7,583	4,730	5,882	4,274
Laborers, except farm	6,135	3,960	5,065	3,740
Farmers and farm managers	5,122	2,580	1,928	2,277
Farm laborers and farm foremen	3,628	2,440	2,501	1,938
Service workers, except private household	6,381	3,465	5,073	3,426
Private household workers	3,118	1,482	2,763	1,500
Total experienced civilian labor force	8,517	4,715	5,937	3,812

Source: U.S. Bureau of the Census, *U.S. Census of Population: 1970, Detailed Characteristics United States Summary,* Tables 227 and 228.
Note: Full-time workers were those who worked fifty weeks or more.

stantially less than males.[8] Negro males earned considerably less than white males in all occupations, and the gaps were especially large in the managerial, professional, sales, and craft occupations. Very little variation in female earnings appeared to be associated with race.

Table 19–5 shows median income for selected educational levels by race and sex. For all education levels except postcollege, the average income of white females was less than one-half the average income level of white males. At each level of education, Negro males earned substantially more than Negro and white females but considerably less than white males. Table 19–5 presents no evidence of discrimination in earnings favoring white females over Negro females.[9]

It is clear from Tables 19–4 and 19–5 that Negro male earnings are

[8] The figures in Table 19–4 are for full-time workers, i.e., those who worked at least fifty weeks in 1970.

[9] The figures in Table 19–5 include all individuals who earned any income in 1970, and, therefore, they include all part-time as well as full-time workers. The percentage of white females with college or postcollege training who worked part-time was much greater than that for Negro females, and this accounts for the higher earnings for Negro females at advanced levels of education.

Table 19-5 Median Income for Selected Education Cells, by Race and Sex, 1970

Education Cell	Total Male	Total Female	White Male	White Female	Negro Male	Negro Female
Elementary School						
Less than 5 years	$ 2,605	$1,231	$ 2,746	$1,291	$2,214	$1,046
8 years	5,340	1,705	5,458	1,703	4,232	1,707
High School						
4 years	7,502	3,126	7,693	3,129	5,444	3,082
College						
4 years	11,192	4,936	11,374	4,803	7,608	6,085
5 years or more	12,718	7,203	12,852	7,145	9,897	8,019

Source: *U.S. Census of Population: 1970, Detailed Characteristics, United States Summary,* Table 249.

substantially below those of their white counterparts. The low income of Negroes is reflected in poverty statistics; in 1970, 29.9 percent of all Negroes and 8.6 percent of all whites were below the poverty level.[10] Other evidence of inequality is shown by the large racial differences in unemployment rates.[11] In 1973, the following unemployment rates were reported: white males, 3.9 percent; nonwhite males, 7.9 percent; white females, 4.9 percent; and nonwhite females, 9.7 percent.[12]

The wealth of research that has been directed at analyzing racial discrimination suggests that earnings differences between whites and Negroes reflect differences in occupational structure and educational attainment.[13] The gap in formal schooling between Negroes and whites has narrowed in recent years, but it is still large. (See Table 19–6.) It should also be stressed that the average schooling figures shown in Table

---

[10] Poverty thresholds are estimated according to family size, sex of family head, residence (farm and nonfarm), and age. In 1970, poverty thresholds ranged from $1,487 (individual female over 65 living on a farm) to $6,116 (nonfarm family with seven or more persons with male head). See *U.S. Census of Population: 1970 Detailed Characteristics, United States Summary,* Table 347 and Appendix B, pp. 25–27.

[11] The unemployed include all those who are seeking work and do not have a job.

[12] *Statistical Abstract,* 1973, p. 224.

[13] For recent empirical studies of racial discrimination, see the following: Barbara R. Bergman and Jerolyn R. Lyle, "The Occupational Standings of Negroes by Areas and Industries," *Journal of Human Resources,* Fall 1971; James Gwartney, "Changes in the Nonwhite/White Income Ratio—1939–67," *American Economic Review,* December 1970; James Gwartney, "Discrimination and Income Differentials," *American Economic Review,* June 1970; James Gwartney, "Discrimination, Achievement, and Payoffs of a College Degree," *Journal of Human Resources,* Winter 1972; Dave M. O'Neill, "The Effects of Discrimination on Earnings: Evidence from Military Test Score Results," *Journal of Human Resources,* Fall 1970; and Leonard Weiss and Jeffrey G. Williamson, "Black Education, Earnings, and Interregional Migration: Some New Evidence," *American Economic Review,* June 1972.

Table 19-6 Median Years of School Completed, by Race and Sex, 1960-72

Population Group	1960	1970	1972
White Males	10.7	12.2	12.3
White Females	11.2	12.2	12.3
Negro Males	7.7	9.6	10.1
Negro Females	8.6	10.2	10.4
Total Population	10.6	12.2	12.2

Source: *Statistical Abstract*, 1973, p. 115.

19–6 understate the real educational gap between Negroes and whites. Several recent studies have shown that Negro education is generally inferior to white education, and, therefore, elimination of the educational gap between whites and Negroes will require an increase in Negro participation in education and an improvement in the quality of Negro education.[14] Even if equality in education is attained, it is doubtful that Negro earnings will reach parity with white earnings unless there is a change in attitudes on the part of employers to open high-paying occupations to Negroes.[15]

Sexist earnings differences are generally attributed to differences in occupational structure.[16] The labor market, through employer prejudice and employee preference, segregates according to sex and concentrates females in low-paying female-dominated occupations.[17] Employers discriminate against women because of fluctuating labor force participation habits, inability or unwillingness to work overtime, geographical immobility due to family ties, sexist attitudes as to what is appropriate for women, and other factors. Many females segregate themselves into fe-

---

[14] Estimates of the quality difference between Negro and white education are found in Joseph S. Coleman et al., *Equality of Educational Opportunity* (Washington, D.C.: U.S. Department of Health, Education and Welfare, Office of Education, 1966), pp. 274–75; also see O'Neill, "The Effect of Discrimination," and Gwartney, "Discrimination, Achievement, and Payoffs."

[15] See Bergman and Lyle, "The Occupational Standings of Negroes"; Lester C. Thurow, *Poverty and Discrimination* (Washington, D.C.: Brookings Institution, 1969); and Christopher Jencks, *Inequality* (New York: Basic Books, 1972).

[16] For recent empirical studies of sexist discrimination, see the following: Malcolm S. Cohen, "Sex Differences in Compensation," *Journal of Human Resources*, Fall 1971; Victor Fuchs, "Differences in Hourly Earnings Between Men and Women," *Monthly Labor Review*, May 1971; Juanita Kreps, *Sex in the Marketplace* (Baltimore: Johns Hopkins, 1971); and Isabel V. Sawhill, "The Economics of Discrimination Against Women: Some New Findings," *Journal of Human Resources*, Summer 1973.

[17] Again, it should be stressed that the occupational categories in Table 19–4 are broadly defined; it is generally within these categories that occupational segregation takes place. Female-dominated occupations are those in which the majority of the jobs are filled by women, and they include elementary school teaching, nursing, secretarial work, etc.

male-dominated occupations because their job choice is restricted by family considerations which dictate hours, working conditions, and location.

Equality for women will require a major revision in attitudes toward sex roles. The current labor market perceives women as placing primary importance on their family life and secondary importance on their worklife outside the home. As long as these attitudes prevail, there will most likely not be any significant movement toward economic equality for the sexes.

The Economics of Crime

In addition to its social costs, crime imposes a considerable economic burden on society by directly siphoning off income and requiring expenditures for crime control.[18] Table 19–7 estimates that the cost of crime to society in 1965 was approximately $21 billion. Crime rates have increased sharply in the past two decades, and, in the nation as a whole, crime rates for all major offenses have at least doubled between 1952 and 1970. (See Figure 19–1.) The increase in crime has been especially severe in urban areas, and Table 19–8 shows that the crime rate for each major offense at least tripled between 1950–71; for robbery, the rate increased almost tenfold. Participation in crime, especially in robbery, burglary, larceny, and auto theft, is heaviest among young males, and arrest rates for nonwhites are much higher than for whites.[19] In conjunction with the rise in crime rates, there has been a decline in effectiveness in solving crimes as measured by the ratio of convictions to arrests.[20]

The accelerating crime rates lowers the quality of life for all Americans and demands immediate attention. For those crimes where it is possible to isolate causal forces, a direct attack should be made on the conditions that breed crime. For example, many crimes against property are rooted in discrimination, poverty, and unemployment. Young urban blacks are the heaviest participants in crime, and, in 1971, the unemployment rate for urban black teen-agers was almost 35 percent. A direct attack on discrimination and poverty should pay dividends by lowering the crime rate for offenses such as crimes against property. At the same time, the decline in police effectiveness suggests that improved means of crime control also are essential to lowering crime rates.

---

[18] An excellent review of the socio-economic impact of crime is presented by Llad Phillips, "The War on Crime: Prevention or Control," in Phillips and Votey, *Economic Analysis of Pressing Social Problems,* and I have drawn heavily from this source.

[19] In 1967, the arrest rate per 10,000 population for larceny was 268.0 for nonwhites and 93.1 for whites; see Phillips, "The War on Crime," pp. 317–21.

[20] See Figure 12–2 in Phillips, "The War on Crime."

Table 19-7 Economic Impact of Crimes and Crime-Related Expenditures, 1965 (millions of dollars)

Crime or Crime-Related Expenditures	Millions of Dollars
Crimes Against Persons	$ 815
Homicide	750
Assault and other	65
Crimes Against Property	3932
Unreported commercial theft	1400
Fraud	1350
Robbery, burglary, larceny, auto theft	600
Arson and vandalism	300
Embezzlement	200
Forgery	82
Illegal Goods and Services	8075
Gambling	7000
Narcotics	350
Loan sharking	350
Prostitution	225
Alcohol	150
Other Crimes	2036
Driving under the influence	1816
Abortion	120
Tax fraud	100
Public Law Enforcement	4212
Police	2792
Corrections	1034
Courts	261
Prosecution and defense	125
Private Costs Related to Crime	1910
Prevention services	1350
Insurance	300
Prevention equipment	200
Private counsel, bail, witness expenses	60
Total Cost of Crime and Crime-Related Expenditures	20980

Source: The President's Commission on Law Enforcement and Administration of Justice, *Task Force Report: Crime and its Impact—An Assessment,* 1967, Ch. 3.

Summary

Despite the current problems that face the American economy, the ability of the economy to solve problems in the past suggests that there are strong grounds for optimism. For example, the sources of discrimination

Figure 19-1 Offense Rates per 100,000 People for Seven Major Felonies

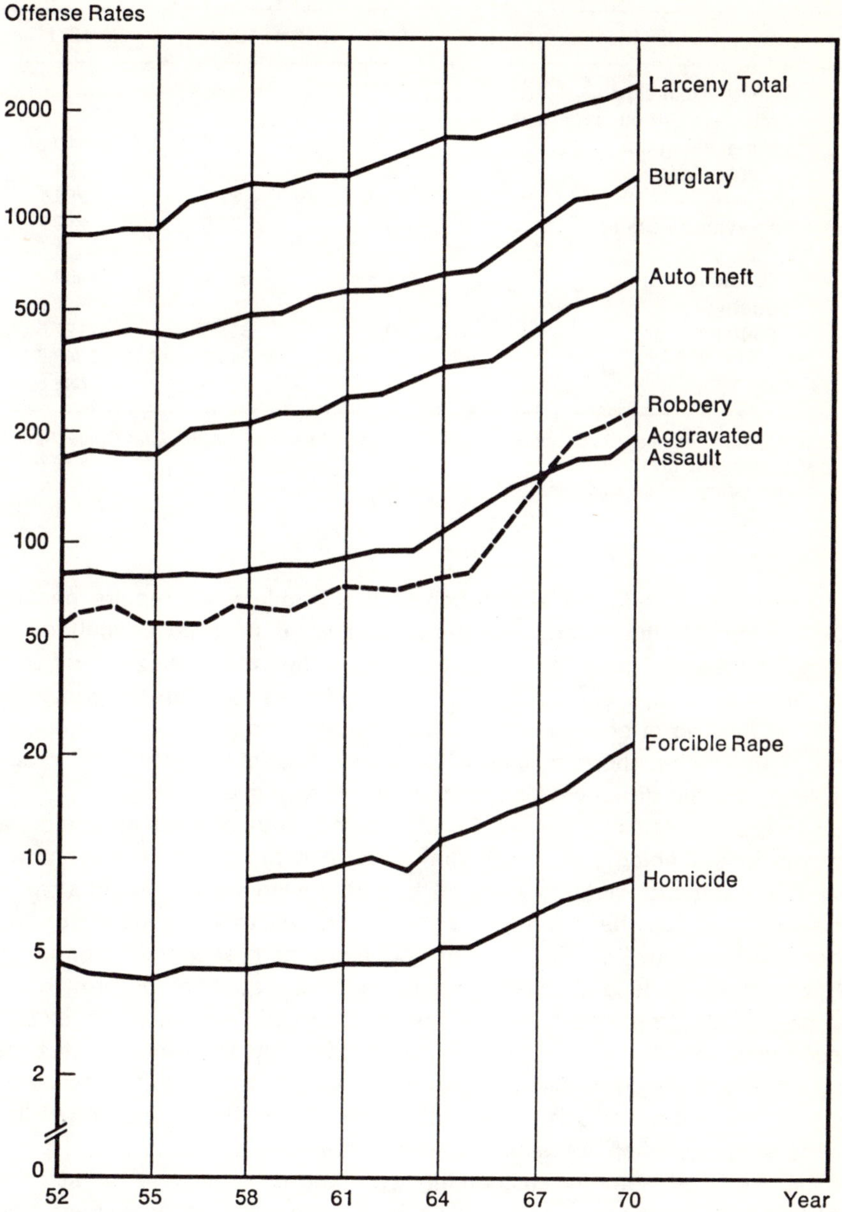

Source: Llad Phillips, "The War on Crime: Prevention or Control," in *Economic Analysis of Pressing Social Problems*, Llad Phillips and Harold L. Votey, Jr. (Chicago: Rand McNally College Publishing, 1974).

Table 19-8 Urban Crime Rates, 1950, 1960, and 1971 (rate of offense per 100,000)

Offense	1950	1960	1971
Criminal Homicide			
Murder and non-negligent manslaughter	2.8	4.6	10.3
Forcible Rape	6.0	8.8	24.5
Robbery	30.0	61.4	284.1
Aggravated Assault	39.4	87.6	219.7
Burglary			
Breaking or entering	211.5	558.1	1432.3
Larceny			
$50 and over	499.1[a]	346.5	1127.6
under $50		1040.5	1648.6
Auto Theft	83.8	241.5	643.6

Source: U.S. Department of Justice, Federal Bureau of Investigation, *Uniform Crime Reports*, 1950, 1960, and 1971.
[a] Includes larceny of all amounts.

are identifiable, and the elimination of this problem will require changes in employer attitudes and adequate funding of minority education. For most crimes, the methods of control are rather clear, and reduction in crime will require elimination of the conditions that breed crime and proper funding of crime control and enforcement agencies. This does not mean that either the problems of crime or discrimination will be readily solved, but the direction for effective policy action is clear.

The problems related to the environment demand massive improvements in technology, and they may require a fundamental restructuring of the traditional notions of growth and development. Quantitative increases in output have traditionally been viewed as the visible sign of a healthy economy. Under present technical and economic conditions, however, there is a distinct trade-off between quantity of growth and quality of life. In the past, technology has adapted very quickly to existing economic conditions, and, through new technology, the United States may be able to continue to expand both the quantity of output and the quality of life. However, if this is not possible, and if zero aggregate growth is a necessary condition for a healthy environment, Americans may have to completely restructure their thinking regarding progress and the standard of living. In the past, improvements in the standard of living have been achieved by generating higher levels of per capita consumption; in the future, improvements in the standard of living may be achieved by attaining cleaner air and water.

Suggested Reading

Becker, Gary S., *The Economics of Discrimination,* 2nd ed. Chicago: University of Chicago Press, 1971.

Bergman, Barbara R., and Jerolyn R. Lyle, "The Occupational Standings of Negroes by Areas and Industries," *Journal of Human Resources,* Fall 1971.

Cohen, Malcolm S., "Sex Differences in Compensation," *Journal of Human Resources,* Fall 1971.

Fuchs, Victor, "Differences in Hourly Earnings Between Men and Women," *Monthly Labor Review,* May 1971.

Gwartney, James, "Changes in the Nonwhite/White Income Ratio—1939–67," *American Economic Review,* December 1970.

———, "Discrimination and Income Differentials," *American Economic Review,* June 1970.

Jencks, Christopher, *Inequality.* New York: Basic Books, 1972.

Kreps, Juanita, *Sex in the Marketplace.* Baltimore: Johns Hopkins, 1971.

Mead, Walter J., "Oil, Energy, and Environmental Concern," in Llad Phillips and Harold L. Votey, Jr., eds., *Economic Analysis of Pressing Social Problems.* Chicago: Rand McNally College Publishing, 1974.

Phillips, Llad, "The War on Crime: Prevention or Control?" in Phillips and Votey, eds., *Economic Analysis of Pressing Social Problems.*

President's Commission on Law Enforcement and Administration of Justice, *Task Force Report: Crime and Its Impact—An Assessment.* Washington, D.C.: U.S. Government Printing Office, 1967.

Rottenberg, Simon, ed., *The Economics of Crime and Punishment.* Washington, D.C.: American Enterprise Institute for Public Policy Research, 1973.

Sawhill, Isabel V., "The Economics of Discrimination Against Women: Some New Findings," *Journal of Human Resources,* Summer 1973.

Thurow, Lester C., *Poverty and Discrimination.* Washington, D.C.: Brookings Institution, 1969.

Glossary

anti-trust Policy actions of government concerned with curbing restraint of trade or restrictions of competition.

balance of payments Financial statement showing a countrys' international receipts and payments. It includes trade in goods and services, gold transactions, and capital movements. If payments exceed receipts, a deficit exists in the balance of payments; if receipts exceed payments, a surplus exists.

balance of trade The portion of the balance of payments dealing with merchandise imports and exports. If exports are greater than imports, there is a favorable balance of trade; if imports are greater than exports, there is an unfavorable balance of trade.

balanced budget The government's budget is balanced if revenues equal expenditures. If revenues are greater than expenditures, there is a budget surplus; if expenditures are greater than revenues, there is a budget deficit.

bank, central The official financial institution of a government that controls the monetary side of the economy by regulating credit conditions and the money supply.

bank, commercial Financial intermediary generally referred to simply as a bank. Commercial banks serve as depositories for savings and demand deposits, and they use these funds to make loans, buy securities, and maintain checking services.

bank notes Paper currency issued by banks. In the antebellum period, most bank notes were issued by state chartered commercial banks, and they generally circulated at a discount *vis-à-vis* gold.

barrier to entry Institutional, legal, financial, or other factors that make it difficult or impossible to enter a particular industry.

benefit-cost ratio A measure (expected benefits/expected costs) used to determine the advisability of various investment projects. The major problem in benefit/cost analysis is the difficulty in achieving accurate measurement of all benefits and costs.

bimetallism The use of two metals (generally gold and silver) as a legal monetary standard.

boycott Effort (usually by organized labor) to persuade people not to deal with a particular firm.

capital The collection of man-made machines, buildings, and other durable assets that are used in the productive process.

capital formation Net additions to the capital stock achieved through investment expenditures.

capital intensive Production process that uses a high amount of capital relative to other inputs.

capital requirements Amount of capital required to enter an industry.

collective bargaining Union-management negotiations regarding wages, working conditions, and other employee grievances.

collusion Agreement between firms to restrict competition by fixing prices and controlling production and distribution.

comparative advantage Production of items in which one's relative efficiency is greatest compared to other producers. To maximize the benefits from trade, a region should concentrate production on items in which it has the greatest relative efficiency.

competition The degree of competition indicates the extent of control over price and output by firms. Perfect competition is a market structure with a large number of small firms such that no one firm is large enough to control price or output. Imperfect competition is a market structure where firms are large enough to influence price and output.

concentration ratio Measure of the degree of control of an industry by the four (eight) leading firms. Usually shows the leading firms' share of output or assets.

conglomerate A combination of firms in different industries under one central management. Conglomerates generally are formed to spread risk through product diversification.

conspicuous consumption (prestige demand) Lavish spending intended to enhance one's social prestige.

constant dollars Measures of economic activity that adjust for price changes over time.

contraction A period of declining economic activity.

corporation A type of business organization that joins one or more associates to act as a legal entity. Courts view a corporation's operation and liabilities as independent from its owners.

cost per ton-mile Rate charge in transportation indicating the cost of transporting one ton one mile.

counterfactual proposition Statement contrary to fact used as a research tool by economic historians. For example, what if the railroads had not been built until the twentieth century?

craft unions Organization of labor in a particular skill or trade such as printers, shoemakers, carpenters, etc.

credit creation Function of banks involving the use of deposits to make loans.

current dollars Measures of economic activity that make no adjustment for changes in prices over time.

customs See tariff.

cycle Periodic fluctuations of expansion and contraction in overall economic activity.

deficit spending Usually refers to deliberate imbalance in the federal government's budget (expenditures greater than receipts) whereby the government engages in "pump priming" activities to stimulate the economy.

deflation A decline in the average price level of all goods and services.

demand A schedule showing the quantity of a good or service that buyers plan to consume at various prices.

demand deposits Money on deposit in banks subject to withdrawal by check, i.e., checkbook money.

devaluation An act making a country's currency cheaper in terms of gold or foreign currencies. Devaluation is generally intended to increase a nation's exports and reduce its imports.

diminishing returns With fixed technology, successive increases in one factor input, other inputs being held constant, will lead to smaller and smaller increases in output.

distribution of income Measure of the degree of concentration of income among the population. If the bulk of an economy's income is concentrated in the hands of a small number of wealthy individuals, the income distribution is characterized by a high degree of inequality; if an economy's income is not concentrated among the wealthy, the income distribution is characterized by a high degree of equality.

division of labor See specialization.

durable goods Goods, such as industrial equipment, machines, and large household appliances, which have a relatively long expected worklife.

econometrics Branch of economics that uses mathematics and statistics to formalize and test the hypotheses of economic theory.

economic development A level of economic progress in which per capita income is above some floor level, modern technology is being adopted, the system of economic organization is efficient, and social, political, and cultural institutions are consistent with economic progress.

economic growth Increase in the aggregate level of economic activity, generally measured by changes in G.N.P.

economic organization Relationship between the various sectors of the economy (households, firms, and government) and the social, political, legal, and institutional framework within which economic activity takes place.

economics Social science concerned with the allocation of scarce resources among alternative ends.

economies of scale Increased efficiency in the conversion of inputs into output that results from an increase in the size of a firm or plants operation.

efficiency Achievement of maximum output relative to input.

embargo A government edict restricting foreign trade.

entrepreneur The "risk bearer" (individual or institution) who perceives business opportunities and determines business policy.

estate and inheritance taxes State and federal taxes imposed on the transfer of property after death.

excise taxes Taxes imposed on the manufacture, sale, or consumption of commodities such as liquor, gasoline, tires, and cigarettes.

exports Foreign sales of goods and services.

extractive industries Industries yielding commodities requiring very little processing whose value is largely determined by nature. Includes most agriculture, mining, fishing, and forestry.

factor substitution Process of replacing one productive resource with another. Within certain boundaries, labor and capital may be substituted for each other. For example, a ditch may be dug by many men by hand, by several men with shovels, or by one man with a machine.

factors of production Productive resources are classified into four broad categories: labor, capital, resources (including land), and entrepreneurship (risk).

financial intermediaries All institutions that receive funds from households and firms and make them available for investments. Financial intermediaries include all banks, savings and loan associations, insurance companies, and other financial institutions.

firm The standard decision-making unit of business enterprise.

fiscal policy Government taxing and spending policies.

full employment Situation in which no more than a small accepted percentage (generally 4 percent) of the labor force is unemployed.

gold standard System that uses gold as the basic monetary unit. Currency is defined in terms of gold; the exchange ratio between currency and gold is fixed; and there are no restrictions on the coinage or circulation of gold.

greenbacks Noninterest bearing notes without specie backing issued by the federal government to help finance the Civil War.

gross national product (G.N.P.) The total value of all goods and services produced for final sale in a given year.

holding company Type of business organization created by acquiring stocks or securities of other firms.

horizontal integration Consolidation of firms producing similar products and selling in similar markets. This type of merger is generally aimed at achieving control over final product markets.

human capital View of the population (number, knowledge, and skill) as a resource that can be increased and improved by investment in education, training, and other programs.

hyperinflation Especially rapid increase in the average level of prices of all goods and services.

hypothesis A tentative theory adopted to explain certain facts and to aid in the investigation of others.

imports Domestic consumption of foreign goods and services.

import substitution Attempt to substitute domestic production for foreign production of certain items currently being consumed.

incidence Refers to the impact of a policy, especially taxation, on various groups in society.

index numbers Figures that show the relative change from a base period, where the base is set equal to 100 and other figures are expressed as percentages of the base.

industrial union Organization of labor in a particular industry, such as steel workers or glass workers, without regard for skill.

infant industry Early stages of an industry's development when it is most in need of protection from foreign competition.

inflation Rise in the average level of prices of all goods and services.

injunction Court order requiring a party to refrain from certain actions or to take certain actions.

innovation Adoption of a new technique of production, new product, new form of business organization, or new method of distribution.

interest 1) Factor payment to capital; 2) Payment for borrowed funds.

investment Business expenditures for plant, equipment, and inventory accumulation.

isoquant A curve showing constant output and the various combination of factor inputs that could be used to generate that level of output.

labor force Includes all people 16 years of age or older who are employed plus all those who are unemployed but actively searching for a job.

labor intensive Production process that uses a high amount of labor relative to other inputs.

laissez faire A system of economic organization characterized by little or no government intervention.

land-labor ratio Refers to the supply of land and resources relative to the population.

linkages Refers to the effects of expansion in one industry on other industries. As one industry expands it creates needs for additional inputs (backward linkages), and it also creates demand for other industries (forward linkages).

margin requirements Percentage of the purchase price of stock required as a down payment.

market economy Economic system in which basic decisions regarding production and distribution are determined without government intervention.

market ratio The exchange rate between gold and silver established in the money market.

merger Consolidation of two or more firms under a single management. Mergers are generally achieved by horizontal combinations (firms producing similar products and selling in similar markets), vertical combinations (firms at various stages of production in a given industry), and formation of conglomerates (firms in different industries).

mint ratio The official exchange rate between gold and silver offered at the mint.

mixed economy Economic system in which basic decisions regarding production and distribution are determined by the joint operation of the free market and government intervention.

model Formal statement of hypotheses generally shown by mathematical specification.

monetary policy The collective powers of the Federal Reserve system to influence output and employment by controlling credit conditions and the money supply.

monopoly market structure characterized by a single firm producing a product for which there are no close substitutes.

monopoly power Control by large firms over price and output.

moving average, five-year A data series that shows the average value of the series over a five-year period centered on the middle year.

national income Total income paid to the factors of production (wages, interest, rent, and profit).

national market A market with diversified production and relative independence from foreign trade.

new economic history Approach to economic history that emphasizes the use of economic theory and statistics.

nondurable goods Goods such as food and clothing, that have a short expected life and are consumed on a rather regular basis.

oligopoly Market structure composed of a small number of firms selling similar (perfect) or differentiated (imperfect) products. The steel and copper industries are examples of perfect oligopolies; the automobile and cigarette industries are examples of imperfect oligopolies.

open market operations Federal Reserve purchase and sale of government securities.

opportunity cost The implicit cost of choosing one alternative rather than another. In making a choice, the benefits from all other possible choices are foregone, and these foregone benefits are opportunity costs.

overproduction Situation in which current production of goods and services exceeds current consumption.

parity An index (1910–14 = 100) of the ratio of prices received by farmers to prices paid by farmers.

participation rate An index of the percentage of the population currently participating in the labor force.

partnership A type of business organization formed by two or more partners who are joint owners and legally responsible for the operations and liabilities of the business.

per capita income The ratio of total income to total population. This is the most commonly used index of economic welfare.

plant Standard production unit in business enterprise. A firm may be comprised of several plants.

pool A type of business organization popular in the 1880s and early 1890s. Pools were loose agreements in which firms tried to acquire some degree of market control by dividing the market or by pooling output and sharing profits.

poverty level Poverty levels vary according to family size, sex of family head, residence (farm and nonfarm), and age. In 1970, the range of poverty levels was from $1,487 (individual female over 65 living on a farm) to $6,116 (nonfarm family with seven or more persons with male head).

prestige demand See conspicuous consumption.

private enterprise system See market economy.

private returns Gain to the individual or firm resulting from a particular course of action.

private sector The household and business sectors. The total economy excluding government.

production function Technical relationship between inputs and output.

productivity Productivity is the ratio of output to input. Common productivity measures include labor productivity (output per employee and output per manhour), capital productivity (output per unit of capital), and total factor productivity (output per unit of total factor input).

profit Return to the entrepreneur or "risk bearer." Residual income share after deducting wages, interest, and rent.

proprietorship A type of business organization with a single owner who is responsible for the operation and liabilities of the business.

public sector All levels of government.

quantity theory of money Theory of the relationship between changes in the money supply and the price level. According to the theory, for a given level of output and a constant velocity of money circulation, increases in the money supply are transmitted directly into increases in the price level.

ratio (logarithmic) scale Scale on a chart where equal percentage changes are represented by equal distances.

real Used to designate variables that have been deflated to take into account price changes. For example, real G.N.P. measures the increase in the output of goods and services after price inflation has been taken into account.

rediscount rate Interest rate charged by Federal Reserve Banks on loans to member banks.

regression analysis Statistical procedure that provides an analysis of the functional relationship between variables so that one or more variables (independent) can be used to explain variations in another (dependent). Simple regression involves only one independent variable; multiple regression involves several independent variables.

rent Factor payment to land and resources.

reserve ratio Percentage of a commercial bank's total assets held in the central bank. A minimum ratio of reserves to assets is generally specified by the central bank.

reserve requirements Legal minimum amount of reserves a bank must hold to cover its deposit liabilities.

reserves (energy) Term used to designate energy supplies that are recoverable under present revenue and cost conditions.

resource intensive Productive process that uses a high amount of resources relative to other inputs.

resources (energy) Term used to designate energy supplies that are not recoverable under present revenue and cost conditions.

sales tax A fixed percentage tax on final retail sales.

savings Portion of income not spent on consumption.

scale The size of a plant or firm's operation is generally referred to as the scale of operation.

silver certificates Paper currency issued by the federal government against its deposits of silver coin.

social returns Gain to society as a whole resulting from a particular course of action.

specialization (division of labor) Concentration of production on particular activities. Regions and individuals attempt to concentrate their efforts on activities in which their relative efficiency is greatest; in this way, total output is maximized because everyone is doing what he does best. The gains of specialization are spread through the economy by trade.

specie Tangible form of money, generally gold or silver.

stock Certificates of corporate ownership.

strike Collective agreement among laborers to stop working; weapon used by labor unions to achieve their goals.

structural change Change in industrial composition of output such as a rise in manufacturing and a decline in agriculture.

supply A schedule showing the quantity of a good or service that producers plan to market at various prices.

tariff (custom) A government tax on imports of foreign commodities. Tariffs are generally passed to protect domestic industries from foreign competition, but, in the nineteenth-century United States, tariffs were also a major means of raising federal government revenue.

taxes A government levy used to raise money for the public sector. Taxes are regressive (progressive) if they take a larger (smaller) share of income from low income individuals than from high income individuals. Taxes are proportional if they take the same share of income from individuals at all income levels.

technology The current state of the arts of production.

technological change A change in the arts of production that results in an improvement in the efficiency with which inputs are converted into output.

tenant farming Type of agricultural organization in which a farmer works land owned by another and pays rent either in cash or in crops.

terms of trade, net barter Ratio of change in the prices received for exports to the change in the prices paid for imports. This ratio shows changes in a country's international price position. If prices received for exports rise faster than prices paid for imports, the terms of trade have improved; if prices paid for imports rise faster than prices received for exports, the terms of trade have deteriorated.

theory The general principles of any body of knowledge. Hypotheses used to explain certain phenomena.

treasury note A currency note issued by the U.S. Treasury in payment for silver bullion.

trust A type of business organization popular in the 1880s and early 1890s. Trusts were formed by several companies in a particular industry by granting control of their stock to a group of trustees. By controlling the voting stock of several companies, the trustees could control the industry.

underconsumption Situation in which current consumption fails to clear the market of goods and services.

underemployment Situation in which labor is not being used in the most efficient manner. Underemployment exists when laborers are working below their skill level, when laborers are working part-time but are seeking full-time employment, and when laborers have stopped looking for work because they were unable to find a suitable job.

unemployment Situation in which some laborers who are seeking work are unable to find a suitable job. The unemployment rate is defined to include those workers who are unemployed and are seeking work.

union An organization of workers seeking to achieve solidarity against management.

value added Defined as the gross value of output minus intermediate production expenses (materials, fuel, etc.). Value added measures the net contribution to output at each stage of production.

velocity Measure of the rate at which money circulates in the economy.

vertical integration Consolidation of firms at various stages of production in a particular industry.

wages Factor payment to labor.

Bibliography

The bibliography presented in the following pages shows the sources that I used most heavily in writing this text. To all of these scholars, I am sincerely indebted. The bibliography is in no way exhaustive, and the interested student is urged to supplement this listing by consulting bibliographical references in other works and the indexes of the major journals in economic history: *Journal of Economic History, Explorations in Economic History, Business History Review,* and the *Economic History Review.*

Books

Aitken, Hugh G. J., ed. *The State and Economic Growth.* New York: Social Science Research Council, 1959.

Andreano, Ralph L., ed. *New Views on American Economic Development.* Cambridge; Mass.: Schenkman Publishing, 1965.

———. *The Economic Impact of the American Civil War,* 2nd ed. Cambridge; Mass.; Schenkman Publishing, 1967.

Associated Universities, Inc. *Reference Energy Systems and Resource Data for Use in the Assessment of Energy Technologies.* Upton, N.Y.: Brookhaven National Laboratory, April, 1972.

Aydelotte, William, et al., eds. *Dimensions of Quantitative Research in History.* Princeton: Princeton University Press, 1972.

Baldwin, Robert E. *Economic Development and Growth,* 2nd ed., New York: Wiley, 1972.

Barger, Harold. *Distributions' Place in the American Economy Since 1869.* Princeton: Princeton University Press, 1955.

Batchelder, Alan B. *The Economics of Poverty,* 2nd ed. New York: Wiley, 1971.

Beard, Charles A. *An Economic Interpretation of the Constitution of the United States.* New York: Macmillan, 1913.

———, and Beard, Mary R. *The Rise of American Capitalism.* New York: Macmillan, 1930.

Becker, Gary S. *The Economics of Discrimination,* 2nd ed. Chicago: University of Chicago Press, 1971.

Bernard, William S., ed. *American Immigration Policy,* New York: Harper and Bros., 1950.

Berry, Thomas Senior. *Western Prices before 1861: A Study of the Cincinnati Market,* Cambridge, Mass.: Harvard University Press, 1943.

Bidwell, P. W., and Falconer, J. I., *A History of Agriculture in the Northern United States, 1620–1860.* Washington, D.C.: Carnegie Institution, 1925.

Bishop, J. Leander. *A History of American Manufactures.* Philadelphia: Edward Young, 1864.

Bogue, Allan G. *From Prairie to Corn Belt.* Chicago: University of Chicago Press, 1963.

———. *Money at Interest.* Ithaca, N.Y.: Cornell University Press, 1955.

Bolles, Albert S. *Industrial History of the United States.* Norwich, Conn.: Henry Bill Publishing, 1881.

Bowman, John D. "Trends in Midwestern Farm Values, 1860–1914." Ph.D. dissertation, Yale University, 1964.

Bromwell, William J. *History of Immigration to the United States.* New York: Augustus M. Kelley, 1969.

Brown, Robert E. *Charles Beard and the Constitution.* Princeton: Princeton University Press, 1956.

Bruchey, Stuart, ed. *Cotton and the Growth of the American Economy.* New York: Harcourt, Brace, and World, 1967.

———. *The Roots of American Economic Growth, 1607–1861: An Essay in Social Causation.* New York: Harper & Row, 1965.

Burns, Arthur F. *Production Trends in the United States Since 1870.* New York: National Bureau of Economic Research, 1934.

Callender, Guy Stevens. *The Economic History of the United States, 1765–1860. Boston:* Ginn and Co., 1909.

Cameron, Rondo. *Banking in the Early Stages of Industrialization.* New York: Oxford University Press, 1967.

Carstensen, Vernon, ed. *The Public Lands.* Madison: University of Wisconsin Press, 1963.

Catterall, Ralph C. H. *The Second Bank of the United States.* Chicago: University of Chicago Press, 1902.

Chandler, Alfred D., Jr., *Strategy and Structure: Chapters in the History of Industrial Enterprise.* Cambridge, Mass.: M.I.T. Press, 1962.

———. *The Railroads: The Nation's First Big Business.* New York: Harcourt, Brace, and World, 1965.

Chandler, Lester V. *American Monetary Policy, 1928–1941.* New York: Harper & Row, 1971.

———. *America's Greatest Depression, 1929–1941.* New York: Harper & Row, 1970.

Clark, Victor S. *History of Manufactures in the United States,* 3 vols. New York: McGraw-Hill, for the Carnegie Institution of Washington, 1929.

Cochran, Thomas C. *The American Business System: A Historical Perspective, 1900–1955.* Cambridge, Mass.: Harvard University Press, 1965.

———, and Miller, William. *The Age of Enterprise.* New York: Macmillan, 1942.

Coleman, Joseph, et al. *Equality of Educational Opportunity.* Washington, D.C.: U.S. Department of Health, Education, and Welfare, Office of Education, 1966.

Commons, John R., et al. *History of Labor in the United States.* New York: Macmillan, 1935.

Conrad, Alfred H., and Meyer, John R. *The Economics of Slavery and Other Studies in Econometric History.* Chicago: Aldine, 1964.

Danhof, Clarence H. *Change in Agriculture: The Northern United States, 1820–1870.* Cambridge, Mass.: Harvard University Press, 1969.

Davis, Lance E.; Easterlin, Richard A.; Parker, William N.; et al. *American Economic Growth.* New York: Harper & Row, 1972.

Davis, Lance E., and North, Douglass C. *Institutional Change and American Economic Growth.* Cambridge: At the University Press, 1971.

Denison, Edward F. *The Sources of Economic Growth in the United States and the Alternatives Before Us.* New York: Committee for Economic Development, 1962.

Dewey, Davis R. *Financial History of the United States.* New York: Augustus M. Kelley, 1968.

Dewhurst, J. Frederick, and Associates. *America's Needs and Resources.* New York: The Twentieth Century Fund, 1947.

Dillard, Dudley. *Economic Development of the North Atlantic Community.* Englewood Cliffs, N.J.: Prentice-Hall, 1967.

Douglas, Paul H. *Real Wages in the United States, 1890–1926.* Boston: Houghton Mifflin, 1930.

Easterlin, Richard A. *Population, Labor Force, and Long Swings in Economic Growth: The American Experience.* New York: Columbia University Press, 1968.

Elkins, Stanley M. *Slavery: A Problem in American Institutional and Intellectual Life.* Chicago: University of Chicago Press, 1959.

Evans, George H., Jr. *Business Incorporations in the United States, 1800–1943.* New York: National Bureau of Economic Research, 1948.

Fabricant, Solomon. *Basic Facts on Productivity Change,* Occasional Paper 63. New York: National Bureau of Economic Research, 1959.

Fels, Rendigs. *American Business Cycles, 1865–1897.* Chapel Hill: University of North Carolina Press, 1959.

Fenstermaker, J. Van. *The Development of American Commercial Banking, 1782–1837. Kent, Ohio:* Kent State University Press, 1965.

Fishlow, Albert. *American Railroads and the Transformation of the Ante-Bellum Economy.* Cambridge, Mass.: Harvard University Press, 1965.

Fite, Gilbert C., and Reese, Jim E. *An Economic History of the United States.* Boston: Houghton Mifflin, 1973.

Floyd, Joe S. *Effects of Taxation on Industrial Location.* Chapel Hill: University of North Carolina Press, 1952.

Fogel, Robert W. *Railroads and American Economic Growth: Essay in Econometric History.* Baltimore: Johns Hopkins, 1964.

———. *The Union Pacific Railroad: A Case in Premature Enterprise.* Baltimore: Johns Hopkins, 1960.

———, and Engerman, Stanley L. *The Reinterpretation of American Economic History.* New York: Harper & Row, 1971.

———. *Time on the Cross.* Boston: Little, Brown, 1974.

Frickey, Edwin. *Production in the United States, 1860–1914.* Cambridge, Mass.: Harvard University Press, 1947.

Friedman, Milton, and Schwartz, Anna Jacobson. *A Monetary History of the United States, 1867–1960.* New York: National Bureau of Economic Research, 1963.

———. *The Great Contraction, 1929–1933.* Princeton: Princeton University Press, 1965.

Galbraith, John Kenneth. *The Great Crash, 1929.* Boston: Houghton Mifflin, 1954.

———. *The New Industrial State.* Boston: Houghton Mifflin, 1967.

Gates, Paul W. *The Farmer's Age: Agriculture, 1815–1860.* New York: Holt, Rinehart and Winston, 1960.

Genovese, Eugene D. *The Political Economy of Slavery.* New York: Pantheon Books, 1965.

Gilchrist, David T., and Lewis, W. David, eds. *Economic Change in the Civil War Era.* Greenville, Del.: Eleutherian Mills-Hagley Foundation, 1965.

Goodrich, Carter, ed. *Canals and American Economic Development.* New York: Columbia University Press, 1961.

———. *Government Promotion of American Canals and Railroads, 1800–1890.* New York: Columbia University Press, 1960.

———. *The Government and the Economy, 1783–1861.* Indianapolis: Bobbs-Merrill, 1967.

Gras, N. S. B. *Industrial Evolution.* Cambridge, Mass.: Harvard University Press, 1930.

Gray, Alexander. *The Development of Economic Doctrine.* New York: Wiley, 1961.

Gray, L. C. *History of Agriculture in the Southern United States to 1860.* Washington, D.C.: Carnegie Institution, 1933.

Gray, Ralph, and Peterson, John M. *Economic Development of the United States.* Homewood, Ill.: Richard D. Irwin, 1974.

Habakkuk, H. J. *American and British Technology in the Nineteenth Century.* Cambridge: At the University Press, 1967.

Hacker, Louis M. *The Course of American Economic Growth and Development.* New York: Wiley, 1970.

———. *The Triumph of American Capitalism. New York: Columbia* University Press, 1940.

Hammond, Bray. *Banks and Politics in America from the Revolution to the Civil War.* Princeton: Princeton University Press, 1957.

Handlin, Oscar, and Handlin, Mary Flug. *Commonwealth: A Study in the Role of Government in the American Economy, Massachusetts, 1774–1861.* New York: New York University Press, 1947.

Harris, Seymour, ed. *American Economic History.* New York: McGraw-Hill, 1961.

Hartz, Louis. *Economic Policy and Democratic Thought: Pennsylvania, 1776–1860.* Cambridge, Mass.: Harvard University Press, 1948.

Hibbard, Benjamin Horace. *A History of Public Land Policies.* Madison: University of Wisconsin Press, 1965.

Higgs, Robert. *The Transformation of the American Economy, 1865–1914.* New York: Wiley, 1971.

Hines, Lawrence G. *Environmental Issues: Population, Pollution, and Economics.* New York: W. W. Norton, 1973.

Holt, Charles F. *"The Role of State Government in the Nineteenth Century American Economy, 1820–1902: A Quantitative Study."* Ph.D. dissertation, Purdue University, 1970.

Hourwich, Isaac A. *Immigrant Labor.* New York: G. P. Putnam's Sons, 1912.

Hughes, Jonathan. *Industrialization and Economic History: Theses and Conjectures.* New York: McGraw-Hill, 1970.

Hunter, Louis C. *Steamboats on the Western Rivers.* Cambridge, Mass.: Harvard University Press, 1949.

Jencks, Christopher. *Inequality.* New York: Basic Books, 1972.

Jenkes, John; Sawers, David; and Stillerman, Richard. *The Sources of Invention,* 2nd ed. New York: W. W. Norton, 1969.

Jenks, Jeremiah W., and Lauck, W. Jett. *The Immigration Problem.* New York: Funk and Wagnalls, 1926.

Jensen, Merrill. *The New Nation.* New York: Alfred A. Knopf, 1950.

Jerome, Harry. *Migration and Business Cycles.* New York: National Bureau of Economic Research, 1926.

Josephson, Matthew. *Robber Barons: The Great American Capitalists, 1861–1901.* New York: Harcourt, Brace, and World, 1934.

Kendrick, John W. *Productivity Trends in the United States.* Princeton: Princeton University Press, 1961.

Kirkland, Edward C. *Industry Comes of Age: Business, Labor, and Public Policy, 1860–1897.* New York: Holt, Rinehart and Winston, 1961.

Kolko, Gabriel. *Railroads and Regulation, 1877–1916.* New York: W. W. Norton, 1970.

Kreps, Juanita. *Sex in the Marketplace.* Baltimore: Johns Hopkins, 1971.

Kuznets, Simon. *Capital in the American Economy.* Princeton: Princeton University Press, 1961.

———, ed. *Income and Wealth of the United States, Trends and Structure.* Cambridge: Bowes & Bowes, 1952.

Kuznets, Simon, and Rubin, Ernest. *Immigration and the Foreign Born,* Occasional Paper 46. New York: National Bureau of Economic Research, 1954.

Kuznets, Simon, et al. *Population Redistribution and Economic Growth, United States, 1870–1950,* 3 vols. Philadelphia: American Philosophical Society, 1957.

Landes, David S. *The Unbound Prometheus.* Cambridge: At the University Press, 1969.

Lebergott, Stanley. *Manpower in Economic Growth: The American Record Since 1800.* New York: McGraw-Hill, 1964.

Leuchtenburg, William E. *Franklin D. Roosevelt and the New Deal, 1932–1940.* New York: Harper & Row, 1963.

Lewis, H. G. *Unionism and Relative Wages in the United States.* Chicago: University of Chicago Press, 1963.

Long, Clarence D. *Wages and Earnings in the United States, 1860–1890.* Princeton: Princeton University Press, 1960.

Lord, Clifford L., and Lord, Elizabeth L. comps. *Historical Atlas of the United States.* New York: Henry Holt, 1944.

Macavoy, Paul W. *The Economic Effects of Regulation: The Trunk Line Railroad Cartels and the Interstate Commerce Commission Before 1900.* Cambridge, Mass.: M.I.T. Press, 1965.

MacGill, Caroline E., et al. *History of Transportation in the United States Before 1860.* Washington, D.C.: Carnegie Institution, 1917.

Mansfield, Edwin. *Technological Change.* New York: W. W. Norton, 1971.

———. *The Economics of Technological Change.* New York: W. W. Norton, 1968.

Marcus, Edward, and Marcus, Mildred Rendl. *Economic Progress and the Developing World.* Glenview, Ill.: Scott, Foresman, 1971.

Martin, Robert F. *National Income in the United States, 1779–1938.* New York: National Industrial Conference Board, 1939.

McGrane, Reginald C. *Foreign Bondholders and American State Debts.* New York: Macmillan, 1935.

Mishan, E. J. *The Costs of Economic Growth.* New York: Frederick A. Praeger, 1967.

Mitchell, Broadhus. *Depression Decade: From New Era Through New Deal, 1932–1940.* New York: Harper & Row, 1969.

Mitchell, Broadus. *Depression Decade: From New Era Through New Deal, to the Economic Consequences of Their Issue, 1862–65.* Chicago: University of Chicago Press, 1903.

———. *Gold, Prices, and Wages Under the Greenback Standard.* Berkeley: University of California Press, 1908.

Moody, John. *The Truth About the Trusts.* New York: Moody Publishing, 1904.

Nelson, Ralph L. *Merger Movements in American Industry, 1895–1956.* Princeton: Princeton University Press, 1959.

Nettels, Curtis P. *The Emergence of a National Economy, 1775–1815.* New York: Holt, Rinehart and Winston, 1962.

Niemi, Albert W., Jr. *State and Regional Patterns in American Manufacturing, 1860–1900.* Westport, Conn.: Greenwood Press, 1974.

North, Douglass C. *Growth and Welfare in the American Past.* Englewood Cliffs, N.J.: Prentice-Hall, 1974. Revised ed.

———. *The Economic Growth of the United States, 1790–1860.* New York: W. W. Norton, 1966.

Nutter, G. Warren, and Einhorn, Henry Adler. *Enterprise Monopoly in the United States: 1899–1958.* New York: Columbia University Press, 1969.

Owsley, Frank L. *Plain Folk of the Old South.* Baton Rouge: Louisiana State University Press, 1949.

Parker, William N., ed. *The Structure of the Cotton Economy of the Antebellum South.* Washington, D.C.: The Agricultural History Society, 1970.

Paullin, Charles. *Atlas of Historical Geography of the United States.* Washington, D.C.: Carnegie Institution and the American Geographical Society of New York, 1932.

Perlman, Selig. *A History of Trade Unionism in the United States.* New York: Macmillan, 1922.

Phillips, Llad, and Votey, Harold L., Jr., eds. *Economic Analysis of Pressing Social Problems.* Chicago: Rand McNally, 1974.

Phillips, Ulrich B. *American Negro Slavery.* London: D. Appleton, 1918.

Ratchford, B. U. *American State Debts.* Durham, N.C.: Duke University Press, 1941.

Rees, Albert. *Real Wages in Manufacturing, 1890–1914.* Princeton: Princeton University Press, 1961.

Robbins, Roy M. *Our Landed Heritage: The Public Domain, 1776–1936.* Princeton: Princeton University Press, 1942.

Robertson, Ross M. *History of the American Economy,* 3rd ed. New York: Harcourt Brace Jovanovich, 1973.

Rosenberg, Nathan. *Technology and American Economic Growth.* New York: Harper & Row, 1972.

———, ed. *The American System of Manufactures.* Edinburgh: Edinburgh University Press, 1969.

Rosovsky, Henry, ed. *Industrialization in Two Systems.* New York: Wiley, 1966.

Rostow, W. W. *The Stages of Economic Growth: A Non-Communist Manifesto.* Cambridge: At the University Press, 1960.

Rottenberg, Simon, ed. *The Economics of Crime and Punishment.* Washington, D.C.: American Enterprise Institute for Public Policy Research, 1973.

Salter, W. E. G. *Productivity and Technical Change,* 2nd ed. Cambridge: At the University Press, 1966.

Samuelson, Paul A. *Economics,* 9th ed. New York: McGraw-Hill, 1973.

Scheiber, Harry N. *Ohio Canal Era.* Athens: Ohio University Press, 1969.

Scherer, F. M. *Industrial Market Structure and Economic Performance.* Chicago: Rand McNally, 1970.

Schiller, Bradley R. *The Economics of Poverty and Discrimination.* Englewood Cliffs, N.J.: Prentice-Hall, 1973.

Schlesinger, Arthur M., Jr. *The Age of Jackson.* Boston: Little, Brown, 1945.

Schmookler, Jacob. *Invention and Economic Growth.* Cambridge, Mass.: Harvard University Press, 1966.

Schurr, Sam H., and Netschert, Bruce C. *Energy in the American Economy, 1850–1975.* Baltimore: Johns Hopkins, 1960.

Shannon, Fred A. *The Farmer's Last Frontier.* New York: Holt, Rinehart and Winston, 1963.

Shaw, William H. *Value of Commodity Output Since 1869.* New York: National Bureau of Economic Research, 1947.

Shepherd, James., and Walton, Gary. *Shipping, Maritime Trade, and the Economic Development of Colonial North America.* Cambridge: At the University Press, 1972.

Smith, Adam. *The Wealth of Nations.* New York: Random House, 1937.

Smith, Walter B., and Cole, Arthur H. *Fluctuations in American Business, 1790–1860.* Cambridge, Mass. Harvard University Press, 1935.

Soule, George H. *Prosperity Decade.* New York: Holt, Rinehart and Winston, 1947.

Stampp, Kenneth M. *The Peculiar Institution: Slavery in the Ante-Bellum South.* New York: Alfred A. Knopf, 1956.

Starobin, Robert S. *Industrial Slavery in the Old South.* New York: Oxford University Press, 1970.

Strassman, W. Paul. *Risk and Technological Innovation: American Manufacturing Methods During the Nineteenth Century.* Ithaca, N.Y.: Cornell University Press, 1959.

Strauss, Frederick, and Bean, Louis H. *Gross Farm Income and Indices of Farm Production and Prices in the United States, 1869–1937,* Technical Bulletin 703. Washington, D.C.: U.S. Department of Agriculture, 1940.

Studenski, Paul, and Krooss, Herman E. *Financial History of the United States,* 2nd ed. New York: McGraw-Hill, 1963.

Swierenga, Robert P. *Pioneers and Profits; Land Speculation on the Iowa Frontier.* Ames: Iowa State University Press, 1968.

Taylor, George R. *The Transportation Revolution, 1815–1860.* New York: Holt, Rinehart and Winston, 1951. (Reprinted by Harper & Row, Publishers, 1968.)

Taussig, Frank W. *Some Aspects of the Tariff Question.* Cambridge, Mass.: Harvard University Press, 1934.

———. *The Tariff History of the United States.* New York: Johnson Reprint Corporation, 1966.

Temin, Peter. *Iron and Steel in Nineteenth Century America: An Economic Inquiry.* Cambridge, Mass.: M.I.T. Press, 1964.

———. *The Jacksonian Economy.* New York: W. W. Norton, 1969.

Thomas, Brinley. *Migration and Economic Growth.* Cambridge: At the University Press, 1954.

Thorp, Willard L., and Crowder, Walter. *The Structure of American Industry,* Temporary National Economic Committe Monograph 27. Washington, D.C.: U.S. Government Printing Office, 1941.

Thurow, Lester C. *Poverty and Discrimination.* Washington, D. C.: Brookings Institution, 1969.

Tocqueville, Alexis de. *Democracy in America.* New York: Century Company, 1898.

Tostlebe, Alvin S. *Capital in Agriculture: Its Formation and Financing since 1870.* Princeton: Princeton University Press, 1957.

Turner, Frederick J. *The Frontier in American History.* New York: Henry Holt, 1920.

Vatter, Harold G. *The U.S. Economy in the 1950's.* New York: W. W. Norton, 1963.

Ware, Norman. *The Industrial Worker, 1840–1860.* Boston: Houghton Mifflin, 1924.

Warren, George F., and Pearson, Frank A. *Prices.* New York: Wiley, 1933.

Wicker, Elmus R. *Federal Reserve Monetary Policy, 1917–1933.* New York: Random House, 1966.

Williamson, Harold F. *The Growth of the American Economy,* 2nd ed. Englewood Cliffs, N.J.: Prentice-Hall, 1951.

Wolman, Leo. *Growth of American Trade Unions, 1880–1923.* New York: National Bureau of Economic Research, 1924.

Woodman, Harold D., ed. *Slavery and the Southern Economy.* New York: Harcourt, Brace, and World, 1966.

Woytinsky, W. S. *Employment and Wages in the United States.* New York: Twentieth Century Fund, 1953.

———. *Labor in the United States.* Washington, D.C.: Committee on Social Security, Social Science Research Council, 1938.

Articles

Abramovitz, Moses. "Resource and Output Trends in the United States Since 1870." *American Economic Review,* 46 (May 1956): 5–23.

Adams, Donald R., Jr. "Wage Rates in the Early National Period: Philadelphia, 1785–1830." *Journal of Economic History,* 28 (September 1968): 404–26.

Adams, Walter. "The Military-Industrial Complex and the New Industrial State." *American Economic Review,* 58 (May 1968): 652–65.

Arnould, Richard J. "Changing Patterns of Concentration in American Meat Packing, 1880–1963." *Business History Review* 45 (Spring 1971): 18–34.

Baack, Bennett D., and Ray, Edward John. "Tariff Policy and Comparative Advantage in the Iron and Steel Industry: 1870–1929." *Explorations in Economic History* 11 (Fall 1973): 3–24

Bateman, Fred. "Improvements in American Dairy Farming, 1850–1910: A Quantitative Analysis." *Journal of Economic History* 28 (June 1968): 255–73.

———. "Labor Inputs and Productivity in American Dairy Agriculture, 1850–1910." *Journal of Economic History* 29 (June 1969): 206–29.

———; Foust, James D.; and Weiss, Thomas J. "Large-Scale Manufacturing in the South and West, 1850–1860." *Business History Review* 45 (Spring 1971): 1–17.

Battalio, Raymond C., and Kagel, John. "The Structure of Antebellum Southern Agriculture: South Carolina, A Case Study." In William N. Parker, ed., *The Structure of the Cotton Economy of the Antebellum South* pp. 25–38. Washington, D.C.: Agricultural History Society, 1970.

Becker, Gary S. "Crime and Punishment: An Economic Approach." *Journal of Political Economy* 76 (March/April 1968): 169–217.

———. "Under-Investment in College Education." *American Economic Review* 50 (May 1960): 346–54.

Bergman, Barbara R., and Lyle, Jerolyn R. "The Occupational Standings of Negroes by Areas and Industries." *Journal of Human Resources* 6 (Fall 1971): 411–43.

Bjork, Gordon. "Weaning of the American Economy: Independence, Market Changes, and Economic Development." *Journal of Economic History* 24 (Decembr 1964): 541–60.

Bogue, Allan G., and Bogue, Margaret B. "Profits and the Frontier Land Speculator." *Journal of Economic History* 17 (March 1957) 346–54.

Bowman, John D. "An Economic Analysis of Midwestern Farm Land Values and Farm Land Income, 1860 to 1900." *Yale Economic Essays* 5 (Fall 1965): 317–52.

Bowman, Mary Jean. "The Land Grant Colleges and Universities in Human Resource Development." *Journal of Economic History* 22 (December 1962): 523-46.

Brady, Dorothy. "Relative Prices in the Ninteenth Century." *Journal of Economic History* 24 (June 1964): 145–203.

Broeze, Frank J. A. "The New Economic History, the Navigation Acts, and the Continental Tobacco Market, 1770–90." *Economic History Review* 26 (November 1973): 668–78.

Broude, Henry W. "The Role of the State in American Economic Development, 1820–90." In Hugh G. J. Aitken, ed., *The State and Economic Growth,* pp. 4–25. New York: Social Science Research Council, 1959.

Brown, E. Cary. "Fiscal Policy in the Thirties: A Reappraisal." *American Economic Review* 46 (December 1956): 857–79.

Brozen, Yale. "The Future of Industrial Research." *Journal of Business* 34 (October 1961): 434–41.

Budd, Edward C. "Factor Shares, 1850–1910." In *Trends in the American Economy in the Nineteenth Century,* Conference on Research in Income and Wealth, Studies in Income and Wealth, National Bureau of Economic Research, Vol. 24, pp. 365–406. Princeton: Princeton University Press, 1960.

Chandler, Alfred D., Jr. "The Beginnings of 'Big Business' in American Industry." *Business History Review* 33 (Spring 1959): 1–31.

———. "The Structure of American Industry in the Twentieth Century: An Historical Overview." *Business History Review* 43 (Autumn 1969): 255–98.

Cochran, Thomas C. "Business Organization and the Development of an Industrial Discipline." Harold F. Williamson, ed., *The Growth of the American Economy,* pp. 279–95. Englewood Cliffs, N.J.: Prentice-Hall, 1951.

———. "Did the Civil War Retard Industrialization." *Mississippi Valley Historical Review* 48 (September 1961): 197–210.

Cohen, Malcolm S. "Sex Differences in Compensation." *Journal of Human Resources* 6 (Fall 1971): 434–47.

Cole, Arthur. "Cyclical and Sectional Variations in the Sale of Public Lands, 1816–1860." *Review of Economics and Statistics* 9 (January 1927): 41–53.

Conrad, Alfred H., and Meyer, John R. "The Economics of Slavery in the Antebellum South." *Journal of Political Economy* 66 (April 1958): 95–130.

Cranmer, H. Jerome. "Canal Investment, 1815–1860." In *Trends in the American Economy in the Nineteenth Century,* Conference on Research in Income and Wealth, Studies in Income and Wealth, National Bureau of Economic Research, Vol. 24, pp. 547–70. Princeton: Princeton University Press, 1960.

Danhof, Clarence H. "Farm-Making Costs and the Safety Valve: 1850–1860." *Journal of Political Economy* 49 (June 1941): 317–59.

David, Paul A. "Learning By Doing and Tariff Protection: A Reconsideration of the Case of the Ante-Bellum United States Cotton Textile Industry." *Journal of Economic History* 30 (September 1970): 521–601

———. "The Growth of Real Product in the United States Before 1840: New Evidence, Controlled Conjectures." *Journal of Economic History* 27 (June 1967): 151–97.

———. "The Mechanization of Reaping in the Antebellum Midwest." In Henry Rosovsky, ed., *Industrialization in Two Systems.* New York: Wiley, 1966. Pp. 3–39.

———. "Transport Innovation and Economic Growth." *Economic History Review* 22 (December 1969): 506–25.

———. and de Klundert, T. H. Van, "Biased Efficiency Growth and Capital-Labor Substitution in the United States, 1899–1960." *American Economic Review* 55 (June 1965): 357–94.

Davis, Lance E. "'And It Will Never Be Literature': The New Economic History, A Critique." *Explorations in Entrepreneurial History* 6 (Fall 1968): 75–92.

———. "Capital Immobilities and Finance Capitalism: A Study of Economic Evolution in the United States, 1820–1920." *Explorations in Entrepreneurial History,* Fall, 1963. 88–105.

———. "The Investment Market, 1870–1914: The Evolution of a National Market." *Journal of Economic History* 25 (September 1965): 355–99.

———, and Legler, John. "The Government in the American Economy, 1815–1902: A Quantitative Study." *Journal of Economic History* 26 (December 1966): 514–55.

Davis, Lance E., and North, Douglass C. "Institutional Change and American Economic Growth: A First Step Towards a Theory of Institutional Innovation." *Journal of Economic History* 30 (March 1970): 131–49.

Demsetz, Harold. "Toward a Theory of Property Rights." *American Economic Review* 57 (May 1967): 347–59.

Denison, Edward F. "United States Economic Growth." *Journal of Business* 35 (April 1962): 109–21.

DuBoff, Richard B. "The Introduction of Electric Power in American Manufacturing." *Economic History Review* 20 (December 1967): 509–18.

Easterlin, Richard A. "Interregional Differences in Per Capita Income, Population, and Total Income, 1840–1950." In *Trends in the American Economy in the Nineteenth Century,* Conference on Research in Income and Wealth, Studies in Income and Wealth, National Bureau of Economic Research, Vol. 24, pp. 73–140. Princeton: Princeton University Press, 1960.

———. "Regional Income Trends, 1840–1950." In Seymour Harris, ed., *American Economic History, pp. 525–47.* New York: McGraw-Hill, 1961.

Eckler, A. Ross, and Zlotnick, Jack. "Immigration and the Labor Force." *Annals of the American Academy of Political and Social Science* 262 (March 1949): 92–101.

Ellis, David M. "Comments on 'The Railroad Land Grant Legend in American History Texts.'" *Mississippi Valley Historical Review* 32 (March 1946): 557–63.

Engerman, Stanley L. "Human Capital, Education, and Economic Growth." In Robert W. Fogel and Stanley L. Engerman, eds. *The Reinterpretation of American Economic History,* pp. 241–56. New York: Harper & Row, 1971.

———."Some Economic Issues Relating to Railroad Subsidies and the Evaluation of Land Grants." *Journal of Economic History* 32 (June 1972): 443–63.

———. "The Antebellum South: What Probably Was and What Should Have Been." In William N. Parker, ed., *The Structure of the Cotton Economy of the Antebellum South,* pp. 127–42. Washington, D.C.: Agricultural History Society, 1970.

———. "The Economic Impact of the Civil War." *Explorations in Entrepreneurial History* 3 (Spring 1966): 176–99.

———. "The Effects of Slavery Upon the Southern Economy: A Review of the Recent Debate." *Explorations in Entrepreneurial History* 4 (Winter 1967): 71–97.

Evans, Robert, Jr. "The Economics of American Negro Slavery." In *Aspects of Labor Economics,* National Bureau of Economic Research, pp. 185–243. Princeton: Princeton University Press, 1962.

Feller, Irwin. "The Urban Location of United States Invention, 1860–1910." *Explorations in Economic History* 8 (Spring 1971): 285–304.

Fenichel, Allen H. "Growth and Diffusion of Power in Manufacturing, 1838–1919." In *Output, Employment, and Productivity in the United States after 1800,* Conference on Research in Income and Wealth, Studies in Income and Wealth, National Bureau of Economic Research, Vol. 30, pp. 443–78. New York: Columbia University Press, 1966.

Fischbaum, Marvin, and Rubin, Julius. "Slavery and the Economic Development of the American South." *Explorations in Entrepreneurial History* 6 (Fall 1968): 116–27.

Fisher, Franklin M., and Temin, Peter. "Regional Specialization and the Supply of Wheat in the United States, 1867–1914." *Review of Economics and Statistics* 52 (May 1970): 134–49.

———. "Regional Specialization and the Supply of Wheat in the United States, 1867–1914: A Reply." *Review of Economics and Statistics* 53 (February 1971): 102–3.

Fishlow, Albert. "Antebellum Interregional Trade Reconsidered." In Ralph L. Andreano, ed., *New Views on American Economic Development,* pp. 187–200. Cambridge, Mass.: Schenkman Publishing, 1965.

———. "Discussion of Bjork Paper." *Journal of Economic History* 24 (December 1964): 561–66.

———. "Levels of Nineteenth Century American Investment in Education." *Journal of Economic History* 26 (December 1966): 418–36.

———. "Postscript on Antebellum Interregional Trade," In Ralph L. Andreano, ed. *New Views on American Economic Development,* pp. 209–12. Cambridge, Mass.: Schenkman Publishing, 1965.

———. "Productivity and Technological Change in the Railroad Sector, 1840–1910." In *Output, Employment, and Productivity in the United States after 1800,* Conference on Research in Income and Wealth, Studies in Income and Wealth, National Bureau of Economic Research, Vol. 30, pp. 583–646. New York: Columbia University Press, 1966.

———. "The American Common School Revival: Fact or Fancy." In Henry Rosovsky, ed., *Industrialization in Two Systems,* pp. 40–67. New York: Wiley, 1966.

———, and Fogel, Robert W. "Quantitative Economic History: An Interim Evaluation, Past Trends and Present Tendencies." *Journal of Economic History* 31 (March 1971): 15–42.

Fite, Gilbert C. "Daydreams and Nightmares: The Late Nineteenth Century Agricultural Frontier." *Agricultural History* 40 (October 1966): 285–94.

Fleisig, Heywood. "The Union Pacific Railroad and the Railroad Land Grant Controversy." *Explorations in Economic History* 11 (Winter 1973–74): 155–72.

Fogel, Robert W. "American Interregional Trade in the Nineteenth Century." In Ralph L. Andreano, ed., *New Views on American Economic Development,* pp. 213–24. Cambridge, Mass.: Schenkman Publishing, 1965.

———. "A Provisional View of the 'New Economic History.'" In Ralph L. Andreano, ed. *New Views on American Economic Development,* pp. 201–9. Cambridge, Mass.: Schenkman Publishing, 1965.

———. "A Quantitative Approach to the Study of Railroads in American Economic Growth: A Report of Some Preliminary Findings." *Journal of Economic History* 22 (June 1962): 163–97.

———. "The Reunification of Economic History with Economic Theory." *American Economic Review* 55 (May 1965): 92–98.

———. "The Specification Problem in Economic History." *Journal of Economic History* 27 (September 1967): 283–308.

———, and Engerman, Stanley L. "A Model for the Explanation of Industrial Expansion During the Nineteenth Century With An Application to the American Iron Industry." *Journal of Political Economy* 77 (May/June 1969): 306–28.

———. "The Economics of Slavery." In Robert W. Fogel and Stanley L. Engerman, eds., *The Reinterpretation of American Economic History,* pp. 311–41. New York: Harper & Row, 1971.

———. "The Relative Efficiency of Slavery: A Comparison of Northern and Southern Agriculture in 1860." *Explorations in Economic History* 8 (Spring 1971): 353–67.

Fogel, Robert W., and Jack Rutner. "The Efficiency Effects of Federal Land Policy, 1850–1900: A Report of Some Provisional Findings." In William Aydelotte et al.; ed., *Dimensions of Quantitative Research in History,* pp. 390–418. Princeton: Princeton University Press, 1972.

Foust, James D., and Swan, Dale E. "Productivity and Profitability of Antebellum Slave Labor: A Micro Approach." In William N. Parker, ed., *The Structure of the Cotton Economy of the Antebellum South,* pp. 39–62. Washington, D.C.: Agricultural History Society, 1970.

Fuchs, Victor. "Differences in Hourly Earnings Between Men and Women." *Monthly Labor Review* 94 (May 1971): 9–15.

Galambos, Louis. "The Agrarian Image of the Large Corporation, 1879–1920: A Study in Social Accommodation." *Journal of Economic History* 28 (September 1968): 341–62.

Galloway, Lowell E., and Vedder, Richard K. "Emigration from the United Kingdom to the United States: 1860–1913." *Journal of Economic History* 31 (December 1971): 885–97.

———, and Shukla, Vishwa. "The Distribution of the Immigrant Population in the United States: An Economic Analysis." *Explorations in Economic History* 11 (Spring 1974): 213–26.

Gallman, Robert E. "Commodity Output, 1839–1899." In *Trends in the American Economy in the Nineteenth Century,* Conference on Research in Income and Wealth, Studies in Income and Wealth, National Bureau of Economic Research, Vol. 24, pp. 13–71. Princeton: Princeton University Press, 1960.

———. "Gross National Product in the United States, 1834–1909." In *Output, Employment, and Productivity in the United States after 1800,* Conference on Research in Income and Wealth, Studies in Income and Wealth, National Bureau of Economic Research, Vol. 30, pp. 3–76. New York: Columbia University Press, 1966.

———. "Self Sufficiency in the Cotton Economy of the Antebellum South." In William N. Parker, ed., *The Structure of the Cotton Economy of the Antebellum South,* pp. 5–24. Washington, D.C.: Agricultural History Society, 1970.

———. "Trends in the Size Distribution of Wealth in the Nineteenth Century: Some Speculations." In *Six Papers on the Size Distribution of Wealth and Income,* Conference on Research in Income and Wealth, Studies in Income and Wealth, National Bureau of Economic Research, Vol. 33, pp. 1–25. New York: Columbia University Press, 1969.

———, and Weiss, Thomas J. "The Service Industries in the Nineteenth Century." In *Production and Productivity in the Service Industries,* Conference on Research in Income and Wealth, Studies in Income and Wealth, National Bureau of Economic Research, Vol. 34, pp. 287–352. New York: Columbia University Press, 1969.

Gates, Paul W. "Charts of Public Land Sales and Entries." *Journal of Economic History* 24 (March 1964): 22–27.

———. "The Homestead Act: Free Land Policy in Operation, 1862–1935." In Howard W. Ottoson, ed., *Land Use Policy and Problems in the United States,* pp. 28–46. Lincoln: University of Nebraska Press, 1963.

———. "The Homestead Law in an Incongruous Land System." *American Historical Review* 41 (July 1936): 652–81.

———. "The Role of the Land Speculator in Western Development." In Vernon Carstensen, ed., *The Public Lands, pp.* 349–67. Madison: University of Wisconsin Press, 1963.

Genovese, Eugene D. "Commentary: A Historian's View." In William N. Parker, ed., *The Structure of the Cotton Economy of the Antebellum South,* pp. 143–48. Washington, D.C.: Agricultural History Society, 1970.

———. "The Significance of the Slave Plantation for Southern Economic Development." *Journal of Southern History* 28 (November 1962): 442–37.

Gilboy, Elizabeth W., and Hoover, Edgar M. "Population and Immigration." In Seymour Harris, ed., *American Economic History,* pp. 247–80. New York: McGraw-Hill, 1961.

Gitelman, H. M. "Perspectives on American Industrial Violence." *Business History Review* 47 (Spring 1973): 1–23.

Goodrich, Carter. "Internal Improvements Reconsidered." *Journal of Economic History* 30 (June 1970): 289–311.

Griliches, Zvi. "Hybrid Corn and the Economics of Innovation." In Robert W. Fogel and Stanley L. Engerman, eds. *The Reinterpretation of American Economic History,* pp. 207–13. New York: Harper & Row, 1971.

———. "Research Costs and Social Returns: Hybrid Corn and Related Innovations." *Journal of Political Economy* 66 (October 1958): 419–31.

Gunderson, Gerald. "Southern Ante-Bellum Income Reconsidered." *Explorations in Economic History* 10 (Winter 1973): 151–76.

Gwartney, James. "Changes in the Nonwhite/White Income Ratio—1939–67." *American Economic Review* 60 (December 1970): 872–83.

———. "Discrimination, Achievement, and Payoffs of a College Degree." *Journal of Human Resources* 7 (Winter 1972): 60–70.

———. "Discrimination and Income Differentials." *American Economic Review* 60 (June 1970): 396–408.

Haites, Erick F., and Mak, James. "Ohio and Mississippi River Transportation, 1810–1860." *Explorations in Economic History* 8 (Winter 1970–71): 153–80.

———. "The Decline of Steamboating on the Antebellum Western Rivers: Some New Evidence and an Alternative Hypothesis." *Explorations in Economic History* 11 (Fall 1973): 25–36.

Hammond, Bray. "The North's Empty Purse, 1861–62." *American Historical Review* 67 (October 1961): 1–18.

Handlin, Oscar, and Handlin, Mary F., "The United States." In *The Positive Contribution by Immigrants,* International Sociological Association, pp. 17–48. Paris: Unesco, 1955.

Harbeson, Robert W. "Railroads and Regulation, 1877–1916: Conspiracy or Public Interest?" *Journal of Economic History* 27 (June 1967): 230–42.

Harper, Lawrence. "The Effects of the Navigation Acts on the Thirteen Colonies." In Richard B. Morris, ed., *The Era of the American Revolution,* pp. 3–39. New York: Columbia University Press, 1939.

Heath, Jim F. "American War Mobilization and the Use of Small Manufacturers, 1939–1943." *Business History Review* 46 (Autumn 1972): 295–319.

Henry, Robert S. "The Railroad Land Grant Legend in American History Texts." *Mississippi Valley Historical Review* 31 (September 1945): 171–94.

Higgs, Robert. "American Inventiveness, 1870–1920." *Journal of Political Economy* 79 (May/June 1971): 661–67.

———. "Race, Skills, and Earnings: American Immigrants in 1909." *Journal of Economic History* 31 (June 1971): 420–28.

———. "Race, Tenure, and Resource Allocation in Southern Agriculture, 1910." *Journal of Economic History* 33 (March 1973): 149–69.

———. "Railroad Rates and the Populist Uprising." *Agricultural History* 44 (July 1970): 291–98.

———. "Regional Specialization and the Supply of Wheat in the United States, 1867–1914: A Comment." *Review of Economics and Statistics* 53 (February 1971): 101–2.

Hoover, Ethel D. "Retail Prices after 1850." In *Trends in the American Economy in the Nineteenth Century,* Conference on Research in Income and Wealth, Studies in Income and Wealth, National Bureau of Economic Research, Vol. 24, pp. 141–90. Princeton: Princeton University Press, 1960.

Hutchinson, Edward P. "Immigration Policy Since World War I." *Annals of the American Academy of Political and Social Science* 262 (March 1949): 15–21.

Hutchinson, William K., and Williamson, Samuel H. "The Self Sufficiency of the Antebellum South: Estimates of the Food Supply." *Journal of Economic History* 31 (September 1971): 591–612.

Jeremy, David J. "British Textile Technology Transmission to the United States: The Philadelphia Region Experience, 1770–1820." *Business History Review* 47 (Spring 1973): 24–52.

Kendrick, John W. "Productivity Trends: Capital and Labor." *Review of Economics and Statistics* 38 (August 1956): 248–57.

Landes, William M., and Solomon, Lewis C. "Compulsory Schooling Legislation: An Economic Analysis of Law and Social Change in the Nineteenth Century." *Journal of Economic History* 32 (March 1972): 54–91.

Lebergott, Stanley. "United States Transport Advance and Externalities." *Journal of Economic History* 26 (December 1966): 437–61.

———. "Wage Trends, 1800–1900." In *Trends in the American Economy in the Nineteenth Century,* Conference on Research in Income and Wealth, Studies in Income and Wealth, National Bureau of Economic Research, Vol. 24, pp. 449–99. Princeton: Princeton University Press, 1960.

Le Duc, Thomas. "History and Appraisal of United States Land Policy to 1862." In Howard W. Ottoson, ed., *Land Use Policy and Problems in the United States,* pp. 1–27. Lincoln: University of Nebraska Press, 1963.

Lerner, Eugene M. "Southern Output and Agricultural Income, 1860–80." *Agricultural History* 33 (July 1959): 117–25.

Linden, Fabian. "Economic Democracy in the Slave South: An Appraisal of Some Recent Views." *Journal of Negro History* 31 (April 1946): 140–89.

Lindstrom, Diane L. "Southern Dependence Upon Interregional Grain Supplies: A Review of the Trade Flows, 1840–1860." In William N. Parker, ed., *The Structure of the Cotton Economy of the Antebellum South,* pp. 101–14. Washington, D.C.: Agricultural History Society, 1970.

Livesay, Harold C., and Porter, Glenn. "The Financial Role of Merchants in the Development of U.S. Manufacturing, 1815–1860." *Explorations in Economic History* 9 (Fall 1971): 63–87.

———. "Vertical Integration in American Manufacturing, 1899–1948." *Journal of Economic History* 29 (September 1969): 494–500.

Loschky, David J. "Studies of the Navigation Acts: New Economic Non-History." *Economic History Review* 26 (November 1973): 689–91.

Macesich, George. "International Trade and United States Economic Development Revisited." *Journal of Economic History* 21 (September 1961): 384–85.

———. "Sources of Monetary Disturbances in the United States, 1834–1845." *Journal of Economic History* 20 (September 1960): 407–34.

Mak, James, and Walton, Gary. "Steamboats and the Great Productivity Surge in River Transportation." *Journal of Economic History* 32 (September 1972): 619–40.

Markham, Jesse W. "Survey of the Evidence and Findings on Mergers." In *Business Concentration and Price Policy,* National Bureau of Economic Research, pp. 141–82. Princeton: Princeton University Press, 1955.

Martin, David A. "Metallism, Small Notes, and Jackson's War with the Bank of the United States." *Explorations in Economic History* 11 (Spring 1974): 227–48.

———. "1853: The End of Bimetallism in the United States." *Journal of Economic History* 33 (December 1973): 825–44.

Mayhew, Anne. "A Reappraisal of the Causes of Farm Protest in the United States, 1870–1900." *Journal of Economic History* 32 (June 1972): 464–75.

McClelland, Peter D. "On Navigating the Navigation Acts with Peter D. McClelland: A Reply." *American Economic Review* 60 (December 1970): 956–58.

———. "Railroads, American Growth, and the New Economic History: A Critique." *Journal of Economic History* 28 (March 1968): 102–23.

———. "Social Rates of Return on American Railroads in the Nineteenth Century." *Economic History Review* 25 (August 1972): 471–88.

———. "The Cost to America of British Imperial Policy." *American Economic Review* 59 (May 1969): 370–81.

———. "The New Economic History and the Burdens of the Navigation Acts: A Comment." *Economic History Review* 26 (November 1973): 679–86.

McCormick, William W., and Franks, Charles W. "A Self-Generating Model of Long-Swings for the American Economy, 1860–1940." *Journal of Economic History* 31 (June 1971): 295–343.

McDougall, Duncan. "Machine Tool Output, 1861–1910." In *Output, Employment, and Productivity in the United States after 1800,* Conference on Research in Income and Wealth, Studies in Income and Wealth, National Bureau of Economic Research, Vol. 30. New York: Columbia University Press, 1966.

Mead, Walter J. "Oil, Energy, and Environmental Concern." In, Llad Phillips and Harold L. Votey, Jr., eds., *Economic Analysis of Pressing Social Problems,* pp. 38–69. Chicago: Rand McNally College Publishing, 1974.

Meeker, Edward. "The Improving Health of the United States, 1850–1915." *Explorations in Economic History* 9 (Summer 1972): 353–73.

———. "The Social Rate of Return on Investment in Public Health, 1880–1910." *Journal of Economic History* 34 (June 1974): 392–421.

Meerman, Jacob. "The Climax of the Bank War: Biddle's Contraction, 1833–34." *Journal of Political Economy* 71 (August 1963): 378–88.

Mercer, Lloyd J. "Building Ahead of Demand: Some Evidence for the Land Grant Railroads." *Journal of Economic History* 34 (June 1974): 492–500.

———. "Land Grants to American Railroads: Social Cost or Social Benefit?" *Business History Review* 43 (Summer 1969): 134–51.

———. "Rates of Return for Land Grant Railroads: The Central Pacific System." *Journal of Economic History* 30 (September 1970): 602–26.

Meyer, John R., and Conrad, Alfred H. "Economic Theory, Statistical Inference, and Economic History." *Journal of Economic History* 17 (December 1957): 524–53.

Miller, William L. "A Note on the Importance of the Interstate Slave Trade of the Ante-Bellum South." *Journal of Political Economy* 73 (April 1965): 181–87.

Mills, Frederick C. "The Role of Productivity in Economic Growth." *American Economic Review* 42 (May 1952): 545–57.

Musgrave, R. A., and Culbertson, J. M. "The Growth of Public Expenditures in the United States, 1890–1948." *National Tax Journal* 6 (June 1953): 97–115.

Niemi, Albert W., Jr. "A Closer Look at Canals and Western Manufacturing in the Canal Era: A Reply." *Explorations in Economic History* 9 (Summer 1972): 423–424.

———. "A Further Look at Interregional Canals and Economic Specialization: 1820–1840." *Explorations in Economic History* 7 (Summer 1970): 499–520.

———. "Interregional Canals and Manufacturing Development in the West Before 1840." *Revue Internationale D'Histoire De La Banque* (1974).

———. "Structural and Labor Productivity Patterns in United States Manufacturing, 1849–1899." *Business History Review 46* (Spring 1972): 67–84.

———. "Structural Shifts in Southern Manufacturing, 1849–1899." *Business History Review* 45 (Spring 1971): 79–84.

———. "The Development of Industrial Structure in Southern New England." *Journal of Economic History* 30 (September 1970): 657–62.

———. "The Role of Immigration in United States Commodity Production, 1869–1929." *Social Science Quarterly* 52 (June 1971): 190–96.

North, Douglass C. "Early National Income Estimates of the United States." *Economic Development and Cultural Change* 9 (April 1961): 387–96.

———. "Institutional Change and Economic Growth." *Journal of Economic History* 31 (March 1971): 118–25.

———. "Ocean Freight Rates and Economic Development, 1750–1913." *Journal of Economic History* 18 (December 1958): 537–55.

———. "Quantitative Research in Economic History." *American Economic Review* 53 (March 1963): 128–30.

———. "Sources of Productivity Change in Ocean Shipping, 1600–1850." *Journal of Political Economy* 76 (September/October 1968): 953–70.

———. "The State of Economic History." *American Economic Review* 55 (May 1965): 86–91.

———. "The United States Balance of Payments, 1790–1860." In *Trends in the American Economy in the Nineteenth Century,* Conference on Research in Income and Wealth, Studies in Income and Wealth, National Bureau of Economic Research, Vol. 24, pp. 573–627. Princeton: Princeton University Press, 1960.

———, and Thomas, Robert Paul. "An Economic Theory of the Growth of the Western World." *Economic History Review* 23 (April 1970): 1–17.

Nugent, Walter T. K. "Some Parameters of Populism." *Agricultural History* 40 (October 1966): 255–70.

Olmstead, Alan L. "Investment Constraints and New York City Mutual Savings Bank Financing of Antebellum Development." *Journal of Economic History* 32 (December 1972): 811–40.

O'Neill, Dave M. "The Effects of Discrimination on Earnings: Evidence from Military Test Score Results." *Journal of Human Resources* 5 (Fall 1970): 475–86.

Overmeyer, Philip H. "Westward Expansion Before the Homestead Act." In Harold F. Williamson, ed., *The Growth of the American Economy,* 2nd ed., pp. 91–115. Englewood Cliffs, N. J.: Prentice-Hall, 1951.

Parker, William N. "Slavery and Southern Economic Development: An Hypothesis and Some Evidence." In William N. Parker, ed, *The Structure of the Cotton Economy of the Antebellum South,* pp. 115–26. Washington, D.C.: Agricultural History Society, 1970.

———. "Sources of Agricultural Productivity in the Nineteenth Century." *Journal of Farm Economics* 49 (December 1967): 1455–68.

———, and Klein, Judith. "Productivity Growth in Grain Production in the United States, 1840–60 and 1900–10." In *Output, Employment, and Productivity in the United States after 1800,* Conference on Research in Income and Wealth, Studies in Income and Wealth, National Bureau of Economic Research, Vol. 30, pp. 523–79. New York: Columbia University Press, 1966.

Parker, William N., and Whartenby, Franklee. "The Growth of Output Before 1840." In *Trends in the American Economy in the Nineteenth Century,* Conference on Research in Income and Wealth, Studies in Income and Wealth, National Bureau of Economic Research, Vol. 24, pp. 191–216. Princeton: Princeton University Press, 1960.

Passell, Peter. "The Impact of Cotton Land Distribution on the Antebellum Economy." *Journal of Economic History* 31 (December 1971): 917–37.

———, and Schmundt, Maria. "Pre-Civil War Land Policy and the Growth of Manufacturing." *Explorations in Economic History* 9 (Fall 1971): 35–48.

Phillips, Llad. "The War on Crime: Prevention or Control?" In Llad Phillips and Harold L. Votey, Jr., eds. *Economic Analysis of Pressing Social Problems,* pp. 309–38. Chicago: Rand McNally College Publishing, 1974.

Phillips, Ulrich B. "The Economic Cost of Slaveholding in the Cotton Belt." *Political Science Quarterly* 20 (June 1905): 257–75.

Pope, Clayne. "The Impact of the Ante-Bellum Tariff on Income Distribution." *Explorations in Economic History* 9 (Summer 1972): 375–422.

Porter, Patrick G., and Livesay, Harold C. "Oligopoly in Small Manufacturing Industries." *Explorations in Economic History 7* (Spring 1970): 371–79.

Post, John D. "A Study in Meteorological and Trade Cycle History: The Economic Crisis Following the Napoleonic Wars." *Journal of Economic History* 34 (June 1974): 315–49.

Poulson, Barry W. "Estimates of the Value of Manufacturing Output in the Early Nineteenth Century." *Journal of Economic History* 29 (September 1969): 521–25.

Primack, Martin L. "Farm Capital Formation as a Use of Farm Labor in the United States, 1850–1910." *Journal of Economic History* 26 (September 1966): 348–62.

———. "Farm Fencing in the Nineteenth Century." *Journal of Economic History* 29 (June 1969): 287–91.

———. "Land Clearing Under Nineteenth Century Techniques: Some Preliminary Calculations." *Journal of Economic History* 22 (December 1962): 484–97.

Ramsdell, Charles W. "The Natural Limits of Slavery Expansion." *Mississippi Valley Historical Review* 16 (September 1929): 151–71.

Ransom, Roger. "A Closer Look at Canals and Western Manufacturing in the Canal Era." *Explorations in Economic History* 8 (Summer 1971): 501–10.

———. "A Rebuttal." *Explorations in Economic History* 9 (Summer 1972): 425–26.

———. "British Policy and Colonial Growth: Some Implications of the Burden from the Navigation Acts." *Journal of Economic History* 28 (September 1968): 427–35.

———. "Canals and Development: A Discussion of the Issues." *American Economic Review* 54 (May 1964): 365–76.

———. "Interregional Canals and Economic Specialization in the Antebellum United States." *Explorations in Economic History* 5 (Fall 1967): 12–35.

———. "Social Returns from Public Transport Investment: A Case Study of the Ohio Canal." *Journal of Political Economy* 78 (September/October 1970): 1041–60.

———, and Sutch, Richard. "Debt Peonage in the Cotton South After the Civil War." *Journal of Economic History 32* (September 1972): 641–69.

Rasmussen, Wayne. "The Impact of Technological Change on American Agriculture, 1862–1962." *Journal of Economic History* 22 (December 1962): 578–91.

Reading, Don C. "New Deal Activity and the States, 1933 to 1939." *Journal of Economic History* 33 (December 1973): 792–810.

Redlich, Fritz. "New and Traditional Approaches to Economic History and Their Interdependence." *Journal of Economic History* 25 (December 1965): 480–95.

———. "Potentialities and Pitfalls in Economic History." *Explorations in Entrepreneurial History* 6 (Fall 1968): 93–108.

Reid, Joseph D. "On Navigating the Navigation Acts with Peter D. McClelland: Comment." *American Economic Review* 60 (December 1970): 949–55.

———. "Sharecropping As An Understandable Market Response—The Post-Bellum South." *Journal of Economic History* 33 (March 1973): 106–30.

Robertson, Ross M. "Changing Production of Metalworking Machinery, 1860–1920." In *Output, Employment, and Productivity in the United States after 1800,* Conference on Research in Income and Wealth,

Studies in Income and Wealth, National Bureau of Economic Research, Vol. 30, pp. 479–96. New York: Columbia University Press, 1966.

Rockoff, Hugh. "Money, Prices, and Banks in the Jacksonian Era." In Robert W. Fogel and Stanley L. Engerman, eds., *The Reinterpretation of American Economic History,* pp. 448–58. New York: Harper & Row, 1971.

Rosenberg, Nathan. "Factors Affecting the Diffusion of Technology." *Explorations in Economic History* 10 (Fall 1972): 3–34.

———. "Technological Change in the Machine Tool Industry, 1840–1910." *Journal of Economic History* 23 (December 1963): 414–43.

Rothstein, Morton. "America in the International Rivalry for the British Wheat Market." *Mississippi Valley Historical Review* 47 (December 1960): 401–18.

———. "Ante-Bellum Wheat and Cotton Exports." *Agricultural History* (April 1966): 91–100.

———. "The Ante-Bellum South as a Dual Economy: A Tentative Hypothesis." *Agricultural History* 41 (October 1967): 373–82.

———. "The Cotton Frontier of the Antebellum United States: A Methodological Battleground." in William N. Parker, ed., *The Structure of the Cotton Economy of the Antebellum South,* pp. 149–65. Washington, D.C.: Agricultural History Society, 1970.

Royd, J. Hayden, and Walton, Gary M. "The Social Savings from Nineteenth Century Rail Passenger Services." *Explorations in Economic History* 9 (Spring 1972): 233–54.

Salsbury, Stephen. "The Effects of the Civil War on American Industrial Development." In Ralph L. Andreano, ed., *The Economic Impact of the American Civil War,* pp. 161–68. Cambridge, Mass.: Schenkman Publishing, 1967.

Saraydar, Edward. "A Note on the Profitability of Ante Bellum Slavery." *Southern Economic Journal* 30 (April 1964): 325–32.

Sawhill, Isabel V. "The Economics of Discrimination Against Women: Some New Findings." *Journal of Human Resources* 8 (Summer 1973): 383–96.

Schaefer, Donald, and Weiss, Thomas. "The Use of Simulation Techniques in Historical Analysis: Railroads versus Canals." *Journal of Economic History* 31 (December 1971): 854–84.

Shannon, Fred A. "The Homestead Act and the Labor Surplus." *American Historical Review* 41 (July 1936): 637–51.

Scheiber, Harry N. "Economic Change in the Civil War Era: An Analysis of Recent Studies." *Civil War History* 11 (December 1965): 396–411.

———. "Property Law, Expropriation, and Resource Allocation by Government: The United States, 1789–1910." *Journal of Economic History* 33 (March 1973): 232–51.

———. "State Policy and the Public Domain: The Ohio Canal Lands." *Journal of Economic History* 25 (March 1965): 86–113.

Schmidt, Louis B. "Internal Commerce and the Development of a National Economy Before 1860." *Journal of Political Economy* 47 (December 1939): 798–822.

Schmookler, Jacob. "The Changing Efficiency of the American Economy, 1869–1938." *Review of Economics and Statistics* 34 (August 1952): 214–31.

Schultz, Theodore W. "Capital Formation by Education." *Journal of Political Economy* 68 (December 1960): 571–83.

———. "Investment in Human Capital." *American Economic Review* 51 (March 1961): 1–17.

Segal, Harvey. "Canals and Economic Development." In Carter Goodrich, ed., *Canals and American Economic Development,* pp. 216–48. New York: Columbia University Press, 1961.

———. "Cycles of Canal Construction." In Carter Goodrich, ed., *Canals and American Economic Development,* pp. 169–215. New York: Columbia University Press, 1961.

Sellers, James L. "The Economic Incidence of the Civil War in the South." In Ralph L. Andreano, ed., *The Economic Impact of the American Civil War,* pp. 98–108. Cambridge, Mass.: Schenkman Publishing, 1967.

Shepherd, James. "Commodity Exports from the British North American Colonies to Overseas, 1768–1772: Magnitudes and Patterns of Trade." *Explorations in Economic History* 8 (Fall 1970): 5–76.

———, and Walton, Gary. "Trade, Distribution, and Economic Growth in Colonial America." *Journal of Economic History* 32 (March 1972): 128–45.

Simon, Matthew. "The United States Balance of Payments, 1861–1900." In *Trends in the American Economy in the Nineteenth Century,* Conference on Research in Income and Wealth, Studies in Income and Wealth, National Bureau of Economic Research, Vol. 24, pp. 629–715. Princeton: Princeton University Press, 1960.

Solmon, Lewis C. "Estimates of the Costs of Schooling in 1880 and 1890." *Explorations in Economic History* (Supplement, 1970).

———. "Opportunity Costs and Models of Schooling in the Nineteenth Century." *Southern Economic Journal* 37 (July 1970): 66–83.

Solow, Robert M. "Technical Change and the Aggregate Production Function." *Review of Economics and Statistics* 39 (August 1957): 312–20.

Soltow, Lee C. "Evidence on Income Inequality in the United States, 1866–1965." *Journal of Economic History* 29 (June 1969): 270–86.

Starobin, Robert S. "The Economics of Industrial Slavery in the Old South." *Business History Review* 45 (Summer 1970): 131–74.

Stigler, George J. "Monopoly and Oligopoly by Merger." *American Economic Review* 40 (May 1950): 23–34.

Sutch, Richard. "The Profitability of Ante Bellum Slavery—Revisited." *Southern Economic Journal* 31 (April 1965): 365–77.

———, and Ransom, Roger. "The Ex-Slave in the Post-Bellum South: A Study of the Economic Impact of Racism in a Market Environment." *Journal of Economic History* 33 (March 1973): 131–48.

Swierenga, Robert P. "Land Speculator Profits Reconsidered: Central Iowa as a Test Case." *Journal of Economic History* 26 (March 1966): 1–28.

Sylla, Richard. "American Banking and Growth in the Nineteenth Century: A Partial View of the Terrain." *Explorations in Economic History* 9 (Winter 1971–72): 197–228.

———. "Federal Policy, Banking Market Structure, and Capital Mobilization in the United States, 1863–1913." *Journal of Economic History* 29 (December 1969): 657–86.

Taylor, George R. "American Economic Growth Before 1840: An Exploratory Essay." *Journal of Economic History* 24 (December 1964): 427–44.

———. "American Urban Growth Preceding the Railway Age." *Journal of Economic History* 26 (September 1966): 309–39.

Temin, Peter. "A New Look at Hunter's Hypothesis About the Ante-Bellum Iron Industry." *American Economic Review* 54 (May 1964): 344–51.

———. "Labor Scarcity and the Problem of American Industrial Efficiency in the 1850's." *Journal of Economic History* 26 (September 1966): 277–98.

———. "Labor Scarcity in America." *Journal of Interdisciplinary History* 1 (Winter 1971): 251–64.

———. "Steam and Waterpower in the Early Nineteenth Century." *Journal of Economic History* 26 (June 1966): 187–205.

———. "The Economic Consequences of the Bank War." *Journal of Political Economy* 76 (March/April 1968): 257–74.

Thomas, Robert Paul. "A Quantitative Approach to the Study of the Effects of British Imperial Policy Upon Colonial Welfare: Some Preliminary Findings." *Journal of Economic History* 25 (December 1965): 615–38.

———. "British Imperial Policy and the Economic Interpretation of the American Revolution." *Journal of Economic History* 28 (September 1968): 436–40.

Timberlake, Richard H., Jr. "The Specie Circular and Distribution of the Surplus." *Journal of Political Economy* 68 (April 1960): 109–17.

———. "The Specie Circular and Sales of Public Lands: A Comment." *Journal of Economic History* 25 (September 1965): 414–16.

———. "The Specie Standard and Central Banking in the United States Before 1860." *Journal of Economic History* 21 (September 1961): 318–41.

Towne, Marvin W., and Rasmussen, Wayne. "Farm Gross Product and Gross Investment in the Nineteenth Century." In *Trends in the American Economy in the Nineteenth Century,* Conference on Research in Income and Wealth, Studies in Income and Wealth, National Bureau of Economic

Research, Vol. 24, pp. 255–315. Princeton: Princeton University Press, 1960.

Trescott, Paul B. "The United States Government and National Income, 1790–1860." In *Trends in the American Economy in the Nineteenth Century,* Conference on Research in Income and Wealth, Studies in Income and Wealth, National Bureau of Economic Research, Vol. 24, pp. 337–61. Princeton: Princeton University Press, 1960.

Uselding, Paul J. "Conjectural Estimates of Gross Human Capital Inflows to the American Economy, 1790–1860." *Explorations in Economic History* 9 (Fall 1971): 49–62.

———. "Factor Substitution and Labor Productivity Growth in American Manufacturing, 1839–1899." *Journal of Economic History* 32 (September 1972): 670–81.

Vartanian, Pershing. "The Cochran Thesis: A Critique in Statistical Analysis." *Journal of American History 51* (June 1964): 77–79.

Walton, Gary. "New Evidence on Colonial Commerce." *Journal of Economic History* 28 (September 1968): 363–89.

———. "Sources of Productivity Change in American Colonial Shipping, 1675–1775." *Economic History Review* 20 (April 1967): 67–78.

———. "The Burdens of the Navigation Acts: A Reply." *Economic History Review* 26 (November 1973): 687–88.

———. "The New Economic History and the Navigation Acts." *Economic History Review* 24 (October 1971): 533–42.

Weiss, Leonard, and Williamson, Jeffrey G. "Black Education, Earnings, and Interregional Migration: Some New Evidence." *American Economic Review* 62 (June 1972): 372–83.

Weiss, Thomas. "The Industrial Distribution of the Urban and Rural Workforces: Estimates for the United States, 1870–1910." *Journal of Economic History* 32 (December 1972): 919–37.

Wicker, Elmus R. "Federal Reserve Monetary Policy, 1922–33: A Reinterpretation." *Journal of Political Economy* 73 (August 1965): 325–43.

———. "Railroad Investment Before the Civil War." In *Trends in the American Economy in the Nineteenth Century,* Conference on Research in Income and Wealth, Studies in Income and Wealth, National Bureau of Economic Research, Vol. 24, pp. 503–45. Princeton: Princeton University Press, 1960.

Willcox, Walter F. "The Distribution of Immigrants in the United States." *Quarterly Journal of Economics* 20 (August 1906): 523–46.

Willett, Thomas D. "International Specie Flows and American Monetary Stability, 1834–60." *Journal of Economic History* 28 (March 1968): 28–50.

Williams, William V. "A Measure of the Impact of State and Local Taxes on Industry Location." *Journal of Regional Science* 7 (Summer 1967): 49–60.

Williamson, Jeffrey G. "International Trade and United States Economic Development, 1827–1843." *Journal of Economic History* 21 (September 1961): 372–83.

———, and Swanson, Joseph A. "The Growth of Cities in the American Northeast, 1820–1870." *Explorations in Entrepreneurial History* (Supplement 1966).

Wittke, Carl. "Immigration Policy Prior to World War I." *Annals of the American Academy of Political and Social Science* 262 (March 1949): 5–14.

Wolman, Leo. "Wages in the United States Since 1914." *Proceedings of the Sixth Annual Meeting,* Industrial Relations Research Association, 1953, pp. 40–46.

Woodman, Harold D. "The Profitability of Slavery: A Historical Perennial." *Journal of Southern History* 29 (August 1963): 303–25.

Wright, Gavin. "An Econometric Study of Cotton Production and Trade, 1830–1860." *Review of Economics and Statistics* 53 (May 1971): 111–20.

———. " 'Economic Democracy' and the Concentration of Agricultural Wealth in the Cotton South, 1850–1860." In William N. Parker, ed., *The Structure of the Cotton Economy of the Antebellum South,* pp. 63–94. Washington, D.C. Agricultural History Society, 1970.

———. "New and Old Views on the Economics of Slavery." *Journal of Economic History* 33 (June 1973): 452–66.

Yasuba, Yasukichi. "The Profitability and Viability of Plantation Slavery in the United States." *The Economic Studies Quarterly* 12 (September 1961): 60–67.

Government Documents

Board of Governors of the Federal Reserve System. *All Bank Statistics, United States, 1896–1955.* Washington, D.C.: U.S. Government Printing Office, 1959.

———. *Banking Studies,* Second Reprint. Washington, D.C.: U.S. Government Printing Office, 1948.

———. *The Federal Reserve System.* Washington, D.C.: National Capital Press, 1939.

Comptroller of the Currency. *Annual Report of the Comptroller of the Currency, 1919,* Vol. II. Washington, D.C.: U.S. Government Printing Office, 1920.

Federal Trade Commission, Bureau of Economics. *Economic Papers, 1966–69.* Washington, D.C.: U.S. Government Printing Office, 1970.

Federal Trade Commission. *Report of the Federal Trade Commission on Changes in Concentration in Manufacturing, 1935 to 1947 and 1950.* Washington, D.C.: U.S. Government Printing Office, 1954.

President's Commission on Law Enforcement and Administration of Justice. *Task Force Report: Crime and Its Impact—An Assessment.* Washington, D.C.: U.S. Government Printing Office, 1967.

United Nations Statistical Office. *Yearbook of National Accounts Statistics, 1971,* Vol. III. New York: United Nations, 1973.

U.S. Bureau of the Census. *A Compendium of the Seventh Census.* Washington, D.C.: Senate Printer, 1854.

———. *Compendium of the Ninth Census.* Washington, D.C. U.S. Government Printing Office, 1872.

———. *Eighth Census of the United States: 1860, Agriculture.* Washington, D.C.: U.S. Government Printing Office, 1864.

———. *Eighth Census of the United States: 1860, Manfactures.* Washington, D.C.: U.S. Government Printing Office, 1865.

———. *Eighth Census of the United States: 1860, Population.* Washington, D.C.: U.S. Government Printing Office, 1864.

———. *Eleventh Census of the United States: 1890, Report on Real Estate Mortgages.* Washington, D.C.: U.S. Government Printing Office, 1895.

———. *Fifteenth Census of the United States: 1930, Manufactures,* Vol. I. Washington, D.C.: U.S. Government Printing Office, 1933.

———. *Fifteenth Census of the United States: 1930, Population,* Vol. II. Washington, D.C.: U.S. Government Printing Office, 1933.

———. *Fourteenth Census of the United States: 1920, Population,* Vol. IV. Washington, D.C.: U.S. Government Printing Office, 1922.

———. *Historical Statistics of the United States, Colonial Times to 1957.* Washington, D.C.: U.S. Government Printing Office, 1960.

———. *Long Term Economic Growth, 1860–1965.* Washington, D.C.: U.S. Government Printing Office, 1966.

———. *Ninth Census of the United States: 1870, Population.* Washington, D.C.: U.S. Government Printing Office, 1872.

———. *Sixteenth Census of the United States: 1940, Manufactures,* Vol. I. Washington, D.C.: U.S. Government Printing Office, 1942.

———. *Sixteenth Census of the United States: 1940, Population, Comparative Occupation Statistics, 1870–1940.* Washington, D.C.: U.S. Government Printing Office, 1943.

———. *Statistical Abstract, 1968.* Washington, D.C.: U.S. Government Printing Office, 1968.

———. *Statistical Abstract, 1972.* Washington, D.C.: U.S. Government Printing Office, 1972.

———. *Statistical Abstract, 1973.* Washington, D.S. U.S. Government Printing Office, 1973.

———. *Thirteenth Census of the United States: 1910, Agriculture.* Washington, D.C.: U.S. Government Printing Office, 1913.

———. *Thirteenth Census of the United States: 1910, Manufactures.* Washington, D.C.: U.S. Government Printing Office, 1913.

———. *Thirteenth Census of the United States: 1910, Population,* Vol. I. Washington, D.C.: U.S. Government Printing Office, 1913.

———. *Twelfth Census of the Untied States: 1900, Agriculture,* Parts I and II. Washington, D.C.: U.S. Government Printing Office, 1902.

———. *Twelfth Census of the United States: 1900, Manufactures,* Vol. VIII. Washington, D.C.: U.S. Government Printing Office, 1902.

———. *U.S. Census of Agriculture: 1940, General Report, Statistics by Subject.* Washington, D.C.: U.S. Government Printing Office, 1943.

———. *U.S. Census of Agriculture: 1950,* Vol. II, *General Report.* Washington, D.C.: U.S. Government Printing Office, 1952.

———. *U.S. Census of Agriculture: 1959,* Vol. II, *General Report, Statistics by Subject.* Washington, D.C.: U.S. Government Printing Office, 1962.

———. *U.S. Census of Agriculture: 1969,* Vol. II, *General Report,* Chapter 3, *Farm Management, Farm Operators.* Washington, D.C.: U.S. Government Printing Office, 1973.

———. *U.S. Census of Population: 1970, Detailed Characteristics, United States Summary.* Washington, D.C.: U.S. Government Printing Office, 1973.

U.S. Congress, Joint Economic Committee. *Hearings,* Part 2, "Historical and Comparative Rates of Production, Productivity, and Prices," 86th Congress, 1st Session, 1959. Washington, D.C.: U.S. Government Printing Office, 1959. Testimony of Raymond Goldsmith, pp. 230–79.

U.S. Department of Agriculture. *Agricultural Statistics, 1971.* Washington, D.C.: U.S. Government Printing Office, 1972.

———. *Yearbook, 1921.* Washington, D.C.: U.S. Government Printing Office, 1922.

———. *Yearbook, 1922.* Washington, D.C.: U.S. Government Printing Office, 1923.

U.S. Department of Commerce. *Annual Survey of Manufactures, 1951.* Washington, D.C.: U.S. Government Printing Office, 1953.

———. *1967 Census of Manufactures,* Vol. I. Washington, D.C.: U.S. Government Printing Office, 1971.

U.S. Department of Justice, Federal Bureau of Investigation. *Uniform Crime Reports, 1950.* Washington, D.C.: U.S. Government Printing Office, 1950.

———. *Uniform Crime Reports, 1960.* Washington, D.C.: U.S. Government Printing Office, 1960.

———. *Uniform Crime Reports, 1971.* Washington, D.C.: U. S. Government Printing Office, 1971.

U.S. Department of Labor. *Manpower Report of the President, 1973.* Washington, D.C.: U.S. Government Printing Office, 1973.

U.S. National Resources Committee. *The Structure of the American Economy.* Washington, D.C.: U.S. Government Printing Office, 1939.

Name Index

Subject Index